"Christian teachers and preachers, leaders and ministers have been waiting years for a good, contemporary, and freshly inspiring work on Romans. Simon Ponsonby was destined to write such a book. Here it is at last, vital, readable, and just what we all needed. Great teaching from a great teacher."

– Canon Robin Gamble, Evangelist, Author and Founder of Leading Your Church into Growth

"St Paul's rhetorical question to the Romans 'What does the scripture say?' (4:3) has always been the gold standard by which Simon Ponsonby has lived and served the Body of Christ, both as a highly effective pastor-teacher and a rigorous theologian. He writes as he speaks, with great flair and invaluable insight, with perfectly-judged illustrations and not a little humour. Simon tackles the towering truths contained within the letter to the Romans with freshness and immediacy, even with courage; and as always, he causes our hearts to be 'strangely warmed' as he makes us think, even sometimes to think again. This book will fall into the 'must have' category for preachers and teachers and believers alike, and deserves the widest readership possible."

– Eleanor Mumford, Co-Founder of Vineyard Churches UK

"If I could only choose one person to hear preach the whole way through the Book of Romans, I honestly think Simon Ponsonby would be at the top of my list. Simon is one of the very best communicators of the gospel I know, and reading God is For Us *has been my opportunity to sit at the feet of a brilliant theologian, story-teller, pastor and passionate follower of Jesus as they diligently unpack this epic Epistle. I've loved the opportunity, and have no doubt in my mind that you will too!"*

– Revd Pete Hughes, Pastor Kings Cross Church, Leader New Wine 18–30s

"Reading a book on Romans that is based on a sermon series makes me think that this is how all biblical commentaries should be written. Simon Ponsonby's engagement with this life-changing, history-making book of the Bible is thoroughly scholarly and unerringly pastoral. It is full of spiritual insight and compassion, with Simon's natural touches of

humour. This book is for anyone and everyone, and it will open up the treasures of Romans for all who wish to mine them."

– Dr Lucy Peppiatt, Theologian, Author, Church Planter, Dean of Studies, Westminster Theological Centre

"Like many pastors, I have about two dozen volumes on the book of Romans in my library. This one by Simon Ponsonby will be in my top three of 'go-to' volumes every time I preach Romans! While showing great familiarity with contemporary Romans scholarship, this is a volume aimed not only at the intellect, but also at the heart and will. Ponsonby's God is For Us *is incredibly useful for reading as a daily devotional. It also is a treasure trove of preaching and teaching illustrations for pastors and church leaders. Not since Dr Martyn Lloyd-Jones produced his Romans series have I read a volume of such powerful, motivating, and inspiring lectures on the book of Romans."*

– Dr Rich Nathan, Senior Pastor, Vineyard Columbus, Ohio

"An erudite piece of work interestingly written that may stand alongside some of the better treatments of Romans. Anyone who wants to learn more about Romans – or to teach it – should read this book."

– Dr R. T. Kendall

"For centuries, commentaries on Romans have built on assumptions and preconceptions inherited from previous generations, each layer further burying Paul's original voice. To this calcified deposit comes a biblical scholar at the peak of his game, lifting the accretions of the years with a forensic skill at once breath-taking and utterly compelling. Reading God is For Us *is like watching the restoration of some majestic Leonardo mural hidden beneath later paintwork – an exhilarating, spine-tingling adventure of wonder and encounter with the New Testament's own masterpiece here revealed as never before.* God is For Us *is the book this supremely gifted theologian was born to write."*

– Revd Paul Langham, Author, Bible Teacher, Vicar of Christchurch Clifton

God is For Us

52 Readings from Romans

Simon Ponsonby

Monarch
Books

Oxford, UK & Grand Rapids, Michigan, USA

Published by Monarch Books
an imprint of
Lion Hudson plc
Wilkinson House, Jordan Hill Road,
Oxford OX2 8DR, England
Email: monarch@lionhudson.com
www.lionhudson.com/monarch

ISBN 978 0 85721 328 0
e-ISBN 978 0 85721 461 4

First edition 2013

Acknowledgments
Unless otherwise stated, Scripture quotations are taken from The Holy Bible, English Standard Version® (ESV®) copyright © 2001 by Crossway, a publishing ministry of Good News Publishers. All rights reserved.
Scripture quotations marked "NIV" are taken from the *Holy Bible, New International Version*, copyright © 1973, 1978, 1984 International Bible Society. Used by permission of Hodder & Stoughton, a member of the Hodder Headline Group. All rights reserved. "NIV" is a trademark of International Bible Society. UK trademark number 1448790.
Scripture extracts marke "KJV" are taken from The Authorized (King James) Version. Rights in the Authorized Version are vested in the Crown. Reproduced by permission of the Crown's patentee, Cambridge University Press.

A catalogue record for this book is available from the British Library

Printed and bound in the UK, April 2013, LH27.

To St Aldates Church family – who taught me so much more than I taught them

Contents

Introduction

I have divided this book into fifty-two short chapters, enough for one a week for a year; or, if you are keen, one a day for fifty-two days. This book on Romans began as a series of sermons preached over twenty months between September 2010 and May 2012 at St Aldates Church, Oxford. I want to thank Charlie and Anita Cleverly for their enthusiastic encouragement of this project, as well as other colleagues at Aldates who vacated the pulpit on Sunday evenings, as well as the congregation who stuck with a sermon series that was uncharacteristically lengthy by modern standards. A friend and respected evangelical leader recently said that if you want to grow a church, you need mini-series of four sermons on current themes to keep people keen. The Vatican have suggested sermons be no longer than eight minutes, and the bishop of Lichfield wants to limit whole services to under fifty minutes. I struggled to preach my *sermons* each week in under fifty minutes. If short and sweet sermons were in fact what my church wanted, they were gracious enough not to say so – and eager enough to turn out weekly for just over a year and a half to study Romans.

I must thank publisher Tony Collins and editors Richard Herkes and Jenny Ward, who had confidence in this project and wrestled my sermons into book format. I am perpetually thankful to God for my dad Jeffrey Ponsonby; he is a model of Berean faithfulness to God's word (see Acts 17:10–12), and who has prayed without ceasing for me as I worked on, and preached through, Romans. Special mention must be made of my great friend Mark Davies, a former SAS sergeant major who, as a new convert, read straight through all of Martyn Lloyd-Jones's books on Romans. Our long and strong discussions over the meaning of texts in Romans have been as profitable to me as any single commentary – even when we failed to reach consensus.

The initial encouragement for this project came from my former colleagues Joanna Braithwaite and Gordon Hickson. Joanna, now with the Lord, believed Aldates needed to dig solid foundations through sound doctrine; Gordon, a revivalist, understood how God had singularly used Romans to stir fires throughout the centuries, and he longed for the fire to fall at Aldates. I dismissed their enthusiasm for this idea, and took comfort that my bosses Charlie and Anita would undoubtedly quash the notion on their return from sabbatical. Imagine my shock, then, when they agreed it would be a good idea! Charlie has often commented that he wanted church to be a place of "doctrine on fire" and believed a series of sermons on Romans would help stoke the fires for us in Oxford. I was somewhat thrown when, shortly after, Charlie said, "I think you can begin preaching Romans next week!"

Why was I so reluctant? Well, it was not simply that Romans is the longest epistle in the New Testament (which is why it comes first in Paul's letters in our Bibles[1]); nor was I reluctant because Romans is widely regarded as the summation and masterpiece of Pauline theology; it was simply because the task seemed too daunting. The master expositor Dr Martyn Lloyd-Jones put off preaching Romans for years because he claimed he did not understand chapter 6. I was well aware I had not fully resolved in my own thinking many of its grand themes on divine revelation in creation, justification, sanctification, the Law, election, Israel, church–state politics – all of which have long provoked disagreement over interpretation.

I felt rather like a Lake District fell-walker being asked to summit Everest. To follow the metaphor, there are in fact two approaches to an ascent of Everest: one called the siege method and the other the Alpine method. In the siege method a large team is established, carrying supplies for many weeks – even months. The team takes time to acclimatize, get fit, and make short recces of the mountain until, after many weeks, when the conditions are right, a select few seek the summit. An example of this would be the 1974 Italian assault that employed 2,000 porters, 100 sherpas, and a team of sixty-four mountaineers, plus soldiers, doctors, and pilots, and 60 tonnes of food. Dr Lloyd-Jones modelled the siege approach when he delivered 353 sermons over fourteen years, eventually published as fourteen volumes – and even then covering only chapters 1–14!

The alternative – the Alpine approach to surmounting Everest –

was modelled by the famous Reinhold Messner in 1980. He flew in to base-camp with a small support team and climbed the mountain in only three days – solo, and without oxygen!

While for the members of St Aldates who followed the series it may have seemed at times like a siege approach, the twenty months of sermons preached were able to fit just one volume, making this clearly a brisk Alpine ascent, keeping to the main route with no time to explore many of the mountain's vistas on the way up. Having now seen the view from the top, I feel ready to tackle it again. I think I know now how to surmount Romans even more quickly, but also know where I would like to pause and spend more time.

So, while covering the whole of Romans, this set of studies makes no claims to be exhaustive or comprehensive. It is not a commentary – there are many excellent ones across the traditions that have journeyed with me. Even if I did not always follow their route map through the epistle I have especially appreciated the insights from pre-eminent church scholars such as Douglas Moo, C. E. B. Cranfield, James Dunn, Joseph A. Fitzmyer, and Thomas R. Schreiner. (The Reformed theology web site www.preceptaustin.org is one of the best-kept secrets for sermon cribs and soul preparation.)

All the material that has made up this book has been "preached" first as a Sunday sermon, with a couple of exceptions that were given as lectures in a more formal classroom setting. They are mainly exegetical and expository, with a few being more thematic. Each week, I taught what I had seen over the last seven days as I searched the Word; each week I taught what, at that time, I felt led by the Spirit to draw out and in turn to apply to my listeners. Thus, having been written to be spoken, not read, the style of the text is more rhetorical than it is literary.

Certain emphases may seem laboured to some, while other texts are either passed over or hastily treated. As I preached, I wanted as much to be prophetic as systematic. I wanted my congregation to encounter God, through hearing me re-present Paul's ancient words, penned from Corinth, directed to a small church in Rome, as he was setting out on a fateful journey to Jerusalem. That said, I hope I have caught the major themes and major thrust of Paul. I include one memorable sermon preached in the series by my old friend, author and director of CMS (Church Missionary Society), the Revd Joseph Steinberg. Joe is a messianic Jew who embraced Christ at no small personal cost. He is also a former director of a mission to the Jewish people, and as such I believe he is uniquely placed to expound Paul's thoughts in Romans 10 on the necessity and priority of evangelism to God's first covenant people, the Jews.

The reader will soon recognize that I do not follow Protestant and evangelical tradition in seeing the central purpose of Romans as a presentation of Paul's gospel or of the doctrine of justification by faith. Far less do I see Romans as containing Paul's systematic theology. To me, it is clearly a pastoral letter addressing theological and practical issues that have arisen in the Roman house-church between Jewish and Gentile church members. In the epistle, Paul is laying down theological principles to work through the problems of the church. I believe the central issue in Romans concerns the Jews and their relationship to God, the Torah, the Gentiles and the future.

The benefit in preaching expository series, and teaching consistently through a book, is that the preacher must move out from the comfort and control of familiar or favourite subjects to tackle texts and themes that might otherwise be ignored. In Romans I have enjoyed reflecting on the ongoing role of Moses' law in the life of the church, Abraham as our father of faith, Israel in God's plans, the church and politics, and women in leadership, to name a few. Many of these themes are contentious, and some of my conclusions and applications have precipitated not just a little heat from the initial hearers. No preacher or teacher is inerrant – only God's Word is – for we prophesy in part. I have tried to be faithful to Paul, and to the Spirit who inspired Paul, in this privileged task of teaching Romans. However, as Bishop Richard Harries said, perhaps prophetically, at my induction as Oxford Pastorate Chaplain in 1998: "Perfection is a predicate of divinity," – his point being not to expect it from me. Thus my understanding and application of Paul's epistle will always be inadequate. To quote Martyn Lloyd Jones: "I am just a little expositor of this Word, and if you can prove to me that I am doing any violence to what the great Apostle teaches, I will give in and admit that I am wrong."[2]

In the preface to his groundbreaking commentary on Romans,

Karl Barth claimed he was following the Reformer John Calvin's method of approaching Scripture:

> *How energetically Calvin, having first established what stands in the text, sets himself to re-think the whole material and to wrestle with it, till the walls which separate the sixteenth century from the first become transparent! Paul speaks, and the man of the sixteenth century hears.*[3]

That must be the method and goal of every preacher, teacher, and student of God's Word, to allow the word written by the apostle or prophet then and there, to be heard as God's word to me, here and now. That expositors and exegetes can vary, and even disagree over what they see and hear in Paul, means we must be humble enough not to claim we have "got it" – and it also suggests the word is dynamic, free and polyvalent: it cannot so easily be claimed or confined to one hermeneutic. It is living and active, not static – it stands over us, we do not stand over it. When preachers' thoughts on Paul are long forgotten, and teachers' books on Paul are gathering dust, Paul's words – God's words – will still be exciting, directing and strengthening God's people.

Paul concludes his letter to the Romans with a benediction – a spoken blessing to the God who has so blessed them: "Now to him who is able to strengthen you according to my gospel and the preaching of Jesus Christ... to the only wise God be glory forevermore through Jesus Christ! Amen" (16:25, 27). Surely that encapsulates the heart of Paul's purpose in writing this epistle: that his readers may be established, made strong by the gospel of Jesus Christ, and that being thus blessed they may give glory to God. And my hope and prayer is that all who read these studies in Romans may grasp and be grasped by the glorious gospel of Jesus Christ, and so live to give glory to the God who is "for us".

1

The Journey Begins

We have fifty-two chapters ahead of us. Why is it worth spending so long studying this epistle so closely? When anyone asked that question over the many months of Sundays that I preached on it, my answer was simple: "Because we don't have any longer."

As I began this study, a former graduate student, who had attended the distinguished New Testament professor Howard Marshall's Greek language class at Fuller Theological Seminary, told me that he began his study on Romans with these words: "First, never teach a course on Romans; second, if you have to teach a course on Romans, never try to teach all of Romans." Why so reluctant?

Well, intellectually and theologically, Romans is massive. It is Paul's magnum opus, his masterpiece, and also the longest church epistle in the New Testament. The question of which is the best route to scale such a mountain has entertained the church for centuries – many of its greatest theologians have attempted it. In heaven I suspect there's a Bible-study group with Origen, Augustine, Aquinas, Wesley, Barth, Lloyd-Jones and many others all debating it.

Let's consider some introductory questions.

Authorship

Romans begins, "Paul, a servant of Christ Jesus, called to be an apostle..." The letter claims to be from Paul and there is no evidence to suggest otherwise. Despite the tendencies of historical critical theology to not take everything biblical at face value, Paul's authorship of this epistle has never seriously been in question, and, unlike certain other New Testament epistles, there is no scholarly assertion that it could be pseudonymous. It is true that in 16:22 it states, "I Tertius, who wrote this letter, greet you in the Lord" but most scholars assume that Tertius was the scribe to whom Paul dictated the letter, despite the odd one or two scholarly claims to the contrary.

Some commentators have questioned whether Romans 16 was part of the original letter at all. Some speculate that that particular chapter, at least, *was* written by Tertius. But the major reason for suggesting the last chapter has been added on is that the author seems fully acquainted personally with at least twenty-six people in the Roman church, whom he names and to whom he sends personal greetings. It is therefore asked: how could Paul know so many people there if he had not founded or even visited the church? (Paul's known visits to Rome were made after this letter was written.)

This is not a problem that should cause any serious questioning. Rome was the centre of the empire – an empire in which many moved quite freely for trade. Paul could well have known or met some of those named in other major cities as they were about their trade, before they found themselves in Rome (notably Epaenetus (16:5) who is called "the first convert to Christ in Asia"). We are well aware that all Jews were expelled from Rome some years prior to Paul writing, and some of those named may have been Jewish believers who fled to cities and joined the churches where Paul was ministering. While Paul names twenty-six individuals, he does not claim to know all of them personally: three he says are "relatives"; two "dear friends"; three he calls "fellow workers"; one he "loves in the Lord" and one has been a "mother" to him. It is possible the rest he knew about, had heard of, and as apostle to the Gentiles was daily in prayer for, as he says: "God ... is my witness how constantly I remember you in my prayers at all times" (1:9–10). Such constant carrying of them in his heart before God in prayer meant he knew them, loved them, and wanted to greet them – even if he had never met them!

The occasion

In 15:25–26 we read that Paul is shortly to take a trip to Jerusalem, where he will hand over funds raised by the churches in Macedonia and Achaia to assist the struggling saints in Israel (Acts 19:21). Paul says he intends afterwards to go on apostolic mission to Europe, starting in Spain, visiting the Roman church on the way, and hopes they will furnish his mission trip – presumably with prayer support, financial backing, and even colleagues to accompany him.

We may triangulate this statement with two other passages to pinpoint the time and occasion of this letter. In 2 Corinthians 1:16 Paul states that he intends to visit the Corinthian church before going to Judea, collecting their contribution to the gift for the struggling church in Jerusalem (2 Corinthians 8). In Romans 16:1–2 Paul commends Phoebe to them; she is part of the leadership in the church of Cenchreae and is entrusted with carrying this letter to the church in Rome. Cenchreae is a seaport in northern Corinth. So we may deduce that Paul wrote this letter on his visit to Corinth, just before his visit to Rome, at the end of his third missionary journey. This would date the writing of the letter sometime between AD 55 and 57. He was arrested in Jerusalem, and after appealing to Caesar was taken to Rome, placed under house arrest and, we believe, eventually executed around AD 62. Interestingly we have two very early manuscripts with scribal ascriptions saying the letter was written by Paul from Corinth.

The recipients

Chapter 1, verse 7, addresses the letter "To all in Rome who are loved by God and called to be saints". This is the only letter in Scripture that Paul wrote to a church he didn't found. There had never been a formal apostolic mission to Rome. The origins of this church – or more accurately a network of house churches in Rome[4] – are not presented in Scripture, although we may attempt some reasonable deductions about it. We know there was a large Jewish community in Rome in the early first century AD with upwards of 50,000 members, including many who had been taken there as slaves following Pompey's subjugation of Palestine in 62 BC. Some made the major pilgrimage to Jerusalem for the sacred Pentecost festival – Acts 2:10 tells us that there were visitors from Rome present on the day of Pentecost. They would have witnessed the Spirit being poured out and heard Peter's sermon, and we may naturally assume they were among the 3,000 converted that day. If so, these would form the nucleus of the church or churches on their return to Rome. Acts 8:1 informs us of a severe persecution that broke out following Stephen's stoning in Jerusalem, and the church was scattered; again it is plausible that some of those Christians found their way to Rome and either founded or supported the embryonic church there.

An important insight into the origins of the church in Rome is offered by the fourth-century writer Ambrosiater:

> *It is established that there were Jews living in Rome in the times of the Apostles, and that those Jews who had believed [in Christ] passed on to the Romans the tradition that they ought to profess Christ but keep the law [Torah] ... One ought not to condemn the Romans, but to praise their faith, because without seeing any signs or miracles and without seeing any of the apostles, they nevertheless accepted faith in Christ, although according to a Jewish rite.*[5]

This is significant. Jewish believers had passed on the faith to Roman Gentiles, but with a Jewish bent – keeping the law! It's possible that issues raised by this provoked Paul's writing of this letter and shaped its particular content. At times Paul is clearly addressing Jewish believers (2:17; 4:1; 7:1) and at other times Gentile believers (11:13), and he probably has Jewish believers in mind in 2:1 – 3:8 and 7:1–6; and is addressing Gentile believers in 9–11. In chapter 14 he appears to be saying to both groups who have been squabbling, "Come on, shake hands, play nice."

The purpose

As with many letters or emails we might write, there is often more than one motive behind them and more than one message contained within them. I think Paul has several reasons in writing to the Roman church.

First, as the "apostle to the Gentiles" (Romans 11:13; see also Acts 9:15) it would be appropriate that he should be connected to the church in the capital of the Gentile empire. This letter serves as a formal introduction to the church and a preparation for his hoped-for coming (1:11, 15:29).

Secondly, Paul intends to embark on a fourth mission, up into Spain, and needs to establish a support base for that in Rome. This letter serves to introduce himself and his intention to them for consideration of support (15:24).

Thirdly, Paul wants to commend Phoebe to the Roman church leadership (16:1) and he exhorts them to assist her. We do not know the nature of the assistance she requires, but his letter, delivered by Phoebe's hand, with so many personal greetings attached to it, would hopefully mean that their hearts and hands would open to her.

Fourthly, Paul states that he has wanted to come and preach the gospel to them but has been hindered from doing so (1:13–15). Unable at this moment to come and preach personally, he may well be dictating something of his gospel, so that at least he will be heard, and his message conveyed, as it is read aloud to the congregations.

Fifthly, and centrally, Paul is writing to resolve a pastoral tension in the church, precipitated by theological disagreement between Gentile and Jewish camps, which he has caught wind of (11:17–25; 12:16; 14:3). This is the work of one exercising his ministry of reconciliation (2 Corinthians 5:18).

As noted above, the church in Rome almost certainly began among the Jewish community and took on a Jewish flavour and Jewish leadership. But in AD 49 the Jews were expelled by Emperor Claudius (Acts 18:2) over strife about someone the writer Suetonius later calls "Chrestus" – that is, "Christus". It's fair to assume that, when the Jewish Christians were expelled, Gentile leadership modified the Jewishness of the church theology and worship. When the Jews were welcomed back to Rome in the mid-fifties, the Jewish church leaders and members returned, and tensions arose over such issues as the place of Jews in God's economy (Romans 9–11), the role of the law (Romans 4–7), Jewish food regulations, sabbath days, and so on (Romans 14). Paul is thus seeking to bring rapprochement between two ethnic groups by means of different expressions of theology and spirituality. The church has struggled ever since to hold together the Jewish roots of the Christian faith in a predominantly Gentile culture with Gentile church leadership.

Lastly, Paul would shortly be a prisoner, under house arrest in Rome. Though he did not foresee this, in God's economy making contact with the church would be pragmatically beneficial. Under house arrest in Rome they could tend to his needs and engage in mutual encouragement (Acts 28:15f; 30f).

The major themes

The distinguished church historian, Philip Schaff, wrote that Romans

> *is the most remarkable product of the most remarkable man. It is his heart. It contains his theology, theoretical and practical, by which he lived and died.*[6]

This tends to have been the general consensus, certainly among evangelicals and Protestants for centuries – that this is the fullest, clearest expression of Paul's theology; his gospel, his systematic doctrine. The Reformer Philipp Melancthon called it "a compendium of Christian doctrine".[7] But are these views right?

While the letter is skilfully and carefully crafted, that this is Paul's systematic theology seems unlikely – there are huge omissions in this letter which he explicates elsewhere. Noticeably it lacks any clear doctrine of the church as we see it in Ephesians 2–4; it lacks any expanded Christological statements as we see in Colossians 1:15–20 and Philippians 2:6–11; it makes little mention of eschatology as we find in 1 Thessalonians 4:13 – 5:11; 2 Thessalonians 2:1–12; and it has little to say on personal ethics, as we find in Ephesians 5–6. Its relative paucity in the areas of Christology, ecclesiology, and eschatology would suggest it is not an attempt at systematic theology. Furthermore, its particular and lengthy emphases on matters pertaining to the Jews and the Jewishness of Christianity suggest that it is dealing with a context-specific issue, although one of universal importance to the church. At times it appears almost as an apologetic for the Jewishness of the church; at other times a lengthy apologetic for the sovereignty of God.

For years scholars have debated what is at the centre or "heart" of Paul's thought. New Testament professor C. K. Barrett goes so far as to say that one would not be wrong in seeing the verses 1:16–17 as "a summary of Paul's theology as a whole".[8] But that view is not one that is shared by most other theologians. It is surely significant that great theologians and movements that have focused on Romans have all emphasized different themes and portions of Romans as being at the centre. For Augustine it was Romans 5 and original sin; for Martin Luther it was Romans 3–4 and justification by faith; for John Calvin it was Chapter 9 and God's sovereignty; for John Wesley it was Romans 6–8 and entire sanctification; for Karl Barth it was Romans 1–2 and God's righteousness;[9] for David Watson it was Romans 6 and being dead to sin.

All this simply goes to show that this letter to the Romans cannot be lightly handled or easily claimed by any one tradition or interpretation. What we may confidently say at the outset of this study is that Romans is foundational.

Romans lays foundations

Martin Luther, whose encounter with Romans led to a personal revival and the subsequent European Reformation, wrote in the preface to his commentary on the letter:

> *This Epistle is really the chief part of the New Testament and the very purest gospel, and is worthy not only that every Christian should know it word for word, by heart, but occupy himself with it every day as the daily bread of the soul. It can never be read or pondered too much, and the more it is dealt with, the more precious it becomes and the better it tastes.*[10]

Romans is the first epistle in the New Testament and, as mentioned earlier, the longest. It is arguably the most important and most influential. Few other epistles come close to covering the breadth and depth of ground that Romans does. While the majority of Paul's letters may go into greater length on certain issues like Christ's divine nature, church life, eschatology, circumcision, no other epistle has the scope and depth, touching on most major themes in theology and church life: from God's revelation, to creation, to salvation, to sanctification, to mission, to church relations, to spiritual gifts, politics, and ethics.

My great friend Mark is a warrior who distinguished himself

over twenty-three years of military service, including seventeen in the famed SAS. While in a semi-drunk state, following a two-week drinking binge celebrating his success and survival in the First Gulf War, he was convicted of sin and converted to Christ while randomly flicking through TV channels in his room. He had paused to listen to a TV evangelist, who was staring as through the screen, and, in a Spirit-inspired moment, described Mark's life, failures, and successes and need for Christ who alone satisfies and saves. Mark followed the evangelist's prayer of commitment. He wept over his sins for an hour, fell asleep, and woke up sober and saved.

Mark knew next to nothing about the faith, but was determined to live all for Christ. The first day back at Hereford Camp he incurred ridicule from his SAS colleagues as he bowed his head and said grace in the food hall. Jeers, derision, and amazement followed – he told me it was one of the toughest things he ever did, up there with Special Forces selection! Immediately his womanizing, drinking, fighting, and swearing ceased. He was perhaps the only declared Christian out of the 250 soldiers serving in the SAS, and he walked a lonely road for many years.

Shortly after his conversion, he was posted to help run the infamous Belize Jungle warfare training school for six months as its chief instructor. Given the unusual nature of his career, which he believed God told him to stick with, he was unable to attend church regularly or be discipled in the regular manner. Special Forces require special discipling. But he was an avid reader, and just as he was about to take his jungle posting, he walked into a bookshop and spotted a fourteen-volume set of books called *Romans*. As a soldier, he was interested in military history, and he assumed they were a comprehensive account of the rise and fall of the Roman empire. Of course it turned out that this was no military history, but the whole collection of over 350 sermons on Romans by Dr Martyn Lloyd-Jones. For the next six months in Belize's swamps and jungles, while being devoured by leeches, Mark himself devoured all fourteen volumes of Lloyd-Jones's series. When he was subsequently posted to Bosnia's nightmare, Mark often had a volume of *Romans* tucked in his Bergen rucksack. God trained him, discipled him, and theologically educated him as he studied Romans. Not knowing how to preach but sensing he should share his faith, Mark would visit prisons and simply read aloud the latest Lloyd-Jones sermon to engage his listeners. He began to see people come to faith in Christ, and even saw healings occur as he prayed for others. There were also miracles of divine deliverance and providence in his own life. Isaiah 54:13 prophesies that one day "all your children will be taught by the Lord", and indeed, in twenty-five years of ministry, I have seldom met anyone like Mark – someone who has been taught by God, taught through Romans.

Mark recalls that he was reading a Lloyd-Jones volume as a new believer on a boat trip, having some R&R, when a fellow soldier's wife asked what he was reading. When he said it was about the Bible, she mocked him for reading this "God-stuff". He replied that if she didn't shut up, he'd throw her into the water and feed her to the sharks. Noting he was an SAS instructor, the mocking ceased. Mark later admitted it was not the best witness, but he was a new Christian, and as he says: "I hadn't yet got to Lloyd-Jones on holiness in Romans 6–7." God had remarkably discipled Mark through his study of Romans; it was the best possible discipleship course and theological education this warrior could have received, and he emerged – not from the desert but from the jungle – a man of God.

Few reading this book will go to theological college for sustained study of theology. And such academic study is certainly no guarantee you will know any more about God or look any more like God. But I can guarantee this: if you master Paul's epistle to the Romans, and if its truths master you; if you pray and study and apply your way through it; then you will not only know more biblical theology than most ministers of religion, you will bear more fruit, such that you can freely sing with the psalmist, "I have more understanding than all my teachers" (Psalm 119:99).

Why not, on your own or with a small group of friends or family, read the whole book in one sitting, aloud, and try to summarize in one sentence what stands out to *you* as its central subject?

2

A Life-Changing Letter

Though many claim Romans is the heart of Paul's theology, as we have stated, there is no consensus on what exactly that heart is, with different themes and different texts competing to be the core.

Romans and the gospel?

Many New Testament commentators tell us Romans is essentially Paul's gospel, a gospel that centres on Christ. Were this so, we would be forced to ask: why does it not resemble any gospel sermon in Acts that Paul gave? And why is Jesus Christ, who is the centre of the gospel, clearly not the central theme of the letter? Granted, God's righteousness as gift received by faith is part of Paul's gospel and a major part of this letter, but we must be careful not to dogmatically assert that Romans *is* the gospel, for that will determine what we preach as gospel, as well as precipitating concerns about an apparent dissonance between Paul's message here and in Luke's summaries of his gospel sermons in Acts 14 and 17. As we will see in the next study, the gospel is integral to this letter as it is integral to the man who wrote it – Paul bled the gospel – but Romans is more nuanced, more pragmatic, and more context-specific. Romans is far more than the gospel, the "kerygma" Paul preached; it clearly addresses salvation history in both its wider frame and its narrower application.

If you compare Romans to Paul's other letters there are marked differences, and if you compare Romans to Paul's recorded sermons in Acts, those differences become even starker – most noticeablely because of its more oblique referencing to Christ's resurrection as vindication of his lordship, and to the sinner's repentance, which are at the forefront of his gospel message. Sure, these themes are presented, but they are present in Paul's presuppositions. Baptist Bible teacher David Pawson does not overstate matters when he says:

> *There is nothing in Romans about heaven or hell; there is nothing about Jesus' return; there is nothing about the kingdom or the church; there is just nothing of what he normally preached. Yet people say Romans is Paul's gospel. It is no such thing. It is part of his gospel.*[11]

Romans and the universal

Word studies and word counts may not always get us to the heart of a letter, but they do shine some light – they can indicate where the weight of an author's argument lies. What is interesting in Romans is the distribution of words used and their difference from Paul's other letters – all highly suggestive of a very particular reason for writing.

The major words and their cognates that give access to the major themes of Romans are telling. Consider this list of the most iterated words, with the number of times they appear shown in brackets: God (153), every/all (79), Law/law (74), Christ (67), justified/righteous (64), sin (48), Lord (43), faith (40), Jesus (36), Spirit/spirit (34), flesh (26), death (25), Jew/Israel (22), word (19), grace (18), hope (16), Father (14), life (14), in Christ (13), gospel (11).

We will return to the theme of God as the centre of the letter, but for a moment, let us consider the second highest word group, "every/all". This gives an indication as to the intention of Paul's writing. The Roman church is experiencing tensions between the Jewish and Gentile believers. Perhaps the Gentile Romans considered themselves superior to the Jews who had rejected Christ and whose branch had been broken. It's possible these Roman Gentile believers have fallen prey to something of the élitist spirit of Rome, even believing that Jerusalem has made way for Rome, and that the Jews have made way for Gentiles. At the same time, the Jewish believers may have thought themselves superior to the Gentile Christians, being heirs of the promises and descendants of the patriarchs. They may have traded on the fact that Jesus was Jewish and that it was from the Jews the gospel came to Rome. Power-playing and posturing from both sides were resulting in a tense and torn church.

Paul's emphatic and sustained universalizing, his constant refrain of "every/all", seeks to remove this tension and division by rejecting racial poles and underscoring what unites them: the same God is revealed to all, whether by creation or conscience or Torah; the same God is sinned against by all; the same God is revealing his wrath to all; the same God freely justifies all who believe; the same God makes all who believe heirs of Abraham; God's Son was freely given up for us all; all Israel will be saved; all food is clean. Jew and Gentile stand all together before God, whether as sinners or as saved; for as Paul states, "there is no distinction: for all..." (Romans 3:22–23).

The "Pax Romana" would be the Roman empire's attempted social construct to unite the disparate nations that belonged to it, establishing unity under the emperor, but it is in fact only the kingdom of heaven through obedience to the shared gospel that can genuinely and freely unite Jew and Gentile under Christ.

Romans is theological – God's word about God

The word "theological" is a conjunction of two Greek words, *theos* meaning "God" and *logos* meaning "word". Romans is profoundly theological, not simply because it is an inspired word *from* God, but because it is a sustained word *about* God. God is thus the central theme in Romans. The word "God" occurs more often than far more typical words like the verb "to be", more than standard prepositions like "into/to/of". In fact the word "God" occurs 153 times in Romans – more often than in any other New Testament book, with the sole exception of Acts where it occurs 166 times. However, Acts has twenty-eight long chapters while Romans has only sixteen generally shorter ones; the word "God" occurs in Acts every 110 words while in Romans it occurs every forty-six words.

Romans is saturated with talk of God. It is pure theo-logy. Like the proverbial stick of Blackpool rock, wherever you break it it says "Blackpool" – and wherever you open Romans, whatever theme it is addressing, God is at the heart. New Testament professor Leon Morris goes so far as to say:

> *No other book in the New Testament has this same concentration on the God-theme... No book in Scripture is as God-centred as this. Fundamentally, Romans is a book about God.*[12]

Paul can speak of: God's gospel; God's Son; God's wrath; God's revelation; God's glory; God's truth; God's judgment; God's decree; God's kindness; God's reward; God's impartiality; God's law; God's relationship; God's name; God's words; God's faithfulness; God's truthfulness; God's offering. It's all about God – he's the point, and he's the subject.

The Roman empire had more gods than any previous empire. Their religious modus operandi was to incorporate all their defeated enemies' gods into their own pantheon – so, for instance, the Roman gods included the gods of Egypt and of Greece. In addition, the Romans believed every home and family had its own familial gods. In 27 BC, at the heart of Rome, a giant Pantheon building to house and honour all the various idols was erected. Roman life was certainly dominated by the differing deities.

To the church in Rome, Paul's letter is polemic and prophetic: all peoples, Jews and Gentiles alike, are summoned and saved by the one and only God, revealed through the gospel. These Christians living in the polytheist power centre of the world are reminded by relentless repetition in this epistle that there is only one God. Paul presses the point 153 times: God is not one among many gods, but *the* God, and he embraces Jew and Gentile through Christ. The Romans hated this and persecuted the church for it – ironically the very term "atheist", meaning literally "without the gods", was coined by the Romans to describe early Christians who rejected the polytheism that was ingrained into Roman culture and who instead worshipped only one God.

Christians across the ages and across the traditions are often tempted to think they are the centre of religion – that somehow it's all about them, all for them. Spirituality and theology becomes ego-centred – God is there to serve them, wait on them, meet their needs and fulfil their aspirations. It all goes to form a Christianity where first-person pronouns dominate – me, my, I – my journey, my sexuality, my becoming, my gifting, my vision, my prosperity, my healing. Romans roundly rebukes this self-centred Christianity and turns us outward and upward to God.

Romans is transformational – God's truth transforms

After the Gospels, the book of Romans is unparalleled in the New Testament for bringing spiritual and theological awakening. A list of those who have encountered Romans and been transformed by God through it, and subsequently become transformers themselves, reads like a potted who's who of church history.

One of the most famous bishops and preachers of the faith in the early church, John Chrysostom, had Romans read aloud to him twice a week (sometimes more), so important did he consider it in laying foundations.[13]

In the fifth century Augustine of Hippo became the great architect of Western theology. He brilliantly described the Trinity, gave a robust defence against the Pelagian heresy of salvation by works, and carefully demarcated the nature of church and kingdom as it overlapped with the philosophies, cultures, and constructs of the Roman empire. As a young man interested only in philosophy and sexual indulgence, he was brought to tears, weeping profusely over the awareness of his own sin and yet confronted with the notion that he was powerless to change himself. Suddenly he heard a child's voice from a neighbouring house saying repeatedly, "Pick it up and read," and he noticed a collection of Paul's writings that had been left on his garden bench by a friend. As he read Romans, God grabbed him, and filled his soul with light and hope. He began a new life serving Christ and his church.

In the sixteenth century the Reformation was triggered through a young, troubled German monk called Martin Luther. Though an Augustinian, he had never grasped the doctrines of salvation by grace; he knew God called him to be righteous, but he didn't know how to become righteous, despite his best efforts, and was tormented by his own sense of sin and guilt and traumatized by the fear of judgment. It was when he was reading Romans that the words in 1:17 were made by the Spirit to stand out to him: "the righteous shall live by faith". In an instant he understood the righteousness God requires is that which he offers to those who simply trust in him by faith. He found rest in God, and the rest is history.

John Wesley was a brilliant eighteenth-century Oxford scholar who returned from America with his tail between his legs after a fruitless mission trip. He longed for God and, like Luther, gave his best efforts to making himself holy. But he knew he failed. As he crossed the Atlantic and went through a severe storm, he was struck by the peace and trust in God that some Moravian passengers exhibited. On returning to England, he attended a meeting at Aldersgate in London where some Moravians read from the preface to Luther's commentary on Romans. As he did so, his soul embraced the truth and reached out to God. He felt his heart "strangely warmed", and he awoke the next day having, as he himself said, no longer the faith of a slave but that of a son. This newfound faith fuelled both the founding of the Methodist movement and the eighteenth-century English awakening.

In the late nineteenth century the so-called "Keswick movement" was birthed, named after a series of annual conventions held in Keswick in England's Lake District; it was devoted to spiritual renewal and the sanctified life. It was phenomenally influential, adding sparks to the Welsh revival, Pentecostal beginnings, East African revival – indeed twentieth-century evangelicalism worldwide. Central to Keswick's theology and spirituality was Romans 7 and the nature of the spiritual versus the carnal life.

Evan Roberts was a Welsh miner who resigned from the pit to seek God in prayer and who, by God's grace, ushered in and directed the Welsh revival in 1904 that saw over 100,000 new converts added to the churches and chapels. Roberts had himself come into personal renewal and peace with God through a revelation of Romans 5:8 – "God shows his love for us in that while we were still sinners, Christ died for us."

The major twentieth-century theologian Karl Barth trumpeted the death of empty human-centred liberal theology after a sustained preaching through Romans during World War I in which he heralded the God-ness of God against a liberalism that had created a god in its own image. His sermons were turned into a book that shook the church in Europe. One scholar, Karl Adams, described his book *Der*

Römerfbrief ("The Letter to the Romans") as falling like a "bombshell on the playground of theologians". Certainly it put a nail in the coffin of German liberal theology and precipitated a whole sea-change and embrace of the Christ-centred, Scripture-revealed God of Jesus Christ.

In the 1960s a young Anglican curate in Gillingham named David Watson spent weeks wrestling with Romans 6 and what it truly meant to be dead to sin and alive to Christ. As he worked through this theme, his character began to change and his preaching exhibited a new power. A local renewal was fuelled in the church of St Mark's under the rector John Collins, and this renewal grew through the ever-widening teaching and evangelistic ministry of David Watson. The effects of that renewal movement are still enjoyed today, particularly within the Church of England, and seminal to it was a profound encounter with God through a profound engagement with Romans.

Our last example of the impact of Romans on influential people of God is John Piper, a world-renowned Reformed preacher and biblical scholar. Piper was called into the ministry through a sustained study of Romans 9. While on sabbatical in 1979 he meditated on the sovereignty and glory of God depicted in that particular chapter. An academic college professor, he felt provoked by God, as if he were saying:

> *I will not simply be analyzed, I will be adored. I will not simply be pondered, I will be proclaimed. My sovereignty is not simply to be scrutinized, it is to be heralded.*[14]

Piper obeyed, resigning from the academy, and accepting a call to be pastor of Bethlehem Church in Minnesota, from where his teaching, preaching, and writing ministry have gone to influence a generation across the nations.

What are we to make of this who's who of church history? Well, what we can say is that Romans is a book that, if prayerfully and obediently engaged with, can change lives, churches, nations – and even the course of history.

3

Meeting Paul

The history of the world in the last two millennia is inseparable from the person of Jesus Christ and the rise of the community of his followers – the church. The church's faith and Christian belief and practice have been articulated and advanced more by Paul than any other church figure.

In astrophysicist Michael Hart's book *The 100 – A Ranking of the Most Influential Persons in History* Paul is ranked sixth after just Confucius, Buddha, Jesus, Isaac Newton, and Muhammad. However, others would dismiss Paul's influence and he doesn't even get a mention in Michael Pollard's *100 Greatest Men*. There has been a constant drip through history of powerful personalities wanting to appear tall by diminishing Paul, and liberals have long sought to drive a wedge between Paul with his epistles and Jesus with the Gospels. American President Thomas Jefferson wrote that Paul was a "dupe and imposter... the first corrupter of the doctrines of Jesus". English novelist and essayist George Bernard Shaw described Paul's doctrines as "a monstrous imposition upon Jesus". Walter Bauer, the nineteenth-century German father of liberal theology, claimed, "Paul was the only arch-heretic known to the apostolic age." Friedrich Nietzsche in his *The Antichrist* gave Paul the title of "dysangelist", regarding him as the counterfeiter, the herald of bad news, "the very opposite of the bearer of good tidings".[15]

But those close to Jesus and close to Paul saw no such dissonance between the doctrine and ministry of Jesus on the one hand and Paul on the other. In Galatians 2:7–10 the Jerusalem apostles, James, John, and Peter – appointed by Jesus himself – welcomed Paul in friendship, honoured God's grace upon him, encouraged him in his apostolic mission to the Gentiles, and exhorted him to remember the poor!

Later Peter would commend Paul's writings, his epistles, already being shared among the church congregations, as being Scriptures, understood as sacred inspired writings (2 Peter 3:16; 2 Timothy 3:16).

Paul was undoubtedly an intellectual giant, tutored under the famed Jewish lawyer Gamaliel. Fluent in Latin, Greek, and Hebrew, with a mastery of logic and language, he authored half the New Testament epistles. Paul was a member of the most élite and most devout sect within Judaism – the Pharisees. He was a passionate man, before his conversion zealously opposing Christianity, and then after his conversion zealously promoting Christ. He was an influential man – his presence and preaching won converts and caused riots, and he upset both Jewish and Roman authorities. He was also a people's person, at ease debating with rabbis in Jerusalem, with scholars in Athens, with washerwomen at the river bank, jailers in prison, governors, and kings. And he was a courageous man, one who endured rejection, derision, suffering, torture, and ultimately beheading – all because of his desire to live for, and promote the name of, Jesus.

No wonder on one occasion when in Ephesus, as the sons of Sceva attempted to exorcize a demonized man, they employed Paul's name as they commanded the demon to leave "in the name of Jesus whom Paul preaches"; but what *is* remarkable is the response of the demons, as recalled by Luke: "Jesus I know, and Paul I recognize, but who are you?" (Acts 19:15). What an extraordinary thing for a demon to have heard of a preacher! No doubt the hosts of hell had been alerted to this man of God who could expose and expel them in the power of the Spirit of Jesus.

In this chapter we shall consider four nouns that Paul ascribes to himself – his name, his duty, his call, and his purpose.

Consider Paul's name

William Shakespeare famously asked, "What's in a name?" Well, in Paul's name we have the whole gospel in microcosm! For Paul had previously been named Saul, until that fateful day when he met Christ on the road to Damascus. Knocked off his horse (according to later tradition), he had some sense knocked into him. And he realized that the One he had been persecuting was the Lord of heaven and earth. Saul had once been an assassin. He had held the coats of the murderers when they were stoning Stephen, giving his vote of approval to their actions. Off of his own bat, he had sought from the high priest official letters to have any Christians in synagogues arrested, and he was about that very business when he was arrested by Jesus (Acts 22:1–8).

We do not know why Saul took the name Paul – there is no evidence of Jesus giving it to him during the encounter – but the tradition of renaming after an encounter with God is very strong in the Bible. Abram becomes Abraham; Jacob becomes Israel; Simon becomes Peter. A new creation, with a new destiny and a new identity, needs a new name. The name Saul stood for "persecutor of Christ", but now Paul would be the "prosecutor for Christ": no longer sent to kill Christians, but now sent to make Christians; no longer the man most feared by Christians, but now the most feared Christian.

Saul was a Hebrew name meaning "asked for from God" and his conversion is no doubt the result of many prayers asking God either to save him or remove him. But he is renamed Paul from the Latin word for "small". No longer Pharisee Saul, the despiser of Gentile dogs, he is now Paul – for the sake of the gospel romanized, latinized, gentilized – apostle to Gentiles, a humble, little man. I like to think it was Paul who took this name for himself, taking the name in the language of the Gentiles he formerly despised, a name meaning "diminutive". This was the act of a broken man, a born-again man, a humbled man, a man with a new vision: to take the gospel to the Roman empire, not to preserve Temple worship in and for Israel. The gospel had worked a complete revolution. The change from Saul to Paul was a change not just of name but also of nature. It is a 180-degree turn, a volte-face, an about-turn; it is true repentance.

The change of name tells us that Jesus' grace extends to befriend even his sworn enemies. No one, not one, no matter how apparently far from God, or hostile to the gospel, or steeped in sin, is beyond the name-changing, life-transforming power of Christ. The Victorian preacher C. H. Spurgeon, speaking of the power of the gospel to transform, said:

> *This change is radical – it gives us a new nature, it makes us love what we hated and hate what we loved; it sets us on a new road; it makes our habits different; it makes us different in private and different in public.*[16]

For centuries converts at baptism have been given a "Christian" name, one that signifies the new life that God has brought and the transformed life God has wrought in the individual. If God gave you a new name, what would it say about his work in you?

Consider Paul's duty

In his encounter with Paul on the Damascus road Jesus said, "I have appeared to you... to appoint you as a servant and witness" (Acts 26:16). Paul never forgot what he was called to be: first and foremost a servant of Jesus. The Greek term is *doulos*, which generally referred to a bond slave. The ancient world was dominated by a culture of slavery. It is estimated that 20 per cent of the whole Roman empire, and 40 per cent of those living in Italy, were slaves. But Jewish culture stood out among its neighbours, for in Israel slavery was abhorred. Israel had no slaves in the Roman sense, only contracted servants who at the end of seven years were to be set free to return home. However, a provision in the Law given by God says that those servants who "love" their master may of their own volition choose to stay; if so, they were to be taken to a wooden door and have their ear pierced with an awl (Exodus 21:5–6), the blood on their face ratifying the union with their master. We must not miss the prophetic typology: Master Jesus was pierced against the wood, his head bloody, serving the world in love. And Paul willingly becomes a slave to love. A slave is there for his master, puts their wish and will before his own. Paul lived to serve his Lord.

As a young lady my granny was a Norden-trained nanny, responsible for minor members of the royal family. Far from regarding being "in service" as demeaning, she regarded it as a great honour. To be a servant of Jesus is the highest honour this universe affords. Blaise Pascal, the seventeeth-century French philosopher, mathematician, and God-lover, wrote:

> *There are only three types of people; those who have found God and serve him; those who have not found God and seek him; and those who live not seeking, or finding him. The first are rational and happy; the second unhappy and rational; the third foolish and unhappy.*[17]

Paul had found and served God; he was certainly rational and blisteringly happy.

How may we apply this to ourselves? First, we are called to serve Jesus. There is a tendency among some to think Jesus is their personal fairy godmother, waving a magic wand to all their wishes. Or perhaps he is their servant, running at their beck and call, there to meet their needs on demand. Not so. Like Paul, we exist to serve our Saviour. And in our prayers, how about not presenting him with a list but occasionally starting with: "Lord, what can I do for you today?"

Secondly, Paul's first duty is to serve Jesus and only after that to serve Christ's body – the church. Some Christians may not assume God exists for their benefit, but they certainly think that the church and its ministers do. They are there to serve them, cater for their needs, wipe their noses, jump when shouted for. Many become dependent on their ministers, and ministers can become co-dependent on them, needing to be needed. No; the role of a minister is to serve Christ, and only secondarily to serve the church, and that service is intended to produce mature disciples who themselves live to serve Jesus.

Consider Paul's call

Paul was called to be an apostle. He did not take this office to himself; he did not apply or interview for it; it was vocation, a charism, a divine summons.

He was set apart, "a chosen instrument of mine to carry my name before the Gentiles and kings and the children of Israel" (Acts 9:15).

No one can take this apostolic priestly title to themselves, or even have it conferred by others. It is a divine office with a divine sanction. In Ephesians 4:11 and 1 Corinthians 12:28 Paul is clear that apostleship is God-given, an anointing and appointing by the resurrected Christ through the Spirit. This is not a natural talent harnessed by the church, as some modern church movements and thinkers propose; it is not latent "entrepreneurialism"; Richard Branson and Bill Gates are not unconverted apostles! The Greek noun *apostolos* simply means "one who is sent". An apostle is a man on a mission from God, who proclaims the good news of God – he is a herald, an ambassador, a pioneer. Apostle is as apostle does. Note that Paul puts "servant" before "apostle", thus defining the character of an apostle. There is no self-promoting pride, no power play, no preening, but service for his Saviour. Next notice how Paul puts "gospel" after "apostle" (Romans 1:1b), defining the focus of the apostle as one framed by gospel ministry.

Apostles found churches and ground churches in the faith. The church is built on the doctrinal foundations laid by the proclamation of the gospel and explanation of the faith given by the apostle. The first Jerusalem apostles were devoted to teaching doctrine, to prayer and the ministry of word (Acts 2:42; 6:4). Most of Paul's ministry was not planting churches but nurturing them through teaching, for instance teaching for eighteen months in Corinth (Acts 18:11). That's how you build a healthy and strong church – by teaching the faith. Apostles are accompanied by signs and wonders (2 Corinthians 12:12); apostles are first-hand witnesses to Christ's resurrection (Acts 1:22; 4:33; 1 Corinthians 9:1); apostles are despised and rejected, the scum of the earth (1 Corinthians 4:13).

I am always wary when I hear people describe themselves as an apostle (and many do). Certainly it is de rigueur to describe oneself as apostolic. But I repeat, apostle is as apostle does – and most who claim the title exhibit none of the evidences.

Now, do not misunderstand me. I do believe in apostles, just as I believe in miracles. But let us have some integrity and, if we are going to claim the title, let us walk the talk. Paul was actually challenging the super-apostles in Corinth when he wrote that, although they were powerful in word, he would see if they had any real power when he came to visit (1 Corinthians 4:19).

What matters is apostolic success not apostolic succession. Apostolic success depends on apostolic faithfulness to the faith once delivered, and fruitfulness in lives changed, churches planted, the kingdom advancing.

Consider Paul's purpose

An apostle is set apart for the gospel – the gospel defines the apostle. If the gospel is not central for them, they are a false apostle. And there are lots around. There were in the early church, and many of the epistles were written to counter error that had crept in through these false teachers. Paul speaks of being "set apart". The Greek word *aphoridzo* is based on the word for a horizon or demarcating line. It was a term the Pharisees used to describe themselves as set apart *from* the sinful world, but Paul says he is set apart *for* the gospel ministry.

Note Paul speaks of *the* gospel. There are not lots of gospels, not lots of competing truth-claims in a pot pourri of realities – just one good news, as there is one God, Lord, and Saviour. The concept of being "set apart" is probably drawn from the Old Testament priestly office, where in the temple (set-apart place) the Levites (set-apart ministers) offered sacrifices (set-apart animals) to God (set apart from all else). Paul will further expound this theme in Romans 15:16 where Paul says he is in the priestly service of the gospel of God – offering Gentiles as sacrifices, set apart for God. This set-apart, priestly role, this New Testament apostolic ministry, is not essentially pastoral, liturgical, administrative, or even sacramental – it is a gospel ministry. The gospel is the ground of Paul's life. As Professor James Dunn says, "Since his conversion, the gospel had been the dominant and determinative focus of his whole life."[18]

This gospel that transformed his life, he lives to give to others. Remove the gospel from Paul and we have Saul; remove the gospel from Paul and we lose half of Acts and half the New Testament! Remove the gospel from Paul and we do not have churches founded in Corinth, Ephesus, Thessalonica, Philippi, Colossae and the good news heralded throughout Asia Minor. Paul is a gospel man. Seventy-five times in his epistles he directly refers to the gospel. Paul's worship is a response to the gospel; Paul's identity is constituted by the gospel; Paul's energy is spent on presenting the gospel; Paul's writings are an explication and application of the gospel. Paul lived by the gospel and for the gospel, and he died for the gospel.

And what was his gospel? John Piper says, "God is the Gospel"[19]

– his work, his ways, his will. Paul's life and message and life message are all about God.

In conclusion

The ancient Greek proverb says, "The hearts of the great can be changed." Whether great or small, God and his gospel transform lives. Who would ever have thought the assassin Saul could be the apostle Paul? Such graces occurred then, and still do today. Who would ever have thought my friend, now named David, who was once named Abu Bakr, the son of a grand Mufti, himself a Muslim imam and doctor of Sharia law, would ever encounter Christ in a vision in a mosque at prayers, and become a preacher of the gospel to Muslims in Britain? But that is what the gospel does, for that is what God does.

4

The Gospel (1:2–7)

In our last study we considered Paul's introduction and self-description of his identity and ministry: he is Paul, not Saul, a servant of Christ, an apostle, set apart for the gospel of God. Paul was a gospel man: saved by the gospel, he lived by and for the gospel. This gospel of God for which he is set apart underpins this epistle. In Romans, Paul is seeking to explicate and apply the gospel of God to the particular situation facing the church community in Rome. In this chapter we will look at verses 2–7. This is Paul's gospel entrée, his hors d'oeuvre, before the main course.

The gospel is the good news

The gospel is unique. It stands alone and does not compete with or complement other truths. Supreme over all, there is only one gospel – the gospel about God's Son. The world has many religions, many ideologies and truths generally perceived, but only one gospel. The Swiss theologian Karl Barth wrote:

> *The Gospel does not enter into competition with other philosophies and religions... it is not one truth among other truths... it sets the question mark against all other truths.*[20]

In our post-modern, relativistic, pluralistic age people are offered a smorgasbord of religious, philosophical, and ideological options to pick and choose and blend and mould to their lives. The cultural rejection of pure form, of absolute truth systems, leads people to make up their own combinations – a bit of eastern yoga, with a bit of Chinese medicine, with a bit of Jewish Kabbalistic philosophy, with a bit of Jesus' Sermon on the Mount, with a bit of Western capitalism. They do not realize – or even care – that all these truths do not cohere, and that their underpinning worldviews are profoundly contradictory. It's a mark of the muddled thinking of our time. Mix all paints on a pallet, and you are left with mud, not art. Some think it's cool to be intellectually relativistic, pluralistic, and eclectic, but it's stupid. One of Aristotle's three classical laws of thought is the law of non-contradiction. This states that two opposing truth claims may both be wrong but cannot both be right. Opposing conceptions of reality, of divinity, cannot cohere in synthesis. Paul claims his gospel is *the* gospel – it either is or it isn't, but either way it cannot be one gospel among many.

At the heart of the gospel is the scandal of particularity. The gospel will not permit itself to be cut and pasted in among others. The apostles stated, "there is no other name under heaven given among men and earth by which we must be saved" (Acts 4:12). Jesus stated that he was the way, the truth, and the life, with no one coming to the Father except through him (John 14:6). C. S. Lewis rightly saw that such exclusive claims confront us with an option – either Jesus is a lunatic who believed this when it was not true; or he was a liar, knowing it was not true but manipulating and deceiving people; or he was the Lord, truly the revelation and mediation of God. And if he is the Lord, then he is not to share his throne with anyone else and his gospel must be accepted whole, not piecemeal. It's all or nothing. We must not abuse the Christian gospel, or any other religious or philosophical gospels, by thinking they can cohere. They cannot.

The gospel is the greatest news

The term "gospel" translates the Greek word *euangelion,* which is a compound of *eu* (meaning "well" or "good") and *angelion* meaning "message" (an angel is a divine messenger). The term *euangelion* was used in the ancient Greek language to speak of an edict from the king, or a prophecy from the gods, or formal news of victory at war. At the heart of the Christian faith is a gospel – great and glorious and glad-making news. It's the best news the world has ever heard. Sadly, some

Christians look like sour-faced Pharisees, as if they've mistaken the haemorrhoid cream for the toothpaste, rather than tasted that the Lord is good in the gospel.

Occasionally I have found myself shouting aloud in frustration at the news on the TV, "Is that it? Is that all you have to say today? Is there no good news? Have you nothing righteous to say?" The seventeenth-century French poet Jean de la Fontaine once wrote: "Every journalist owes tribute to the evil one." Journalists are bringers of bad news. But Christians are different. They are evangelists, bringers of *euangelion*, the greatest news ever told.

Why is the gospel the greatest news? Because it satisfies all human longing. Intellectual, existential, spiritual, moral, and eternal desires are met. I recall visiting Betel, a drug rehabilitation mission founded by Elliot Tepper in Spain, and now working in several countries worldwide. In the Madrid church, there are several hundred young men, and their mothers and friends and family, who come to church having seen the transformation God has worked in these former vice- and drug-ravaged lives. They are a church full of people who were drug addicts, dealers, prostitutes, and even murderers. Here they met Jesus Christ, found forgiveness of sins, freedom from slavery, a family to belong to and a future to live for. When they worship they shout loudly and dance enthusiastically. Raul was one of the first to be rescued from the hell of heroin addiction. He became a pastor and church leader, but sadly died of HIV contracted through shared needle use. Asked why the *betelitos*, the former addicts in the church, celebrate so enthusiastically, he replied: "We dance because we cannot fly." Such is the overflow from embracing this good news.

The gospel is promise fulfilled

This is the gospel "which he promised beforehand through his prophets in the holy Scriptures" (1:2).

Promises are easily made but not always readily kept. They can be cheap.

George Stephanopoulos, a US political commentator, famously said in a radio interview, "The President has kept all the promises he intended to keep."[21]

The word "promise" in English usage comes from the Latin *promittere,* literally referring to something "sent before" or "sent ahead". A promise is a word or vow sent in advance, a declaration that something will or will not be done. In the Old Testament God sent a word of promise that one day he would send a Son, a Saviour. The gospel is a promise both given and fulfilled. God kept his word. Paul says the prophets in the holy Scriptures were full of expectation of the visitation of God. The realization of that is the gospel of Jesus.

The Old Testament Scriptures contain over a hundred direct prophecies relating to the gospel. They speak of one born of Adam's seed who would crush the snake's head (Genesis 3:15); of one born in Bethlehem (Micah 5:2); one born of a virgin named Immanuel "God with us" (Isaiah 7:14), born of David's seed (Isaiah 11:1; Luke 2:4), a suffering servant who would bear the sins of us all (Isaiah 53:12) – every page of the Old Testament is watermarked with prefigurements ("types") of Jesus: every prophet a type of Jesus the Word of God; every priest a type of Jesus the Great High Priest; every king a type of Jesus the King of kings; every sacrifice a type of Jesus the Lamb of God who takes away the sin of the world; every holy place (altar, Tabernacle, sanctuary) a type of Christ dwelling with us.[22]

The gospel was no bolt out of the blue – it had long been longed for. Year after year seasons came and went, generations were born and died, kingdoms rose and fell, and the promises waited unfulfilled. The word was heard – one day, some day, he will come, God will come... salvation will come. Abraham, Moses, David, Isaiah all saw it from afar. But now, on us, has come the fulfilment of the ages (1 Corinthians 10:11; Galatians 4:4).

The Gospel is Son-centred

This is the gospel "concerning his Son" (verse 3). In 1:3–4 we have what Calvin termed "the definition of the gospel". It is a remarkable summary of the gospel, so succinct and sublime that some scholars believe it to have been an early hymn or creed. It is centred on the Son and presents him in his two natures, human and divine, Son of man and Son of God.

As Son of man he was descended from David "according to the

flesh" (the Greek *kata sarka* is an idiom which literally states "born of the seed"). Jesus is not some distant, deistic divine who walked on sand and left no footprints, abstracted from the realities and frailties of human existence. He was fully human, he shared our flesh and blood.

As Son of man he was designated Son of God "in power according to the Spirit of holiness by his resurrection from the dead, Jesus Christ our Lord". Jesus' divinity was visibly demonstrated through his resurrection in power. The resurrection was the vindication of his claim to be God and his ability to forgive sins. The resurrection was the conclusive event wherein God's power was displayed: accepting atonement, forgiving sins, reversing death, and shattering the demonic.

A hardened old soldier pal of mine struggles with Christianity: he says he wants to believe, claims he would give anything to believe, but knows it all hangs on the resurrection, and at that he balks. He said to me, "I've held bits of dead men; the dead don't come back." But *what if* he who claimed to be God, who lived a sinless life, who uttered the most profound things ears ever heard, who healed the sick with a word, what if such a one *did* come back, never to die again? Surely then we would know God had come among us. Christianity stands or falls on the resurrection. Paul, when he went by the name of Saul, despised the name of Jesus, believing him to be an imposter and a blasphemer; but when he met this risen, death-conquering, glorious Jesus on the Damascus road, everything changed.

Paul's Christology centres on three names; verse 4 states "*Jesus Christ* our *Lord*" (my italics). Jesus is the carpenter from Nazareth, whose name means "God saves" – he is Saviour and Deliverer. Christ is the long awaited anointed one, the Messiah, the King of Israel. The Lord is the name of God. The Saviour Jesus from Nazareth, the anointed king of Israel, the divine Lord... this is the heart of the gospel. The good news is focused on this single person and message, Jesus Christ the Lord. He is the main actor in the drama – he must take centre stage, and he is the one with whom we have to do.

One error of emphasis when presenting the gospel is to focus on mechanics – to try and present all the mysteries and metaphors of the atonement. What is so evident here is the simplicity, clarity, purity, and yet profundity of Paul's cameo of the gospel. How many of us preachers or teachers say far more without saying half as much!

Although it is presupposed in his reference to the resurrection, Paul surprisingly doesn't mention the word "cross" or "crucified" – indeed, the word is not found even once in the whole letter of Romans. The gospel concerns God's Son – Jesus Christ the Lord is the very heart of the gospel. We must be careful not to turn the kerygma into algebra.

The gospel is for his name's sake

Paul writes, "*through* whom we have received grace and apostleship to bring about the obedience of faith for the sake of his name" (verse 5, my italics). If one error is to focus on the gospel mechanically and abstractly, the second error is to focus on it purely subjectively – "What's in it for me?" While the good news certainly is good news "for me", because God has visited and acted for me, to forgive me, to deliver me, and live with me, the gospel is not a Middle-eastern self-help course. It is not a benefit package, some kind of eternal pension scheme, or consumer confectionary. No; it concerns the Son, and it's for his name's sake – for his glory and renown; for his honour and his crown.

I know a church where each week, instead of a creed, they recite a "statement of faith", claiming, among other things, "cheques in the post". When Jesus died without a shirt on his back, smeared in his own blood, he did not die to make us wealthy. He died to make us holy and fit for eternity with God. The gospel is not there to make you healthy or wealthy, but to save you from sin, death, and hell, and present you as a servant to Christ.

The apologist Ravi Zacharias has written a book for disaffected churchgoers called *Has Christianity Failed You*? Ravi is responding to people's feelings that the church has let them down. Sadly there is doubtless truth in that; church can fail people, her ministers and members disappoint. But God and the gospel fail no one. Sometimes expectations have failed, but that's because those expectations were misplaced in the first place. Of course the question whether Christianity has "failed me" would seem to presuppose Christianity is for me, that I am the centre of God's universe. But God is not a moon orbiting me; he saves me for his name's sake.

The gospel is a call from love

Paul writes "to all those in Rome who are loved by God" (verse 7). The presupposition of the gospel call is the love of God. God's love is the internal logic, the "deeper magic" of the gospel. Moses' words for Israel hold true for the church: it was because the Lord loved you that he brought you out of slavery (Deuteronomy 7:7–8). However, the presupposition of God's love does not override our volition: will we love the Lover? As C. H. Spurgeon stated, "The hearing of the gospel involves the hearer in responsibility" – a response to the call from love is required.

There has been a mantra among church growth movements in recent years: "Belong, Believe, Behave." It seeks to express the reality that faith is often a journey that begins with an embrace by the church community, long before faith in Christ is nurtured; and only after that is there a lifestyle change. It certainly challenges us as Christians not to place theological, credal, or moral hurdles for people to jump over before they can even get near church. The church must have a soft fringe, an open door, an open-heart policy. That said, we are also confronted by certain imperatives.

A call to believing obedience (verse 5)

The gospel of God's Son must be believed and received. Paul will develop this more clearly throughout this epistle to the Romans, but faith – a trusting belief – is what we must bring to God's gospel. It is not much, but it is necessary; it is the very ground on which the gospel is effected in us. True faith elicits obedience: to trust is to obey.

A call to belong to Christ (verse 6)

No longer lost, lonely, homeless, wandering. No longer a stranger in the crowd, an outsider looking in. Christ bids us not simply to believe in a creed, but to come home and rest and belong in God's family. The twentieth-century psychologist William Glasser in his "choice theory" famously argued that, as humans, we are driven by the genetically ordered needs of survival, love, and belonging, power, freedom, and fun. All these, and much more besides, come with believing in Jesus.

A call to become saints (verse 7)

A little while ago the pope made a special journey to Oxford to "beatify" Cardinal Newman – to formally institute the former Oxford cleric as a saint. While the Protestant in me protests to some of the Roman Catholic doctrine surrounding saints, the real issue is this: we do not need a special ceremony to make someone a saint after they have died. On the contrary, faith in Jesus' death is the means and the moment when we are declared as saints – set apart as holy, before God and for him. Whoever believes in Christ, belongs to Christ, and is beatified by Christ.

That is the great gift of Christianity. The great challenge of the Christian life is then to become what we are.

Paul concludes his opening greetings with a blessing: "Grace to you and peace" (verse 7). This is no ordinary greeting – it is without precedent in ancient writings, Greek or Hebrew. Grace – *charis* – was the traditional Greco-Roman greeting and blessing. Peace – *eirene* – was and is the traditional Jewish and Semitic greeting (the Greek word *eirene* translates the Hebrew *shalom*). In and through this gospel, centred on God's Son, East meets West and the very best blessings of both worlds come together.

In conclusion

The gospel is the hope of the world – her only hope. The church dare not lose it or abuse it or confuse it.

These are some of the last words the famed Baptist preacher C. H. Spurgeon ever uttered:

> *I may not have many more opportunities of preaching, and I make up my mind to this one thing, that I will waste no time upon secondary themes, but when I do preach it shall be the gospel, or something very closely bearing upon it. I will endeavour each time to strike under the fifth rib, and never beat the air. Those who have a taste for the superfluities may take their fill of them; it is for me to keep to the great necessary truths by which men's souls are saved. My work is to preach Christ*

crucified and the gospel, which gives men salvation through faith. I hear every now and then of very taking sermons about some bright new nothing or another. Some preachers remind me of the emperor who had a wonderful skill in carving men's heads upon cherry stones. What a multitude of preachers we have who can make wonderfully fine discourses out of a mere passing thought, of no consequence to anyone. But we want the gospel. We have to live and to die, and we must have the gospel. Certain of us may be cold in our graves before many weeks are over, and we cannot afford to toy and trifle: we want to see the bearings of all teachings upon our eternal destinies, and upon the gospel which sheds its light over our future.[23]

5

Apostolic Apps (1:8–16)

One of the new words that has entered the vocabulary of my family – and no doubt of many other families – in recent years is the word "app", short for "applications". For Christmas and birthdays, my sons, who have iPods, are often asking for credits for iTunes to buy apps. There are over 700,000 (and rising) apps available, and one of the most popular downloads are weather apps. The weirdest download app I've come across must surely be one called "Hold On". This is a solitaire-type game, and its goal is to see how long your finger can keep pressed down on a virtual button. It times your endurance levels and you can submit your score to your own personal mini-league. Presumably it's important for those who wish to keep their finger on the pulse!

In this study we are considering seven apostolic apps. As we consider this list, ask yourself and God which of these apps you are going to download into your daily routine?

1. I-Thank

"First, I thank my God through Jesus Christ for all of you" (verse 8).

Paul starts rhetorically by saying "first", but like many preachers gets carried away and writes the whole of Romans without ever listing a second or third point! His first point is to thank God – Paul's life and letters are marked by thanksgiving – and among his most repeated catchphrases are "thanks be to God" or "I thank God". Paul never got over the wonder of the gift of God's grace. And Paul never wants us to get over what God has done for us. In Romans 1:18–25 Paul defines two archetypal sins: idolatry and immorality. But, he states, at the heart of sin is the fact that they did not give God thanks (verse 21).

If the hallmark of sin is withholding thanksgiving to God for all his gifts, then the hallmark of a redeemed and sanctified believer must be thanksgiving to God.

The German existentialist philosopher Martin Heidegger was fond of quoting the seventeenth-century German Pietist phrase: "Denken ist Danken" – to think is to thank.[24] We need to constantly remind ourselves of all we have to be thankful for: breath, work, rest, play, food, clothing, shelter, money, friends, heath care, and so much more. And then there's God himself, given to us in love. William Shakespeare prays: "O Lord who lends me life, lend me a heart replete with thankfulness."[25] I sometimes think the angels stand aghast at the paucity of our gratitude to God.

Giving thanks to God is not only his due, it is to our benefit. Thanksgiving is our gift to God that actually gives back to us at some point in the future. Psychologists have repeatedly proven in clinical tests that adopting a thankful attitude each day (even without directing that thanks to God) produces immediate benefits: the thankful person has a greater sense of feeling well; sleeps deeper and longer; has a better marriage; is physically healthier; more optimistic; attains their goals; is more alert; enthusiastic; energetic; and caring towards others.

2. I-Serve

"God... whom... I serve with my spirit" (verse 9).

When Paul speaks of being a servant of God he employs a technical term. The Greek *latreuo* is drawn from the Old Testament priestly Temple ministry. The priests were servants of God, and Paul offers a priestly service through his prayer and preaching, giving to God sacrifices and offerings of Gentiles saved through the gospel (Romans 15:16). This divine service is offered from the heart – "with my spirit" – it is not lip service, nor begrudging duty, and never a mere show for others. Paul serves because his heart is ablaze with love for God. To serve God is the greatest privilege this world affords. Paul knew the perfect freedom of being "On His Majesty's Service".

David Brainerd, the eighteenth-century missionary to the Native Americans, once recorded in his journal: "If I cannot serve God one way I will serve him another – I will never leave off this blessed service." Only someone whose heart has been captivated and captured for Christ could ever write like that. Without this, our service will be duty; whereas with a captivated heart our service will be duty and delight. How sad it is that so many of us do not know this delight – in fact some do not even know this duty. On the contrary, some would apparently rather God serve them than they serve God. The mark of sin is to be self-serving. The hallmark of the redeemed people of God is a life laid down.

3. I-Pray

"I mention you always in my prayers" (verses 9–10).

Paul was a pray-er. The high priest of Israel bore before God the twelve tribes engraved on twelve gemstones on his breastplate as a physical symbol of a people carried in the heart to God. Similarly Paul as a priest in serving God also served the Roman Christians by bearing them on his heart in prayer.

In Chapter 16 of this epistle Paul sends greetings and personal words to twenty-six individuals "by name". These personal addresses reveal his pastoral heart. He clearly knew some, like Priscilla and Aquila, because he had worked with them. He may never have met the others, but he'd certainly heard of them and remembered their names, and as priest and apostle he committed himself daily to pray, "always", for all of them, carrying them, caring, naming them. Paul was an intercessor, a man who walked and talked with God. I am reminded of the evangelical statesman John Stott. Every day he opened an old notebook that contained constantly updated lists of names, some of which had been there for over three decades. Stott prayed every morning between 5 and 6.30 a.m., interceding for individuals and ministries, including many who would never meet him or know of his prayers before eternity. Stott's ministry, mentoring, and writing have influenced thousands, perhaps millions. But only in heaven will we know what influence his daily prayers had.

At theological college over twenty years ago our missions tutor, Howard Peskett, in the very first lecture, handed us all a small, three-inch sized index card, and asked us to write our name and the word "hello" in any language we knew. He then collected them in. He said nothing by way of explanation, and then began his lecture. I wondered what this eccentric act was about, until later I learned that he had a card for every student that he taught – and prayed for them every morning. I'm humbled when I think of my former tutor's prayer life, or read about Paul's prayer life, or John Stott's. What paltry percentage of my prayer life is given for others? How many people do you name before God each day, apart from yourself?

4. I-Impart

"I long to see you, that I may impart to you some spiritual gift to strengthen you" (verse 11).

The Roman church is receiving a letter from Paul that is his longest, most detailed, most sustained presentation, reflection, and contextual application of the gospel. What a gift it is. And yet he also longs to see them in person, so that he can impart something that a letter can't convey. He sends them the word of doctrine, but hopes to come to impart a charism – something "spiritual" – that which belongs to the Spirit of God, to the supernatural not the natural world. "Gift" – *charisma* – is the same word used of the extraordinary grace-gifts in Romans 12:6 and in 1 Corinthians 12. In 2 Timothy 1:6 the word is used of the gift he received through the laying on of hands. This supernatural spiritual charism is what Paul desires for them, so that they may be strengthened, encouraged, and enabled to stand firm.

Paul gives no hint as to what this gift is. Maybe it will be given purely by the sovereignty of God in the moment of unction, or maybe Paul intended to come and observe and see what was lacking and then, with his apostolic authority, to release something to the community.

Apostles impart – they don't seek to impress or impose. Apostles don't come to *receive* but to *leave* something of God. The early Didache ("Didache", meaning "teaching", was a widely used late first-century document which instructed the church on various pastoral matters), claimed someone was a false prophet if they stayed too long and expected money. Apostles seek to equip the church with spiritual gifts for works of service. They see what is lacking in a church and impart a deposit. They reveal the heart of the gift-giving

God. These are unforgettable moments of divine gracing – where heaven touches earth, where Father God comes, arms laden with good things for his children.

5. I-Am Bound

"I am bound to both Jews and Greeks" (verse 14).

The church in Rome appears to be working through tensions and divisions between Jewish and Gentile congregation members. Paul throughout will address himself to Jews and then Gentiles, and show how both are sinners, both are saved by faith, both fit into God's plan and need to get on with one another. Paul is clear that he is a man for both. He won't take sides, and nor must they. Paul says he is *obligated* – he is in debt, he owes himself to both groups. To the Jews he is obligated, as a Jew himself; to the Jews belong the patriarchs, promises, and prophets; from them comes the Messiah, his Jesus. To the Gentiles Paul is obligated because Jesus saved him and commissioned him as apostle to the Gentiles – his existence is graciously grounded in taking the gospel to the Gentiles. As the New Testament scholar Leon Morris says, "An obligation to Jesus Christ who died for him, produced an obligation to all those for whom he died."[26]

We too are obligated to the Jew and the Gentile. We are obligated to the Jews because without them we have no Jesus, no Bible, no gospel. We are obligated to our Gentile ancestors who nurtured and proclaimed and suffered for the gospel, to pass it down through the ages to us today. Tragically, some Christians have replaced the Jewish faith with the Gentile church and sought to exorcize all trace of Judaism, almost to gentilize Jesus. Tragically also, some Christians would have us replace Gentile church with Judaism. Israel zealots want to circumcise and Judaize Western Gentiles. No, like Paul we are indebted to both Jew and Gentile – and what God has joined together let no man put asunder.

6. I-Preach

"I am eager to preach the gospel to you" (verse 15).

As well as imparting an anointing, a special strengthening gift by the Spirit, Paul wants to come and herald the gospel. He wants to reap a harvest among the Gentiles (verse 13), to win people to Christ in the pagan capital. Paul was never content with past successes – he was constantly looking for new places, new opportunities, new people to make Christ known. Rome was the symbolic centre of the world – the heart of the greatest empire ever to rise in the West. Paul thrilled at the prospect of proclaiming that Jesus Christ is Lord as much to the principalities and powers as to the multitudes of pagans.

Preaching is the mark of an apostle. Preaching is the divine economy wherein God is revealed, strongholds are torn down, lives are transformed. When a man or woman, filled with the Spirit of God, stands before a group, opens their mouth, and faithfully declares the full gospel, God also speaks. God comes and wrestles with and for the heart and mind of the listener. In the age of internet, iPhones, iPads, and the iCloud people may dismiss – even despise – I-Preaching as a linguistic dinosaur. But this foolishness of preaching remains the wisdom and the way of God.

When I was considering entering the ministry, I recall a church elder telling me the age of preaching had passed away: now had come the age of... the overhead projector! This remarkable electronic light device would transform the presenting of the Christian message, and millions would flock to Christ through the creative artistry of coloured pens and acetate! Or not! The OHP is fast fading into history, whereas that old-time, old-fashioned preaching remains.

Many years ago, when I was still new to the chaplaincy in Oxford, I was wobbling one day over my calling and feeling insecure. My boss at that time, David MacInnes, said an unforgettable truth, which steadied me then and has done many times since. It is credited originally to various church divines, including Bishop Benson, Philip Brookes, C. H. Spurgeon: "If God has called you to be a preacher, don't stoop to be a king." I myself have often quoted it in gatherings of those who have a call to preach, and seen them visibly roused again to their high calling.

7. I-Am Not Ashamed

"I am not ashamed of the gospel" (verse 16).

Paul can eagerly desire to preach the gospel because he's proud of it, because he knows that in it God's power is revealed for salvation. In civilized Roman culture one was forbidden to even mention crucifixion, as it was the ultimate barbaric punishment reserved for the worst barbarian criminals. And yet Paul glories in it, boasts of it; willingly, publically, unashamedly he announces it to be God's mystery and wisdom. Though Paul does not speak directly of the cross but of the gospel, the cross is the centre of the gospel – the locus of divine revelation and salvation.

Many are ashamed of the cross. Nietzsche mocked the image of Christ crucified as God being like a spider on a wall.[27] Today, many who claim to be Christian are offended by the cross; embarrassed and ashamed they try to mellow its stigma and make it more palatable. They seek to remove from it the status of divine requirement. They approach it from the angle of the injustice of humanity to crucify the Son of God. Or they interpret it as being the identification of God with our sufferings, crying alongside us. But they find it unthinkable that God would actually require the cross as payment for the debt humankind owes him, as satisfaction for justice.

Here are just two recent statements from notable figures who have rejected the traditional New Testament interpretation of the cross as a substitutionary sacrifice for sin, and who reject the notion that God punished Jesus for our sin at the cross. Steve Chalke, Baptist minister and advocate for Christian social action, says that such an action would be more akin to "a form of cosmic child abuse";[28] and even worse is Emergent Church guru Alan Jones's claim: "The church's fixation with the death of Christ as the universal saving act must end."[29] In an attempt to do away with the offence, the "scandal of the gospel", they remove the very heart of the gospel that alone can save. Many haven't the stomach for the cross. They want to avoid its visceral, vicarious nature. They balk at its *sola via ad salum* – the only way to salvation.

It has often been said that one mark of theological liberalism is to give new meaning to old words. But if we are to receive the merit of the cross, we need to embrace the old meaning of the old rugged cross. Of this Paul was not ashamed, and neither must we be. We can have our heads held high at God's Son held high on the ignominious gallows, where love and justice meet, and where Christ is glorified.

Let us with the writer to the Hebrews recall our Jesus who, for the joy set before him, endured the cross, scorning its shame (Hebrews 12:2).

In conclusion

Paul presents a cameo of his ministry and inspires us with his seven apostolic apps: I-Thank, I-Serve, I-Pray, I-Impart, I-Am Bound, I-Preach, I-Am Not Ashamed. Which app is God calling you to download to your life?

6

Concerning His Son (1:3)

What concerns you? In a US survey[30] conducted in 2010, 1,000 adults were asked what concerned them most for the coming year. (The focus was on the political realm.) The results were:

- 98% economy, money, employment
- 25% health
- 24% national security
- 9% immigration and border control
- 4% environment
- 4% education

What occupies your mind, your emotions, your planning? Maybe you are feeling positive and excited, or perhaps you are anxious and apprehensive. This list certainly gives us much to worry about.

The apostle Paul had other concerns, and one dominated all others.

Concern yourself with God's Son

Paul knew that the Old Testament promises and prophecies concerned God's Son. Paul's service as an apostle will concern God's Son. Paul's gospel concerns God's Son (1:3).

The Greek word translated "concerning" is *peri*, literally "about, concerning, regarding, around, near, touching". It is a preposition of proximity or connection.

Like spokes trued into a wheel hub, everything in the Christian life – doctrine, deeds, worship, service, character formation, mission – all must concern and connect to the hub of Christ. One reason Paul is writing this epistle to the Romans is to centre their life together on the Son, to renew their relationship to the gospel. Paul is concerned that the church in Rome's concern is not the right one. They are concerned about many things: they are having an internal leadership dispute, there are tensions over the ongoing role of Jewish roots in the life of Christian so Paul wants to lift their vista, to renew their concern for the gospel of Christ.

It would be a strange soccer fan that paid more attention to the advertising on the sideline or the latest kit-colours than to the players and the game. Yet as Christians we can so easily get sidetracked as we take our eye off the ball and lose what the pastor John Wimber repeatedly called us to: "the main and the plain".

Paul Tillich, the radical 1960s Christian philosopher and theologian, defined religion as "the state of being grasped by an ultimate concern".[31] It's a useful term, for it forces us to ask, "What is the ultimate concern of our Christianity?" And if the answer is anything penultimate, anything less than being in Christ, we have substituted footnotes for the main text.

The gospel concerns God's Son. The Bible concerns God's Son. Jesus said the Old Testament was all about him. When Jesus met the two on the road to Emmaus, "beginning with Moses and all the Prophets, he interpreted to them in all the Scriptures the things concerning himself" (Luke 24:27). Shortly afterwards when Jesus met the Eleven he said, "everything written about me in the Law of Moses and the Prophets and the Psalms must be fulfilled" (Luke 24:44).

I love the cameo of concern in Mary and Martha's responses to Jesus (Luke 10:38–42). Martha is concerned "with many things" – being a good host, making sure everyone has enough to eat, serving her guests. Mary is simply concerned with the Son – she only has eyes for him; he is all her attention. Mary knows her place, and there and then it was not in the kitchen but at the feet of Jesus. Martha resents Mary for not pitching in and offering a helping hand, but Jesus affirms Mary's decision: "one thing is necessary. Mary has chosen the good portion" (Luke 10:42).

All of us can easily leave Christ to one side while we roll with the exigencies of pressurized life in the twenty-first century. It's not that we intentionally ignore Christ, it's that we aren't conscientiously conscious for him. And thus, little by little, he moves to the periphery of our concerns. The Corinthian church sidelined Jesus when it became more concerned with charismatic power, dynamic personalities, and fleshly indulgences. The Galatian church sidelined Jesus when it was more concerned with its efforts to justify itself before the Law. The Colossian church sidelined Jesus with its concern for religious festivals and food, and spiritual phantasms. Very few New Testament epistles do not in some measure address churches in crisis due to being abstracted from Christ by false teachers and false doctrines. What sort of a scriptural canon would the church have collated from the apostles if the church had faithfully concerned itself with living the Gospels and doing Acts of apostles? Of course, God knows the propensity of humankind, even regenerate Christians, and the issues of the church then are the issues of the church always – to concern itself with less than Christ.

The devil would have us concerned with anything but Christ. In C. S. Lewis's *Screwtape Letters* the master demon Screwtape is instructing the junior demon Wormwood:

> *What we want, if men become Christians at all, is to keep them in the state of mind I call "Christianity and". You know, Christianity and the Crisis, Christianity and the New Psychology, Christianity and the New Order, Christianity and Faith Healing, Christianity and Psychical Research, Christianity and Vegetarianism, Christianity and Spelling Reform. If they must be Christians let them at least be Christians with a difference. Substitute for the faith itself some Fashion with a Christian colouring.*[32]

Lewis saw crisply that "Christianity and" soon becomes "not Christianity".

Ask yourself the question: is Jesus the main attraction at your church? Is he the main focus of your faith? Community, building projects, ministry to the poor, creative worship, healing, 24–7 prayer… unless these are inspired by Christ and all directed to him, they are hollow religion. If the first thing to come to mind when you describe a church is not Jesus, then it's not a church! The twentieth-century prophet A. W. Tozer wrote, "for the true Christian, the one supreme test for the present soundness and ultimate worth of everything religious must be the place our Lord occupies in it."[33]

We must frequently heed God's challenges to the seven churches recorded in John's Apocalypse and in particular the word of rebuke to the Ephesian church. Jesus commends their hard work, toil, patient endurance, resisting evil, testing false apostles, and filtering of false doctrines. However, he says, "I have this against you, that you have abandoned the love that you had at first ... repent, and do the works you did at first" (Revelation 2:4–5).

Was there ever such a traumatizing, terrifying word spoken over a church?

Was there ever a time when Jesus was nearer and dearer to you?

Make Jesus all your concern.

God's Son is concerned with you

The physicist Albert Einstein famously stated in an interview, "I cannot believe that God plays dice with the cosmos."[34] There was nothing random about Einstein's notion of the divine. But then there was nothing personal about it either: "I believe in philosopher Spinoza's God who is revealed in the orderly harmony of what exists, not in a God who *concerns* himself with the fates and actions of human beings."[35] That was the deist's view – a God who wound up the world and went walkabout. Not too dissimilar from the ancient Greeks' view of gods whose attitude to humankind they defined as *apatheia* – apathetic, indifferent, a yawning indifference, where humans were mere playthings, pawns to push around and amuse themselves with. Aristotle taught that the Greek gods had no capacity to love humans.

The animists and pagans lived in fear of gods and spirits, believing them to be violent, malevolent and needing to be placated or controlled through sacrifices and spells. How different the biblical presentation of God! As the psalmist muses in amazement: "What is man that you are mindful of him, and the son of man that you care for him?" (Psalm 8:4). The biblical God concerns himself with you. The biblical God has you occupying his mind and heart.

In 2007 Baylor University, in Texas, USA, conducted a three-year national survey around the question, "Is God concerned with my personal well-being?"[36] The responses were as follows:

- 4.7% strongly disagreed
- 7.3% disagreed
- 12% undecided
- 26% agreed
- 50% strongly agreed.

The statistics surprise me, with a total of 76 per cent agreeing or strongly agreeing that God is concerned with their well-being. This reflects the strong presence and influence of the Christian faith in America. By contrast, in the UK in one recent survey, only 38 per cent claimed that they even believed in God, let alone a God interested in their personal well-being.[37]

What do you think? Does God care for you? Do you matter to him?

Jesus once said to Peter: "I have prayed [literally] concerning [*peri*] you" (Luke 22:32). In his high-priestly prayer in John 17 Jesus prays repeatedly "concerning" them. How extraordinary is that? If Jesus is the Lamb of God slain before the foundation of the earth, it's because he was concerned for you before the foundation of the earth! The very presupposition of the gospel is God's concern for you. Hours before his betrayal, arrest, trial, and death he is thinking and praying and concerning himself with his disciples and those who would later follow. Indeed, the whole of the incarnation, crucifixion, and resurrection was an event in which Jesus Christ was concerned for us. And now, in heaven, "he always lives to make intercession" for you (Hebrews 7:25). Think on that: Jesus Christ having a 24-7 prayer meeting... for us. If we could grasp this profound truth, that we are on Jesus' prayer list, on his mind and in his heart, concerned about us and what concerns us, and petitioning the Father for us, we would never worry again!

The Gospels show that Jesus is concerned about whether people have enough to eat and drink and clothes to wear; that he is concerned with the poor, needy, harassed, and helpless; that he is concerned with the widow, the orphan, the leper, the outcast and sinners; that he is concerned with the demonized, the diseased, the dead; that he is concerned with the victims of religious abuse and political injustice; that he is concerned with women caught in adultery; that he is concerned with tax collectors involved in usury; that he is concerned with lost sheep gone astray; that he is concerned with prodigal sons far from home; that he is concerned with the nations of the world; that he is concerned with the nation of Israel and her rejection of him as Messiah; that he is concerned with the broken-hearted and bruised; that he is concerned with the eternal destiny of all; that he is concerned with you.

Jesus Christ concerns himself with you. Concern yourself with Christ.

7

Harvests and Hindrances (1:13)

Paul was the ultimate missions man. He had preached the gospel all the way round from Jerusalem to Illyricum, modern Serbia (Romans 15:19). His stated purpose in writing Romans is to prepare the way for a visit to Roman congregations whom he hoped would equip him for his intended missionary push into Europe.

The letter to Romans is a mission letter from a mission man, revealing a missionary God whose mission is to reach out with the gospel of Jesus Christ to save the world – Jew and Gentile.

We will shortly explore Romans 1:18–25 where we are confronted by three themes: first, the general revelation of God; secondly, the general rejection of God; thirdly, the general condemnation by God. We will see that the rejection of God leads to sin presented in two archetypal structures: *idolatry*, worshipping created things rather than the Creator of all; and *immorality*, taking sex outside of the God-gifted parameters of heterosexual monogamy. Three times in verses 24, 26, and 28 Paul says, "God gave them up to their sin." God let them have their way and live with the consequences. He didn't restrain them.

Having said that, however, although God gave us up to our sin, he never once gave up on us in our sin.

"I am not ashamed of the gospel, for it is the power of God for salvation to everyone who believes, to the Jew first and also to the Greek. For in it the righteousness of God is revealed... as it is written, 'The righteous shall live by faith.'" (Romans 1:16–17). Paul is not ashamed of the gospel because it covers sin's shame (verse 27);

unrighteousness can be covered by God's righteousness (verse 18). The offer is open to all: Jew and Gentile alike. It's inclusive.

No matter how far from God, no matter how dark one's deeds, no matter your morality, history, pedigree, ethnicity, no one, never, nowhere, is beyond the reach of God's love and forgiveness through Jesus. And it is this gospel that pulses through Paul and compels him to go into all the world and make disciples of all nations. This gospel must be heard and held.

Paul's heartache for a harvest

"I want you to know, brothers, that I have often intended to come to you... in order that I might reap some harvest among you as well as among the rest of the Gentiles" (1:13).

Paul tells us in verse 10 that he "prayed" to come to Rome; in verse 11 he "longed" to come; in verse 13 he intended or "planned" to come. There were several reasons, not least his desire to meet and encourage the church, but perhaps the major driver behind his praying, longing, and planning was his burden to preach the gospel to them (verse 15) and consequently reap a harvest among them. Paul always had his eyes on the harvest. (The Greek word *karpon* is literally "fruit" that was ready, ripe for the reaping.) Paul never took his eyes off the harvest to be brought into the barn of God's kingdom through the preaching of the gospel.

Our Jesus had his eyes on the harvest as he hung on Golgotha's gibbet. His heart swelled and his eyes filled with blood, sweat, and tears to the vision of the harvest his death would win and winnow. Right at the outset of his ministry Jesus used this metaphor of the harvest to describe people who were ready for God: "Do you not say, 'There are yet four months, then comes the harvest'? Look, I tell you, lift up your eyes, and see that the fields are white for harvest" (John 4:35).

The Greek uses two different words to reinforce the exhortation to see the harvest – *idou* ("Behold!, Look!, See!, Listen!") and *eparete* ("look up"). Many of us have our eyes closed, or we are looking in the wrong place. So often the church is looking at herself, preaching to herself, tending herself, concerned with herself. A religion of "me, my,

I" – she doesn't see the harvest. Solomon observed, "He who gathers in summer is a prudent son, but he who sleeps in harvest is a son who brings shame" (Proverbs 10:5). We are focused on building bigger and better barns, but where is the harvest to bring in? Paul saw the harvest – he saw the untold millions still untold: they were waiting, longing, hungering, for the gospel he had to offer.

Due to the advance of the gospel there are more Christians today on planet earth than in the preceding twenty centuries since Pentecost, all put together. But due to the exponential population increase, there are more people alive today without Christ than in all the previous twenty centuries since the church was founded, put together. The harvest is vast.

A few things have awakened me recently to the readiness of the harvest. First, I think of the BBC's 2010 TV programme *Big Silence*. It followed a group of religious agnostics as they spent two weeks in silence at a Christian monastery, with times of reflection with a monk. Initially most of the volunteers appeared cynical, indifferent, even mocking of the church. But within a few days, as they ceased from the drivenness of their daily routine and began to examine their own lives, they became aware of an internal mess, of a felt need of God. Two of the group had profound experiences of Christ and converted to Christianity. One of these, a hard-driven businessman, said he intended to sell his businesses and spend time with his family and God! Just taking time to stop, look, and listen, opened people up to a need and desire for God that was so near the surface. "Look, the fields are ripe to harvest."

The second thing to strike me recently was a church member who told me that he had been sharing with some non-church friends about his own faith and trying to gently stir up interest in spiritual matters. He suggested that they might like to get together and read a soft Christian book that considered Christian spirituality and theology in an oblique manner. He recommended Donald Miller's *Blue Like Jazz*. Two of the guys responded in a way that was indicative: "That book sounds interesting, but perhaps we could also read the Bible?" My pal was trying to tread carefully and slowly, whereas these non-Christians were pressing to read our holy book. "Look, the fields are ripe to harvest."

The third example is a man I became friends with through a mutual interest in photography. He knows I'm a vicar, but I've been reluctant to push my faith or even talk about it. Recently, right out of the blue, he said to me, "I don't want to be presumptuous, but can I come to your church?" There was I, treading softly, thinking I'd wait a few months and gently ask if he'd like to come to a Christmas carol service, and then maybe in the new year invite him to an Alpha Course... all nice and slow, taking a year or two to move him along the Engel Scale.[38] But no. "Can I come to your church?" I said yes, and he did. "Look, the fields are ripe to harvest."

We must ask ourselves: where is the harvest before our very eyes? Where is it Jesus directs our gaze and says: "Look, the harvest!" Who can you see nearby, in your family, community, neighbourhood? The evangelist J. John often says: "A missionary is not someone who crosses the sea but who sees the cross" – and, we might add, who sees the lost. Yes, God will call some to reap a harvest overseas – and God will call some from overseas to reap a harvest here; but we will never witness abroad if we haven't learnt to witness at home. Augustine's comment on Jesus' commandment to love our neighbour is apposite: "Pay special regard to those who by the accidents of time or place or circumstance are brought into closer connection with you."[39] Yes, we must get God's heart for the nations – but also for those who are near. We need to ask God to give us eyes to see.

Harvests need harvesting. Harvesting needs harvesters. If the church wants the harvest in the store house of the church, she needs to bring it in. The ripe cannot reap themselves. It's a trendy theological conviction to teach and preach and pray for the so-called "end-time-harvest" – but harvests need to be brought in.

Handbrakes and hindrances

"... thus far [I've] been prevented" (1:13).

There are three occasions when for three different reasons Paul is hindered from harvesting, and these involve the demonic, the divine, and the call of duty.

First, then, the *demonic*. In 1 Thessalonians 2:18 we read that Paul "wanted to come to you ... again and again – but Satan hindered us".

He has just pointed out (verses 15–16) that the Jews "killed both the Lord Jesus and the prophets, and drove us out" and that they displease God "by hindering us from speaking to the Gentiles so that they might be saved".

The devil directly opposed Paul's gospel mission. We can expect direct conflict and contestation whenever we give ourselves to preach the gospel, witness to Christ, or bring in a harvest of souls. Sometimes it will be overt, sometimes subtle, but always and everywhere the devil opposes mission. He does not easily give up those in his grasp. Satan seeks to blind unbelievers to the gospel, and to blind believers to the harvest.

The second handbrake to mission can be *divine*. In Acts16:6–7 Luke tells us that the Holy Spirit hindered Paul and Timothy from entering Asia, and then the Spirit didn't allow them to enter Bithynia. God was hindering Paul reaping a harvest in one place, to enable him to reap a harvest in another. Paul was seeking to minister the gospel in Asia, but the way was not opened; when Paul received a dream of a Macedonian man asking for help, he pushed that door instead – and it opened: they had a fruitful harvest planting churches in Philippi, Thessalonica, and Berea.

When I first felt a call to the ministry, I went to my vicar and told him I wanted to go to YWAM (Youth With a Mission) or YFC (Youth for Christ); I asked for his blessing and perhaps some financial support. To my surprise and disappointment he refused to give it. I was gutted and doubted if I was even called to full-time ministry as I'd supposed. But some months later there was a remarkable convergence of visions given to me and another church member that directly confirmed where I should be and what I should be doing. And so God called me to a far more radical adventure of faith and mission. This time when I told my vicar he acknowledged, "This is God!" and the church prayerfully and financially supported me as I was working as an evangelist. The divine delay was not a "no" but a "not here, not now". A couple of years later I wanted to go to America and be involved in church planting with the Vineyard movement. At a conference in the summer before leaving, again God spoke very clearly, closing the door to America and instead calling me to theological college and training for ordination. Reluctantly I obeyed. Instead of being a Vineyard pastor in the USA I became a vicar in the UK. And yet wonderfully in recent years God has opened up numerous opportunities to teach at various Vineyard conferences, both in Britain and the USA.

God sometimes closes one door before opening another. There was a new church planting initiative we felt called to at St Aldates. We had our eyes set on pioneering church-planting into France and Spain. However, just when we thought these doors were opening, God clearly closed them as the possibility for church-planting in these countries fell through. Then suddenly our "Macedonian man", who was in fact a Scandinavian seminary professor, asked us to help the Scandinavian Lutheran churches in practical preparation for ministry and renewal within the established historic churches. And soon we found God bringing students to us from Denmark, Sweden, and Norway for one-year courses, to be equipped for church-planting in Scandinavia.

The third handbrake to mission is *duty*. In Romans 15:20–22 Paul states that the reason he was "hindered" in coming to Rome was because he had made it his ambition to preach the gospel and reap a harvest where the gospel had not already been preached. Rome had already heard the gospel; a church was already established; and Paul felt both pragmatically and on principle that his time was better spent preaching in virgin territory. Only when he had exhausted pioneering opportunities in other cities, from Jerusalem to Illyricum, did he feel released to come to Rome.

Regrettably much mission activity is looking to harvest in a field already reaped. We are so often just rearranging church chairs and preaching to the choir. It's almost as if Paul lived by the principle that no one should hear the gospel twice until everyone had heard it once. I read a while ago in *Frontiers Mission* magazine that over 50 per cent of all American missionaries in Africa are located in the nation of Kenya – which is the most Christian nation in Africa with a population of upwards of 80 per cent Christian. The most missionaries are where they are least required! Most of them have never led anyone to Christ! Meanwhile 41 per cent of all distinct racial people-groups have yet to see an indigenous church in their own language.

We must ask ourselves and ask God: where is the harvest I am to work in?

Paul's mission experience shows us that his choice of where to go was affected by several factors: demonic opposition, divine direction, or a sense of duty. What other hindrances are there on our fulfilling the great commission? Maybe we don't believe the Bible and need not concern ourselves for the eternal destiny of judgment and hell for all who are outside Christ? Maybe we are ashamed of the gospel and do not really believe it alone is the power to save us. Maybe we are, at heart, simply prejudiced: we differentiate between people groups, like Jew and Gentile, preferring one category over another. Maybe we have forgotten that God gives his Spirit to all and all have a responsibility in ministry, whereas we leave it all to professional clerics instead. Maybe we are so programmed by TV shows such as *X-Factor*, instant-success culture that we are not prepared to put in the long, hard years of faithful service, of ploughing and watering before we reap. The evangelical statesman John Stott once claimed that the greatest single hindrance to evangelism today is the secret poverty of our own spiritual experiences. Perhaps we have tasted that God is good so little ourselves that we have no passion for gospel?

Only when we have God's heart and he has hold of ours will we overcome the hindrances and reap a harvest of lost lives led to God. It's the Spirit-filled who see the harvest field. O church, let us cry to God: send us your Spirit, then send us as labourers into the harvest field.

In conclusion

The apostolic father of the Salvation Army, General Booth, said this:

> *You have enjoyed yourself... long enough. You have had pleasant feelings, pleasant songs, pleasant meetings, pleasant prospects. There has been much of human happiness, much clapping of hands, and much shouting of praises – very much of heaven on earth. Now then, Go to God and tell Him you are prepared as much as necessary to turn your back upon it all, and that you are willing to spend the rest of your days struggling in the midst of perishing multitudes, whatever it may cost you.*[40]

Look, the fields are ripe to harvest. What's hindering you?

8

The Gospel for Christians (1:15)

"I am eager to preach the gospel to you also who are in Rome" (1:15).

The good news is needed as much by those inside church as outside. The good news is not the church's export goods. It is not the freebie leaflet left for visitors at Alpha Courses, Christmas carol, or Easter services. Paul wanted to come and preach the gospel to the Christians in Rome. He had been delayed from doing so partly out of duty, because he did not want to build on another apostle's foundation. And yet he was still stirred by the prospect. He says he was *eager* to do so – the Greek word *prothumon* is a conjunction of two terms: the preposition *pro* meaning "towards" or "before"; and *thumon* meaning "intense emotion, anger, passion, desire". It was a term that was used in ancient Greek of spectacular zeal shown by a warrior in battle. Paul burned with intense desire to herald the gospel to the church in Rome that had already received it.

Some commentators have struggled with why he would want or even say this, and a few have even suggested the original Pauline text has been corrupted in its verb tense and originally read, "Once upon a time I had wanted to come to preach the gospel to you." However, the received texts are reliable and consistent in transmission, and describe Paul's desire to visit the existing church in Rome and preach the gospel to the church.

So we must ask "why?"

Paul had a duty to discharge

Paul defined himself as an apostle "set apart for the gospel of God" (1:1). Paul was a gospel man; the gospel was his raison d'être. The gospel Paul lived *by* he also lived *for*. Like the proverbial stick of Blackpool rock mentioned previously, cut Paul anywhere and you have the gospel. Take the gospel out of Paul and you have a murderer; put the gospel into Paul and you have a martyr. The gospel was the Procrustean bed for Paul's life – if something wasn't relevant to the gospel ministry, it was lopped off. The gospel determined where he went, what he spent, how he lived, how he died. His reference in Romans 15:19 to preaching the gospel from Jerusalem to Illyricum (modern Serbia) spans 1,500 miles and three missionary journeys – and now he wants to pioneer into Europe through the gateway of Spain. Paul's presupposition was this: "For necessity is laid upon me. Woe to me if I do not preach the gospel" (1 Corinthians 9:16). The ancient philosopher Seneca claimed that true happiness comes through understanding our duties to God and men. Paul understood his duty and experienced divine approval as a herald of the gospel.

As for Paul, so for the church. It is the gospel that should define us; it is the gospel that should be our duty, our delight, our Procrustean bed, our very presupposition. In my own church expression, Anglicanism, we have three distinct ministerial orders, all of which are defined by their duty to the gospel. The ordinals describe deacons as servants in the gospel; priests are to proclaim the glorious gospel; bishops are to ordain and commission ministers of the gospel. When this gospel is not the mark of the man or woman holding that office, they fail the office, and must be reminded of their office. That's when they either repent or need to be removed.

The gospel is the criterion that tests everything. A church without a gospel to hold it together and herald is no longer a church. The gospel should be the first and last thing for us. Jesus' so-called "Great Commission" in Matthew 28 commands the disciples to go preach the good news to every creature and to make disciples. If there is no going, no preaching, and no gospel, there can be no disciples and no church.

Paul had a disunity to detox

The church in Rome was divided, disunited, and tearing along the fault line of Jew/Gentile and the ongoing role of "clean versus unclean" in their lives. But Paul knew that true unity would be established not through some pragmatic compromise over dietary laws, or which religious days to follow, but by going much deeper into the most profound shared identity – that of those who live by the gospel. It was not table fellowship but gospel fellowship that would unite them. If they were truly united by the gospel, they could be flexible, undogmatic, and generous on which aspects of Judaism were to be embraced.

The gospel – to the Jew first and then the Gentile – was what united Jew and Gentile. The Jewish Christians and the Roman Gentile Christians would inevitably have different cultural ways of expressing their faith and there must be room for both. The gospel showed there was only level ground at the foot of the cross. It was their shared sin, lostness, trust in Christ, baptism in water and in Spirit. It was their shared new identity in Christ, their shared story, their shared destiny, their shared DNA. It was their shared inclusion, incorporation into God's family. Unity never comes through endless hours spent horse-trading non-essentials at ecumenical meetings. Unity is never about fractions, pursuing the lowest common denominator.

Yes, it is the gospel that unites; but it also divides. We unite around the gospel – rightly defined, rightly defended – or we do not unite at all. But it may lead to an acknowledgment of real division. The irreparable tear within the Anglican Communion in recent years is not over the headline-grabbing issues of gender and sexuality: the issue is whether we believe and live by the gospel. When, in 2003, episcopal bishop Frank Griswold consecrated as bishop a divorced priest who had embraced a practising homosexual lifestyle, he justified it by claiming the episcopal church was being led by the Spirit to "contradict the words of the gospel".[41] One of the protesting African bishops, Archbishop Melango of Central Africa, responded with evangelical conviction: "We are not one. We do not share the same faith or gospel. You should resign."[42] The gospel, as once delivered, tests all – it is a sword that unites and divides.

These were two of Paul's motivations, and they must also be ours. But there are other reasons why we must we keep preaching the gospel in church.

We are constituted by the gospel – it is the diagnostic tool for all we think, say, do, and are. The gospel re-evaluates all values. The gospel brings disorder to our veneer of order and sets in order our disorder. So here are six reasons why we must keep preaching the gospel in church.

1. Many who come to listen need saving

The gospel is the power of God unto salvation (1:16) – it is the only power, it is the very real power, it does save. And it saves both "Jew and Gentile" – its saving power is all embracing. And Paul wants to preach the gospel to the church in Rome because he knows some in the church will need to hear and be saved.

We make a grave mistake if we presume everyone in our church is in God's kingdom. In the 2011 UK government census on religious belief they found that less than half (48 per cent) of those who declared themselves as Christian, when quizzed, actually believed Jesus was the Son of God who died to save their sins and rose from the dead.[43] In other words, half of those who thought they were Christian cannot be, because they don't believe the core tenets of Christian belief. Dietrich Bonhoeffer was a visiting scholar in the USA in the early 1930s. He attended many churches there but was amazed and appalled that in none of them did he hear the gospel, the word of God proclaimed – not until he attended a Black American church did he hear the gospel heralded, heard, and held.

Of course Paul needs to preach the gospel in the church and so do we, because not all who sit in church are saved. Many can sit and sing and enjoy fellowship and do church for years without ever accepting Christ as their Lord. I spoke to Rich Nathan, pastor of the Mega Church Vineyard in Ohio. He told me that at one leaders' meeting in the UK some pastors were grumbling that no one was becoming a Christian. He asked them, "Do you preach the gospel at church?" They answered, "No, why would we? This is not the USA – people don't simply come to church; everyone who comes is Christian." Rich protested, "Every time I preach in UK churches I offer an invitation for people to come to Christ, and every time people do." I am reminded of the autobiographical account of the Victorian Cornish vicar William Haslam, who was himself saved while he was preaching the gospel to his congregation! There are plenty of vicars that need to be saved.

This chapter began life as a talk that I have given on some four separate occasions: twice to clergy and twice at church events. The first time I gave it a man came forward at the end and said he wanted to become a Christian. The last time I gave it, at a New Wine Christian conference, a non-believing husband attended and at the end received Christ and was gloriously baptized as he professed his newfound faith. A sermon designed to encourage Christians to preach the gospel had been the instrument to bring a non-Christian to faith.

2. The church is always misplacing the keys of the kingdom

The church has been given the keys to open heaven and yet she often locks herself and others out. The mid-twentieth century Swiss theologian Emil Brunner rightly bemoaned:

> *At every period in the history of the church the greatest sin of the church, and the one that causes the greatest distress, is that she withholds the gospel from the world and herself.*[44]

It is truly shocking how many of the New Testament epistles are addressed to churches which are in crisis because they have entertained false preachers and false gospels. Jude spends most of his letter lambasting the false apostles with the choicest of language. In Paul's letter to the Corinthians Paul rebukes those who have seemingly graduated from the cross and moved onto "higher things". In his letter to the Galatians Paul is almost incandescent with rage at their replacing grace with law, faith with works, Spirit with flesh. To the Colossians, Paul warns of the deceptions of going after the weird, gnostic, mystical, and legalistic doctrines and practices being propagated among them. He has to remind the Thessalonians that, contrary to what some weirdoes are saying, the second coming hasn't occurred. Paul challenges Timothy to stamp out the false teaching in his church in Ephesus where some were claiming that it had already happened.

In Galatians 1:6–10 Paul states a word that is becoming increasingly relevant for today's church: "I am astonished you are so quickly deserting him who called you in the grace of Christ and turning to a different gospel... But even if we or an angel from heaven should preach to you a gospel contrary to the one you received, let him be accursed." As Manhattan pastor Tim Keller once warned so memorably in a sermon: "If any angel appears to you and announces any other gospel than the one you received from the apostles, no matter how dazzling or blinding he is, grab him and kick him out by the effulgent seat of his pants."

Today it seems to me that two errors predominate: either gospel-minus or gospel-plus. Gospel-minus Christians are found in the retiring old liberals and emerging new liberals who take away from the faith as once delivered; accommodating it to their own preferential truth systems, rejecting orthodox themes of judgment, hell, and the exclusiveness of Christ; and instead creating a pot pourri of their preferred points of view. The gospel-plus is increasingly seen in Neo-Pentecostals who want to claim more from God than God has provided – whether health and wealth, or bizarre experiences with angels or visitations to third heavens and other such unscriptural exotica. Augustine once wrote, "If you believe what you want in the gospel, and take out what you want, it is no longer the gospel you believe but yourself."[45]

People have always sought to baptize their worldview or their flesh with the gospel – no matter whether it's the Pentecostal prosperity "God wants you rich" gospel, the equally flawed Franciscan "God wants you poor" gospel, the South African apartheid "God wants you white" gospel, or the South American Marxist liberation "God wants you rising up against your oppressors" gospel.

There is no "designer gospel", no "bespoke gospel". There is only *the* gospel, a one-size-fits-all-and-saves-all. We must stick to the apostles' gospel, and, as the old hymn goes, "tell the old, old story".

3. The gospel reminds us what we are like

The gospel is a divine study in human anthropology. It reveals the polarity of the human condition – both *wicked* and *beloved*. The gospel is both God's yes and God's no – it shows we are adored and abhorred.

The gospel shows that we are utterly unrighteous and under divine wrath. The gospel's *a priori* is universal transgression and universal condemnation – for all have sinned and fallen short of the glory of God, and the wages of our sin is death (Romans 3:23; 6:23).

Yet that's only half our story – for God shows his love for us in this, that while we were still sinners Christ died for us (Romans 5:8). Most people totally do not get themselves – they are at the same time insecure but sin-secure. As *insecure* they often feel lonely, rejected, ugly, poor, outsiders, afraid. But as *sin-secure* they think they are basically pretty decent, upright, and good. We are so often self-deluded about our own moral goodness. We fail to see just how sinful we are against God's standard of holiness.

I met a chap who, when he learned I was a minister, quickly claimed: "I don't go to church, but I keep the commandments." I replied, "Really? Which ones? Do you love God with all your heart, soul, and strength? Do you love your neighbour as yourself"? His face dropped.

People are deluded about their goodness, their standing before God. The gospel exposes sin. The gospel exposes us as bankrupt, shouting a resounding "no" to our religious efforts at self-improvement and spiritual attainment. And yet, at the very same time, the gospel also sings an eternal "yes" over us – an accepting, forgiving, welcoming, affirming, embracing, yes. Truly, divine love bids us welcome. As the gospel re-evaluates our values, for our insecurity it shows that we are loved by God, while for our sin-security it shows in stark relief that the measure of our sin is the murder of the innocent Son of God.

In the hilarious movie *Trains, Planes, and Automobiles,* John Candy and Steve Martin play two unlikely travel companions trying to get home for Thanksgiving by any and all means of transport. Candy inadvertently sets a car on fire with a cigarette while he's driving along. It is totally burnt out, yet mechanically manages to move. As they drive along the highway in the still smoking wreck, they are pulled over by the traffic police who inspect the vehicle and ask the driver: "You feel this vehicle is safe for highway travel?" Candy replies, "Yes, I do. It's not pretty, but it'll get you where you wanna go." The officer is not impressed: "The vehicle will be impounded." Often we have no real sense of self-awareness, of just what a wreck we are. A car's capacity for movement does not mean it is roadworthy; even so, our modest spiritual or moral leanings do not cover a multitude of sins. God asks us: do you feel fit for heaven? Many say, "Yes, I really do." God says, "Wrong, impounded!"

4. The gospel reveals to us what our God is like

We have seen that Paul speaks of "the gospel of God" (1:1). The gospel reveals God. It demonstrates what God is like at the core of his being and doing – a God of holiness and love, a God of justice and forgiveness. The gospel is the defining revelation of God, the mystery and wisdom of God… God in a stable, God on a gibbet, God in my place, God for me.

The atheist writer and philosopher, Voltaire, famously quipped, "If God has made us in his image, we have more than repaid the compliment." Voltaire believed we had simply visualized God as a larger version of ourselves. Ironically, this very same critique was levelled by the great theologian Karl Barth who felt that very often we had indeed constructed a small God, like the Greeks and Romans before us – an anthropomorphized divine, man writ large.

But this big-man-little-god is not the God revealed in the gospel. The God here is incarnate and visceral – fully human and yet also incomparable and incomprehensible. Karl Barth thundered a resounding "no" against this big-man-little-god of optimistic liberalism, speaking of "the infinite qualitative distinction" between God and humanity, Creator and creature. No, God is not like us; he is for us, but he is not like us.

Today old liberalism in trendy new clothes continues to infect the church. It continues to present a projection of the big-man-little-god they want God to be, a god in their image, bloodless, sentimental, limp, and pallid, bearing little resemblance to the God of the Bible, the all-conquering Lion of Judah. We too easily accommodate God to our own preferential truth systems, baptizing God in our name and putting him to work for us. The gospel's God confounds us all! The gospel shows God's great loathing of sin and great love for sinners. The gospel shows God personally taking responsibility for the human sin he loathes. The gospel shows a God intimately involved in human history. The gospel shows us God is going to return to consummate human history.

5. The gospel inspires true worship

The gospel shows us who we worship and why. The particular how of worship, which we spend most of our time debating or defending, is far less important than the who and the why and the when. This is what true "gospel music" is all about, as the gospel inspires in us a response to God of praise, worship, love, adoration, and service.

Seeing the great lengths of the love of God to save sinners, we worship.

Contrary to popular opinion, I believe the climax of Romans is not the end of Chapter 8 – "Who shall separate us from the love of Christ?" – but the doxology at the end of Chapter 11 – "Oh, the depth of the riches and wisdom and knowledge of God!" When we have encountered God in the gospel, our souls soar, they sing.

Were the whole realm of nature mine,
That were an offering far too small;
Love so amazing, so divine,
Demands my soul, my life, my all.

ISAAC WATTS

If we lose sight of the biblical gospel, we will lose biblical worship. We may even begin to worship worship, settling for entertainment – something for our benefit.

6. The gospel motivates us to mission

The gospel reveals that we live in a loved, lost world. The church is God's "lost and found" department. If we really grasp the gospel we will want to go-spell it out, and tell it out, to the world. Life is fragile. The week I wrote this present chapter, three people in their twenties each told me about a friend who had recently died: one had been murdered; one hit by a lorry; and one died of a brain tumour. And I wondered if anyone had ever shared the gospel with any of those three whose lives were tragically cut short. Ignorance is not bliss, it is hell.

In 1732 two men who lived in Copenhagen felt called to be missionaries. They were members of the Moravian Church. One was a potter named John Leonard Dober, the other a carpenter named David Nitschman. What made them unique was their method: they sold themselves into slavery to an English slave-owner in the West Indies who had 3,000 slaves. These slaves had no access to the gospel. One of the men left his wife and children begging on the wharf for him to reconsider and stay. But the call and the heart of God for these slaves in the West Indies were even greater than the pull of home.[46] As the ship pulled away from the docks, and the sail unfurled, the men linked arms, and one lifted his hand and shouted, "May the Lamb that was slain receive the reward of His suffering."

In conclusion

At the very moment I began typing up this chapter from the original talk, as I sat in my favourite coffee shop in Oxford, I received a text message from a young man on retreat before his ordination into the priesthood the following day. He told me he was currently listening to the very talk I had given, and was stirred by the great and weighty call being given him. He had somehow managed to get my mobile number and texted me anonymously to encourage me. And it *did* encourage me. But it also seemed to me to be a divine token, a yes to the theme I have, with my faltering words and shallow insights, tried to convey here. The gospel is the hope of the world. It is the only hope. And God's eyes range throughout the world, searching out men and women who will give their all to proclaim this good news to all, to pluck burning brands from the flames and to beautify a glorious bride for the return of the Bridegroom King.

9

Going for God's Gospel (1:16–17)

Some years ago, I met a minister from a more conservative tradition. He introduced himself with the comment, "I've just met the Revd so-and-so, who told me you were a gospel man." That was the first time I had heard that phrase and I was not sure what to make of it. But the more I have reflected, the more I am proud to be described that way. I believe it is a title every Christian and every church should want to wear. The Greek word for "gospel" – *euangelion* – gives us our word "evangelical". A gospel person is an evangelical; an evangelical is a gospel person. This is someone whose life is framed by the gospel – living by it, living for it. Paul was pre-eminently a gospel man. His whole intellect and energy were brought to bear on presenting the gospel and, through the gospel, presenting people to God. His worship and devotion were enjoyment and employment of the gospel. His teaching and writing were an exhortation and description of the gospel.

Though Romans is not a clear presentation of his gospel, as we have already suggested, it nevertheless directs us to Paul's passion *for* the gospel.

1:1– Paul... set apart for the gospel of God.

1:9 – For God is my witness, whom I serve with my spirit in the gospel of his Son.

1:15 – I am eager to preach the gospel.

1:16 – I am not ashamed of the gospel.

15:16 – A minister of Christ Jesus... in the priestly service of the gospel of God.

15:19 – Fulfilled the ministry of the gospel of Christ.

When I began studying theology as an ordinand, my first New Testament essay was on this very text, Romans 1:16–17.[47] It was a great place to start my theological training, since such a text ought to frame the whole of a ministry. I recall being disappointed that I did not get a very good mark and I've never forgotten that the tutor scribbled across the paper more than once "too preachy"! I knew then that my future did not lie as an academic but as a minister. The gospel is not something simply to be dissected, but to be declared.

As a minister of the gospel Paul writes about being without shame, without blame, and without strain.

Without shame

First, Paul writes, "I am not ashamed of the gospel." This gospel was so glorious that there was never a moment, never a person, never a situation that caused Paul to question it. He proudly proclaimed this gospel in market places, homes, synagogues, prisons, before beggars, rulers, kings – he loved it, he lived it, he died for it. Paul had absolute confidence in it: it was a tried and tested formula. It had changed his life, it had changed others' lives, it had imparted glory, dignity, eternity. That's why it was called "gospel" – simply *great news*, the greatest news.

The Greek word here is *epaischunomai* – and means "to experience a painful feeling or sense of loss of status because of some particular event or activity, be ashamed" (so the Greek–English lexicon of Bauer, Arndt, Gingrich and Danker). How strange that some cannot feel this way about that which came sent from heaven with divine power. This is a gospel that silences every other gospel. It calls every other religious truth claim and worldview into question. Paul recognized that the gospel was foolishness to the Greeks and a stumbling block to Jews and yet it was also the power of God to save all who believe (1 Corinthian 1:23–24). And it was the only one.

Some may feel ashamed of the gospel and seek to disassociate themselves from it because the cross is:

- *a religious offence* – it claims that all your religious devotion and good works are futile and achieve nothing towards justifying you before God;
- *a moral offence* – it claims that justice is met by an innocent man

dying for the guilty, and that is an alien justice;

- *a metaphysical offence* – it claims the particularity of one man in one place at one time can be said to have universal and eternal relevance;
- *an existential offence* – it says that you, even though you may think you ain't half bad, are such a sinner that you deserve to die for your sins;
- *a theological offence* – it says that God's eternal Son became flesh and in weakness carried the sin of the world and died separated from his Father;
- *a cultural offence* – for it says God demands a bloody sacrifice, a flesh-and-blood substitute for your sin.

Paul wasn't ashamed to share it, but sadly many who call themselves Christians are. Why is that?

Perhaps it's *a matter of experience* – some have not really tasted that the Lord is good, and they are not sure if the gospel is really good news; they are still tempted by the sirens of the world who often seem more attractive than a life serving Jesus.

Perhaps it's *an issue of evidence* – they are aware that their own lives do not measure up; there are moral inconsistencies, they often fail, and so they think that if they share their faith they will be accused of being hypocrites.

Perhaps it's a worry over *intelligence* – a concern that the gospel may not stand up to intellectual scrutiny, that it needs explaining and defending and they have not got the answers.

Or perhaps it's a misplaced *tolerance* where some have bought into the cultural liberal or post-modern pressure to believe that all conviction is wrong, and that to hold firmly and exclusively to a religion is to be a bigot, and to claim one's religious view as right is arrogant and intolerant. I suspect some who are embarrassed by the gospel have in fact never known it. For who could be ashamed of what has brought them life?

Along with the hymn writer Isaac Watts, let us never be ashamed to own our Lord or to defend his cause. Not ashamed of him who, for us and for our salvation, endured the cross, scorning its shame, that he might win a people for God. To stand for him who hung for us, wearing only humanity and our sin, mocked, scourged, bruised, bleeding. And let us be clear that if before men and women we are ashamed of Christ and his gospel, on judgment day he will be ashamed of us, and then our shame can never be removed.

Without blame

The gospel is "the power of God for salvation... in it the righteousness of God is revealed" (1:16–17).

Paul's confidence in the gospel was rooted in its power. This power is perfect, sourced in God himself, and able to fulfil what it promised – to annul sin, to effect a radical moral change in human nature, and to bring humankind into a personal relationship with the distant, unknown God.

Paul knew his gospel was not all talk and no action. It had changed him at the very core of his being, from a racist murderous rabbi into a man who lived and died to share gospel with Gentiles. Paul speaks here of two core aspects of the gospel: salvation and righteousness.

The gospel brings salvation

This has been the universal longing ancient and modern. All peoples at all times have sought to find salvation. The Greek philosopher Epicurus claimed that salvation lay in obedience to his teaching. The Roman statesman Seneca claimed all men and women are looking for salvation... "for a hand to lift them up". Buddha taught that we must work out our own salvation and not depend on others. The Qur'an states that no one can pay for another's sins; the Hindu poet Rabindranath Tagore says that we "gain freedom when we have paid the price in full".

In stark contrast to all these, in the Bible the salvation we desire but do not deserve is the salvation gifted to us. God comes to save us for himself; we do not save ourselves for God.

A. W. Tozer put it this way: "The gospel message declares that the wronged God took the wrong upon Himself in order that the one who committed the wrong might be saved."[48]

The Bible describes salvation (*soteria*) in terms of freedom from sin (Matthew 1:21), escape from danger (Matthew 8:25), wholeness

(Matthew 9:21), the lost being found (Matthew 18:11), restoration of lost glory (Romans 3:23; 8:21); removal of a curse (Galatians 3:13), release from the grip of the Law (Galatians 5:1), rescue from flames of God's wrath and judgment (Romans 5:9; Jude 23).

Salvation has three tenses: in the *past* we were saved (2 Timothy 1:9, for example) at the point we embraced Jesus in his gospel and were born again; in the *present* we are being saved (1 Corinthians 1:18) as the Spirit works in us the benefits of Christ's death; and in the *future* we will be saved (1 Peter 1:5) when Jesus returns to bring the fullness of what he won for us at Calvary. Salvation is an accomplished and guaranteed positional fact when we trust in Christ; salvation is an ongoing implementation as we are conformed into Christ's likeness; salvation is a future hope as we anticipate resurrection, acquittal before the final bar of God, entry into and eternity in God's new heaven and new earth.

The gospel brings righteousness

Salvation is the consequence of being righteous (*dikaios*). We are saved having first been declared and established as righteous. The word "righteousness" is synonymous with the word "justification" – and the gospel makes us right or just or justified before God's justice, rightness, righteousness.

First, it is a gospel of righteousness because it reveals the very righteousness of God which must be satisfied, his moral law that must be upheld, and indeed was upheld when Jesus, the morally perfect Son of man, took God's just judgment upon himself to satisfy God's justice and turn aside God's right wrath from us.

Secondly, it is a gospel of righteousness because, through it, the uprightness or justness of God is imputed to us on the basis of faith in Christ's death. This establishes us in a right standing with God. Having satisfied the demands of God's justice, settling the account and accusation against us, we are freed from condemnation, acquitted on all charges, no longer law-breakers and sinners but friends of God (Romans 3:21–26).

Thirdly, the good news is of the righteousness of God because, through embracing the gospel, we receive the Spirit so that the legal *imputation* of a righteous standing with God is co-joined with the active *impartation* of the Spirit of righteousness, the seed of a moral transplant that begins to bring the fruit of righteousness into our lives.

Without strain

The gospel is addressed to "everyone who believes... to the Jew first and also to the Greek ... from faith for faith ... the righteous shall live by faith" (1:16–17).

Justification, righteousness, salvation... these are the great goals of God's gospel. And to whom is this remarkable offer made available? Not merely a Semitic élite. Paul is clear about the all-embracing scope of the gospel. It is for everyone, and the word *everyone* in Greek means everyone. No one is outside of God's gracious gift. No one need look for an alternative way to righteousness and salvation. There are no alternative gospels for other peoples. This gospel is for everyone, and its condition of acceptance – faith – is the same for all. No matter what our past, our failings, backslidings, sins, rejections of God... "everyone" means that salvation is to be found in this gospel alone. No one can find it anywhere else. Everyone may be saved, everyone must be saved, through gospel (Acts 4:12).

The gospel is to the Jew first and then to the Gentile

This underscores the universality of the gospel, because "Jew and Gentile" is a term that in the Hebrew mindset means "everyone". There are not two gospels for two different people groups; both Jew and Gentile are saved on the same basis. The Jews are first because of their placing in salvation history. They are the womb in which the gospel was conceived – theirs the patriarchs, prophets, promises and Messiah. The gospel went out from Jerusalem, Judea, Samaria, to the world. The gospel is for everyone, but stems from the Jewish religion. Ours is the Jewish God. The Jews were first in terms of God's affections, and of his ordinations. Israel is spoken of as God's firstborn son, Israel the firstfruits of the gospel. They were the first to embrace it, and God loved them first. Shame on the church that forgets or despises its older brother.

Salvation is for everyone "who believes". We bring nothing to God but empty hands. We believe, and so we receive. If there is anything else in our hands then they are not free to receive God's gift. Our justification cannot be achieved on the basis of our merit – hard work, good works, religious works. No, we accept it on the basis of faith alone in Christ alone.

Belief in this sense is an assent that "you alone can save me". It is surrender. The fifth-century English bishop Pelagius was rightly denounced as a heretic over his belief that we give God a helping hand in our salvation. Many of us are essentially Pelagian, thinking we can save ourselves, or at least bring something to the deal. Never! All the drowning person can do is reach out in desperation. They must be taken hold of and lifted to safety.

The gospel is from faith for faith

The Christian life begins, continues, and finishes with faith (1:17). We never graduate from faith – there is never a point where we can think that our works work our salvation. Certainly faith puts us to good work, but no matter how long we are a Christian we must never cease to rejoice and rest in the gift of faith that gifts our justification.

Martin Luther was an Augustinian monk and biblical scholar who was tormented by his own sense of sinfulness and impending divine judgment. The term "righteousness of God" filled him with abject dread and terror. He was ever conscious that he was a sinner living under the sword of God's just judgment. He fasted over a hundred days a year, brutalizing his body and soul through devotions, vigils, disciplines. He whipped himself to atone for his sin; he even climbed the steps of the Scala Santa (Holy Stairs) in Rome on his bloodied knees. He once said, "If anyone could be saved through monkery it was I." Read his testimony:

> *Night and day I pondered until I saw the connection between the justice of God and the statement that "the just shall live by faith." Then I grasped that the justice of God is that righteousness by which through grace and sheer mercy God justifies us through faith. Thereupon I felt myself to be reborn and to have gone through open doors into paradise. The whole of Scripture took on a new meaning, and whereas before the "justice of God" had filled me with hate, now it became to me*

> *inexpressibly sweet in greater love. This passage of Paul became to me a gate of heaven… If you have a true faith that Christ is your Savior, then at once you have a gracious God. For faith leads you in and opens up God's heart and will, that you should see pure grace and overflowing love.*[49]

This verse in Romans changed Luther's life, delivering him from striving and bringing him the peace with God for which he had longed and fought. It directly precipitated the Reformation.

10

The God Who Would Be Known (1:18–21)

God is "by his nature continuously articulate". So said A. W. Tozer.[50] "For what can be known about God is plain to them, because God has shown it to them" (1:19).

Having introduced himself as God's apostle to the Gentiles – a man set apart to serve Christ by ministering the gospel – and having introduced his general theme of the righteousness of God revealed to Jew and Gentile alike by faith; Paul begins to construct the first pillar of his argument in Romans 1–2. In these first two chapters he addresses the knowledge of God to which both Jew and Gentile actually had access, and the failure of both Jew and Gentile alike to respond rightly to that revelation, resulting in a shared unrighteousness and a shared need for God's justification. The argument is more spiral than linear, as Paul often loops back to a thought previously shared, or steps aside in parenthesis to highlight another thought that comes to mind. That said, broadly speaking, 1:18–21, 32 and 2:14–16 relate to the Gentile's access to general revelation through creation, conscience, and an awareness of divine decrees, while 2:1–29 relates to the Jew's access to special revelation through the Law.

The Gentile will be judged according to their response to general revelation in the structures of creation and conscience, while the Jew will be judged according to their response to special revelation in the commands of the law (2:12). Paul will show that both Jew and Gentile fail to live up to the standard revealed and required (3:9–18) and consequently God is fully justified in judging and condemning both (3:23). In our next chapter we will look more closely at the specific rejection of, or failure to comply rightly with, revelation. In this current chapter we will confine our attention to the nature of this revelation.

The unknown God willing to be known

"For the wrath of God is revealed from heaven against all ungodliness and unrighteousness of men, who by their unrightoeusness suppress the truth. For what can be known about God is plain to them, because God has shown it to them. For his invisible attributes, namely, his eternal power and divine nature, have been clearly perceived, ever since the creation of the world, in the things that have been made. So they are without excuse. For although they knew God, they did not honour him as God…" (1:18–21).

Before Paul specifically details the static structures of revelation in creation, he states that God has already initiated a new dynamic disclosure against the Jew and Gentile who have failed to respond appropriately to that revelation. We must not miss Paul's emphasis on special revelation of God's purposes in his brief treatment of the general revelation of God.

We have seen that the "righteousness of God" is being *revealed* (Greek *apokalupto* 1:17) in order to satisfy the wrath of God that is also being revealed (Greek *apokalupto* 1:18) against those who have rejected the power and divinity of God *made plain* to them (*phanero* 1:19) in creation. The new age has dawned, a new disclosure of God's purposes made manifest. This is a dynamic revelation, centred on Christ and the gospel: negatively, in judgment, divine wrath is poured out on sin; positively, in atonement, God himself provides a substitute for sin.

The difference Paul assumes between "revealed" (*apokalupto*) and "made plain" (*phanero*) is that, while both refer to a divine disclosure, *phanero* concerns something naturally plain to see, whereas the force here of *apokalupto* is of a sudden disclosure of something previously hidden from view. The righteousness and the wrath of God are revealed in the gospel, righteousness and wrath presupposing each other and both being central to atonement and final judgment. These particular and proper disclosures are not part of the more general divine disclosure already made plain in and through the created order. God's wrath and righteousness are particularly seen in certain dynamic, historical events, while God's power and divinity are traced in general natural structures.

What can be known about God

"What can be known about God" (*gnoston* 1:19) suggests both a knowing and a limit to that knowledge. Divine knowledge is real but partial. Not everything about God can be known, only what he chooses to reveal. God is not knowable in himself, only indirectly through his works and acts (Exodus 33:20; Deuteronomy 4:12; Colossians 1:15; 1 Timothy 1:17). This knowing is not the intimate knowing of lovers, for that is available only through Christ by the Spirit (Ephesians 3:14–19). There is a clear disclosing, a knowing of God through creation where God has made a plain showing of himself. But we must not expect too much from this, or build too much on it. The active verb in "God has made it plain to them" shows that this divine revealing to human knowing is not merely a characteristic spin-off of creation but was willed and caused by God.[51] The revelation of God through the structuring of creation was intentional, not accidental and not automatic. Its subsequent rejection makes human sin all the more shocking and humans all the more culpable.

Drawing on both Greek and Jewish ideas, Paul is clear that the natural world, being made by God, discloses something of the nature of God. This knowledge is not hidden and needing to be found by the spiritual or intellectual; it is there for all to see, plainly. There is a general revelation in creation generally available to all. Cranfield says, "God is objectively manifest; his whole creation declares him."[52]

This knowledge of God through creation has generally been known by two names – either natural theology or general revelation. I think we can make a helpful distinction between the two. While natural theology refers to the initiative of humans to seek traces of God *through* creation, general revelation prefers to emphasize the initiative of God choosing to reveal himself *in* creation.[53] And this is important because we must emphasize that the revelation of God in creation is only there because God places it there. It is not, as some philosophers would want to argue, because effects disclose causes; it is not accidental. No, it is revelation because God choses to reveal. He controls what we may see of him in creation. We do not stumble over God in the dark. He is revealed.

Ever since the beginning of creation

This divine disclosure is not some new addition – not a veneer – it is structured into the very fibre of the universe. It has always been there from the start, for God willed that the "invisible things" (*ta aorata*) in his nature – "his eternal power and divine nature" (1:20) – should be knowable, at least in part. Thus the visible creation speaks of the invisible Creator.

This is an oxymoron, as invisible attributes of the unseeable God are seen. Jewish tradition was clear that no one could see God and live, yet his invisible qualities were understood to be mirrored in his great work of nature. The term "eternal power and deity" is found only here in the New Testament. It is not clear how exactly Paul thinks we see these qualities of eternal and divine power. Perhaps it is in reflecting on the powerful creation that we can deduce a more powerful Creator. A creation exhibiting great power is made by a Creator of greater power; a creation that came forth in time is made by a Creator before time; and so forth.

Paul says that these attributes of God can be "clearly perceived" (*kathoratai*) and "understood" (*nooumena*) in the things that have been made (1:20). Paul speaks of both a "seeing" and a "perceiving", a visualizing and a comprehending – the fusion of the faculty of the senses and the intellect in knowing something of God. For those with eyes to see and minds to comprehend, God's existence and aspects of his nature are evident. From "what is made" (that is, the fact that things are made) we know there is a Maker, and from what is made (the content of nature) we know something of that Maker. We know he is *not* the same as what he made, for as the one who made it he must stand over and distinct from it. But at the same time something of the mind of God may be inferred from the matter he has made. Creation's power, complexity, beauty, diversity, glory, productivity, symbiosis… all draw lines from God and tell us something about God.

The known God unknown

Paul says that humankind is "without excuse" (1:20). On the day God appoints to judge the world, no one can claim ignorance of God. Atheism is not the logical position. Those who haven't seen have chosen to shut their eyes and close their minds. The sociologist Max Weber has rightly said, "It is not humanity's insufficiency that brings judgment and wrath down upon himself, it is guilt."[54]

Paul claims they clearly knew God: "Although they knew God they did not honour him" (1:21). He was no stranger to them. His existence was no surprise, his requirements not news. This knowledge is obviously partial, falling short of true intimate knowledge – a knowing of the affections. It is more a knowing *about* than a knowing *of*. But although it is not the knowing of person to person in encounter, it is a form of knowing nonetheless. It is a knowing unresponded to, a knowing left unknown, which leaves them culpable, sinful.

John Calvin wrote, "That there is some God is naturally inborn in us all, and is fixed deep within as it were in the very marrow."[55] Tragically, this inchoate knowing became a futile knowing. It led nowhere. It did not lead to worship and the honour of God; instead it led away from God to idolatry. Indeed, far from honouring God, they sought to "suppress the truth" (1:18) in order to justify their actions. The concrete structures of revelation were countered by a willing concealment – ignore the evidence, hide the evidence, and live as we choose. Ungodliness and wickedness, described by Paul in characteristic terms of idolatry and homosexual activity, are the fruits of rejecting revelation and rejecting God.

And so this general revelation has a negative effect. Far from leading people to God it indirectly led them to act against God. Far from leading to worship and relationship, it led to rebellion and immorality and idolatry, resulting in God's wrath necessarily being poured out. Paul is clear that this universal revelation is universally rejected.

God in creation? Yes, but no, but yes![56]

The great weight of church tradition has affirmed the revelation of God in creation. Augustine says memorably:

> *Some people read books in order to find God. Yet there is a great book, the very appearance of created things. Look above you; look below you! Note it; read it! God, whom you wish to find, never wrote that book with ink. Instead, He set before your eyes the things that He had made. Can you ask for a louder voice than that? Why, heaven and earth cry out to you: "God made me!"*[57]

The Orthodox scholar St John of Damascus wrote in the eighth century: "The whole earth is a living icon of the face God." Catholicism subscribes to this view, notably through the great works of medieval scholar Thomas Aquinas, and recently articulated through Pope John Paul II in a sermon on World Youth Day:

> *The visible world is like a map pointing to heaven… We learn to see the Creator by contemplating the beauty of his creatures. In this world the goodness, wisdom and almighty power of God shine forth…* [58]

Parts of the Reformed tradition go even further. The great father of the Reformation, Martin Luther, ascribed to creation not just knowledge of God as Creator but even as Redeemer: "God writes the gospel, not in the Bible alone, but also in trees and in the flowers and clouds and stars." John Calvin, in his famous *Institutes of the Christian Religion,* structures his doctrine of revelation by treating first the knowledge of God the Creator, then secondly the knowledge of God the Redeemer. But, along with Paul in Romans, Calvin emphasizes the failure of humankind to respond to creation revelation:

> *Although the Lord represents both himself and his everlasting kingdom in the mirror of his works with very great clarity, such is our stupidity that we grow increasingly dull toward so manifest testimonies and they flow away without profit.*[59]

French Catholic writer René Latourelle claims that "since creation, the world is like an open book in which we constantly read the perfections of God."[60] The philosopher and mathematician Blaise Pascal points to the nature of creation as revelation – where God is seen as the unseen, the elusive presence: "What can be seen on earth points to neither the total absence nor the obvious presence of divinity, but to the presence of a hidden God. Everything bears this mask."[61] Even the great modern scientists, like the Jewish physicist Albert Einstein, have a sense of God through creation: "That deep emotional conviction of the presence of a superior reasoning power, which is revealed in the incomprehensible universe, forms my idea of God."[62]

This is the general church position – acknowledging creation as an actual witness, albeit a modest and insufficient one that would not lead far, even if it were rightly acted upon. The historic Reformed creed, the *Westminster Confession*[63] 1:1, states:

> *Although the light of nature, and the works of creation and providence, do so far manifest the goodness, wisdom, and power of God, as to leave men inexcusable; yet are they not sufficient to give that knowledge of God, and of his will, which is necessary unto salvation.*

Others would take an even more negative view – the most vociferous being the famous twentieth-century Swiss Reformed theologian, Karl Barth.

In his 1930s polemic Barth thundered a resounding *Nein* (*No!*) to any and all notion of the revelation of God in creation, declaring himself to be "an avowed opponent of all natural theology".[64] For Barth, only God can reveal God – and God reveals himself to men only in and through Jesus Christ. And creation, by virtue of its being creat*ed*, has not the capacity to disclose its Creat*or*. Barth limited revelation to the category of a personal encounter in an event with Christ, and thus no static structure in a tree, a sunrise, or dung beetle can be credited with revelatory capacity, for it was neither personal nor divine nor dynamic.[65]

Barth's prior position on this would not allow him to read Romans 1 in its plain obvious sense, and verses18–25 were exegeted creatively to exclude any hint of revelation in creation. Barth actually made the text say the opposite of what it actually says, manipulating the plain meaning so as to suggest Paul was preaching part of his gospel, and that man sees creation as divinely made only after he has been confronted with that witness of the gospel. Thus, Romans 1:18–21 is taken by Barth to be a matter of special not general revelation. For him creation is just the context for revelation in Christ, which comes only when someone finds faith through the preaching of the gospel.

Barth was eager to point out that, without special revelation, we certainly get nowhere near perceiving God as he really is in himself – neither as Trinity nor as the One who became human in order to redeem us. The centre of the Christian understanding of God cannot in any way be grasped through this natural, general revelation. Perhaps we can do no more than grope our way towards a vague awareness of nature being created by a powerful and eternal divinity; but that is enough to hold man accountable for not honouring God as such, for reducing the Creator, who clearly cannot be the created, into an inanimate object, an idol, a thing far less than a creature. How easily humankind has substituted the glory of God for a gilded image of an insect or animal, and prostrated itself before this lifeless lump. Such absurd idolatry must lead to condemnation. Idolatry is the worst blasphemy.

God is revealed, but only partially and indirectly

Now, we might well ask, "What exactly of God may we potentially see in his creation?" We must be careful not to draw simple lines of deduction from creation to Creator. Care is needed here, as the creation is fallen, and groaning, and itself awaiting the day of redemption. Not all we see in creation is as God ordained. Much is anti-God – an unravelling, a deviation, a destruction. Yes, there is beauty and creativity and mutuality and power and regeneration. But equally there is violence, erosion, disasters and death, nature red in tooth and claw. Does this speak of God too?

It is certainly true that, whatever revelation of God is given in creation, it has often served to lead to idolatry. The innate human desire for the divine has led to a worshipping of the created rather than the Creator – or of a creator made in the image of the created. Whatever revelation of God we may discern from creation, we must be cautious before we attribute it to God. It simply does not work that way. But what we see must lead us to awe and wonder… and direct us away from what we see to the unseen Creator God.

Furthermore, given that creation is God's handiwork, then for us to mar, spoil, abuse, or simply use creation without honour or reference to God, is to do the work of the demonic, of the un-creator. Those who understand that creation is the handiwork of God, which he made to provide a space for covenant relationship with his people – the bridal suite for the Lamb and his bride – must grace this place.

Finally, Paul's whole point in referring to the structuring of creation as a revelation of God is to show that humanity is universally guilty of failing to honour God. He revealed himself, but they did not rightly follow revelation. They are culpable of sin. God's judgment is just.

11

Wicked is as Wicked Does (1:18–32)

Tory frontbencher Iain Duncan Smith, a devout Roman Catholic, precipitated a press outcry in 2010 when he claimed that to be unemployed but not to take available jobs is "surely a sin". To speak of "sin" was to employ a religious category, a moral absolute requiring divine back up, and such a value judgment was deemed unacceptable in secular twenty-first-century Britain.

In our modern Western society we have largely abandoned the category of sin.

We are governed by a scientific Darwinian paradigm that defines humans as mature mammals – and animals do not have morals. Morality and ethics, right and wrong, are taken to be merely socially constructed, self-serving, pragmatic principles, needed to order our relationships. Or so we are told.

And really it is the only real alternative to the view that morality is divinely ordained. The nineteenth-century German philosopher Friedrich Nietzsche believed there was no objective right or wrong, just the law of the jungle, survival of the fittest, dog-eat-dog, the rule of the gun. Indeed, categories of sin, of moral right and wrong, were meaningless to him. Many major thinkers from atheist Nietzsche to theist Fyodor Dostoyevsky have observed that "where there is no God, all is permissible". When we no longer have categories of sin or evil defined as a deviation from a divine standard of moral perfection, we struggle to understand the wrong we see – and the wrong we do. We blame sin on poor environment and living conditions, inadequate education or emotional privation – any excuse to avoid accepting personal responsibility.

The English Philosopher John Locke claimed that education begins the gentleman. In similar vein Jean-Jacques Rousseau said that man is a noble savage – nature's gentleman. But the battlefields of the twentieth century put the lie to that, as probably the most cultured and educated nation in the world brought hell to earth with two world wars. Civilization is far crueller than the jungle.

Is the young soccer hooligan in need of education or punishment? Is the banker who invests recklessly for his quick bonus in need of governmental regulation or punishment? If people were basically good, they would only need a leader or a teacher; but if people are basically sinful, then they need a saviour. And they are sinful, and they do need saving. Malcolm Muggeridge, the journalist and satirist, claimed, "The depravity of man is at once the most empirically verifiable fact but also the most resisted by the human mind."[66]

1. God and sin don't mix

"The wrath of God is revealed from heaven against all ungodliness and unrighteousness of men" (1:18). Unrighteousness is paired here with ungodliness – the lack of God with the presence of evil. Sin is a theological category; it has to do with God, or the disregard of God.

Verse 17 shows that God is righteous; verse18 shows us humankind is unrighteous. Three times in 1:18 and 1:29 Paul speaks of the human condition as *adikian* – a conjunction of two Greek words, *a* meaning anti/absent/against and *dike* meaning righteousness or justice. *Adikian* may be translated as "wickedness" (NIV) or "unrighteousness" (ESV). This is Paul's anthropology; his definition of the condition of humankind. First and foremost wickedness is a theological category. It is not essentially a psychological, emotional, sociological, or social condition; it is about how we are with God. While this section (verses 18–32) mentions "wickedness" three times, it mentions "God" thirteen times! Sin is a theological category; God's perfection is the reference point.

Sin is a refusal to worship God (verse 21): "they knew God, but they did not honour him as God or give thanks to him". Sin is a substituting of God for idols (verse 23): they "exchanged the glory of the immortal God for images". Sin is a rejection of God's truth (verse 25): "they exchanged the truth about God for a lie". Sin is a refusal to accept God's version of reality. Sin is atheism (verse 28): "they did not see fit to acknowledge God". The word here is *dokimazo*, which was used of testing the purity of metals; Paul is saying that they refused to prove the reality of God. Sin is a despising of God (verse 30): they are "haters of God".

During the Diet of Augsburg Luther wrote to Melancthon, "Sin is essentially a departure from God."[67] God is the point of it all, God's holiness the benchmark, God's law the test. When we sin God takes it personally. Sin is not merely *what* we do wrong but *against whom* we do wrong. When we sin we are making a statement about our relationship to God, what we think of him and his law. Of course no one likes to be thought of as sinful, or to think of themselves as wicked – against the good and against God. We are quick to make comparisons: "Well, they're worse... I've never done that... " But the comparison is not against people we consider wicked; it's against God. The plumb line is God's nature, his character and Law. And against that we are all crooked.

2. Sin is driven by the will

Paul tells us that people "by their unrighteousness *suppress* the truth" (1:18, my italics). On judgment day no one can claim, "I never knew," or, "I couldn't help it." Paul says to such people, "You lie", for "they are without excuse" (1:20). God's laws are written into creation (1:32) and on our conscience (2:15), but we still get to choose whether or not to obey. The Edwardian Indian apostle, Sadhu Sundar Singh, wrote: "Sin is to cast aside the will of God and to live according to one's own will."[68] Sin is not accidental, nor is it incidental; it is wilful, intentional, and volitional. Sin is a decision. It involves suppressing the revelation of God's will, silencing the moral conscience and ignoring the voice of the Spirit. Jesus in Gethsemane said, "Not my will but thine be done." Every time we sin we are saying, "Not thy will but mine be done."

Anyone who has had children knows about the rebellious will. Children go through a phase sometimes called "the terrible twos" (which some never grow out of) when they shriek and hurl themselves down in the supermarket aisle just to get a chocolate teddy-bear or lolly. Their will makes demands and their mind has learned that, if they scream and scream, their embarrassed parents will give in. And when we sin, we are not that different from the spoilt infant kicking and screaming and making a scene to get our own way. We aren't interested in what some divine moral parental authority figure may think is best for us; we aren't prepared to wait; we want, and we get.

3. Sin is justified intellectually

Paul tells us that "they exchanged the truth about God for a lie..." (1:25). The sinful will is strengthened and supported by the corrupt mind – "they became futile in their thinking, and their foolish hearts were darkened. Claiming to be wise, they became fools" (1:21–22). The will suppresses truth; the mind substitutes truth for a lie. A debased mind leads to sinful conduct (1:28).

The ancient Greek philosopher Socrates claimed that sin is ignorance – literally, a lack of knowledge. Paul would say that such a definition lacks knowledge, because sin is not ignorance, it is defiance. Sin is justified by a base mind. In criminal law one of the essential elements to establish guilt is defined as *mens rea* (Latin for "a guilty mind"). The act does not make a person guilty unless the mind is also guilty. Thus, to be an *actus reus*, a guilty act, there must first be a *mens rea*.[69] I read of a tragic case where a man, suffering years of chronic sleep disorder, strangled his wife to death in her bed, in his sleep, because he thought in his dream she was a burglar. This poor man was acquitted because he did not have *mens rea* – a guilty mind... only a broken heart. And so too in biblical theology, sin is an *actus rea* following from a *mens rea*. It is the selfish will justified and rationalized by the depraved mind.

Wickedness replaces the truth with lies. There is an intellectual exchange. This intellectual shift leads to a moral shift. An alternative narrative, an alternative conception of reality with an alternative ethic, is substituted for the now suppressed truth given in creation and conscience. Here is a demonic spiral: first, our will wills against God's will; secondly, divine truth is suppressed; thirdly, our thoughts become futile and our minds darkened as we justify an alternative reality; finally, our conduct becomes improper.

The mind must be set to sin – a sinful "mindset". Actions follow beliefs. Thoughts affect actions. Beliefs are formed to justify actions. As the mind, so the person. To use some rather stark illustrations: at a political level, years of "education" and intellectual propaganda format innocent children into suicide bombers in the Middle East; iterated intellectual indoctrination turn Hutus into mass murderers of their Tutsi neighbours – just as cultured Germans turned into clinical exterminators of their Jewish fellow humans who were soon seen as little more than cockroaches. When Hitler's *Mein Kampf* becomes a bestseller in some of the Arab nations, one can expect that the strife will long continue over Israel.

In *A Dictionary of Thoughts,* nineteenth-century American theologian Tryon Edwards rightly said:

> *Thoughts lead on to purposes;*
> *purposes go forth in action;*
> *actions form habits;*
> *habits decide character;*
> *and character fixes our destiny.*

And we live at a time and place where God's thoughts are suppressed. Now, even if we had an education totally conforming to a biblical ethic, we would still expect evil, because sin comes from within the heart of man; but when that evil propensity is educated, the evil is exaggerated.

This theme of the link between act and thought Paul will return to repeatedly. He knows that the way of the sinful mind is death and hostility to God (8:6–7) and that if we are not to be conformed to this world then we must be transformed by the renewing of our minds (12:2).

4. Sin does not negate but relocates the religious impulse

Paul writes about an exchange, a relocation. Sinful humanity has "exchanged the glory of the immortal God for images resembling mortal man and birds and animals and creeping things" (1:23). They have also "exchanged the truth about God for a lie and worshipped and served the creature rather than the Creator" (1:25).

The mark of wickedness is not atheism but paganism; not the removal of all gods, but a replacement of the one and only God with other gods. Whether these surrogate gods are divine is immaterial: an idol is anything to which we bestow what belongs to God alone. Wickedness is not irreligious. It is simply misdirected religion. When we remove the God of revelation, we do not become godless, we simply create gods of our own fabrication. Idolatry rushes into the vacuum left by exorcising Yahweh. We may not call them gods, we may not worship them in temples or chapels, but they take a place in our affections and emotions and actions that is rightfully God's own throne.

The mark of this kind of religion, of idolatry, is futile thinking and senselessness. The "exchange" involves a transfer of affection and devotion from the eternal to the temporal, from the Creator to the creature, from truth about God to lies about God, from the divine to the mundane, from glory to earthly, from extraordinary to the ordinary. Idols of animals and reptiles and insects – creatures which, in the hierarchy of creation, are so far beneath humankind – are given veneration. The created is venerated when the Creator is abandoned. Adam was called to name and tame creatures; fallen man tends to worship them. It is the ultimate blasphemy, the great work of wickedness.

Paul's brief treatment of the human condition, deviant in worship and ethics, is utterly disparaging. There is no hint of trying to find a point of contact with other religions, as any fragmentary revelation they might possess only serves to make them "without excuse" and in need of a Saviour. Paul doesn't regard these pagans, these polytheists or animists, as anything other than wilfully deceived. Their religious expression is evidence of their rejection of God, not signs of their seeking God. Their idolatry is wickedness not commendable spirituality. Paul does not stand alongside them as the follower of one path among many to the top of the spiritual mountain. He condemns their ignorance and idolatry. Such a tone is one that does not sit well in our relativistic, pluralistic, twenty-first-century world. Nor would it have sat well in first-century Rome, with all its cultural, moral, and spiritual diversity. Rome made room for every idol. Paul made room for none.

Sin is a serious business. And if we are ever to understand the nature of God and the work of Christ, we must settle the matter of sin. We must see it and call it for what it is. Sin must be exposed before it can be expelled. And that is what Paul is doing here. Before he explains the cross of Christ, we need to see what caused it. Sin in you. Sin in me.

12

The Spiral of Sin (1:18–32)

The spiral of sin moves from the suppression of truth, to the substitution of false gods, to moral corruption. Paul speaks three times of an *exchange*:

- Spiritually, sin exchanges the worship of Creator for that of creatures.
- Intellectually, sin exchanges believing the truth for embracing a lie.
- Morally, sin exchanges an appetite for natural sex for unnatural sex.

Sexing sin?

Please read my reflections on this difficult and painful subject in the light of my wider observations later in this chapter: none of us may set ourselves up as judge. Let him who is without sin cast the first stone.

As Paul develops his argument he does not shy away from giving examples. And so he makes explicit the kind of thing he has in mind: how "their women exchanged natural relations for those that are contrary to nature; and the men likewise gave up natural relations with women and were consumed with passion for one another, men committing shameless acts with men" (1:26–27).

The famous expositor Dr Martyn Lloyd-Jones, despite preaching over 300 sermons on Romans, skimmed over this passage. We can only guess at why such a careful teacher avoided it. I have been tempted to do the same. Few passages in Scripture are more likely to precipitate protest from a politically correct and morally permissive society. The Christian has to decide before God and his Word whether culture or

Scripture will frame their values. Since the changing of the English law in 1967, when sodomy was legalized, and with the introduction of civil partnerships in 2004, the society in which I live has embraced homosexual relationships as entirely normative. In forty years we have seen the law do a complete about-turn, from prosecuting those who commit homosexual acts to prosecuting those who object on religious or moral grounds to such acts. Today, to raise a question over someone's sexual proclivity on theological, moral, or psychological grounds is to invite condemnation as a bigot and, in some cases, legal prosecution. Where sexual matters are concerned freedom of sexual expression stands over freedom of speech. But we are faced with this biblical text, and so we must be faithful to hear what Paul, and indeed what God through Paul, is saying. The constraints of our format here regrettably do not permit more than a cursory comment.

First, Paul is clearly referring to homosexual *acts* – intimate relations not inclinations. Paul claims these acts violate the natural order of things, the way God decreed and designed them. Surprisingly, and indeed rarely, Paul refers to both lesbian and male homosexual acts. Paul says both are an exchange of the natural for the unnatural. Paul's term "contrary to nature", rendered "unnatural" in some Bibles, translates the Greek *para physin* meaning "against or contrary to the natural or physical". Thus, for Paul, such acts circumvent the divine ordering of nature's purpose and function. Paul not only critiques such acts as unnatural, a contravention of divine design, but also as "dishonourable" or immoral (1:26) and "shameless" (1:27). For Paul, homosexual and lesbian acts deviate from the divine design and thus from divine sanction.

In this passage Paul links homosexuality with idolatry. Karl Barth made much of the fact that the image of God is revealed in humankind as "male and female" (Genesis 1:26). Thus, in the unity, mutuality, and diversity of human sexuality – male with female – God is revealed. Could Paul be suggesting that male with male relations, or female with female, analogously subverts the mutuality and diversity within God, and thus is ultimately blasphemy?

Various attempts have sought to escape the plain reading of this text – for understandable reasons. A popular but flawed reading of the text in some theological circles suggests that the "natural/unatural" motif relates not to divine nature and the order of things, but whether the homosexual actor is acting according to their nature or not. They suggest Paul is claiming that these "unnatural" homosexual relations are those of people who are not "naturally" homosexually inclined and who are thus acting against their own heterosexual orientation. This is followed up by suggesting that those for whom homosexual desire is "natural" must not be encouraged to "unnatural heterosexual" expression but must be allowed to be who they are and practise same sex. But are we really to believe that heterosexuals were choosing to have homosexual sex against their will and natural desire? That seems preposterous. Let us not miss Paul stating that those involved were "consumed with passion for one other" (1:27). This is their desire.

Another major argument suggests that what is in view is not mutual homosexual acts but pederasty, the exploitative adult male having abusive relations with a younger boy, rather than the consensual expression of love between two persons of the same sex. Several points within the text prove that pederasty is not the issue here.

First is the fact that Paul talks of men with men and not men with boys. If the issue were pederasty Paul would have had several words available to make this clear!

Secondly, the fact that Paul speaks of women shows it is not simply male homosexual acts in view, but also female.

Thirdly, there is an implicit mutuality and reciprocity, rather than abuse of power, suggested in Paul's statement about being "consumed with passion for one another" (1:27). It is inescapable that Paul is identifying consensual homosexual and lesbian acts, both of which Paul says incur "due penalty" (Greek *antimisthia* meaning "repayment"). There is punishment for their "error" (the Greek word is *plane* which refers to one who wanders or is led astray). Just as idolatry is declared wicked by Paul, though it was normative in Rome, so Paul declares homosexual acts as wicked, even though that too was an accepted part of social sexual fabric in first-century Rome. Paul's views on idolatry and homosexuality were as politically incorrect then as they are now. Paul highlights homosexuality and idolatry as illustrative sins, and perhaps chooses to focus on these because they are indicative of the public sins that marked the Roman culture to which he writes. We need to ask ourselves what sins he would highlight if he directly addressed us today in the twenty-first-century Western world.

Paul's conception of homosexuality is consistent with his training as a rabbi in the Torah, with its unequivocal prohibition of homosexual acts, as well as the Torah's establishment of male–female monogamy as the only sanctioned biblical paradigm for sexual relations. Orthodox Christians must also recognize that Paul is writing truth, teaching revelation, inspired by the Spirit of God and recorded in sacred Scripture. Theologically we must heed Paul's treatment. Today's cultural norms do not give us licence to disregard the more difficult scriptural passages.

Having said that, pastorally and ethically we must not close ourselves to modern contributions that regard homosexuality as an authentic expression of nature itself, or the long-term, deeply ingrained consequence of nurture, which becomes a "second nature" for some. Paul does not deal with the issue of "sexual orientation" but implies that homosexual "acts" are a matter of choice, in which the individual consciously and wilfully exchanges divinely designed natural sexual relations for unnatural sexual relations in rebellion against God. And because Paul believes it is a choice, it is one they can choose not to pursue. The choice is either to disobey God and obey the desires of the flesh for homosexual sex; or obey God and not act upon the desire of the flesh. We must give due heed to the scientific data probing the question of whether homosexuality is a choice or biogenetically determined. I have listened to many male homosexuals and lesbians who would say they had no choice in their attraction or orientation and were acting not unnaturally but in fact consistently with their own sexual nature; they certainly did not conceive their behaviour as wilful rebellion against the design of a Creator. Indeed, as I wrote this very section, I received an unsolicited email from a friend in a covenanted lesbian relationship who feels rejected by the church in God's name: "God knows, and I mean that in a literal sense, I did not choose this, although I have integrated and am now comfortable with being gay these days. The journey to get here was excruciatingly painful and certainly not the product of choice."

Granted that homosexual desire is generally not a choice but a profound orientation, as powerful as heterosexual orientation and attraction, the fact remains that *acting out* this desire is always a choice. And Paul believed that the choice to act homosexually is the wrong one.

The church has often been quick to condemn but slow to help. I believe homophobia is a worse sin than homosexuality – the hatred of others is far worse than what may be regarded as misdirected sexual affection. The church must be a place of grace, welcome, and space for us all to journey into wholeness through Christ. Homosexual acts may be condemned as sinful according to Romans 1, but that is no basis for homophobia, which just adds sin to sin. While idolatry and homosexuality are clearly singled out here, Paul's point is not to isolate one or two sins but to show that we are *all* guilty of sin. Indeed, his list of sins does not end with homosexuality in verse 28 but with a catalogue of sins in verses 29–31. We must not highlight idolatry and homosexuality and pass over those of which we are all too often guilty. Romans 1:24–28 is the briefest sketch on the issue of homosexuality – as such it is a very incomplete basis for a Christian response to this issue. While this inspired text must inform our theological and moral understanding of homosexual acts, we must not read it in isolation from other texts that speak of God's intention in creation, the brokenness of humankind seeking fulfilment, the forgiveness of God, and the transformation of desire.

In a recent interview, the leading evangelical preacher and writer Vaughan Roberts, who had revealed that he himself wrestled with same-sex attraction, was asked if he defined himself as homosexual. He replied emphatically no, and I close this section with his words:

> *The brokenness of the fallen world afflicts us all in various ways. We will be conscious of different battles to varying degrees at different moments of a day and in different seasons of our lives. No one battle, of the many we face, however strongly, defines us, but our identity as Christians flows rather from our relationship with Christ.*[70]

When we judge others for their sin, we condemn ourselves for ours

They were filled with all manner of unrighteousness, [defined as] evil, covetousness, malice. They are full of envy, murder, strife, deceit, maliciousness. They are gossips, slanderers, haters of God, insolent, haughty, boastful, inventors of evil, disobedient to parents, foolish, faithless, heartless, ruthless.

1:29–31

Paul highlights idolatry and immorality as archetypal sins, but does not stop there. (Sadly many Christians do!) Paul catalogues a whole vipers' nest of sin and wickedness that marks humankind in its rejection of God. It is truly tragic that many evangelicals have pointed the finger at homosexuality yet never see the finger pointing back at their own sins of pride, boasting, gossiping, dishonouring parents, covetousness, and envy. What surprises in this list of nineteen sinful conditions is just what Paul lumps together, making no apparent ethical distinction between, say, murder, and boasting, categorizing all of them as simply "unrighteousness". If we make a categorical hierarchy of sins with homosexuality or idolatry at the top, we can be tempted to assume that simply being heterosexual and evangelical makes us righteous. Not so. Paul will not allow us to slip off the hook. He makes it clear that if we are proud, arrogant, slanderers, gossips, or envious, then we are lumped in with murderers and God-haters. *Kyrie eleison* ("Lord, have mercy").

Sin is never private

Sin is social, communal, and relational; it is not a private thing. All the sins listed by Paul are actions or attitudes that affect others detrimentally. In every case someone would be on the receiving end, the damage end. In so-called chaos theory, the concept of the "butterfly effect" describes how minor things done in one place can have major repercussions far away. A butterfly's flapping wing in Canada might cause a tiny change in the atmosphere that starts a chain of atmospheric events that ultimately redirect a tornado thousands of miles away in Japan – bringing chaos! Your demand for cheaper clothes means the poor suffer in sweat-shops in India; your lust for internet porn means some Romanian child's mum is paraded and degraded on your lap-top screen; your temper outburst ultimately leads to your family tip-toeing round you with anxiety and fear.

Sin is a universal condition

> *Therefore you have no excuse, O man, every one of you who judges. For in passing judgment on another you condemn yourself, because you, the judge, practise the very same things.*
>
> 2:1

Paul's whole point in cataloguing sins has not been to point out sinful individuals, but to show that we are all universally sinful and guilty. Later Paul will say that "none is righteous, no, not one" and "all have sinned and fall short of the glory of God" (3:10, 23). Sinfulness, wickedness, unrighteousness, this is the universal condition. The story is told about writer Sir Arthur Conan Doyle who loved practical jokes, and who once sent a telegram to twelve of his friends, all senior establishment figures. It simply said, "Flee at once. All is discovered."[71] Within twenty-four hours ten had left the country! What guilty secrets do you carry?

The psychiatrist Dr Karl Menninger wrote a bestseller called *Whatever Became of Sin?*[72] In it he recalls a sunny day in September 1972, when a stern-faced, plainly dressed man stood still on a busy street corner in Chicago, and as pedestrians hurried by on their way to lunch or business, he would solemnly lift his right arm and, pointing to the person nearest him, state loudly one word: "Guilty!" The effect of this on the passing strangers was extraordinary. They would stare at him, hesitate, look away, look at each other, and then at him again; then hurriedly continue on their way. One man turned to another and exclaimed: "But how did he know?" No doubt many others had similar thoughts. God knows and God points and God says, "Guilty!" – to *all* of us.

Sin has disastrous consequences

The wrath of God is being revealed against all ungodliness and wickedness...

1:18

By your hard and impenitent heart you are storing up wrath for yourself on the day of wrath when God's righteous judgment will be revealed.

2:5

Sin against God is no small thing. You really don't want to find yourself on the wrong side of God. Paul speaks of "the day of wrath" (2:5) – the Greek word is *orgao* meaning to swell with emotion, anger, and indignation. God in his holy love cannot turn a blind eye to evil for ever. He has set a day when he must break out in righteous wrath, a just judgment against our sin. Not to do so would be to negate his very being as God.

We see here that God's judgment of sin is both temporal and eschatological – it is experienced now and consummated at the end when Christ returns. Paul speaks of both. There is eschatological judgment when Christ returns and judges everyone's every thought, word, and deed. And there is temporal judgment, seen in the catalogue of sin in Romans 1:18–32 which is structured around the thrice repeated "exchange" and thrice repeated "God gave them up" (1:24, 26, 28). God lets them have it – their desire, their way. In 1:27, when Paul says that they were "receiving in themselves the due penalty for their error", he is explaining that sin is its own reward, and its own judgment. Sin is itself part of the curse of sinning. Eden's forbidden fruit was bitter.

Sin is its own terrifying reward. In Christopher Marlowe's play, *Doctor Faustus*, the character Faustus desires to make a pact with devil: his soul in hell for eternity in exchange for powers in the here and now. Notably even the demon Mephistopheles attempts to dissuade him, conscious of the consequences. Oscar Wilde's *The Picture of Dorian Gray* is a tale of a young prince charming who has an oil portrait painted of himself. This painting becomes a true mirror of Dorian, for as he gives himself to every debauchery and remains visually unmarred, the oil painting takes on the aging and marring of sin vicariously. As Dorian continues to indulge in every kind of wickedness the painting strangely changes and becomes sinister, marred, and ugly. Finally Dorian, seeing how depraved and hideous he has become in the painting, takes a knife and slashes the picture; yet as he does so he falls down dead, the knife in his own heart. Wilde concludes the story with these stark words: "He was withered, wrinkled and loathsome of visage. It was not till they had examined the rings that they recognized who it was."[73] G. K. Chesterton saw it clearly: "We have sinned and grown old."[74]

Sin brings its own reward, judgment now and judgment in the future.

The promise of grace

Before we conclude this study on sin, which ends so solemnly with the foreboding of judgment, let's not miss the hope here too. Romans 1:18 begins "the wrath of God is *revealed* from heaven against all ungodliness" – but look at the parallelism of the preceding verse: "the righteousness of God is *revealed*". Before ever a word of judgment is uttered there is a word of grace. Before Paul mentions the condemnation on unrighteousness, he already anticipates the promise of the gift of righteousness to any and all sinners who believe the gospel of Jesus Christ. Grace before judgment.

13

The Conscience Compass (2)

I woke feeling bad, an invisible weight on me. No peace. I turned my thoughts to God, but prayer was foggy. I had my breakfast, went to answer Facebook messages, and saw the name and photo of someone who had come up in a conversation I'd had the day before. This person had, on several occasions, offended some friends of mine, and I rehearsed how he had upset me too, and quoted a few things I had heard about him. When I saw the Facebook image, the Spirit reminded me of the harsh things I had said and listened to. My conscience condemned me. There was no peace, no sense of God, until confession.

What is your conscience telling you?

The first two chapters of Romans show us that God has revealed himself; he has revealed himself especially through his commands and oracles to the Jews and generally through creation to all humankind.

He has also revealed himself – his moral code – through human conscience.

Indirect revelation of God comes through his commands, his creation, and his writing on our conscience. Consequently no one on judgment day, when their wrongdoing is exposed and judged, can ever claim, "I never knew God. I never knew right from wrong." Which is why Paul can say, "All have sinned."

1. Conscience is *activated* in the soul of humankind

Paul writes: "Though they know God's righteous decree that those who practise such things deserve to die, they not only do them but give approval to those who practise them" (1:32). Later he says,

"For when Gentiles, who have not the law, by nature do what the law requires, they are a law to themselves... They show that what the work of the law is written on their hearts, while their conscience also bears witness, and their conflicting thoughts accuse or even excuse them" (2:14–15).

The Gentiles who do not possess God's moral prescriptions given in the written Law (2:27) nevertheless are not ignorant of the moral law. They have a divine moral directive written on their "conscience" (Greek *syneidesis* literally means "knowledge or discernment with"). This internal moral knowing, this conscience, is activated in the human heart and mind, registering right and wrong. Our response to it either accuses or excuses us.

The Old Testament does not have a term for conscience – after all, the people of the time had the explicit divine decrees in Moses' Law; but they did speak of the guilty heart, or of feeling the hand of the Lord against them, due to moral failure. David, after he committed adultery with Bathsheba and murdered her husband Uriah the Hittite, wrote of his tortured conscience which had physical as well as spiritual effects: "For when I kept silent, my bones wasted away through my groaning all day long. For day and night your hand was heavy upon me; my strength was dried up as by the heat of summer" (Psalm 32:3–4).

In Modern Hebrew the word for "conscience", *matspun,* is interestingly almost identical to the Hebrew word for "compass", *matspen.* This is not a semantic accident. The artist Vincent Van Gogh said, "Conscience is a man's compass."[75] Conscience is a moral intuition, not a cognition; it is felt rather than thought, an internal voice indicating beforehand whether an act or thought or speech will be right or wrong, and afterwards whether it was right or wrong. Where did this moral knowing at the deeps of our personality come from? Charles Darwin believed every animal would eventually develop a conscience. Some theologians say it's part of being made in the image of God, unlike animals who are governed by instinct and sex, survival and sustenance drives. We have a moral code, which we are free either to obey or not obey. Some believe it came into existence when Eve ate the fruit of the tree of knowledge of good and evil. It's possible that it is the voice of the Holy Spirit, who in his preserving grace seeks to stem the tide of evil, ordering society, convicting of sin, righteousness, and judgment (John 16:8). The German philosopher Immanuel Kant called this the "categorical imperative", the internal "I ought". The human "I ought" is rational, yet it precedes Descartes' "I think". Children are not taught conscience. It's not the programming by parents, although the educating of children may underline or undermine the innate conscience. Both my boys confessed to me at the age of seven that during school SAT tests they had looked at their friends' answers – and felt bad. I had not ever told them not to cheat, as I had no idea they were sitting tests and wouldn't have entertained the idea! Yet somehow innate sin in their flesh made them cheat, while innate moral conscience (no doubt strengthened through their upbringing) made them feel guilty. Both then confessed to their teachers!

2. Conscience is *predicated* on the existence of God

The Victorian Oxford scholar priest, John Henry Newman, wrote that "conscience implies a relation between the soul and something exterior, something superior".[76] Indeed, conscience implies that there are moral absolutes, and these absolute standards seem to require a referee, a moral judge, who will reward or rebuke on a day of reckoning. Our conscience gives us the sense that we have transgressed an ancient Law and deserve judgment and punishment by the ancient Law-keeper. This internal law may not be reflected in the law of the land, or in the moral law we have constructed or been weaned on and nurtured in; it seems like a deeper, older, more universal law.

Paul's point is that God writes *his* decrees, commands, and ordinances into the human heart. This internal, universal moral register may be recognized or formalized in laws constructed by communities, or completely ridiculed and rejected by them – but its genesis is in the human soul, and it is not easily erased. There is a general universal knowing that "murder is wrong" and "adultery is wrong" and "marriage is good" and "education, protection, and provision for children is right". Even where people violate these moral norms, even where society collectively and legally acts contrary to them, they are not easily silenced. Even atheists protest the Holocaust, and its perpetrators sought to dissociate themselves from guilt or responsibility. If there are inalienable human rights, they rely on essential moral presuppositions requiring a divine underpinning. Conversely, if there is no God, there are no moral absolutes, and ethics are merely utilitarian. We have already seen how the philosopher Nietzsche saw crystal clearly that, where there is no God, everything is morally permissible. But he said conscience was a *bad* product of evolution, "man turned in on himself". Conscience was seen as a handbrake on the engine of evolution. If there is no God, no moral referee, no basis to claim rights and wrongs; if we are just evolved fish, upright mammals who walked out of the jungle, then violence, abuse, self-interest, and oppression are just "monkey business".

The moment you say an act is wrong you appeal to an absolute moral right, and for that to be meaningful there must be a source and an ultimate arbitrator. Our consciences are speaking to us. They are saying, "God is watching, God is keeping account, and one day you will give an account."

3. Conscience is *negated* or *exaggerated* by sin

Paul states of the sinful that "though they know God's decree" they "give approval to those who practise them" (1:32). Elsewhere he writes of consciences that are "seared" (1 Timothy 4:2) and "defiled" (Titus 1:15).

This moral register is not a special gift for an enlightened few. It is a universal given, it is part of the possession of humanity. Paul's whole point in referring to it here in Romans is that all have it, though none fully comply with it, and all are condemned by their own consciences. I have only ever met one person who claimed there was no such thing as right and wrong and who believed that he therefore had never "sinned" in any regard. When pressed, it was clear he was either completely psychotic or demonic, or both, as he asserted that gross crimes such as rape and murder were not "sin".

Conscience is a voice not a power. Conscience does not act in controlling sin – the power over sin resides in our will, and many have their will in bondage to sin. The main reason smoke alarms do not work is because people disconnect the batteries. So too Satan tries to unplug the batteries to our conscience so that it won't raise the alarm to sin. The enemy of our souls loves to lead us into sin – to make us disobey God's decree, to silence the conscience, to demagnetize the moral compass. He has done a pretty good job in society, where systemic idolatry and immorality and injustice all point to a smothering of conscience.

The opposite of negating the conscience is to exaggerate it. Whereas the enemy tends to negate the conscience in non-Christians, he often does the opposite for Christians.

C. S. Lewis long ago pointed out that there are two equal and opposite errors regarding the demonic – either to disbelieve in it or to focus too much on it. Similarly, the conscience that may have been largely ignored or suppressed when we were not Christians can suddenly be the focus of too much attention and scrupulous scrutiny for the keen Christian – to the point of neurosis. I have often counselled devout believers who are over-sensitive and over-attentive to their conscience, and the enemy of their souls fosters this, robbing them of peace and the joy of forgiveness, anxiously digging around all the time for signs of sin. This happens especially with those whom Paul describes as having a weak conscience (1 Corinthians 8:7, 10), when the demonic turns the conscience's gentle voice into an intrusive, relentless siren, constantly examining, constantly condemning. The conscience turns from teacher to taskmaster. It is clear our conscience is being exaggerated when, despite confession and godly counsel, no peace and no comfort come. It's quite clear that, if conscience continues to condemn after confessing, it's the work of the enemy. There is no condemnation for those who are in Christ Jesus (Romans 8:1).

This trait is often seen in those who have grown up in a strict, rule-based, legalistic church tradition, whether an authoritarian Protestantism or strict Catholicism (they both meet round the back), where spirituality and obedience to God are often motivated by guilt, shame, or fear. There is now a recognized psychological category called "Catholic guilt", for such religion can format the conscience to internal, obsessive-compulsive, moral nit-picking… a permanent soul-trawling constantly on the look-out for what deserves judgment.

In the US comedy series *30 Rock*, in the episode "The Fighting Irish", Jack Donaghy comments on his experience of growing up Catholic:

> *Even though there is the whole confession thing, that's no free pass, because there is a crushing guilt that comes with being a Catholic. Whether things are good or bad, or you're simply eating tacos in the park, there is always the crushing guilt.*

This is not limited to Catholicism, of course. I've seen it in conservative evangelicals and charismatics. In all such cases we are dealing with a false guilt, an over-active conscience. And many Christians need to really hear Jesus saying, "I forgive you – it's dealt with."

4. Conscience is *elasticated* in its subjective application

While we do not believe in moral relativism – right is objectively right and wrong is objectively wrong – the conscience is not an infallible guide to determining moral rights from wrongs. The conscience is more a compass indicating a general direction than a GPS signal offering an exact moral grid reference. On lesser matters Paul even allows Christian consciences to contradict each other, while insisting on a higher unity in Christ. In Romans 14 he addresses the issue of flexible conscience and personal conviction:

"One person believes he may eat anything, while the weak person eats only vegetables" (14:2); "One person esteems one day as better than another, while another esteems all days alike. Each one should be fully convinced in his own mind" (14:5). "Who are you to pass judgment on the servant of another. It is before his own master [God] that he stands" (14:4). "Why do you pass judgment on your brother?" (14:10).

In 1 Corinthians 8:9–13 Paul applies the same principle to meat offered to idols. He says his conscience allows him to eat it, but he won't if it causes someone to stumble, for if someone eats meat offered to idols, following Paul's example, while themselves believing it to be a sin, they are condemned for acting against their conscience. Thus, even if the person's conscience is wrong to prohibit a certain act, or to justify another, if they do not act according to their conscience, in faith and obedience, then they condemn themselves. Where there is no direct biblical prohibition or prescription, just basic Christian principles as laid down and deduced from Scripture should get us through, and Christians need to act according to their own consciences – not someone else's. However, they must not impose the dictates of their conscience on others.

Conscience issues, then, are to be determined by the individual believer. This will include practical and ethical issues such as politics and voting, bearing arms or pacifism, tithing, dating, clothing, Sunday trading, smoking and drinking, the death penalty, birth control, to name a few. When a conclusion cannot be clearly drawn from an obvious reading of Scripture, then one's conscience dictates.

As long as we are seeking God's will, obedient to clear biblical principles, and attentive to our conscience, we are free to live before God as we see right.

5. Conscience is *exonerated* by the blood of Jesus

A guilty conscience can be like a heavy weight: "their conscience also bears witness, and their conflicting thoughts accuse" (2:15).

Shakespeare's brilliant insight into the guilty conscience is portrayed in Lady Macbeth who, in his play *Macbeth*, manipulates her husband to kill King Duncan and gain the crown. But no sooner has he done this than her guilty conscience, and that of her husband, cannot be silenced. They both begin to lose their minds. Having trouble sleeping, they are terrified by dreams and delusions. Macbeth sees ghosts, while Lady Macbeth groans, "What, will these hands ne'er be clean?"[77] She asks her doctor for a drug to ease the torment, but the doctor tells her that the problem is spiritual not physical. Finally, overwhelmed by her condemning conscience, Lady Macbeth commits suicide.

I recall reading about a man in Rwanda who, in the period of mass genocide, murdered and buried his neighbour, only to have sleepless, tormented days and nights for years. Finally, going half-insane with guilt, he dug up the body and handed both it and himself in at the police station.

Such can be the weight of a guilty conscience. But the promise of God is that our hearts can be sprinkled clean from all this by Jesus' blood (Hebrews 10:22). The accusing, condemning voice can be silenced, the stain of sin cleaned, and peace can come. Paul was once Saul. If anyone should or could have had a bad conscience, it was he. Saul initiated the violence against the church. He despised and blasphemed Christ. Then Jesus knocked this assassin off his high horse on the Damascus road. And he turned his life around. How could this murderer sleep – this blasphemer, this opponent of Christ? How could he ever preach the gospel? And yet, towards the end of his life, Paul can assert that he keeps "a clear conscience toward both God and man" (Acts 24:16). How? Because Paul had heard Jesus speak forgiveness, and had drunk deeply of grace. Paul had received the Spirit who testified that he was God's son and heir. He knew there was now no condemnation for him in Christ. Paul knew his guilt had been removed, his justly deserved punishment revoked. His guilty slate was clean, and his conscience was clear.

Is yours? It can be. Let Jesus clear it!

14

Judgment Day (2:1–16)

Like a lawyer Paul has persuasively presented the case for the prosecution. In Romans 1 and 2 he has shown that God has revealed himself to all humankind, whether through creation, conscience, or the commands of the Law. No one is without some witness to the divine. Nevertheless, not only has humankind consistently failed to honour the revelation of God in righteous living, they have wilfully disobeyed the divine laws and embraced sin, living to themselves, living against others, and without regard to God. Therefore all humankind is culpable and liable for divine judgment.

Romans 2:1–16 is about judgment. This is a theme many would rather not entertain. Einstein once wrote,

> *I cannot conceive of a personal God who would directly influence the actions of individuals or would directly sit in judgment on creatures of his own creation.*[78]

But what matters is not Einstein's conception of God, but God's conception of Einstein! Even the greatest minds can be fools. Ignoring or rejecting the notion that God will judge us is like sleeping when your house is on fire.

In fact it turns out that judgment is a concept many accept and most live their lives by. So called "existentialists" believe judgment occurs every day, through every act we make, the act determining its own consequence or judgment. Buddhists and Hindus believe in the reincarnation cycle of karma, that what you do in this life determines what you return as in the next. The three monotheistic religions – Judaism, Christianity, and Islam – all believe that a day is set apart when history will end and eternity begin, with universal and personal judgment as the fulcrum between the two.

The philosopher Immanuel Kant argued that humankind has a deep knowing that justice will be done: guilt punished, wrong righted, right rewarded. He posited that, since justice is manifestly not seen in this life, there must be a day of reckoning in the afterlife. Certainly anyone who has sat with the dying, as I have, will know that those who die without faith in Christ often die in fear. Could this be a dark foreboding, as they go through the veil to a judgment that awaits? They do not go easily into the next life; while their physical and mental faculties may be dying, their soul is often awakened, their consciences heightened, and, in the words of Dylan Thomas, they "rage, rage against the dying of the light".[79]

It is claimed by the nurse who tended him in his last few hours that the atheist Voltaire died a terrible death: "For all the wealth in Europe I wouldn't want to see another unbeliever die. All night long he cried out for forgiveness."[80] David Hume, the atheist philosopher famous for his empiricism and scepticism of religion, cried aloud on his deathbed, "I am in flames!" It is said that his "desperation was a horrible scene". Contrast that with the Wesley brothers who were known to boast, "Our people die well."[81] My godly great-grandfather's last words were, "I've found a friend."

Paul writes of "that day when, according to my gospel, God judges the secrets of men by Christ Jesus" (2:16). The day of judgment is part of the gospel. Perhaps we have so whittled away at the gospel, so accommodated it to people's palate, that we have lost the context of it: Christ will judge the living and the dead. This verse seems alien to us because, in large part, we have only preached a small part of the gospel. We want a feel-good, self-help, bless-me, me-centred gospel. But that's no gospel. The gospel can only be understood against the backdrop of judgment day. I want us to consider Paul's phrase that judgment takes place "by Jesus Christ" and suggest this implies three crucial aspects to judgment: Jesus is judge; Jesus is the basis of judgment; Jesus is judged.

1. Jesus judges on judgment day

To listen to much God-talk these days, it would seem we humans think it our role to put God in the dock. This is close to blasphemy! German New Testament scholar Oscar Cullmann wrote: "Judgment is the primary eschatological function of the Son of Man."[82] It's why he's returning. Paul, preaching at the Areopagus (Acts 17) to intellectual Greeks, attempted to make a point of contact with them by appealing to their religious, philosophical, and poetic sensibilities. He got a hearing. Then he dropped the bombshell: this abstract deity they grope after, called the "unknown god", "has fixed a day on which he will judge the world in righteousness by a man whom he has appointed; and of this he has given assurance to all by raising him from the dead" (Acts 17:31). They listened to Paul's apologetics, but they didn't like his gospel conclusion! It's one thing to believe in God, quite another to agree that he will judge us.

The Anglo-Saxons called this judgment day "Domisday" – Doomsday; Paul in Romans 2:5 calls it "the day of wrath". It is the day of reckoning, the day when wrongs are righted, and right is rewarded; the Day of days. It is a day diarized deep in the human soul and psyche. Many of the English literary giants reflect on it: Chaucer, Milton, Blake, Byron, Browning. Great artists seek to portray it: Michelangelo, Bosch, Tinteretto, Giotto, Burns Jones. The prophet Joel prophesies the coming of "the great and awesome day of the Lord" (Joel 2:31). It is the great hope for Christian believers, our walk and war cry: *Maranatha!* "Come, Lord Jesus."

But what woe this contains for unbelievers, for those who turn away from God! Truly terrifying. Our Doctor Faustus, at the end of his life in Marlowe's play, having lived his life for himself and having made a pact with evil, cries:

> *Mountains and hills come, come, and fall on me,*
> *And hide me from the heavy wrath of God.*[83]

In the folk tale *Chicken Licken* Henny Penny is full of anxiety about the sky falling in. I sometimes wonder if the deep angst that marks the human condition is not a foreboding of the sky falling in, but of Christ returning in the clouds as Lord.

This judgment was actually initiated through his incarnation, ministry, death, resurrection, and ascension, but it will be consummated, as the ancient creed succinctly states, when "he will come again to judge the living and the dead". Let the world tremble. On his return Jesus will take his rightful place and execute his just judgment. It is Jesus' Day, the day when he takes centre stage, when every soul is brought before his throne – every thought, word, and deed weighed by him. Jesus knows all and will judge all. His decree will be final – there is no court of appeal. No longer meek and mild, not the nursery book image of a shepherd carrying a lamb on his shoulders. Not the carpenter of Nazareth, but the warrior King, the Son of the Most High God, the Judge of all the earth, blazing in glory and majesty, eyes like the sun, feet of burnished bronze, a sword in his mouth, seated on a white throne, gathering the nations to kneel to his feet.

Many don't want this picture of Jesus. They want the "beautiful fool", as Kathy Mattea's song of the same name describes him, a sweet, gentle martyr like Gandhi or Martin Luther King. Not so. It is with this Judge Jesus on Jesus' judgment day they will have to do. In the words of the poet T. S. Eliot, "In the juvescence of the year came Christ the Tiger."[84]

2. Jesus is the criterion of judgment

There is much we can learn about God's judgment from Romans 2:

- It will fall rightly, justly, legitimately (verse 2a).
- It will fall on those who practise the things listed in 1:29–31 (verse 2b).
- It will fall on those who judge others but act similarly (verse 3).
- It will fall on those who reject the kindness of God in Christ (verse 4a).
- It will fall on those who refuse to repent of their sins (verse 4b).
- The stubborn and sinful will experience the wrath of God on the day of wrath (verse 5a).
- The day of wrath is a revelation of our sin and God's righteousness (verse 5b).

- It will be a day of reward and rebuke – eternal life for those who have done good and sought glory and immortality; tribulation and distress for all who have done evil (verses 6–10).
- Judgment is based on the knowledge of those judged: those with the Law judged by the Law; those without the Law judged without the Law (verse 12).
- The very secrets of our hearts will be judged (verse 16).

Judgment comes "by" or "through" (Greek *dia*) Jesus Christ. He is the ground or basis on which judgment is made. So Paul's gospel says that God will judge by Jesus as executor and executer *and also* by Jesus as the measure, the basis of judgment. Not only do we have Jesus as judge, we have Christ as criterion of judgment. We are judged by Jesus, but also on the basis of our response to Jesus. "On that day many will say to me, 'Lord, Lord …' And then will I declare to them, 'I never knew you; depart from me'" (Matthew 7:22–23); "whoever denies me before men, I also will deny before my father" (Matthew 10:33); "as you did not do it to one of the least of these, you did not do it to me" (Matthew 25:45).

Jesus is the criterion for judgment. Do you know Jesus? Did you serve Jesus? Have you acknowledged Jesus before men? Our relationship with Jesus before judgment day determines his response to us on judgment day. Where we have loved Jesus, lived for him and served him by serving the poor, naked, oppressed, imprisoned, then we are welcomed. But he won't welcome a stranger into heaven.

Jesus judges us on the basis of himself. I do like the saying in the Jewish Talmud (a collection of ancient rabbinical instructions central to Hebrew spiritual thought and practice): "A person will be called to account on judgment day for every permissible thing they could have enjoyed but did not."[85] The greatest judgment will be on those who could have known and enjoyed Jesus but who ignored him and the pleasure that he brings.

3. Jesus is the judge judged in our place

This is Karl Barth's famous statement summarizing the work of Christ at Calvary.[86] Not only is Jesus the judge, not only is Jesus the criterion of judgment, but he is also the judge who takes on himself his pronouncement of judgment against our sin.

When Paul states that God judges us through Jesus Christ, the Greek wording can mean that Jesus is both judge and that we are judged with him or in him. I believe Paul here, as elsewhere, uses language that is deliberately ambiguous, conveying several layers of meaning. The great mystery and marvel of the gospel is not only that Jesus is judge, nor that Jesus will judge us on the basis of our response to him, but that he is the judge who has taken the penalty of his just judgment on himself.

The judgment on our sin is revealed here as death and separation for eternity from God. All our merits, all our efforts at being and doing good, could never cover our sin. Sin separates the sinner from a holy God. Sin draws down upon itself the just punishment from a just God. But two millennia ago, on a bleak hill, outside the city gates of an occupied city in the armpit of the Roman empire, on Love's judgment day... God in Christ, God in the flesh, God with us, joyfully volunteered to pay the price of human sin, death, and hell. On Calvary's tree Judge Jesus dies for you and me – the sinner's substitute, the sinner's Saviour. He who knew no sin became sin for us (2 Corinthians 5:21) as God laid on him the iniquity of us all (Isaiah 53:6). There Jesus said to charge to his account what we owe (Luke 10:35). The Judge of heaven is the Lamb of God who takes away the sin of the world (John 1:29).

C. S. Lewis beautifully portrays this in *The Lion, the Witch and the Wardrobe* when Edmund is sentenced to death by the White Witch and Aslan volunteers to take his place, a willing substitute and sacrifice for Edmund's sin. Aslan is laid on the stone altar and stabbed to death by the Witch. He dies in Edmund's place; he dies Edmund's deserved death. But in so doing, Aslan unwinds the White Witch's wickedness, for a deeper magic, an older law, is at work. Lewis writes: "... when a willing victim who had committed no treachery was killed in a traitor's stead, the Table would crack and Death itself would turn backwards."[87]

Have you ever heard of a judge who passed sentence and then paid the fine?

I have, only once, when a woman who stole the milk off doorsteps (which shows how old this story is!) to feed her poor kids was fined for theft. The magistrate offered to pay the fine. I trawled the internet for other illustrations of such a thing – and found none. Why not? I think it's because judges do not pay criminals' fines! It just doesn't happen. Judges judge, they don't embrace the judgment for the judged. But One did. God did it for you and me.

Paul's gospel – the only gospel, our gospel – points to judgment day when Jesus sits as judge: when he judges us for our response to him, and whether we have said yes to him, trusting that he was judged in our place.

15

I'm a Jew on the Inside (2:17 – 3:4)

In our last chapter we reflected on the theme of divine judgment that forms the central theme of Chapter 2:1–16. In this passage, the word "judge" or "judgment" occurs nine times, and Paul labours the point so that we do not miss the point. God revealed himself through the creation, the conscience, and the commandments. None have responded rightly. No one is without excuse, no one may claim ignorance. Atheism is not ignorance, it is rebellion. Every person, one way or another, has made a judgment about God: whether to love God or leave him out of their lives; whether to acknowledge and follow his revelation, or ignore it and go their own way. And God has fixed a day when he will make a judgment on each human for the judgment they made about him.

Having considered the themes of revelation and judgment on all, Jew and Gentile alike, Paul anticipates a hand going up in protest: "Just a minute, Paul – what's all this about God showing no partiality (verse 11)? We are Jewish! We have a "special relationship" with God, don't you know?"

Paul responds to this in three ways.

1. Possession is not nine-tenths of the law

Paul writes:

> *But if you call yourself a Jew and rely on the law and boast in God and know his will and approve what is excellent, because*

you are instructed from the law; and if you are sure that you yourself are a guide to the blind, a light to those who are in darkness, an instructor of the foolish, a teacher of children, having in the law the embodiment of knowledge and truth – you then who teach others, do you not teach yourself?

2:17–21

You who boast in the law dishonour God by breaking the law. For, as it is written, "The name of God is blasphemed among the Gentiles because of you."

2:23–24

The Jewish people possessed the law, but the law did not possess them. The Jewish people boasted about their having a special relationship with God, but God was unable to boast about a special relationship with them. The Jewish people boasted in promises, patriarchs, covenants, law, the dwelling of God with them, in the tabernacle and temple. Yet the sad fact is that most missed the fulfilment of their faith when Messiah came, all the while boasting in possessing the hope. Something special, already theirs, in their grasp, was to no avail.

It's like the undergraduate who proudly boasts about getting into Oxford University, who swaggers around town in a scarf and gown... but never attends a tutorial, never writes an essay, and gets sent down after failing their first-year exams. It's like the homeless man I once read about who lived a pauper beggar's life, always weighed down by his heavy old overcoat; when he died they found thousands of pounds in gold sovereigns stitched into the coat lining. He was a walking bank, but he never drew on it.

In the Western movie *Open Range*, shortly before the climactic gun-fight, the cowboy, played by Robert Duvall, visits the hardware shop. "Morning, I'm thinking about some candy. I want something special... what's the most expensive you've got?"

The shopkeeper replies: "This is dark chocolate – comes all the way from Switzerland in Europe."

Duvall asks, "You tried it?"

"No," the shopkeeper replies. Duvall breaks it and hands him a piece, and tut-tuts: "Sitting right in front of you and you never even tried it. Shame to go for ever without taking a taste of something."

What a tragedy the Jewish community failed to avail themselves of the very thing entrusted to them. And how tragic that we, the people of God – the church – all too often fail to avail ourselves of the God in Jesus Christ given to us in Scripture and sacrament by his Spirit.

The most scathing indictment Paul levels against the Jewish community is that the very God they claim as their God is blasphemed, cursed, mocked, and rejected because of them (2:24). They were uniquely called to lead people to Yahweh, to be a light to the nations, and yet they have actually put people off God. Not only did they not avail themselves of their own Messiah, their unrighteous religious ways turned others from God.

But we must ask how many folk on judgment day will point a finger at the church and say, "I blasphemed God, because of the way the church portrayed him. I wanted Christ, but church withheld him from me! I rejected God because the Christians made me think him cruel, vindictive, petty, joyless, mean. They lived just the same life as me – their faith made no difference whatsoever – so I concluded their message was empty!"

Today, as I write this, I have had a deep conversation with a young lady who knew I was a priest and explained that she had been turned off church because of what she claimed was the sinfulness of the most Christian and church-going people she knew. She didn't explain the details, but she said enough to make it clear that she and her family suffered a great hurt by professing Christians, and it has turned her from taking Christians seriously. I wonder how many people have been turned away from Christ, even to being blasphemers, because of the wicked witness of those who claim Christ's name. I read of a 2009 report[88] on Catholic Institutions in Ireland that said: "Catholic nuns and priests for decades terrorized thousands of children in workhouse-style schools."[89] Many of them on judgment day will point an accusing finger at the church… and so will Christ.

One of the great inverse ironies, when considering this passage in Romans, is that most Jews today will reject Jesus because of the church's failure to witness and the church's withholding of the gospel to them through the church's systemic abuse of Jews for 1,700 years. Now it is Jesus who is blasphemed among the Jews because of the church. When they see a cross they see a swastika; one Jewish lady told me that she believed if she looked at a church cross she would go to hell – somehow it was akin to making a contract with the devil.

The Jews in the time of Paul were criticized for possessing the law but not obeying and appropriating the law. Today, the church faces the same condemnation: we withhold from ourselves and from others the very thing that gives us life. Possession is not nine-tenths of the law; God's law must possess us.

2. What matters is whether you are a Jew on the inside

> *For no one is a Jew who is merely one outwardly, nor is circumcision outward and physical. But a Jew is one inwardly, and circumcision is a matter of the heart, by the Spirit.*
>
> 2:28–29

What is a Jew? Who counts? Is it a racial, genetic, religious, or geographical identity? Today the question is pressing the authorities in Israel as many Eastern Europeans, notably Russians, seek to claim Jewish ancestry and emigrate to Israel. In New Testament times Jews celebrated their ability to trace their ancestry back to Abraham; their genealogies, family history, proof of bloodlines, mattered a great deal to them, not least on their return from exile (Nehemiah 7:64). After the Roman expulsion of all Jews from the land of Israel, the Jewish people never lost their sense of identity, and by AD 500 they had developed a unique categorizing of a Jew as anyone whose mother was Jewish. This issue of Jewish identity was central to the Nazi regime who, in the notorious Nuremberg laws of 1935, defined a Jew as anyone with three Jewish grandparents, or anyone born to a Jewish parent, or anyone married to a Jew. For most in German occupied territories such a pedigree meant death.

Paul, a former Pharisee (the strictest, most élite Jewish sect) shockingly, and against all convention, says that a Jew is not one merely outwardly, according to race or religion. There is more to being Jewish than ancestry. Here he anticipates 9:6 – "For not all who are descended from Israel belong to Israel."

For Paul a true Jew is not one who possesses the Law but who is possessed by the God of the Law. A true Jew is not one who is circumcised in their private parts but in their heart. One is a true Jew not physically but spiritually, not outwardly but inwardly. The rite of circumcision involving the most physically intimate part of a man was always a prophetic symbol, pointing to a deeper circumcision, a more intimate incision and separation to God of the heart. The first cut is not the deepest – the deepest cut is.

Paul is not saying anything new here – he is triangulating several Old Testament texts and themes, such as the words of Moses who said, "Circumcise... the foreskin of your heart" (Deuteronomy 10:16); and Samuel: "man looks on the outward appearance, but the Lord looks on the heart" (1 Samuel 16:7); and Jeremiah: "this is the covenant that I will make with the house of Israel... I will put my law within them, and I will write it on their hearts" (Jeremiah 31:33); and Ezekiel: "I will put my Spirit within you, and cause you to walk in my statutes" (Ezekiel 36:27). Embracing the new covenant of the circumcised heart, inscribed by the Spirit, occurs when Jew or Gentile trusts not in their circumcision blood but in Christ's blood.

Paul implies that the Jew who is circumcised in the flesh but whose heart has not been circumcised by the Spirit to Christ is not a true Jew, for the true Jew is the Jew or the Gentile who has entered a new covenant in Christ, through his shed blood, undergoing new birth according to the Spirit and not natural birth according to the ancestry of Abraham. Unless God's Spirit has made a deeper incision on your heart, circumcision is little different from the memorable case of Laurence Sterne's *Tristram Shandy* who was circumcised when the window fell on him while going to the toilet.

A marriage covenant takes a ring as the external symbol of the union. The ring symbolizes something precious (gold), a union (two ends become one), and eternal (an endless circle). But for many, the ring becomes meaningless and promises made, covenants entered, are ruined – people often wear a ring despite having an affair. The covenant symbol is empty if it is not lived by. The English Standard Version Study Bible notes on this section state succinctly: "True Jewishness and true circumcision are not ethnic or racial matters but matters of the heart and a work of the Spirit." The Jew on the inside receives his praise "not from man but from God" (2:29). This is a Semitic pun, a play on words, for the word "Jew" is from the Hebrew "Judah" meaning "praise". Paul is saying that the Jew who receives praise from God is the spiritual Jew – the inward, heart-circumcised Jew.

3. God's yes to Israel trumps Israel's no to God

The true Jew, the Jew on the inside, dare not despise the Jew after the flesh for they remain the apple of his eye.

Paul's distinction between "outward Jew and inward Jew" has tragically been misused and abused. Some Christians, who thought they were the true Jews, the true circumcision, the true new Israel, have despised and oppressed those who were Jewish outwardly after the circumcision in the flesh. They boasted in their replacement of Israel and their fulfilment of the Law.

The history of anti-Semitism is perilously close to the history of the church. The church forgot that the gospel is always to the Jew first. The church forgot that Christians are the in-grafted olive branch. The church failed to pray for the Jews, to thank God for them, honour and evangelize them. St Melito of Sardis in the late second century was perhaps the first to assert that all Jews were perpetually guilty of the crucifixion of Christ, as deicide was an unforgivable sin. He was the first to say that the church had replaced the Jews.

Rhetoric made way for violence. In the first Crusade, in the early Middle Ages, those claiming the name of Christ hacked their way through Europe – in many major cities in Germany and France (Worms, Mainz, Cologne, and so on) a huge number of the Jewish populalation were killed. Arriving in Jerusalem they infamously filled a synagogue with Jews, barred the door, set the place alight and, while hundreds burned to death, they knelt and sang the "Te Deum".

Christendom banned Jews from citizenship, creating the "wandering Jew". In England they evicted them, having first stolen all their wealth. They concocted lies to accuse and abuse them, they even hung them from cathedral spires. In Spain one can still see ancient chains hanging outside some medieval churches where Jews were hung and tortured – simply for being Jews. Luther in his famous tract *Of the Jews and Their Lies* exhorted the readers to burn the synagogues, ban the Talmud, put Jews to hard labour, and threaten death to rabbis if they taught Judaism.

In late nineteenth-century Russia the Orthodox Church incited the murder of many thousands of Jews and made two million homeless. Their racist pogroms were normally stirred up by priests on religious high days like Christmas Day, Good Friday, and Pentecost. Every single edict of the Nazis against the Jews has a precedent in church history. Indeed, Hitler once told Pope Pius XII that he was merely doing what the church had done for 1,500 years. Oh, how the church must repent of her racism, her anti-Semitism, her pride, her withholding the gospel from Jews. (We will return in more detail to this demonic thread in the church in Chapters 35–37.)

Paul anticipates the question: if the true Jew is inward not outward, if many Jews face judgment by God – a severe judgment for not complying with the law – is there any point in being a Jew? "Then what advantage has the Jew?" (3:1) He answers his own question: "Much in every way... the Jews were entrusted with the oracles of God. What if some were unfaithful? Does their faithlessness nullify the faithfulness of God? By no means!" (3:2–4).

First, Jews are privileged with being stewards of the oracles of God – his revelation through the prophets. They got to hold them and to herald them. The Jews were uniquely called to this privileged position as priests, God's representatives, manifesting him to the world.

Secondly, Jews are privileged as the recipients of God's promises: Paul says that God is faithful even if Israel are largely unfaithful. Their "no" to God by rejecting Christ cannot undo God's yes to them as sons of Abraham, Isaac, and Jacob.

Moses affirmed God's faithfulness, "who keeps covenant and steadfast love... to a thousand generations" (Deuteronomy 7:9). Israel's faithlessness can never negate God's faithfulness; indeed, Israel's faithlessness will serve only to magnify God's faithfulness. God has kept every promise he ever made.

Bible teacher David Pawson tells of meeting a man whose wife was repeatedly unfaithful shortly after they were married – not unlike the prophet Hosea (see Hosea 1:2). She contracted a sexually transmitted disease and acted unspeakably against her covenant partner. Friends told him to divorce her and find a faithful wife. He refused. His covenant love for her meant he would not forsake her, even if she deserved it, even if she had forsaken him. Pawson applies this to God's covenant love with Israel. Despite the fact that Israel was unfaithful, many rejecting their Messiah, nevertheless God says, "If you break it, Israel, you will not break me; I will hold on."[90]

And Paul anticipates a theme to which he will devote three entire chapters (9–11) – the most sustained theme of the whole letter – which will show that God has not rejected Israel; ultimately, though the Gentiles have been grafted into Israel's olive tree, and though some Jewish branches have been broken off, one day they will look on the one whom they pierced and mourn, and then all Israel will be saved, and life from the dead will begin.

16

Even if You are Faithless, God Remains Faithful (3:3)

Paul asks, "What if some were unfaithful? Does their faithlessness nullify the faithfulness of God? By no means! Let God be true though every one were a liar..." (3:3–4a).

This is no empty rhetorical question. Israel's faithfulness has already been called into question and exposed as fickle. No sooner are they led out of the iron cage of Egypt than they begin complaining at their lot and criticizing their God, wanting to be back in Egypt; or they turn their appetites to whoring after the Moabite gods and gals. No sooner has God miraculously fed and watered them than they are complaining that they have no garlic or cucumber. No sooner has God bared his mighty arm in deliverance than they are prostrate before a golden calf. A cursory reading of the Old Testament demonstrates the constant wandering from faithfulness to Yahweh – abandoning the covenant to prostitute themselves with pagan gods and pagan sensualities.

The grace of God does not stop their faithlessness for long. The rebuke of God through the prophets does not curb their spiritual adultery. Only exile ever brings them to their senses and restores them to their God, and then it is only for a season. But God is not like Israel: he responds not in kind but with kindness. His faithfulness is tested and demonstrated as true. Israel may break covenant with God; God does not break covenant with Israel. The history of Yahweh and Israel is one of God's faithfulness despite her faithlessness; as Paul wrote to Timothy, "if we are faithless, he remains faithful – for he cannot deny himself" (2 Timothy 2:13). Great is his faithfulness.

Unfaithful by nature

All humankind has been unfaithful to the revelation of God given in creation, conscience, and commandment. Jesus once called Israel a "faithless and twisted generation" (Matthew 17:17) – surely a term applicable to most generations of most nations. Was there ever a people faithful to God? The Bible is an honest book. It makes it clear that all have been faithless in response to what God required and deserved.

Even the great patriarchs and prophets of Scripture are portrayed as having failed God:

- Adam and Eve disobeyed the command of God and it's been a family trait since
- Abraham was dishonest with the Egyptians and distrusting of God with Hagar
- Esau was faithless, selling his divine birthright and blessing for a bowl of stew
- Jacob (Israel) was faithless, deceiving and manipulating his way through life
- Moses failed to give God honour for the miracle of water from the rock
- Samson destroyed the Philistines and then was defeated through lust
- David committed adultery with Bathsheba, then murdered her husband
- Solomon built the temple for God, then built high places for idolatry, and temples for his pagan wives
- Jonah, having been called by God to Nineveh, fled in the opposite direction
- the twelve disciples, having lived with Christ, deserted and denied him when he was arrested;
- almost all Paul's letters include correction for failings within the churches
- six of the seven letters to the churches in Revelation are rebuked for sin: "I have this against you."

Failure therefore seems to be a feature of most believers' lives. American soccer coach M. H. Alderson once said, "If at first you don't succeed, you're running about average."

Our response to our faithlessness

How do we respond to our own failure at following God faithfully?

Pretence

The term "cover-up" was perhaps invented to describe what Adam and Eve attempted. When their sin exposed their nakedness, they made coverings from fig leaves. They further pretended they weren't there by hiding in the trees when God came for his early evening stroll with them. David attempted a cover-up when he got Bathsheba pregnant, by trying to make it seem as if it could have been Uriah's child. The sinful flesh will often try to cover up, to sweep under the carpet its own faithlessness.

Transference

When God confronted Adam and Eve, hiding behind the trees and the leaves, and confronted them with their sin, they tried to pass the buck. Adam blamed Eve and Eve blamed the snake. Adam even implied it may be God's fault: "the woman whom *you* gave to be with me." Rather than put their hands up, admit and confess their guilt, they sought to deflect it onto someone else.

Penance

This comes from the Latin term meaning penalty. We know we have failed God and others, and sometimes we inflict or invite punishment on ourselves. Historically, the religious would punish themselves through self-harm such as acts of flagellation or beatings or hair shirts or self-denials or fastings. We want somehow to suffer for our failure.

We are seeing an epidemic of self-harming in our day, especially among young women. I'm sure there is a complex causation, but I believe this is partly a way of punishing one's perceived wrongs or anticipated judgments, removing guilt and shame, for those with no religious mechanism for confession. One self-harmer wrote:

> *I would say there is a definite punishment element involved in my self harm, a feeling that I have to take things out on myself, to drive the bad feelings away, punish myself for what I let happen to me, and to get the badness out.*[91]

Oh, how we need to grasp that our punishment was laid on him: by his stripes we are healed, and his blood, not our blood, avails for us.

Repentance

Stephen D. King has pointed out, "You don't drown by falling in water, you drown by staying there."[92] Repentance is a drowning man reaching for a life buoy. The prodigal son knew he was drowning, and he came running to his father – shabby, filthy, empty handed, with the husks of the pig fodder still between his teeth, crying, "Father, I have sinned against heaven and before you" (Luke 15:21). And the Father embraced him in loving mercy.

To repent is to admit that we have failed God – failed his standard, failed his decree. Sadly, though repenting should be the first thing we do, it is often the last thing. Richard Nixon was repeatedly asked why he never apologized or asked forgiveness of Americans for Watergate. He said that he refused to grovel. "Watergate was worse than a crime, it was a blunder."[93] That may be regret, but it's not repentance.

God's response to our faithlessness

How does God respond to our failure at fidelity?

God is understanding

God is not shocked by our failure or our sin. It comes as no great surprise. God doesn't get caught out. He is omniscient – nothing we have done or will do is outside his knowledge. God remembers that our days are like grass; that we are but dust (Psalm 103:14–15).

A few years ago, I was feeling overwhelmed by my sin – I was weeping, so aware of failing God yet again. I was thinking, "How can I be in ministry when my character is still so fallen? What a disappointment I am to God! If he'd known how weak I would prove to be, how fickle, how frail, he'd never have called me into ministry."

And then he spoke to me. It was one of those rare, unforgettable moments, branded in my soul. God said, "Nothing you do takes me by surprise. I know all the sins you have committed and will ever commit, and I have already paid for them."

God is uncompromising

Though he knows we will trip over the bar of his perfections, of his call to be holy as he is holy, he does not lower that bar. The standard is set. It corresponds with the righteousness of God's character; to lower the bar would be to contradict his being. The standard stays, because God cannot set less than best for us, and that is only found by clearing the bar. Of course, it is only Jesus who is able to clear that bar.

God is forgiving

The devil reminds us of our failures, whereas God remits our failures. Anton Chekhov stated that "women can't forgive failure".[94] Not true. My wife Tiffany manages to forgive my failure on a daily basis. No matter how badly or how often we fail, God will always be ready to forgive – and he does so on a massive scale. He is in the forgiveness business. He forgives seventy times seven. As soon as God hears the words, "Father… I am no longer worthy to be called your son", his grace, forgiveness, love, and mercy flow from his throne.

God is restoring

There is a wonderful poem by Louise Fletcher Tarkington which begins:

I wish that there were some wonderful place
Called the Land of Beginning Again
Where all our mistakes and all our heartaches
And all of our poor selfish grief
Could be dropped like a shabby old coat by the door
And never be put on again.[95]

This is the longing of many. And it is the offer God in Christ makes to us all – the kingdom of God, entered by faith in Christ, is the land where we begin again at the beginning.

When we come to God in sorrow for our sin, he is quick to

forgive, to restore, and transform. The prodigal son who returned in repentance exchanged pigswill for barbecued calf, pauper's rags for a prince's robe. Among my two favourite popular Christian writers are Jamie Buckingham and Brennan Manning. Their books powerfully impact my life with the message of God's forgiving and restoring grace. They understand it. They have both drunk deeply of God's grace. Manning is a repeatedly failing alcoholic ex-priest and divorcee. Buckingham was a pastor disgraced for serial adultery. Both became great God-lovers who wrote from their lived learning of the reality of divine mercy. How have you failed God? How do you respond? How does God respond? However much our failing God's standard grieves him, when we run to him ... he runs to us.

God is ever faithful

Paul is clear that, regardless of Israel's faithlessness to God, God himself is ever faithful. Indeed, Paul says that though everyone be a liar, God is true – true to his word, true to his promises, true to his covenant, true to himself. Sin cannot nullify God's faithfulness.

His mercy is fathomless. God has not failed us once. I recall hearing a remarkable tape-player recording of an old homeless man who lived on the streets and in doss houses around London. When others broke into song, fuelled by alcohol, he would contribute, soberly, hopefully, a song that had long sustained him: "Jesus' blood never failed me yet, never failed me yet; there's one thing I know, for he loves me so, Jesus' blood never failed me yet."[96]

Everything human fails. Every human fails. Nothing remains untouched by the un-creating of the Fall. But God is faithful, and his love endures for ever.

Human weakness does not make God weak.

Some reading this may feel that God has let them down and deserted them. They may feel abandoned, disappointed, betrayed, or confused. Like the disciples in the boat amid the storm on Galilee, you have cried out, "Lord, don't you care if we drown!" and it has seemed as if the Lord stayed asleep and did not wake up to still the storms raging around you!

Perception is often not true to reality. God never fails us. Rather, it is our image of who God is and how God acts that fails us. We sometimes need to reformat or rework our image and, with Job, get to that place where we can say, "Though he slay me, I will hope in him" (Job 13:15).

God is faithful to his covenant

The prophet Isaiah comforted Israel under the shadows of exile: "Can a woman forget her nursing child?... Even these may forget, yet I will not forget you. Behold, I have engraved you on the palms of my hands" (Isaiah 49:15–16). God would not forget the covenant with Israel made at Sinai. He would always keep a remnant in Israel and would restore them to the land. And he does not forget the covenant he made with his bride, the church, when Jesus took the cup and said, "This cup that is poured out for you is the new covenant in my blood" (Luke 22:20).

There is no way back through Calvary, the veil cannot be re-hung. Christ's death was the irreversible, decisive act of God establishing his love for us for all eternity. His faithfulness to Israel was sealed in Passover blood and circumcision blood; his faithfulness to the believer in Christ was sealed in his own blood.

God is faithful to his Word

Joshua declared to the people of Israel as they entered the land, "you know... that not one word has failed of all the good things that the Lord your God promised concerning you. All have come to pass for you; not one of them has failed" (Joshua 23:14). King Solomon declared the very same thing 500 years later. A further 700 years passed and Paul could state, "it is not as though the word of God has failed" (Romans 9:6). God speaks his word and keeps his word. The great missionary to China, J. Hudson Taylor, could speak from long experience: "There is a living God, he has spoken in the Bible; he means what he says, and will do what he has promised."

God is faithful in his mercies

"Because of the Lord's great love we are not consumed, for his compassions never fail. They are new every morning" (Lamentations 3:22–23, NIV). Every night while we are asleep, God is at work for our good the next day. Even as the sun rises, God's goodness greets us anew every morning. He is the God of fresh manna: there is nothing stale in God's economy, no yesterday's stale loaf, just freshly baked, daily bread; new grace, new love, new mercies. The Catholic monk Thomas Merton said, "A saint is not someone who is good, but someone who experiences the goodness of God"[97] – and the good God wants us all to know his goodness.

God is faithful in his presence

Moses promised that God would "not leave you or forsake you" (Deuteronomy 31:6, 8; Joshua 1:5). The phrase appears three times, and is repeated in Hebrews 13:5 where the Greek term rendered "leave" (*ano*) means to untie chains or ropes. God won't let go. He won't leave us. By his Spirit he abides in us, he remains with us. No matter what situation, circumstance, trial, or tribulation we may find ourselves in, he goes with us, to strengthen and to sustain.

Pre-eminently, the divine faithfulness to Israel and to the whole human race is demonstrated in the sending of his Son to die for our sins: God with us, God for us, God faithful to us. We sinned, we rebelled, we deserved judgment, we violated the covenant in creation, Israel violated the covenant God established with her through the patriarchs but it was never violated from God's side. He never forsakes; he works and reworks to restore us to himself.

Such faithfulness must surely lead us to worship the Lord; it must lead us to work for the Lord; and it must lead us to walk faithfully with the Lord. He is the rock on which we stand. Elisabeth Elliot, missionary and wife of martyr Jim Elliot who was killed by the Auca Indians of Ecuador, once wrote, "God has never promised to solve all our problems; God never promised to answer all our questions; He has promised to go with us."[98]

The God who was faithful to Israel in the past will remain faithful. Despite her failure to God by her general rejection of the Messiah and the gospel, nevertheless God's love still stands, God's word still stands, God's covenant still stands. In the end, we can depend on God.

"If we are faithless, he remains faithful – for he cannot deny himself" (2 Timothy 2:13).

17

The Righteousness of God (3:21–26)

We have arrived at what the Reformer Martin Luther called "the chief and very central place of the epistle and of the whole Bible".[99] I think of Romans more as a mountain range than a single mountain, and so I see many peaks, but this surely is one of them. Some scholars believe Paul is quoting a fragment of an early church hymn at this point, for while the language and theme is Pauline and it fits the flow of his argument well, it is certainly also the stuff of worship and praise and thanks and celebration. This was the truth the Reformation grasped, and a truth we need to grasp anew in every generation.

What do you prefer to hear first – the good news or the bad news?

A chap wakes up after surgery and his doctor says, "I've got some good news and some bad news; which would you like first?"

The patient answers, "Give me the bad news!" The doctor says, "We cut off the wrong leg!"

The patient pauses in shock then screams in horror. Steadying himself, he asks, "And the *good* news?"

The doctor replies: "Your other leg's getting better!"

In the argument so far, Paul began by stating the good news, and then he has informed us of the bad news. Now he restates the good news in more detail.

The good news of 1:16–17 was that the gospel is the power of salvation, and the just will live by faith. The bad news of 1:18 – 3:20 is of universal revelation, universal transgression, universal condemnation. The good news of 3:21–25 is that *we are justified by the just act of a just God.*

1. We are justified

> *... the righteousness of God has been manifested ... the righteousness of God through faith in Jesus ... for all have sinned and fallen short of God's glory and are justified.*
>
> 3:21–24

The central theme of verses 21–26 focuses on the word group we translate by the words "righteousness" and "justified"; it is repeated no fewer than seven times in these five verses. The Greek noun *dikaiosyne,* the adjective *dikaios,* the verb *dikaioo,* are all from the root *dikē,* which we met in Chapter 11. In ancient Greek this word referred to just punishment – it was a battle cry when going into combat, as if to say, "Here comes your come-uppance!" *Dikē* was also the name for the Greek god of moral justice.

This word group was forensic, drawn from the law courts: if you were *dikaios* you enjoyed the legal status of being innocent. If you were judged according to the law and declared by a judge as just, or "justified", you were "free to go" – not guilty, acquitted, innocent of all charges.

Paul's choice of this term and its use here in the argument clearly reflects this Greek background of the law-courts. We are looking at *the judicial character of the gospel.* But Paul is a Jew, and so he also reflects the Hebrew conception of righteousness as "relational", referring to a state of belonging within the covenant community. The Hebrew equivalent of *dikaios* is *tsedeq,* which describes when we conform to the conditions needed to live in covenant relationship with Yahweh.

Now, the Greek word group *dikaios* and the Hebrew *tsedeq* are reflected in two English word groups as well. From the Latin we have "just"; and from the Germanic we have "right". In our context here these are synonymous. To be justified is to be righteous; justice is all about righteousness.

When the Bible is translated into English, from its Hebrew and Greek Scriptures, the translators will use these synonymous word groups interchangeably. They may use either "just" or "righteous", "justice" or "righteousness", "justified" or "made righteous". For the verb they can only use "justify" as we do not have a verb "to righteous-ify" – this is why translators will use "justify" even when they are currently using the "righteous" word group.

Paul strikingly states "None is righteous, no, not one" (3:10). Every single individual has violated God's moral law and been judged and found guilty. Following the Greek judicial metaphor we have been condemned; following the Hebrew covenant-relational metaphor we have failed the criteria for inclusion in the covenant filial relations. Despite our best efforts at self-improvement, at attaining righteousness through obedience to the Law, "by the works of the law no human being will be justified in his sight" (3:20).

If the story ended there, we would all be doomed – condemned by God's law, guilty, judged, without God, without hope, without the prospect of life.

But now

Martyn Lloyd-Jones wrote of this couplet in verse 21:

> *There are no more wonderful words in the whole of Scripture than these two words: "But now" – what vital words they are.*[100]

Because of these two words and where they lead, everything changes: our universal guilt, our estrangement from God, our deserved punishment for sin, the Law's powerlessness to lift a finger to help. But now!

But what? "The righteousness of God has been manifested" (verse 21); "for all have sinned and fall short of the glory of God, and are justified" (verses 23–24). We have stood before a holy God and been exposed as sinful. We have been weighed in the scales of justice and found wanting. We have been judged at the judgment seat and been found guilty. We have been measured against the perfect law and exposed as law-breakers. We have violated the covenant conditions and been barred from being God's people. But now... God himself has acted, God has justified us, God has acquitted us.

By a quirk of the English language we can say that to be "justified" is shorthand for "*just as if I'd* never sinned". We are declared innocent. It's a passive verb, referring to something that is done to us and for us, not something that we do ourselves. God gives us what we do not have; God makes us what we are not. We the unrighteous are made righteous; we the unjust are made just. God the righteous gives to us out of his righteousness. God *imputes* to us what we did not previously possess – he gives us what is his – his righteousness, his holiness, his perfect standing. Luther called it an "alien righteousness" – something outside our sinful nature, unnatural to us, has been instilled in us.

It is as though God has credited to our account his justness, his moral status, his uprightness. We were in debt to God, morally bankrupt, but God deposits into our deficit moral account his own righteousness. In 2008 the British banks were in debt. They had loaned out considerably more than their deposits and, when the loans faltered, the banks began to collapse. The government (that is, the taxpayers!) bailed out the banks to the tune of £100 billion. They took the debt on themselves – they gave the banks credit that was not theirs. Banks were credited with funds, bailed out of debt due to their own weakness, incompetence, and greed.

Analogously, our sin, our ignorance and greed, has led to our collapse. But God does not bankrupt us; he puts us further in debt to him as he makes a deposit to pay what we owed him. On the basis of God's gracious gift we have been imputed with God's own righteousness so that we are acquitted of transgression and relationally restored to him and his people. (Of course the analogy with the banks breaks down because God really did pay the debt once and for all, whereas UK taxpayers continue to pay for the bank's bail-out.)

2. We are justified by the just act

On what basis did God justify us? Has he simply postponed judgment? Or did he simply write off the bad debt? Neither. He has neither obviated the need for judgment nor dismissed the matter as unworthy of judgment. No, he himself paid the debt in full. Paul says we are "justified by his grace as a gift, through the *redemption* that is in Christ Jesus, whom God put forward as a *propitiation* by his blood, to be received by faith" (3:24–25). We have here two wonderful words that make all the difference in the world: redemption and propitiation.

Redemption

This is a term frequently used in the Bible to refer to the deliverance of the Israelites from slavery in Egypt. The word here refers to a ransom paid to secure the release of a slave, or a deposit made to settle a debt.

In 1646 Charles I left Oxford to surrender to the Scots rather than to Oliver Cromwell's Roundheads. The Parliament paid the Scots £400,000 ransom (worth about £60 million today) to release King Charles into their hands. The king scoffed that he was worth more!

Two thousand years ago, the people did not pay to release a king. That King paid with his life to release the people. Our redemption from slavery to sin, death, and hell is achieved by the payment made by Christ in giving his life to secure our life. The famous Hindu Poet Rabindranath Tagore wrote that "We gain freedom when we have paid the price in full."[101] That is certainly the logic of most religions and the expectation of most people. But Christianity is the celebration of freedom gained because *Jesus* paid the price in full.

Propitiation

This is a rare word scripturally and even rarer in our culture. The Greek word *hilasterion* conveys both the sense of "expiation" – the covering of guilt and sin – and "propitiation" – the appeasing of divine wrath. We have already seen in Romans 1 and 2 that the wrath of God against the sinfulness of humankind is a major theme of Paul's argument.

The stain of sin does not disappear with time; it needs cleansing. God's righteous wrath cannot simply dissipate; it must be satisfied. God's holiness means sin must be cleansed; his righteousness means sin must be punished. And so God's justice is made to fall on God's Son Jesus, the willing substitute, the sufficient sacrifice, the satisfaction and propitiation for sin, and his shed blood becomes the means of the expiation of our guilt.

Significantly, the term *hilasterion* is used in the Septuagint (the Greek version of the Old Testament) for the mercy seat that was above the ark of the covenant. There, on Yom Kippur, the Day of Atonement, the high priest went into the presence of God and sprinkled blood on the cover over the ark, and that blood availed for the sins of the nation (Exodus 25:17–21; Leviticus 16:14–16). This is a powerful picture of what Christ achieved for us at Calvary – his blood sprinkled before the justice seat of God, cleansing sin, turning aside divine judgment. The animal slain at Yom Kippur was insufficient to fully atone, such that this act needing to be repeated each year; but Christ's death was perfect and permanent (Hebrews 9:25–27).

On 26 November 2008 a gang of radical Islamist terrorists stormed the Taj Mahal Palace Hotel in Mumbai, India. After the carnage many were left dead and injured. A reporter interviewed a guest who had been at the hotel for dinner that night and remarkably survived. The guest described how he and his friends were eating dinner when they heard gunshots. Someone grabbed him and pulled him under the table. The assassins came striding through the restaurant, shooting at will, until everyone (so they thought) had been killed. Miraculously, the man survived. When the interviewer asked the guest how he lived when all else at his table had been killed, he replied, "I suppose because I was covered in someone else's blood, and they took me for dead."[102]

Well, we must not push the analogy. God is no terrorist – the devil is! But sin brings God's wrath and our death. The condemning law as an angel of death passes over us if, by faith, we hide in Christ's ever warm blood.

3. We are justified by the just act of a just God

> *This was to show God's righteousness, because in his divine forbearance he had passed over former sins. It was to show his righteousness at the present time, so that he might be just and the justifier.*
>
> 3:25–26

God cannot ignore sin and still be God. If God ignores sin, he sins. God, who sees all, cannot turn a blind eye to sin – it is ever before him. His justice means he must deal justly with sin – it is an inviolable law of his universe. A judge who doesn't judge is not a judge. If our sin is not judged and punished, then it is God who is undone. For a season God in his grace and forbearance overlooked sin, but sin cannot be overlooked for ever. God left a temporary, pragmatic, and prophetic sacrificial temple system to deal with sin on a daily basis – but it was always only temporary… until Jesus the perfect sacrifice came. We are saved from the wrath of God by the wrath of God – as it is satisfied and spent on the Son in our place.

It is often protested: how can an innocent pay the penalty of the guilty? How can God's requirement of his Son's death for a sinner's life be just?

As we have seen, some have even accused such a notion, were it true, of being tantamount to cosmic child abuse. Certainly the Old Testament is clear that Yahweh is distinguished from pagan gods for not accepting human sacrifices, and the Law states that an innocent cannot be punished for a guilty person. Ancient rabbis actually protested against Christianity for their presentation of a God who accepted human sacrifice as being more like Molech than Yahweh.

And I agree… if Jesus were just a man, even a perfect man, a willing sacrifice. Then indeed his death for our sins would be unacceptable, an injustice. If God had passed punishment for the guilt of the world on a mere mortal, it would be unjust.

However, if God himself becomes a man and takes the punishment on himself, then who can gainsay it? If Jesus dies not just as Son of man but as Son of God – if God was in Christ reconciling the world to himself – if God suffers, if God atones, if God sets the terms and meets them, then let God be God and all the world fall silent. Messianic Bible teacher Dwight Pryor said, "The Satisfaction of God comes through the Substitution of God."[103] God gives what God demands. We are justified by the just act of a just God.

The cross demonstrates that God is both just and justifier. At Calvary God is shown to be righteous, morally upright. His holy law is upheld, sin is condemned, dealt its due, and righteous wrath is spent. At the cross God's justice is not compromised but fully satisfied.

At Calvary God is also shown as justifier – he stands in our stead, paying our penalty, imputing his righteousness to us, justifying the unjust. Justice and mercy, wrath and love meet. The motive is not simply the satisfaction of his justice; it is also the satisfaction of his affections, for he has set his desire on us.

What is the source of this justification? It comes "by his grace as a gift" (3:24). God's loving-kindness is the drive of salvation. His goodness is the motive.

And if the basis on which we are justified is the grace of God, then it is not on the basis of any merit, credit, or effort on our part. It is *charis* – grace, a divine gift. Grace is the outrageous generosity of God, whereby he gives us what we lack and what we do not deserve. God graced us with redemption not because he had to, but because he willed to. The grace of the cross is God's active mercy triumphing over God's active wrath.

What is the means of securing this justification? It is through "faith in Jesus" (3:26). Yes, that's all – just faith, belief, trust in Jesus as God's Son, sin's sacrifice and our Saviour.

What is the scope of this justification? It is "for *all* who believe" (3:22) – Jew and Gentile, everyone and anyone.

There is a universal awareness of sin and longing for forgiveness. Many years ago I visited a dear man who had attempted suicide and was in a psychiatric hospital. He was filled with guilt, shame, and fear of God's judgment for something he had done years before. When I arrived he seemed fine, and when I enquired how he was, he said. "It's all right, I'm forgiven." I was surprised but delighted. I asked: "When did this happen, how do you know you are forgiven?" His answer shocked me: "There's a guy in the next room, and for a packet of cigarettes he'll forgive you your sins."

The guy next door cannot forgive your sins. You and I sinned against God and only God can forgive us. And he will do so, willingly, freely, and joyfully – and not for the price of anything we can give. It cost much more. It cost the death of his Son.

How do we respond to this? C. H. Spurgeon said,

> *Too many think lightly of sin and therefore think lightly of the Saviour. He who has stood before his God, convicted and condemned, with a rope about his neck, is the man to weep for joy when he is pardoned, to hate the evil which has been forgiven him, and to live to the honour of the Redeemer by whose blood he has been cleansed.*[104]

18

Faith Alone in Christ Alone (3:21–31)

Woody Allen once declared, "If only God would give me some clear sign – like making a large deposit in my name in a Swiss bank."[105] Well, that's exactly what God has done. He has made a large deposit on our behalf, only in a far safer vault than a Swiss bank… in the eternal heart of God.

In Romans 1–3 Paul presents us with his anthropology, which concludes that all humankind has fallen short of God's glory through sin. We are utterly unrighteous, under God's wrath and helpless to get ourselves out of this mess. Thank God that the word "guilty" is not the last word on the subject. But now… (3:21) God has intervened; God interfered on our behalf. God has acted to make righteous the unrighteous, to justify the guilty. How so? Jesus becomes the sacrifice, the propitiation for sin and the redemption of sinners – as C. H. Spurgeon put it, "bearing the thunderbolts of the divine opposition to all sin".[106] Christ stands in our stead, credited with our sin, that we might stand in Christ's stead, credited with his righteousness. We are justified by the just act of a just God.

This, then, is the architecture of our great gospel. But how do we now appropriate or activate this offered justification?

We are justified through faith alone, in Christ alone, by grace alone.

1. Through faith alone

Paul repeatedly connects the gift of righteousness with the act of faith, referring to "the righteousness of God though *faith* in Jesus Christ for all *who believe*" (3:22). Jesus is the One "whom God put forward as a propitiation by his blood, to be received by *faith*" (3:25); God justifies "the one who has *faith* in Jesus" (3:26).

Faith justifies. The word "faith" translates the Greek *pistis*, which indicates trust, belief, persuasion, conviction, and faithfulness. Biblical faith is not simply "yes" but "yes please". It is both believing and receiving. It is assent and commitment.

Following Martin Luther, the late sixteenth-century Lutherans in their "Form of Concord" statement of faith declared that the salvation of our souls through justification by faith was "the chief article of the whole Christian doctrine".[107] Subsequent Lutheran scholars like Carl Braaten assert that justification by faith is "the article by which the church stands or falls".[108] The Protestant Reformation saw a return to biblical Christianity after centuries of deviation from justification by faith and accretions of required religious acts aimed at purchasing divine forgiveness. Medieval Christianity came to believe you could literally buy forgiveness – the rich with their money, buying indulgences, giving monies to the church to offset sins. You could even pay monks to pray or do penance for you or your dead family's release from purgatory. The poor were, as always, in trouble, and so their only hope for forgiveness was religious effort, pilgrimage, assisting with the crusades, and wishful thinking.

God was conceived as being little more than a petty-minded bookkeeper holding detailed accounts of our moral debits, which could be offset by putting credit into our account by gifts to the church, religious devotion, blood, sweat, and tears. We have already considered the conversion of Martin Luther, the Augustinian scholar monk from Erfurt in Germany; however, his conversion is so significant and archetypal that it pays to revisit it.

Wracked with guilt, shame, loathing of sin, and abject terror of God's wrath, Luther tried his best to be righteous, to balance the scales in his moral favour. He pursued ruthless asceticism, flagellation, lengthy fasting, slept in the freezing cold without blankets; so extreme was his religious passion that his superiors worried he'd kill himself to save himself. He testified that:

> *I tormented myself to death to procure peace with God for my troubled heart and my agitated conscience; but I was surrounded by horrible darkness, and could find peace nowhere.*[109]

Religious is not the same as righteous – and all Luther's efforts brought no peace with God. Such efforts never will. Luther required a revelation to shatter his delusions that he could justify himself according to his efforts. One day God broke through to him as he read in Romans 1:17 that "The righteous shall live by faith". He saw clearly that the righteousness of God that he both feared and longed for would not come by his own good works, effort, religion, or attempt to accrue merit, but by simply believing, trusting, and receiving. Joy, peace, freedom flooded his soul; he was saved utterly by simple trusting in the grace of God. And that is the essence of faith. God's ways have not changed.

Paul is quite clear: God "will justify the circumcised by faith and the uncircumcised through faith" (3:30). There are not two ways, not two legitimate approaches to justification. The Jew is not justified by the Law of Moses while the Gentile must be justified by faith in Christ; faith alone justifies all.

Once we are justified by faith there can be a subtle undermining of our faith – a retreat to self-justification before God and others by our works. Having begun in faith, we can subtly rely on our effort, our strength, our merit, to please God, and we find ourselves religious and self-righteous again – either proud at our efforts or condemned by our failure. The Vineyard church leader John Wimber would often say, "The way in is the way on." We begin the Christian life by faith and we continue it by faith.

Paul anticipates the protest from the Jewish Christians in the Roman church: What then of the Torah, the Law of Moses? What place obedience and obligations to the covenant commands of God given through Moses? Paul clearly contrasts "the law of faith" with "the law of works" in verse 27, and states that "we hold that one is justified by faith apart from works of the law" in verse 28. However, as Paul will explicate more fully through the letter, God gave the Law and the Law is good. It reveals God's character and framed covenant relations. Even so, the works of the law and the law of works never justify. In fact, they expose our failure.

Only faith saves, only faith justifies, only faith makes us right with God.

For the Jewish believer, though not the Gentile, the particular Mosaic law of works and works of the law given in the Torah may frame their cultural Jewish response to God, but they must beware seeing them as means either of attaining righteousness or boasting in their observance.

We are not justified *by* our good works (Ephesians 2:9); we are justified *for* good works (Ephesians 2:10). Thomas Oden says that our good works "are those that follow from God's own good work of grace on the cross, received by faith, as attested in Scripture ... All talk of good works assumes a due consideration of justifying grace ..."[110] Faith is evidenced in love. Works become our duty, our delight, our worship – true faith works itself out through love (Galatians 5:6). There will be and must be good works, religious works even, but these are evidence of faith, the response of faith. They must never supplement or supplant faith.

2. In Christ alone

Faith needs a focus. Twice in this passage Paul clarifies that saving faith is faith in Jesus (3:22, 26). Saving faith is not simply an existential blind leap of faith into the dark; it is not faith in faith that justifies. And we have seen it can never be faith in oneself or one's own good efforts; it is not even religious faith or faith in a god or gods. Justifying faith is belief and trust in Jesus Christ; it is persuasion, reliance, and faithfulness to Jesus Christ. It is a "yes" to Jesus, who he is as Son of God and Son of man, and a "yes" to what he's done as sacrifice and substitute for our sin. So, while justification is *universal* – it is available for all who have faith – it is also particular: it is only for those who believe in Jesus.

What justifies is not simply the exercise of faith in itself, or being a person of faith, but the object and ground of our faith – Jesus Christ. Many today in our pluralistic age take offence at such exclusive statements. They think it disrespectful, bigoted, judgmental, and intolerant. Many want to hold together all religions as equally valid paths to God. But while emotionally desirable to some, this is intellectually untenable. To somehow claim that all religions and all persons of faith are pretty much the same is a comment based on ignorance of the facts, and does justice to none. Indeed, it violates the law of non-contradiction and seeks to impose a synthesis of opposing truth claims. All religions cannot all be right, as they fundamentally disagree at the most basic levels – on the nature of God, the way to God, and the way to live for God.

Ravi Zacharias, an expert in comparative religions, says that, far from all religions being essentially the same creature with different clothes, they are in fact merely superficially the same and fundamentally different.[111]

Islam says Jesus was a righteous prophet but not God.

Judaism says Jesus was a false prophet and blasphemer of God.

Hinduism says Jesus is one god among millions.

Christianity says Jesus is the one and only God incarnate.

These are not minor nuances. They are fundamental. No well-meaning liberal can hold these together. Yes, the religious are united in their humanity, in their lives shaped by spirituality. But let us not kid ourselves that the religions are much of a muchness.

Christianity is inclusive – it asserts that God justifies *all* who believe; but Christianity is also exclusive – it asserts that God justifies all *who believe* in Jesus.

A popular post-modern preacher has written, "People come to Jesus in all sorts of ways… sometimes people use his name, other times they don't."[112] Sound good? It's what many want to hear. But it's nonsense! And therefore dangerous. It helps no one and misleads many. My wife Tiffany would not appreciate me coming to her and calling her by the name of my secretary Patricia. God saves, he saves through his Son, his Son has a name, that name is Jesus.

Yes, we really can be justified. Justification comes by faith, not works. Faith must be directed towards Jesus as Son of God and sacrifice for sin. Without faith in Jesus there can be no justification. It is not up to us to set the terms or conditions for our justification – it is against God that we have sinned, and God determines how those sins may be forgiven. I am amazed at the arrogance and ignorance of so many who think they can dictate terms to God. It is another symptom of self-willing sin.

It is God's prerogative to set the terms for our justification and salvation, and he says: "To all who did receive him, who believed in his name, he gave the right to become children of God" (John 1:12). The apostles stated: "And there is salvation in no one else, for there is no other name under heaven given among men by which we must be saved" (Acts 4:12). Paul will later enforce this: "if you confess with your mouth that Jesus is Lord and believe in your heart that God raised him from the dead, you will be saved" (Romans 10:9). You cannot come to Jesus without believing and calling on the name of Jesus. We are not to debate it or try and renegotiate it; we must gratefully receive it, and eagerly share this good news with others.

And why is Jesus' the only name that saves? Because he is the only Saviour. He is not like other religious leaders who tell you how to save yourself, he is the one whom God put forward as the propitiation for our sins. It is he and he alone who died for the sins of the world, and whose death as Son of God and Son of man was sufficient to do so. As the Cecil Frances Alexander's hymn goes, "There was no other good enough to pay the price of sin; he only could unlock the gate of heaven and let us in."[113]

I love that we call his very name Jesus, for this is the Greek form of the Hebrew name Joshua or Yeshua meaning "Yahweh saves". Whenever someone called out his name as he grew up, they were declaring the work he would accomplish for the sins of the world. And it is only when we cry, "Jesus – Yahweh's salvation – save me" that we can be saved.

3. By grace alone

Justification is an unmerited, undeserved, unwarranted gift. It is given solely on the basis of grace; it is priceless yet free – "we are justified by his grace as a gift" (3:24). Faith that secures justification is not a work, it is itself a gift. The word Paul uses here is *charis* from which we get our word "charity" – it refers to benevolence, a favour. It is also a term in ancient Greek related to both joy and beauty. Paul emphasizes the free nature of this by enforcing the noun "gift" as being given "freely".

Justification is a freely given grace gift. Grace has been defined by the acronym "God's Riches At Christ's Expense" and that is about the sum of it. What we receive free, Christ paid for with his life. Grace puts an end to striving; grace puts an end to fear of failure; grace puts an end to self-condemnation and self-recrimination. Grace brings us to a place of rest, peace, and contentment.

If justification is a gift of grace – one I couldn't pay for even though I may want to – I just come empty-handed to the cross. No merit of my own I claim. I am a starving man and grace feeds me; I am naked and grace clothes me; I am drowning and grace rescues me; I am lost and grace finds me; I am dead and grace resuscitates me. Grace does for me what I can't do for myself. But the ever-insistent flesh fuels the spiritual equivalent of home schooling. We make an attempt at go-it-alone, do-it-yourself religion, seeking to justify ourselves.

It can't be done. God saves you singlehandedly. We are saved by God or not at all. The moment I think I bring anything but wretched me, I am a robber, a divine glory thief. I forget myself. We must never become fugitives from grace.

There was a major debate in the early fifth century between the African bishop Augustine and the English bishop Pelagius over how much we bring to our salvation.[114] The same issue re-surfaced in the sixteenth century during the Reformation. Indeed, this topic is never far from the surface of religious dispute. We need to keep reapplying the lessons learned because we keep making the same mistakes. The issue in the fifth century was whether or not we participate in our salvation – whether our efforts and works build credit against our sins. Bishop Pelagius thought humankind wasn't half bad, and was able to bring something to God. He believed we are responsible for contributing to our salvation and the only grace necessary is the commands of the law, the demands of which by our own will we can fulfil.

Augustine countered him saying that we were born in sin and utterly dependent on the grace of justification and grace for sanctification. Augustine won the day and Pelagius was rightly denounced as a heretic. We bring nothing to our salvation except ourselves. In fact, we are like the cripple on a mat, lowered down to Christ by his friends through their prayers and witnessing. Brought by grace to grace – Jesus simply said, "Your sins are forgiven" (Mark 2:5).

Fifteen hundred years after the Augustine–Pelagius debate, the theologian Karl Barth said that if he had not been born Swiss he would like to have been English, because, he believed, they enjoyed sitting in front of an open fire, drinking whisky, and talking theology. The problem, though, Barth went on, was that all the English take after Pelagius – refugees from grace, trying to justify themselves, to sanctify themselves. During one of his regular prison visits, he said this:

> *Some of you have heard it said that in the last forty years I have written a great many books and that some of them have been very fat ones [he published 500 works including 40 books]. Let me, however, frankly and even gladly confess that the four words "my grace is enough" say much more, and say it better than the whole pile of paper with which I have surrounded myself.*[115]

Grace is sufficient. Grace is enough for all sinners, and for all sins. John's Gospel (1:16) states of Jesus: "from his fullness we have all received, grace upon grace."

In conclusion

In an extraordinary interview published as *Bono on Bono: Conversations with Michka Assayas*, the lead singer of U2 shows remarkable insight into justification through faith alone in Christ alone by grace alone. He says that we have "moved out of the realm of karma into one of grace". Although the universe is ruled by laws, both physical and moral, where every action is met by an equal or opposite reaction, grace turns this upside down.

> *Love interrupts... I'd be in big trouble if karma was going to finally be my judge... It doesn't excuse my mistakes, but I'm holding out for grace. I'm holding out that Jesus took my sins onto the cross, because I know who I am, and I hope I don't have to depend on my own religiosity.*[116]

We are justified by grace alone, through faith alone, in Christ alone.

19

My Father Abraham (4)

Abraham believed God, and it was counted to him as righteousness.

ROMANS 4:3

In our last study, in Romans 3, we saw that we are universally sinful and have been found guilty before God's holy and just bar. We can be acquitted on all counts of sin and declared righteous by means of God's gracious gift. Christ's death in our stead, for our sin, means that his righteousness is credited to us. We appropriate this and are brought into the new covenant relationship with God on the basis of trusting faith in Jesus.

Here in Romans 4 Paul seeks to show that this is not some radical departure, some paradigm shift in God's economy; indeed, as he has said, "the law and prophets bear witness to it" (3:21). Paul now reveals how Abraham, the supreme patriarch and father of Israel, was himself made righteous by faith, as a gift. Abraham is Paul's prime illustration of a man justified by faith. He is, as Danish theologian Søren Kierkegaard described him, "the Knight of Faith".[117]

Abraham's three steps to heaven

- Abraham *believed* God and it was *counted* (or *credited*) to him as *righteousness* (verse 3).
  - To the one who does not work but *believes* in him who *justifies* the ungodly, his *faith* is *counted* (or *credited*) as *righteousness* (verse 5).

    - Blessed is the one who is *counted* (or *credited*) as *righteous* apart from works of the law (see verses 6–7).
- *Faith* was *counted* (or *credited*) to Abraham as *righteousness* (verse 9).
- Abraham is the father of all who *believe,* so that *righteousness* will be *credited* to them (see verse 11).
    - This is why Abraham's *faith* was *counted* (or *credited*) as *righteousness* (verse 22).
    - It will be *counted* (or *credited*) to us who *believe* in him (verse 24).

In reading Romans 4 it becomes apparent that the whole chapter revolves around a concentration of three word groups:

- *pistis* – "belief" or "faith", occurring seventeen times
- *logizomai* – "to count" or " to credit" or " to reckon", occurring eleven times (27 per cent of all occurrences in the New Testament are in this chapter)
- *dikaios* – "righteous" or "just" occurring eleven times.

These three terms and concepts are the very heart of the gospel. Three little words change the world.

1. Believe

Righteousness is not automatically given to all. The mechanism for receiving this standing is faith – trusting in Jesus. Naturally, as Paul will show in Romans 10, you can't believe if you haven't heard, and on us is laid the responsibility to help people to believe.

In a recent best-selling Christian book the author emphasizes the verse in John 3:17 – "God did not send his Son into the world to condemn the world, but in order that the world might be saved through him." And on the weight of this biblical statement the author argues for a sort of universal salvation based on the decrees of God and death of Christ regardless of the response of the individual. However, the author omits to mention that John immediately goes on to say "whoever believes in him is not condemned, but whoever does not believe is condemned already" (verse 18). Believing in the Christ is all we need bring to receive our free salvation – but bring it we must, for without it we remain lost and dead in sin and divorced from God.

2. *Credited*

This is an accounting term and refers to a deposit put into your account. This is not a salary that's been earned, it is a gift. This is something we receive, not something that is ours by right. It comes from the outside. God credits our moral bank account and takes us from the red into the black.

3. *Righteous*

This is the right *legal* standing with God that brings right *relational* standing with God. It involves both acquittal, the declaring of innocence, and moral uprightness, with an embrace into relational, covenantal, filial standing with God. To be *without* sin is to be *within* God's community.

As we have seen above, there are three steps to heaven: *believe* and *credited* and *righteous*. The Jewish community emphasized three very different steps – Jewishness and circumcision and works of the Law. But without faith *like* Abraham's, rather than faith *in* Abraham, such things are like M. C. Escher's famous architectural drawings of steps that actually lead nowhere

Paul is at pains to show that Abraham was justified by faith, not as a payment for work (verses 4–5). Abraham did not actually do anything for God – no sacrifice, no service; he was justified by faith. Nor was it for being circumcised (verses 9–12), as he was circumcised subsequent to being declared justified. As for the Law, Abraham was justified by faith, not obedience to the Law, which was not given to Moses for another 700 years.

Many seek to be righteous before God on the basis of good works, a religious symbol, or obedience to rules, but these can never cover sin. A right can't cover a wrong. If we are to be declared righteous, it must come from outside of us for we cannot balance the scales in our favour – not even come close. The one reckoned righteous by faith *will* do goods works for God. The one reckoned righteous by faith *will* take the signs and seals of covenant (now baptism). The one reckoned righteous by faith *will* seek to obey the law of God. But the one reckoned righteous by faith knows that these are the right responses of the righteous, never the routes to righteousness.

My Abraham – the father of faith

Advances in IVF technology have resulted in several pregnancies for women in their sixties. The world record for the oldest couple to bear a child by IVF is held by Rajo and Bala Ram, aged seventy and seventy-two respectively. Generally women become infertile in their fifties, while men's sperm and mechanics deteriorate as they age. While there are cases of men in their eighties still being fertile, the oldest recorded woman to conceive naturally was aged fifty-nine.

Abraham was 100 years old and Sarah a similar age when she conceived for the first time. Genesis 17 details the divine visitation to Abraham and the remarkable promise that he, a centenarian, with an elderly barren wife, would sire from his seed a son and heir and descendants as numerous as the stars. A totally absurd proposition... that is, without God. Nevertheless, despite the physical and biological impossibility of a 100-year-old man and an elderly barren woman conceiving, Abraham believed God's word and was reckoned as righteousness. Abraham did not have great faith in God, but he did have faith in a great God, and he knew God was good for his word. He knew that, despite biological impossibilities, the Lord of all life could bring life from his dead loins and Sarah's closed womb. Paul tells us that the words "counted to him" as righteous were not written for his sake alone, but for ours also (Romans 4:23–24); for Abraham is the great archetype of faith-crediting righteousness, and we too will be counted righteous who believe that God can bring life from the dead, raising Jesus.

As I began work on this study I was in a coffee shop when in came a post-grad friend with his father, both secular Jews from New York. My friend asked me what I was working on, and I replied "a talk about Abraham". Immediately the father asked: "My Abraham?"

Whose father is Abraham? All Jews understand Abraham as their father – he is their patriarch, they are his direct ancestors, born of his seed. Abraham begat Isaac, who begat Jacob, who begat twelve sons, who fathered the twelve tribes of Israel. On one occasion the Pharisees argued with Jesus, boasting "Abraham is our father" (John 8:39), and the modern-day equivalent group, Hasidic Jews such as Chabad, speak of "Avrohom Ovinu" – "Abraham Our

Father" – and regard themselves not just as genetic ancestors but as spiritual heirs.[118]

All Arabs claims Abraham as their father, through his first son Ishmael. All Muslims claim Ibrahim as their spiritual father – the Qur'an speaks of Islam as the religion of "your father Ibrahim"[119] (22:78) and Islam teaches that Abraham was the first preacher of pure Islam and the pilgrim father who instituted Haaj (pilgrimage). Both Arabs and Jews can rightly claim Abraham as their father "after the flesh" – and both the religious Muslim and orthodox Jews claim Abraham as their own spiritual father. All Christians claim Abraham as their father, for Paul says Abraham is "the father of all who believe... so that righteousness would be counted to them" (4:11). This is significant in the context of the letter: in the tensions between the Gentile and Jewish believers, the Jewish believers may be making much of their Jewish ancestry. Paul is showing that *all* believers, Jew and Gentile alike, can look to him as their very own spiritual father.

Interest in ancestry is keen these days. TV programmes on celebrities tracing their family roots, online ancestry networks, professional family-tree researchers – all these and more serve the increasing number of people who want to know where they came from, who they are. My father has spent years tracing our family history and family tree and has written a large book on our family roots. He told me recently he had discovered some good news and some bad news. The good news was that we have noble ancestors – Cornish barons who warred against the English when they changed the prayer book from Latin to English! The Cornish noble thought this was a power play of the English, foisting their language on the Celts. The Latin prayer book was universalizing, equalizing, whereas the English prayer book was seen as an insult.

Then Dad shared the bad news. He showed me a wedding certificate of a Victorian ancestor who had put an "X" alongside her printed name – why? Because she could not write! My dad was muted in embarrassment at an illiterate ancestor. I loved it: lords and illiterates, my ancestors. But my ancestor is also Abraham, who sired a child when he was 100, and who believed God's promise which was credited as righteousness. My father, Abraham.

Abraham is the father of all who have faith in God. The Bible devotes the first eleven chapters to the creation of world, to the fall of Adam and Eve, and to the pre-history of humankind up to the introduction of Abram. It then devotes the next fourteen chapters to the story and journey of Abraham alone – so crucial is he to the biblical worldview and an understanding of the life of faith. And because of our faith in Christ, our life, story, and journey are now joined to Abraham's life, story, and journey. There are some Christian healing ministries that seek to cut you off, set you free from all the negative spiritual "hand-me-down genes" from your ancestors, so that their sinful patterns are not repeated in your life. But Paul wants us to awaken to the wonderful truth that, in Abraham, we have an ancestor whose influence we should celebrate and imitate.

My Abraham, the friend of God

The apostle James wrote, "'Abraham believed God, and it was counted to him as righteousness' – and he was called a friend of God" (James 2:23). It is not only the Muslims, Arabs, Jews and Christians who put faith in God and call Abraham "my Abraham" – God himself, in whom Abraham believes, says, "That's my Abraham." That's my boy! Abraham is the only person in the entire Bible to be directly called God's friend, and this is stated three times. James takes exactly the same Old Testament quote that Paul takes from Genesis 15:6 and adds to it the title "the friend of God". Friendship with God is the result of believing in God and being declared righteousness.

The Protestant emphasis on being "righteous" often thinks only in terms of the taking away of moral guilt and a crediting of judicial and moral perfection. But that's only part of the story. The very declaration of moral righteousness finds its goal in relational righteousness – a filial, covenantal relationship. We become friends of God. Righteousness is never a right relationship to the Law, but friendship with the Lord. The moral law is not an end in itself; justification is not an end in itself; it is the basis, the pre-requisite, of covenant relationship.

The Hebrews always understood that righteousness meant friendship with God.

The problem was that the Pharisees became exclusive in keeping this friendship to just the few who attempted to keep the Law as they defined it; and to them righteousness was a law-based clique. If we as Christians emphasize moral rightness over divine friendship, we too miss the point in righteousness – that God wants to be friends with us, and Calvary shows us just how much. Jesus said, "Greater love has no one than this, that someone lay down his life for his friends" (John 15:13). Christ died for us, not just to acquit us of sin, but to admit us into his group of friends.

And then, says Jesus, "You are my friends if you do what I command you" (John 15:14). Declared righteous by faith, and now friends of God, we live righteously.

The Roman philosopher and statesman, Cicero, once said, "Without friendship life is nothing."[120] One study claims we will have 396 friends over a lifetime – but never more than thirty-three at any one time.[121] I imagine it all depends on definitions, but I think that number is way too high. Either that or I'm not very friendly! I have nearly 1,000 Facebook "friends"... but most are just contacts and many I've never actually met. Cyber-friends do not lay down their lives for you.

Research carried out at Duke University in North Carolina in the USA concluded that 25 per cent of Americans have *no one* with whom they can have a meaningful conversation. Not one! And 50 per cent have no more than two people, often only one, of this sort in their lives.[122] A friend is someone we walk through life with, someone we can share everything with, someone who comes running in troubled times. What a remarkable thing that God counts us among his friends. Dr Samuel Johnson said, "Life has no pleasure higher or nobler than that of friendship."[123] That is certainly the case when our best friend is God.

No wonder Paul begins to celebrate – "the blessing of the one to whom God counts [credits] righteousness: 'Blessed are those whose... sins are covered; blessed is the man against whom the Lord will not count his sin'" (4:6–8). The righteous by faith are thrice blessed – thrice favoured by God. Not only are they justified; not only are their sins forgiven, but we are blessed with divine friendship... we are God's friend, just like Abraham.

20

The Gospel of Love (5:5–8)

What immediately comes to mind when you hear the word "love"? I asked a number of people this question and the majority replied by defining love in terms of romantic relations. A few replied with Christian religious motifs: God, cross, sacrifice. Several sang the Beatles' song to me, "All You Need is Love." There were some rather surprising replies like cheese, empty, pain, embarrassment, red, elusive, fear.

In Romans Paul spends the first four long chapters landscaping the gospel. He has explained its necessity, mechanism, appropriation, and benefits. But in all his many words one has been totally absent: love. Why has Paul not used this word? Is it because the notion of love is absent from God's workings in the gospel? By no means! Paul has not mentioned love yet, I believe, because he knows we will respond, "Ah yes, yes, I know about that" and then fail to fully grasp the gospel, projecting onto it our own preconceived notions of love.

Years ago, when I started out preaching, I was told by my mentor, Korky Davey, "There are two rules in life: never invade Russia in winter; and never tell folk what your theme is before you speak; because some will click off, thinking they know it all already."

In truth many today misunderstand the gospel because they have a pre-constructed notion of what it is, and fail to understand it on God's terms, interpreting it in the light of their own unbiblical and pallid concepts of love. Many project their ideas of love onto God and, like Procrustes' bed in Greek mythology, lop off whatever biblical portrayal of God does not fit with their own constructed notion of God as love. Usually it is God's holiness that is excised, or his judgment and wrath – as some fail to see that these are all aspects of love.

But now in chapter 5, having given us the architecture of the gospel, Paul introduces the notion of love as the ground and goal of the gospel. It is a theme he will continue to explore as our distilled experience of God and the hallmark of our life together. Romans 1–4 details the gospel which is the divine display of love – *amor mysticus tremendus dei* – the divine Love which cannot be fathomed without first seeing the wicked "no" of humankind to God, and the repeated "yes" of God to humankind. Pre-eminently divine love is manifested in the visceral, vicarious death of Christ at Calvary. Until we see the cross, until we see the cost, we cannot conceive of love.

We must not project any sentimental notions onto our understanding of divine love. Love is bloody Calvary; love is unconditional gift. Only in the light of the sinfulness of humankind – its idolatries, immoralities, rejection and rebellion against divine revelation – coupled with God's determined advance to embrace us, can we begin to fathom his love. So Paul doesn't mention love until he has first explained love. We must be so careful not to project our conception of words onto God's employment of our words. God's revelation interprets our conception. God's Word interprets our word. We need a re-evaluation of values in the face of the cross.

I want us here to explore God's love as presented in two ways: love as an objective historical event (5:8) and love as subjective existential experience (5:5). The love Paul speaks of is denoted by the word *agapē*. Virtually unused in ancient Greek, its etymology unknown, it was picked up by the early church to define the gospel. A new word was needed to articulate this extreme love. The word conveys "intensity" and "proximity" – you cannot *agapē* from a distance. And so love comes close.

Love planted

"God shows his love for us in that while we were still sinners, Christ died for us" (5:8).

There is a heart at the heart of the universe. Do you see it? Divine love is not some intangible, ethereal, sentimental notion. Divine love is tangible, historical, active – it is a brute fact and involves a brutal fact. Divine love is not the preserve of poets but historians. Divine love demonstrates itself in time and space. Divine love expresses itself through a man, in a life laid down 2,000 years ago on a hill outside Jerusalem. God does not *shout* that he loves us, he *shows* it.

The word translated "shows" in verse 8 is *synistesin* – a conjunction of two Greek words, *syn* meaning "with" and *histemi* meaning "to stand by, make firm, fix, establish". God's love stands with us, by us, for us – love fixed firmly alongside us. "God commendeth his love toward us," as the King James Version of the Bible has it.

Shakespeare celebrates love in his sonnet 116:

Love is not love
Which alters when it alterations finds,
Or bends with the remover to remove:
O no! it is an ever-fixed mark… [124]

Once when I was asked to preach on love at a wedding, the bride and groom meant to ask for sonnet 116 but mistakenly asked for sonnet 16 – which is all about bloody warfare. But actually the unbending love of sonnet 116 is indeed the love that goes to bloody war to save us. God's love is an ever-fixed mark that neither bends nor removes. The cross is a monument – it is a monumental memorial to love. God loved us "while we were still sinners" – he doesn't love us because we are lovely or lovable. He loved us when we were ugly in sin, rebellion, selfishness, and idolatry, with our backs turned on him. He loved us when we despised and dismissed him. He loved us when we were still far off – he saw us from afar and he loved us.

Søren Kierkegaard stated "God loved us first",[125] echoing John's letter which tells us that we love him because he first loved us (1 John 4:19). Two thousand years ago, eighty generations ago, when my Iron Age Celtic ancestors were barbarians pushed around by Rome's armies and living hand to mouth in mud hovels, I was foreseen, foreknown, and foreloved by God.

Catholic scholar Joseph Fitzmyer writes beautifully:

There is no quid pro quo in the love manifested: divine love is demonstrated toward the sinner without a hint that it is repaying a love already shown.[126]

"Christ died for the ungodly" (5:6) – he died for us "while we were sinners" (5:8). Yet unborn but not unloved. He loves us not because he saw us at our best; he loved even while seeing us at our worst.

A sociologist writing a study on parenting interviewed a mother of thirteen children.[127] The interviewer asked: "Do you think all your children deserve full, impartial love?" The mother replied, "Of course." Trying to catch her out, the interviewer asked: "Which do you love most"? The mother answered: "The one who is sick until he gets well, and the one who is away until he gets home." It was when we were sick in sin and far from home that God loved us most, that he was most occupied with us and went out of his way to save us.

Sadly, some neither see nor desire this kind of a God, this kind of love, this kind of a gospel. A vicar friend in London was at a clergy meeting, and a priest was thumbing through a book on the gospel by Australian evangelist John Chapman. This vicar, seeing its evangelical content, spat out the words, "What makes me really angry is when people say Jesus died for our sins." Unbelievably, he was disbelieving the heart of the Christian faith.

Paul throws out a few pointers at what this "love planted" secures for us: peace with God (5:1); access to God (5:2); justification (5:9); salvation from God's wrath (5:9); reconciliation with God (5:10). And without the cross, the converse is true: we are enemies of God, excluded from God, condemned by God, under God's wrath, cut off from God. The cross shows God loving us to death, God standing in our stead, taking our infirmities, bearing our iniquities. Someone once defined love in terms of the marriage vows: "When he says I do, he does."

At the cross love is planted: God stands beside us and says, "I do."

Love poured

"God's love has been poured into our hearts through the Holy Spirit who has been given to us" (5:5).

Calvary is a fixed marker, a planting of God's love in time and space. It is objective, historical, geographical, and monumental – but it's much more! The cold hard facts of love at Calvary become the warm embrace of fire by his Spirit. Paul says that we can know that objective historic display of love subjectively – immediately, intimately, existentially. God doesn't just say, "I love you, look at the cross" – he says "I love you" and gives us himself; he pours himself into our hearts by his Spirit. One of the tragedies in the Christian world is that many have seen God loves them, by looking at Calvary – the objective fact – but have never experienced God's love – the subjective encounter. Oh, how God longs to pour his Spirit out on us – to magnify, to expand his love within us and for us.

God's love has been poured...

The image of pouring conveys a lavish, abundant, extravagant grace of the Spirit given to us. The Greek word is *ekkexytai,* used in the Septuagint to speak of the Levites pouring out the blood of sacrifices in temple offerings. The divine two, blood and Spirit, are inseparable. Out of our Lord's side flowed blood and water. Because Jesus poured out his soul unto death, because he poured out his blood on the rubble before the rabble at Calvary, so he pours into our hearts his Spirit of love. It was used in classical Greek for the overflow of a body of water, and we must not think of this pouring as a mere dribble or drizzle. It's a deluge, a flood.

... into our hearts...

The heart in Hebrew thought was the centre of one's being, one's core (in the Greek world the centre of being is seen as the mind or bowels). The heart is the place of the affections, emotions, and feelings that drive actions. God gives himself to us in love at our very core. It is love experienced, love *felt*. As Mark Stibbe has said, when the dentist says "You won't feel this", don't believe him, and when some Christians say of God's love, "You wont feel this" – don't believe it! Love is an event (Calvary); it is an experience (shed abroad in our hearts).

In a famous account Sarah Edwards, the wife of eighteenth-century revivalist Jonathan Edwards, recalls a remarkable personal encounter with Christ by the Spirit that lasted for several hours as she lay, unable to move, on her bed. She recalls it as:

> *the sweetest night I ever had in my life... all night I continued in a constant, clear, and lively sense of the heavenly sweetness of*

> *Christ's excellent love, of his nearness and dearness to me, and my dearness to him… I seemed to myself to perceive a glow of divine love come down from the heart of Christ… At the same time my heart and soul all flowed out in love to Christ, so that there seemed to be a constant flowing and re-flowing of heavenly love.*[128]

That is what it means for love to be poured into our hearts. Have you ever known that?

… through the Holy Spirit…

God gives us the gift of himself. It is no mere token, instrument, or accessory. God himself gives himself. He comes to abide with us. The gift is the giver. Even as God gave his Son, so he gives his Spirit. The whole Trinity is intimately involved in the outgoing ingathering of God's love. Augustine taught us that the inner life of God is love – love between the Father and Son and Spirit. God loves the world by sending his Spirit, and by that same Spirit draws us in love to God. It's a love affair. The authentic experience of the Spirit is to know God's love and to love God in response.

… who has been given to us

It is a gift given; three times in Romans 5 Paul speaks of the "free gift". It *has* been given. The Spirit has been poured out at Pentecost.

That past event needs appropriating and to be made a daily present experience. The longing of all human life is for love. There is a profound ache that only God sending his Son, then sending his Spirit, satisfies. I so appreciate Samuel Rutherford, the Puritan who wrote from jail in Aberdeen in Scotland about his discoveries of divine love:

> *O thirsty love, wilt thou set Christ, the well of life to thy head and drink thy fill? Drink and spare not, drink love and be drunken with it.*[129]

We must keep coming to the river of divine love and drink until full drunk.

We rejoice

The overflow of "love planted" at the cross and "love poured" into our hearts is that "we rejoice in *hope*" (5:2), "we rejoice in our *sufferings*" (5:3), and "we rejoice in *God*" (5:11). Love brings joy, and joy celebrates.

Irish polymath, Arthur Lynch, once wrote:

> *We must rejoice when love is great, and pardon its excess, for love is the staff of life, and life without love is life in vain.*[130]

God's love testifies that God is with us, God is for us, God has a future for us and we rejoice. And we endure suffering – we persevere and we triumph – because we are loved, and the fiery afflictions and temptations of life cannot quench the joy of love. Those who see love planted at Calvary by God's Son; those who experience love poured into us by his Spirit; really will be the happiest people on earth.

21

Heaven's Hoi Polloi (5:12–21)

Swedish theologian Anders Nygren claimed that Romans 5 is the point "where all the lines of Paul's thinking converge".[131] Chapters 1–4 of Romans have presented us with the need and means of salvation; chapters 6–8 will address the need and means of sanctification. Romans 5 is a transitional chapter – it concludes Paul's meditation on salvation and sets the scene of sanctification, introducing themes important to the doctrine. It's not an easy chapter, as William Barclay notes: "No passage is more difficult for us to understand today. It is difficult because Paul expresses himself in a difficult way."[132]

And it does seem Paul's rhetoric runs away from his logic. But, if we look closely, there are some crucial truths and wonderful treasures here.

If you could choose your parents, would you?

We live in an age where DNA research means we can tweak the genetic structure of our children by modifying the sperm or ovum or foetus – removing hereditary diseases and even determining eye colour and physiology.

It's one thing to tweak your children's DNA, but what if you could do the reverse – retrospectively chose the DNA of your ancestors? It is joked that the first sign of intelligence is to choose your own parents! But we all know that we cannot change what – or who – has gone before us.

In Romans 1–3 Paul has emphasized that we are individually and corporately guilty before God as a result of sin. Though sin is universal, Paul emphasizes our personal responsibility and culpability. However, in Chapter 5 Paul introduces a new actor in the play: Adam. And Paul also introduces a new theme, claiming that our sinful condition stems in part from our spiritual ancestry.

In chapter 4 Abraham is introduced as the father of faith and righteousness; here in in chapter 5 Adam is introduced as the father of death and unrighteousness. Paul says that through the one man Adam (whom he considers both archetypal and the historical progenitor of mankind) we have inherited a spiritual DNA. Adam's DNA leads us towards sin, judgment, condemnation, and death. Our spiritual ancestry determines our moral propensity and eternal destiny. Like father, like son: as heirs of Adam we share his character, which is sinful.

Adam is father and font. He is the head of our race. His DNA of sin has been imputed and imparted to us. I found myself noticing a character weakness in one of my sons that I recognized I have, and it's also a propensity my dad has. I don't think it is simply an environmentally learned thing. We inadvertently receive both the good and the not-so-good from our genetic ancestors.

Paul says that our propensity to sin is not simply an act of rebellion and volition, but a condition we have because our ancestor Adam gave it to us.

The good news is that we are not tied to our ancestry – it can be "genetically modified", so to speak, spiritually re-engineered. Natural, born-to-die sinners after Adam can be spiritually reborn after Christ into righteousness and life. We are imputed Adam's unrighteous DNA at birth, "brought forth in iniquity" (Psalm 51:5); and, praise God, we are imputed Christ's righteous DNA at our new birth, born again to holiness.

God's top trumps

In Romans 5 Paul speaks a lot about which rule and reign we live under. There is a "reign of sin" in Adam (5:21) and a "reign of grace" in Christ (5:21). There is also a "reign of death" in Adam (5:14) and a "reign of life" in Christ (5:17).

We must ask which rule and reign we are living under. Luther's friend Philip Melancthon once wrote, "Old Adam was too strong for young Philip."[133] Indeed we are powerless to overcome the grip of sin and destiny of death that our ancestor Adam has on us. One mightier than he must prise his grip off and cast him aside. And this is exactly what Christ comes and does.

In J. R. R. Tolkien's *The Lord of the Rings* Théoden, the King of Rohan, has come under a spell of evil Saruman, and is oppressed by the curses of Gríma Wormtongue, who acts as his counsellor but really speaks for Saruman. Théoden has become prematurely old, bowed, broken, grey, and paranoid, without hope and full of fear. When Gandalf comes and commands the darkness to flee from him, he is delivered; he rises and stands tall. Colour fills his cheeks, hope fills his heart, a sword fits his hand, and he becomes a man fully alive, ready to do battle against the hoards of evil.

Five times in Romans 5 Paul uses the Greek term for "much much more".

> *For if many died through one man's trespass, much more have the grace of God and the free gift by the grace of that one man Jesus Christ abounded for many.*
>
> 5:15

> *For if, because of one man's trespass, death reigned through that one man, much more will those who receive the abundance of grace and the free gift of righteousness reign in life through the one man Jesus Christ.*
>
> 5:17

> *... where sin increased, grace abounded all the more.*
>
> 5:20

The conflict in us between old Adam's influence and Christ's is an uneven one. A flyweight, Adam is in the ring with a super-heavyweight Jesus.

When they were young my sons were keen players of the card game "Top Trumps." I played it as a youth in the 1970s. A deck of cards covers themes like Top Cars, Top Guns, Top Jets, Top Armies, and so on. Each card describes an item and gives it points out of 100 for how it ranks against others in speed, effectiveness, reliability, and so on. You serve the cards out and then consecutively lay your cards against each other's, and the card with the highest points wins. The lesser card is trumped by the greater one.

Paul in Romans 5 plays spiritual Top Trumps between our life as sinners in Adam and life for righteousness in Christ. Adam lays down the card "sin" – Christ lays down the card "righteousness". Christ is Top Trump. Adam lays down the card "death" – Christ trumps this with the card "life". Adam lays down the card "condemned" – Christ lays down the card "justified – Christ is Top Trump. Whatever card our old Adamic sinful DNA throws at us, Christ has a card to beat it.

Many prefer Adam. Some have suggested that introducing Christ's DNA, far from improving life, actually corrupts that of old Adam. Karl Marx thought Christians were drugged by religion, the opium of the masses. Sigmund Freud thought Christians were dependent – retarded infants groping for a father figure. Richard Dawkins thinks Christians are deluded – living in the dark ages, unenlightened and ignorant.

However, the former president of the Royal College of Psychiatrists, having reviewed a wealth of literature on the benefits of religion on human well-being, wrote this:

> *In the majority of studies religious involvement is correlated with:*
>
> - *well-being, happiness and life satisfaction;*
> - *hope and optimism;*
> - *purpose and meaning in life;*
> - *higher self-esteem;*
> - *better adaptation to bereavement;*
> - *greater social support and less loneliness;*
> - *lower rates of depression and faster recovery from depression;*
> - *lower rates of suicide and fewer positive attitudes towards suicide;*
> - *less anxiety;*
> - *less psychosis and fewer psychotic tendencies;*
> - *lower rates of alcohol and drug abuse;*
> - *less delinquency and criminal activity;*
> - *greater marital stability and satisfaction.*[134]

Grace is... the basis

Granted that Christ has all the winning cards that trump everything that life in Adam can throw at us, but how do we become "upwardly mobile" from this old programmed life in Adam to new life in Christ? The answer is grace.

John Stott wrote, "Grace is love that cares and stoops and rescues."[135] We move from sin and the shadows of death in Adam, to life and holiness in Christ, not on the basis of anything we do, but purely and totally on the basis of grace. Paul cannot help repeatedly introducing grace at every opportunity – that is because he grasps that grace is the Christian life from start to end. Ten times in just six verses Paul states that this is all a gift of grace. And he speaks not simply of grace but of "grace abounding – abundant grace". Grace is a gift. Grace is not grace if you have earned it; a gift is not a gift if you bought it. Grace is not a reward, or a payment, or a due. It is outrageous, underserved, unmerited, divine favouring. The mark of the sinful flesh, of old Adam, is "I did it my way." The mark of the Christian is a dependency on what I receive from God.

Consider: "the grace of God and the free gift by the of grace of that one man Jesus Christ abounded for many" (5:15); "the free gift following many sins brought justification (5:16); how "much more will those who receive the abundance of grace and the free gift of righteousness reign in life" (5:17).

It is in the nature of God to give. I like to give gifts to my sons. When my wife Tiffany says, "You'll spoil them," I reply, "Good! I'm their father – it's what fathers do." It's what Father God does – Paul says elsewhere that he "lavished" the riches of his grace upon us (Ephesians 1:7–8). The seventeenth-century Welsh priest, George Herbert, in his poem "Pulley" describes this abundance of God:

When God at first made man,
having a glasse of blessings standing by,
let us, said he, poure on him all we can.[136]

Twice, in verses 15 and 16, Paul repeats that the "gift is not like the trespass". The gift of Christ's righteousness is not like Adam's transgression. Besides being polar opposites, I believe the gift of righteousness in Christ differs from the gift of transgression in Adam because the Adam's legacy was automatic whereas the gift of Christ needs to be received. The consequences of Adam's disobedience automatically carried over to his ancestors – all Adam's heirs are born in sin, we are born to die. However, Christ's obedience and righteousness do not automatically carry over to all who need it. We did not choose to be born in the flesh, born as heirs of Adam, but we must choose to be born again and become inheritors of Christ's work. Gifts must be received. Conversely, grace can be rejected.

A couple of years ago I saw a notorious Oxford drunk fall hard on the road outside my house, hitting his head on the curb and knocking himself out. He split his head open and lay unconscious and bleeding. I rang the paramedics and one arrived quickly. He began working on the guy who soon came round, sat up and started wrestling with the paramedic aggressively. Perhaps in his drunken state he thought he was being attacked or robbed. The paramedic tried to calm him down and explained he wanted to help, but the drunk was having none of it. Exasperated, the paramedic warned, "If you do this, I will have to leave." Shortly afterwards that is what he did, leaving the guy, drunk, concussed, bleeding, and hurting in his own stubborn stupidity. More recently that same man came into our church drunk and weeping and broken, and we prayed for him. More recently still I saw the man totally transformed – sober, clean-shaven and bright-eyed. It would seem he had finally accepted grace. Rescue requires response. Grace can be rejected, though happily for us it does not always take no for an answer.

Heaven's hoi polloi

Divine grace is *exclusive* in that it can be found nowhere but in God, yet it is the most *inclusive* thing in the world, embracing any and all. Grace knows no élitism; it is not only for the few – it is extended to all.

Twice (in 5:15 and 5:19) we read of grace extended to "the many" – the Greek term here for "the many" is *hoi polloi*. This term simply means "the many", although it has entered the English language as a socially élitist term to describe or dismiss the unwashed masses. God's transforming grace, the grace that invites us to relocate our lives from being dead in Adam to being alive in Christ, is an invitation open to all, including our sense of "hoi polloi". From the highest to the lowest, from the richest to the poorest, from the smartest to the simplest and the best to worst... grace is offered.

"For as by the one man's disobedience the many were made sinners, so by the one man's obedience the many will be made righteous" (5:19).

22

Go, Sin No More (6)

C. H. Spurgeon tells the story of a woman who claimed she had attained "sinless perfection" and had not sinned for years. Then he recalls that someone stood heavily on her toe (was it Spurgeon?) and "her sinless perfection departed her like the morning dew". Paul has explained in chapters 1–3 that the universal human condition is sin, inherited from Adam (chapter 5). To sin is to fall short of the yardstick of Yahweh – deviating from his will and his decree. Sin is doing, saying, thinking, feeling, anything that is not in conformity to God. My sin damages me, it damages my community and it damages my relationship with God.

Paul has now shown (chapters 3–5) that sin is atoned for by Christ's death, the benefits of which are received by faith, by trusting in that death for us. God's love covers God's wrath. The question Paul moves to now in chapter 6 is this: "Given that I am free from the *penalty* of sin on judgment day – having my sins forgiven, my slate wiped clean, my debt to God paid for – is it possible for me to be *practically* free from its presence and its power in my life today?"

Paul will show that, while this side of heaven we will never be free from sin's presence, spoiling our world and tempting our own body and mind, we can indeed be free from sin's power over us, and free to live *practically* the righteousness that is imputed to us *positionally*.

No means no

Twice Paul asks, "Shall we sin?" (6:1, 15), and the answer is not yes! "By no means!" (6:2). Yes, grace abounds to sinners, but that is no licence to sin.

Grace covers sin. God's mercy is greater than his wrath. When God forgives our sin, he is glorified. Experiencing God's grace and mercy in forgiveness elicits our heartfelt worship and praise and thanksgiving. And it's possible that some in the church exercised a strange logic at this point. Or it may be that some outside the church thought this was what was going on – that Christians were choosing to sin in order to ask forgiveness, in order to magnify God's grace yet further.

Martin Luther in a letter to his friend Philipp Melancthon once wrote, "Sin boldly – but believe and rejoice in Christ even more boldly."[137] His point was not to encourage us to sin, but to shock us into realizing that, even if we committed great sins, they greatly glorify the grace of God when they are confessed.

Again, in verse 15 Paul rhetorically asks, "What then? Are we to sin because we are not under law but under grace?" Again the answer is "By no means!" Some cynical and flesh-led Christians may have thought, "Well, we are not under law now but under grace, and if God always forgives sin, we might as well enjoy ourselves sinning." They figured that, if you can get away with sin without being charged, why not? Wouldn't you? The Law can't touch us, we're already saved.

In both these responses, Paul is combating those who may seek to take grace for granted. Paul's answer is a short and sharp "No way!". The Greek is *me genoito* – more literally, "May it not come into being". May this sin never come to birth.

Shall we sin? No, nay, never, no, nay, never no more. Provision of grace for sin is not a resignation to sin. Yes, grace abounds to sinners, but that's no reason to sin. Freedom from the penalty of the law is not permission to break the law.

Indeed, the very provision of grace and freedom from law fortifies us against sin.

Sin is a universal condition (3:23), but could it be that Paul is suggesting here that, for those in Christ, it is possible to be free from sin? Must sin for a Christian be inevitable – like wrinkles, death, and taxes?

In verse 7 Paul reminds his readers that they have been set free from sin; in verse 14 "sin will have no dominion over you" – it is not going to be their master. Paul refuses to entertain any claim that "I just couldn't help it".

I once received a speeding fine. Thinking (mistakenly) that I was driving down a 50 mph country lane, I was caught driving at 36 mph in a 30 mph area. The police sent me a letter stating various excuses that would not be accepted, including: "I did not know the road; I did not see the signs; I have a clean licence; I was late; I didn't know cameras were there; the road was clear; I was momentarily distracted; the car behind forced me to speed up." The law accepts no excuse for speeding!

Paul accepts no excuse for sinning. Though he says Adam influences us, ultimately we are accountable in Christ for our sin, and if we sin we do so volitionally. Shall we sin? No! It is possible not to sin. Does Paul believe we can be free from sin? Yes! Does Paul believe we can live a life, moment by moment, sinless? Yes! Was Paul sinless? No (as Romans 7 will lead us to acknowledge). Have I ever met a sinless person? No. Nevertheless, Paul refuses to take sin for granted – he refuses to resign to its power.

In John 8 a woman is caught in adultery. The Pharisees want her stoned for her sin. But Jesus says that he doesn't condemn her, and then commands her to "sin no more". Do you think she returned to her adultery having been shown grace and heard the direct word of the Lord? I doubt it. And she had not even received the indwelling Spirit.

Paul believes not only that we should hear "I don't condemn you" but also respond to grace and "sin no more". The presence of sin is always with us until Jesus returns, but the penalty and power of sin have been broken at the cross.

It is not that Paul thinks we are unable to sin, but he does think we are able not to sin.

The *New Scientist* recently published an article entitled "10 Impossibilities Conquered by Science"[138] in which they listed ten claims that scientists had once said were impossible but which advances had made possible. Among them were:

- knowledge of the internal constitution of stars and planets
- making an item fly when it's heavier than air
- the creation of force fields
- making an item invisible (we can now in two dimensions)
- teleportation (at the level of atoms)

Scientifically, just because something was previously impossible doesn't mean it is never possible. Similarly, just because you have never met a sinless person, living a perfect life, holy as God is holy, walking in the Spirit, abiding in Christ, that does not mean you won't. Indeed, why don't you become that person? Don't give in to sin before you've even started. If you concede that you will inevitably sin, you will sin.

Free means free

What grounds does Paul offer for such optimism about freedom from sin? Sinlessness is not the result of self-help, self-improvement, or self-hypnosis. The sinful self cannot overcome sin. The Law cannot overcome sin. Freedom not to sin can only come by being free not to sin.

I watched a TV programme in which a lady had a gastric bypass by hypnosis. The therapist led the woman to believe in a trance that she had had the operation. The idea was that this would change her mindset towards food and thus she would eat less and consequently lose weight. She did lose weight, but I think it was because she started running every evening and joined the dieting club! Paul is *not* saying that we have had some kind of bypass operation when we have not – he is not saying we are free from sin when in fact we are not. What he *is* saying is that genuine soul surgery really has taken place to change our nature and our attitude to sin. Paul adopts two metaphors to explain why continuing in sin is nonsense.

First, we do not sin because we are dead to sin; secondly, we do not sin because we are free from sin. It is not just the penalty of sin, but the very power of sin that is removed.

1. Dead men don't sin

How can we who died to it still live in it (6:2)?
The one who has died has been set free from sin (6:7).
You must consider yourselves dead to sin (6:11).

Distinguished New Testament professor, Charlie Cranfield, wrote:

> *the death to sin which Christians are said to have died is, according to Paul, an event which has rendered their continuing in sin as something essentially absurd.*[139]

Sin was a pattern of our old life, as heirs of Adam. But we have died to that. At the cross Jesus took the penalty of our sin and broke its power for us. The resurrection of Christ shows that the power of sin was dealt a death blow at the cross. By belief and baptism into Christ, united with his death for sin and his resurrection over sin, we know not just the forgiveness of sin, but the very freedom from it. We need to recognize that fact and live in the reality of it. Many Christians can go their whole lives without grasping this truth of their identity in Christ.

George Müller, the saintly founder of orphanages and schools, was asked the secret of his success:

> *There was a day when I died,* utterly died*; died to George Müller and his opinions, preferences, tastes and will – died to the world, its approval or censure – died to the approval or blame even of my brethren and friends – and since then I have studied only to show myself approved unto God.*[140]

In similar vein, worldwide evangelist Billy Graham, when asked how he coped being away from his wife with the temptations of travel and fame, commented: "I'm dead to every woman but my wife Ruth."[141]

Victory over sin comes, not through a second and subsequent mystical experience of "dying to sin", but through a revelation that in Christ we are actually dead to sin.

In the Movie *Mission Impossible 2* Tom Cruise plays an über-spy combating global terror. A wicked arms dealer places a microelectronic explosive device in Ethan Hunt's brain and sets it to detonate. The only way it can be deactivated is by Hunt dying, which short-circuits the explosive chip. Hunt's wife electrocutes him to death, thus deactivating the chip, and then brings him to life again with a defibrillator.

Sin is like an implanted explosive chip in our old nature, inherited through Adam and activated by our sin, and it keeps going off. But by belief and baptism into Christ, we are identified with him, in his dying for us at Calvary, his dying for sin, his rising in power to new life. The explosive chip of sin is deactivated, and sin-free we are brought back to new life.

We must, and we may, live like those who are dead to sin and alive in Christ.

2. Freed slaves don't take orders from old masters

We are no longer enslaved to sin (verses 6, 17); sin will no longer be our master (verse 14); we once presented our members as slaves to impurity and lawlessness (verse 19); now we have been set free from sin (verse 22).

We were once in the control, service, and mastery of sin. A slave is at the beck and call of his master. His shackles restrain him from being free. But when the slave is set free from his master and his bonds, he can go where he wants, when he wants, and do what he wants. Paul says that the old slave master of sin has been nullified. He has lost his job, lost his slave. The old slave master may shout, but the freed man need no longer jump. Many of us have been ordered around by sin for so long, we don't know how not to sin. It's an automatic reflex. But we need to learn to walk free.

It can take time for a slave to be reprogrammed from having the mindset and motor-responses of a slave to that of a free man. Often we need prayer, training, ministry, and revelation to help us learn to think and then live free. David MacInnes, my former rector, told me he once met a pastor who had suffered torture under a European communist regime. Once free and in the UK this man nevertheless tensed anxiously every time he saw a police car. He could not easily throw off the association that it triggered, with its thoughts of arrest, pain, and torture. The fact was that he was a free man in England, he was not on the police radar whatsoever; but he had to reprogram his trained fearful impulses.

Do you still take orders from your old boss, your old enemy? Formatted responses to sin need to be reprogrammed. The only authority the slave master sin has over you is that which you give him. You are under new management – you have been transferred from the kingdom of darkness to the kingdom of God's Son (Colossians 1:13). While this side of heaven we will never cease to be plagued by sin, nevertheless we need never again be mastered by it, for now we are the children of God, and no more, never again, the slaves to sin.

Paul adds that we are no longer slaves to sin but slaves to righteousness (6:19). We are no longer bossed about by sin but now we have a new master, a new set of duties. We are freely indentured to the bonds of the love of Christ, and we respond to his commands – not from threat but from love. He calls us to serve holiness and righteousness. If a soccer player is transferred from one team to another, and his old coach rings up and starts telling him what to do, the player can tell him where to go. We are under new management. Our new coach is righteousness.

Second blessing?

The Wesley brothers subscribed to a doctrine that became a significant feature of their Methodist movement's theology and spirituality, giving rise to the subsequent holiness movement in the nineteenth century, which influenced both the Keswick and the Pentecostal movements. They believed that sanctification, a sinless perfection they termed "perfect love", was possible as the result of a "second blessing", a baptism of the Spirit, a single endowment of grace subsequent to conversion. I find no basis whatsoever for this notion.[142] Later in his ministry, John Wesley wrote expressing disappointment that so few attained this perfection; those who had received an experience of grace often could not keep its benefits for more than a year. In his later years Wesley never taught it or even referred to it.

The Bible neither envisages nor urges us to seek a "second blessing" for holiness. We do not have to look forwards, we have to look backwards. Holiness, victory over sin, moral perfection, all comes through what Christ has done through the cross and resurrection, and our union with him at our conversion. It needs appropriating every minute, every, every day. We have crossed the Jordan and entered the promised land. Now we need to possess the land.

Is it possible to live without sin? Peter says, "His divine power has given us everything we need for life and godliness" (2 Peter 1:3, NIV). He has done his part. We must do ours.

23

Red, Amber, Green (6:11–13)

Red–Amber–Green is a universal category. It was introduced as the system for traffic lights in the UK in 1920, and it's been used to grade the dispensing of medicines, school reports, health and safety categories, and more. In this chapter I'm going to apply this convention to three key texts in chapter 6.

Paul has brought us to the point where we can see it may be possible for us to advance through life without being held back by sin. It won't go away, but it need not be our master.

For many centuries Anglican, Orthodox, and Catholic churches have begun their services with a formal confession – recognizing that before we can approach God, we must have clean hands and a pure heart. I recall hearing a visiting African minister comment, in a somewhat bemused fashion, that he had attended a service in the morning and had said confession, so why did we need to begin our evening service with a confession? He couldn't understand what we would have to confess, having prayed only eight hours earlier – surely no one had sinned between the 10:30 and 6:30 services? He was not joking. I sometimes wonder what it would be like to come to the confession and, like going through customs at an airport, have "nothing to declare"! No conscious sin to confess.

Could that ever be possible?

It is often remarked, "Better to ask forgiveness than ask permission" – do as you want and then apologize. Not true. Better never to sin than ask forgiveness! But, as we have seen, the presence of sin remains a reality until Christ returns. It is something that won't simply disappear – we will have to deal with it daily.

Sin is out to get you, to spoil you, even to destroy you, certainly rob you of the blessings in Christ. The prince of preachers, C. H. Spurgeon, once said,

> *As a reigning king sin is dead to you and you to it; but as a sneaking outlaw sin is still lurking within your soul. It is plotting and planning to get back its former dominion over you, and not merely plotting and planning, but it is also warring and fighting to that end.*[143]

If we sin, we have given in. We have chosen to say yes to temptation, to the flesh; somewhere along the line we have partnered with the sinful nature rather than our renewed spirit in Christ. Paul said: "No temptation has overtaken you that is not common to man. God is faithful, and he will not let you be tempted beyond what your ability, but with the temptation he will also provide the way of escape, that you may be able to endure it" (1 Corinthians 10:13). Temptation will come; defeat does not have to.

Paul does not want us to be complacent or passive about sin. He employs powerful imperatives in his instructions on resisting sin. These dos and don'ts make an appeal to our will, exhorting us to exercise tenacity in our struggle against sin. Paul never envisages a passive spirituality, a sort of "let go and let God" or "do not strive". That is utter nonsense. My sons often tell me to "chillax" (a contemporary conjunction of "chill-out" and "relax"), especially when I question the logic of having a smelly sports kit in a moist polythene bag in a dark corner of a bedroom, growing its own eco-system, whose stench is seeping into my study! No, I won't chillax about that. Nor will I chillax about the creep of sin!

John Owen, the luminous Puritan theologian, chaplain to Oliver Cromwell and chancellor of Oxford University, wrote in his magisterial treatise on holiness:

> *Sin does not only still abide in us, but is still acting, still labouring to bring forth the deeds of the flesh. When sin lets us alone we may let sin alone; but as sin is never less quiet than when it seems to be most quiet, and its waters are for the most part deep when they are still, so ought our contrivances against it*

> *to be vigorous at all times and in all conditions, even where there is least suspicion.*[144]

The responsibility of overcoming daily sin is yours and no one else's. Many people want someone else to fight their sin for them. In the medieval church you could actually pay monks to do penance for your sin, and even for the sins of the dead, as if votive prayers, offerings, and masses could speed them along through purgatory. I recall a friend saying he was fed up with blokes confessing their addiction to porn while not trying to stop using porn. He made the point that confessing your sin does not absolve you of your responsibility to deal with it. It is not for the one who hears the confession to deal with sin; it is for the sinner to stop sinning. You must address what you confess.

The goal here is not to be thought of as a negative form of "overcoming sin", but a positive way to be transformed into the likeness of Christ. Twice Paul speaks of the desired goal, or fruit, as leading to sanctification (6:19, 22). We must have this positive goal in mind, not simply a life of "no to sin" but of "yes to sanctification" – the possibility of purity, conformity to Christ, holiness. Otherwise we end up as anxious, fault-finding legalists. We should be known more for what we are *for* than what we are *against*. Like runners in a race, what matters is not the starting line but the finishing line.

So how do we make progress?

Red means *no*

"Let not sin therefore reign in your mortal body, to make you obey its passions" (6:12).

Paul conceives of sin as a kingdom ruling, controlling, and governing our lives and our world. That reign is now broken. The only authority the power of sin has in our life is one we chose to allow it.

Paul says we are not to allow it. Now he would not exhort us to do something we were impotent to enact. It is up to us whether we give in or not. We can choose to be disloyal to our king, Jesus, and to be ruled by another.

In the Cultural Revolution in China (1966–76) the authorities tried unsuccessfully to change the coding of traffic lights and, given their commitment to the national red flag, and Chairman Mao's red book, they wanted the colour red to be seen as positive. So the government changed the order of the colours on the traffic lights, and made red (formerly meaning "stop") mean "go". It was a danger disaster! People were simply too programmed to interpret a red traffic light as anything other than stop. In our cultural moral revolution, people want to say red is green – they are morally colour blind, and want to say that sin is not sin – they call that which is evil good and that which is good evil (see Isaiah 5:20). But red is red; sin is sin; stop is stop! And Paul wants us to see red and stop sinning.

"Do not present the members to sin as instruments for unrighteousness" (6:13). The term Paul uses for "presenting" is the Greek word *paristemi*, which is a conjunction of two words: *par*, a preposition meaning "beside"; and *histemi*, the verb for "to stand". Do not present your members to sin literally means do not stand alongside sin. Do not place yourself and your members in the proximity of sin. The word "members" literally refers to our physical body parts. We are not to place any part of us in the proximity of or alongside the activity of sin. We are not to offer our *eyes* to watch or read that which is sinful – be it violent, deceitful, materialistic, erotic. We are not to fill our *mind* with thoughts of pride, lust, criticism, unforgiveness, self-loathing, fantasy, coveting. We are not to use our *tongues* for speech that is unclean, critical, swearing, smutty, harmful to others.

There is wisdom in the three famous Chinese Confucian monkeys: one has his hands covering his eyes, one covering his ears, the third covering his mouth. See no evil, hear no evil, speak no evil. And occasionally there is a fourth monkey with arms folded meaning "do no evil". God calls us to not allow our eyes, ears, mouth, or hands to be presented to or for sin. These are not to become "instruments" (the Greek indicates means tools or weapons) for unrighteousness.

The tense movie *127 Hours* tells the true story of Aron Ralston. Climbing in the barren Utah desert, his arm became wedged in a crevasse by a falling bolder. Unable to free himself, he was slowly starving to death. Realizing that no one was coming to help, he was faced with a terrible choice: to do nothing and almost certainly die before he was rescued; or to remove his own arm, to free his body to escape. The film graphically depicts him applying a tourniquet and cutting off his own forearm. Jesus said: "If your hand causes you to sin, cut it off" (Mark 9:43); take radical evasive action to avoid sinning. Well, rather than cut your hand off or pluck your eye out to avoid sin, Paul offers us the soft option: just don't give your hand or eye to sin.

Amber means think

"Consider yourselves dead to sin and alive to God" (6:11). The key word here is "consider". The Greek is *logizomai*, which has a range of meanings: to reckon, to count, to compute, to calculate, to take into account. Here it refers to a deliberate and sober judgment of who we are in Christ. Christians are to constantly take account of theirselves, to know themselves in the light of the gospel and in the sight of God. We are the crucified with Christ; therefore we must live as dead to sin and alive to God. When sin tempts us, when old patterns of Adam's flesh try to influence us, we need to stop and think: I'm a dead man, and dead men don't sin. In Monty Pythonesque terms, "This parrot is dead… he's not pinin', he's passed on … no more! He has ceased to be! … This is an ex-parrot!" The old man in Adam is dead. Occasionally he may appear to be resurrected and pining for sin, but we do not permit it.

Sin often begins in the mind. It is rationalized and from there can send a message to our members, the body. We need to retrain the mind to righteousness. Reckoning yourself dead to sin is setting your mind – having a mindset not to sin. The mind controls the will and the will controls the act. We need to train the mind to think: dead to sin, alive to God.

There is an ancient story from the fourth-century Egyptian Orthodox Church which seeks to provoke us to "reckon ourselves dead to sin". A young monk came to the saintly Abba Macarius: "Father, what is the meaning of being dead and buried with Christ?"

Macarius answered, "My son, you remember our dear brother Sinusitis who died, and was buried a short time since? Go now to his grave, and tell him all the unkind things that you ever heard spoken of him, and that we are glad he is dead, and thankful to be rid of him, for he was such a pain to us, and caused much discomfort in the church. Go, my son, and say that, and tell me how he responds." The young man went to the grave, spoke as commanded, then returned.

Macarius enquired, "How did he respond?"

The young monk said, somewhat confused, "He didn't; he's dead."

"Go now again, my son, and repeat every kind and flattering thing you have ever heard of him; tell him how much we miss him; how great a saint he was; what noble work he did; how the whole church depended upon him; and come again and tell me what he says." The young man went again to the grave and spoke all flattering things to the dead man, then returned to Macarius.

"He answers nothing; he's dead and buried."

The old priest said: "Now you know what it is to be dead with Christ. Praises or curses are nothing to him who is really dead with Christ."

Of course, the young monk still remained alive while the dead monk was dead – and while alive he would be tempted to sin and have the opportunity to sin; sin is not dead in him. However, the old abbot Macarius's point was that the young monk was to live "as if" dead to sin – not giving it any credence or control in his life.[145]

And to live as if we are dead to sin, and as if sin is dead in us, is possible. As long as we remain in this fallen world, and in our inherited Adamic bodies, with their flesh programmed to sin, groaning and awaiting the resurrected body, the propensity to sin will be present. However, its power is broken. As we live as those dead to sin, as we walk as those alive to God, sin need not have any influence over us.

Now, it is possible for a computer to operate with two different operating systems – Mac OS and Microsoft Windows, for example; or Windows and Unix. Both are on the hard drive and one is selected over the other. As Christians in not-yet-resurrected bodies, we carry around an old operating system in our flesh full of viruses that would have us sin, while we live under a new operating system that is holiness and conformity to Christ. We have the choice which one controls us. Some Christians seek to move between the two. But we are to reckon ourselves as "dead" to the old operating system of sin, and to refuse it room.

Green means go

"But present yourselves to God… and your members to God as instruments for righteousness" (6:13).

Sin in a Christian's life is evidence that person is presenting themselves to sin rather than presenting themselves to God for good. They are presenting their members to sin rather than to righteousness. To present ourselves to sin, we must turn our back on God. You cannot be living a life towards God and at the same time sin against him. The Christian must choose to live "standing beside God". Consciousness of God, gazing on Christ, would cause all thought of sin to flee away. Just as no one would snort and spit standing beside the Queen, who would sin standing before God? The problem of sin is in part a problem of disorientation from God. Holiness is Godward life. We need to cultivate a Godward grammar – living a life *of, to, for, by, with,* and *from* Christ.

My baptismal verse given by my sponsor to me prophetically was 2 Timothy 2:15 (KJV) – "Study to shew thyself approved unto God, a workman that needeth not to be ashamed, rightly dividing the word of truth." It is a very fitting word. Baptized believers are to present themselves to God – again we have the Greek word *parastemi,* "standing beside" God. Regretfully, for several years following my baptism in my teens, I did not live a Godward posture, but lived facing towards sin.

When Old Testament priests were ordained they were anointed with blood on the right ear lobe, right thumb, and right big toe, cleansing and devoting their extremities to God (Leviticus 8:23). In Anglo-Catholic churches when the Gospel is read, the people often make the sign of the cross three times – on their forehead, mouth and over their heart – symbolizing that their mind, words and affections are consecrated before Christ. It is important to do this, if not physically then spiritually, throughout the day, presenting to Christ all our instruments, offered to righteousness, set apart for God.

The dead man walks in the opposite spirit to the sinful man. A vicar friend of mine told a chap who had confessed addictive lustful sin to him that he was practising the presence of lust, and instead should practise the presence of God. That is wisdom and practical pastoral advice. We are to walk in the opposite spirit to sin. We are to present our members to righteousness where once we gave them to unrighteousness.

I used to struggle with German people. My family went through World War II; Mum was injured as a baby by V2 bombs. We wouldn't buy German or talk to Germans… I was a xenophobe. God convicted me, and I have tried to live in the opposite spirit. So now I drive a German car, have German friends, use a German fountain pen, have a German flag in my study, and pray for Germany. My heart is changing: where once the German accent grated with me and caused deeply racist thoughts to rise, now it draws me. (I can't wait to be invited to preach in Germany!)

Practice makes perfect. My son is having guitar lessons and he enjoys the endless repetition of chord structures and their placing on the frets. All this formats his brain with finger memory. The more he practises the more immediate, natural, and effortless playing becomes. Sin is often a programmed habit, an auto-reflex of the flesh – body members and mind. Holiness can become a habit through habitually presenting yourself and your members to God.

In conclusion

On 29 October 29 1941 Winston Churchill visited his old school of Harrow. At that time Britain was hard-pressed by the Nazis. Churchill gave what became a famous speech in his characteristic style:

> *Never give in, never give in, never never never never, in nothing great or small, large or petty; never give in, never yield to force, never yield to the apparently overwhelming might of the enemy.*[146]

And this is Paul's approach to the problem of persistent sin. Never give in to sin. Never, never, never, never: in sins large or petty, never surrender.

24

The Law of Sinai and the Law of Sin (7:1–6)

In chapter 6 Paul has been strongly calling the church to a life of holiness. The question that he now addresses is: to what extent is the Torah, the Mosaic Law, relevant and helpful in assisting us to live a holy life? Is the Mosaic Law the benchmark of holiness, or do we derive our ethics and standards elsewhere? What is the nature of the relationship between the believer and the Law?

There are some amusing old laws still on the British statute books.[147] For instance, it is illegal to die in the Houses of Parliament. It is illegal to hang washing across the street or beat a doormat after 8.00 a.m. It is illegal to drive a cow when drunk. It is illegal to hail a taxi if you have the plague. It is illegal to pretend to be a pensioner if you live in Chelsea, London. It is illegal to eat mince pies on Christmas Day. It is illegal in Chester for a Welshman to enter the city walls between sunset and sunrise – if they do they may be shot with a crossbow.

Old laws, once enforced, do not quite belong in the twenty-first century.

The question Paul addresses in Romans 7 is whether the old laws of the covenant made with Israel, on the statute books of the Torah, still apply to the Christian in the new covenant; and, if so, how do we apply the rule?

This issue of the relevance of the Torah was prominent in the church in Rome due to the make up of its members. Many were messianic or "fulfilled" Jews – they had embraced Jesus as their long-awaited Messiah. They still sought to maintain their customs and culture, and rightly so. In Romans 14 we will see that they were still following a kosher diet and kashrut law, and were committed to the sabbath. As late as the fourth-century the theologian Ambrosiater said that the Roman Church followed the "Jewish rites", still maintaining its Jewish identity.

For cultural and pragmatic reasons this is right for the messianic Jews, and it is important for the Gentile converts to understand the rock from which we were hewn. However, the presenting question in the first part of Romans 7 is about the Torah, the Mosaic laws, the 613 prescriptions and prohibitions given to the people of Israel in the wilderness and which formed their covenant with Yahweh; and in particular the extent to which the Christian in the new covenant must abide by them, or may be assisted by them, towards curbing sin and conforming to Christ. Can the Law of Sinai curb the law of sin?

Released from the Law

"But now we are released from the law, having died to that which held us captive" (7:6).

When Paul speaks of the Law he is referring to the Torah, which is Hebrew for "instructions" and refers to the 613 *mitzvot*, or commands, recorded in the Pentateuch. Rabbis claim there are 365 prohibitions – "Thou shalt nots" – and 248 prescriptions – "Thou Shalts". The question for us as Christians is: are we obligated to keep these laws? All? Some? None? Is the Torah, the rule book for framing the first covenant, the same rule book for framing the new covenant? Do these laws define the nature of holiness per se, or were they particular for Israel?

Let me say up front that the material in this chapter, taught by me on two occasions, precipitated more heat than all the other talks on Romans preached over eighteen months put together. My interpretation was vehemently disapproved of and disagreed with by a vocal few, who cried in protest and queued to rebuke me. Many insisted we were still bound by the Law. And they certainly were. One even pointed out we were under the law of gravity! Clearly I had not been clear enough exactly what laws I was referring to. I still believe I have rightly read Paul here, but I humbly ask my readers to read my thoughts carefully and to write to me (via my publisher or

St Aldates Church, Oxford) if you can show from Scripture I am awry. We prophesy in part.

Paul clearly says several positive things about the Law in Chapter 7. He describes the Law as: holy, righteous, good (verse 12), spiritual (verse 14), and disclosing what sin is (verse 16); he desires to obey its ways (verse 18) and it is of God (verses 22, 25). But he also says some less than positive things. We died to the Law (verse 4a), we bear fruit (holiness) apart from the Law (verse 4b), the Law brought death to us (verses 5, 9–10), Christ released us from the bondage of the Law (verse 6), it is the old way (verse 6), and it stirred sin in us (verse 7).

Paul employs an analogy. He states that a woman is free from the Law and free to remarry if her husband dies. Similarly, Paul says we are free from the Law because we died in Christ – and Christ died to the Law. The dead are no longer married to their former spouse. We were once wed to the Law, but in Christ we have died to it and become the bride of a new husband, not the Law but of Christ. Many Christians are bigamists – they are married to both the Law and to Christ. In fact, it has been said that a Christian trying to live by the Old Testament law is like someone keeping the dead body of their deceased wife in the living room, even though they have since remarried!

To return to the Law is to return to the tombs. In Paul's main study on the Law, in his letter to the Galatians, he writes, "if a law had been given that could give life, then righteousness would indeed be by the law" (Galatians 3:21). The Law cannot give life, the Law cannot give righteousness; it can only identify sin, increase sin, and condemn us to death.

The Law pointed its finger at sin, but it couldn't lift a finger to remove sin.

What then is the ongoing purpose of the 613 laws of the Old Testament? Since the writings of Thomas Aquinas, the medieval philosopher, both Catholic and subsequent Protestant formularies of faith make a distinction between the *sacrificial, civil,* and *moral* law of the Old Testament. Generally, they then claim that the sacrificial component of the Torah was fulfilled and annulled by Christ at the cross; they claim that the civil component related only to Jews living life in the land (agricultural laws etc); and they assert that the moral laws in the Torah, which reflected eternal divine qualities, are binding on us as Christians.

This sounds reasonable but is ultimately misleading. Paul never makes such a distinction – he simply speaks of the Law, and there is no hint of any categorization. The Jews never made such a tripartite distinction. For the orthodox Jew, wearing *payots* (sideburns) was a moral command. Both sacrificial and civil law were moral to the Jew. Now, some have understandably questioned that if you now allow garments of two different fibres, or you permit people to eat shellfish, we have no basis to prohibit homosexual acts, since all these are forbidden by the Torah. If we base ethics on the Mosaic Law, it's "all or nothing", and we may not be selective.

Many Christians simply whittle the 613 down to Ten Commandments, the Decalogue written on the two tablets of stone and kept in the ark of the covenant. Indeed, some scholars suggest that the other 603 are merely a commentary on the Ten. In one survey of 1,200 American Christians, 88 per cent said that the Ten Commandments form the basis of their ethics.[148] The Vatican II documents of 1962 stated that "all men may attain salvation through faith, baptism and the observance of the [Ten] Commandments".[149] And Protestant fathers have taken similar stances: Bishop J. C. Ryle said, "I cannot find a syllable (in Apostolic epistles) which teach that any one of the Ten Commandments is done away with."[150]

This appears to be the normative view, but is it the one Paul held to? If the 613 – or the ten – are the basis for Christian morals and ethics, we would surely expect them to be exhorted and repeated in the New Testament. So where are they? Even those who make such claims are inconsistent, for since the apostolic era we have not kept the fourth commandment, to keep the Jewish sabbath which is defined as beginning at sundown on Friday until the appearance of the first three stars on Saturday evening. (Keeping this as the holy day of rest has only been maintained by a few Christian sects and has not been normative since the apostles delivered the gospel message to the Gentiles.) If the Decalogue were morally binding, why did Paul say that the Law given on tablets of stone is a ministry of death, transitory, its glory fading (2 Corinthians 3:7–11)?

I personally disagree with the tradition. Biblical professor F. F.

Bruce was, I believe, correct to say, "The believer is not under the law as a rule of life."[151] Nowhere does Scripture allow us to pick and choose over the Law, embracing what we deem moral over the ceremonial. Paul is crystal clear: you cannot take the law piecemeal: "I testify again to every man who accepts circumcision that he is obligated to keep the whole law" (Galatians 5:3).

In Galatians Paul rebukes the church for buying into Torah observance: "O foolish Galatians! Who bewitched you?" (Galatians 3:1). Paul claims the Law of Mount Sinai is analogous to the illegitimate Ishmael, not the true son Isaac of the true Jerusalem (Galatians 4:22–26). For freedom Christ set us free. Freedom from what? From the Law! And consequently Paul says, "Do not submit again to a yoke of slavery" (Galatians 5:1). Do not put the shackles of the Law on again! To the Ephesian church Paul refers to "Christ abolishing the law and commandments" (Ephesians 2:15). The word for " abolish", *katargeo,* means, according to one Greek–English Lexicon of the New Testament: "to cause something to be unproductive, to cause something to lose its power or effectiveness; to cause something to come to an end or to be no longer in existence; to cause the release of someone from an obligation" (Bauer, Arndt, Gingrich and Danker). How can we read that in any other way than "no more law"?

To the Hebrews the author writes that the old covenant (based on Torah commands) is obsolete (*palaioumenon*); it is old, obsolete, ruined, a vanishing shadow, now that Christ has brought a far better covenant (Hebrews 8:13). And again in Hebrews 10:9 he has done "away with the first [the Law] in order to establish the second". In Romans 10:4 Paul states that "Christ is the end (*telos*) of the law", and as the ESV Study Bible notes state, this "probably includes the idea of both goal and termination. The Mosaic law has reached its goal in Christ... and the law is no longer binding upon Christians."[152]

What then is the role of the Law? This has sometimes been explained in terms of the acronym SOS. The Law *Shows Our Sin* and also *Shows Our Saviour.* We would not know what sin was without it (Romans 7:7), yet it also highlights the perfections of Jesus, who fulfilled perfectly all the Law and who satisfied its requirements by bearing the curse of the law for us all.

In Galatians 3:24 Paul likens the Law to a tutor or guardian leading us to Christ – a chaperone who was necessary until we met our beloved, but after which becomes an awkward accompaniment! A road map is important until we reach our destination, but afterwards it becomes unnecessary.

Historically, the church has responded in two polar-opposite ways regarding the Law. In the second century there were two extreme Christian views. The Ebionites were Judaizers, rejecting Paul's teaching as liberal and lax and enforcing the keeping of the Law, maintaining the Jewishness of Christianity. Diametrically opposed were the Marcionites – essentially antinomian, that is, anti-Law – who rejected Matthew's Gospel as too Jewish, too rule-bound, and who rejected the Old Testament as in any way normative or useful for the Christian.[153]

Throughout history church traditions have often leaned toward Ebionitism or Marcionitism – legalism or liberalism. Certain strains within conservative evangelical and Roman Catholic spirituality can breed a spirit of pride, a religious spirit, legalistic and fearful, and inculcate a neurotic form of guilt. Liberal traditions jump on the idea of freedom from Law, which can become freedom to do whatever we like: yes to shrimp, yes to homosexual acts.

A few years ago, when I was preaching in Holland, I felt a real heaviness in every meeting at which I was present. The people seemed unresponsive, the ground hard. Then one man told me he had struggled with church for years, and even for a while stopped attending. He said the reason was that every service began with reciting the Ten Commandments, week in week out, making him feel guilty but offering no help with his sin.

That is the Law. It points out fault but can't lift a finger to help.

I felt the Lord tell me to preach away from the theme I had planned for these Dutch folk, and teach instead on grace and the Spirit-filled life. The Law, delivered cold and hard, crushes the human spirit and quenches the Holy Spirit. As I preached, the formerly stoic congregation began to weep and, during ministry, to collapse in the Spirit. My lovely interpreter whispered: "The Dutch don't do this."

Legalists are refugees from grace; liberals are abusers of grace. Ignatius of Antioch, the late first-century bishop and martyr, wrote:

"If we still live according to Jewish Law, we acknowledge that we have not received grace."[154]

A new way of the Spirit

"We serve in the new way of the Spirit, and not in the old way of the written code" (7:6).

We serve in a new way by a new Spirit, and in a new spirit. Now, it is important to say that this new law and new way will often overlap with the old laws. Indeed, nine of the Ten Commandments are repeated in various forms in the New Testament. But there are also times when the Spirit leads us to serve in a new way, breaking free from the old. The new covenant and therefore the New Testament – not the Old Testament – defines our new way of life.

The fact is, the Law of Sinai cannot curb the law of sin. C. S. Lewis wisely observed, "You cannot make men good by law, and without good men you cannot have a good society."[155]

The Law was like an MRI scan showing up our heart disease. It was good for diagnosis but it could not operate. We needed a heart transplant.

Paul speaks of a new way that is not like the old way of Torah. God's new covenant people do not live by God's old covenant laws. The Torah is not the church's rule book, and so we must not derive our ethics from it without the bigger picture. The Torah was given to define and frame Israel's covenant with Yahweh. The Torah is informative but not normative. Please understand that this "new way" is not lawlessness but a new lawfulness. We the church live in a new dispensation framed by the law of the Spirit on our hearts, the law of Christ, the law of love. Let us consider these three guides.

The new law of the Spirit

This is what Jeremiah prophesied – a new covenant, a new heart, a law within (Jeremiah 31:33). This is what Ezekiel prophesied: a new heart, a new spirit, walking God's way (Ezekiel 36:27).

Paul clearly contrasts the laws of the old covenant with those of the new covenant: "And you show that you are a letter from Christ delivered by us, written not with ink but with the Spirit of the living God, not on tablets of stone but on tablets of human hearts" (2 Corinthians 3:3). Paul is clear: the Ten Commandments came with a glory that is fading, while the New Covenant by the Spirit has come with a glory that is increasing. One cannot hold together the old with the new. The Spirit leads the church to serve God in a "new way" with a "new law" from a "new engraving" on the heart not the tablets of stone. The righteous requirements of the Law are fulfilled in us who walk by the Spirit; that means the Spirit will guide us in these.

In Acts 10 we see the Spirit of God telling Peter he could now eat any and all foods, contrary to the Mosaic Law. In Acts 15 the Jerusalem council said the Spirit led them to say that the Gentile Christians need only abstain from meat offered to idols, sexual immorality, and blood. They did not enforce the Law on the Gentiles, not even circumcision that was the covenant sign of embracing the Law as God's people. They did not say that Gentile believers must keep the 613 commandments – or even the Ten Commandments. The Spirit led them to give just three laws, and then later Paul modifies the Jerusalem council's edict and says they can now eat meat offered to idols (1 Corinthians 8:8).

The new law of Christ

Paul wrote elsewhere that he was "under the law of Christ" (1 Corinthians 9:21). Christ's new commandments are the basis of his way of life, not Moses' old ones. There were times when Jesus abrogated the Mosaic Law. Several times he said: "You have heard that it was said [old Law] but I say unto you (new law) ..." Was this merely his commentary or interpretation on the law, or was he establishing a new law, like a new Moses giving a sermon on a new mount? It seems more like the latter. Under the Old Covenant they stoned sons who brought parents shame, yet the New Covenant is beautifully illustrated by the Father running and embracing the prodigal son who had humiliated him. In the old covenant you stoned adulteresses, yet in the new covenant Jesus said to the woman caught in adultery, "I do not condemn you." This is clear abrogation of the Mosaic Law.

On occasions Jesus actually intensified the Mosaic Law, judging not simply the act but the heart's secret motives. Mosaic Law told us not to commit adultery, yet the Messiah's law says, "Do not even lust." The Mosaic Law said, "Do not murder," yet the Messiah's law says,

"Do not even hate." Salvation Army leader Catherine Booth said: "If Christ cannot supersede the law, then I am lost, and lost forever."[156]

The new law of love

Augustine of Hippo famously said, "*Ama Deum et fac quod vis*" – "Love God and do as you will." His thesis was that, if we genuinely love God, then what we want to do will be what he wants, and our actions will conform with his decrees. Jesus summed up the Law with two commandments: love God and love your neighbour (Matthew 22:36–40). If you love God, then you won't have any gods before him, you won't blaspheme, you won't make graven images, you will keep a time of regular rest and focus on the Lord. If you love your neighbour, you won't dishonour your forebears, commit hate crimes or sexual misdemeanours, steal, lie, or be consumed with envy. Love fulfils the Law. If we love God and love our neighbour, by the Spirit, we will fulfil the moral requirements of the law, and be holy as God is holy. The apostle James said the royal law is to love your neighbour. Paul said love fulfils the law. And love is the fruit of the Spirit.

In conclusion

The writer G. K. Chesterton once argued that true religion should be less a theory and more a love affair. God's New Covenant people, God's new commandment people, are not under the jurisdiction of Moses' laws in their morals and ethics. But we are not lawless; we are led by a new three-fold law – the law of Christ, the law of the Spirit of life written on our hearts, and the law of love. These three cohere and they fulfil the righteous demands of the Mosaic Law. In some respects it is easier to follow the Torah: it is fixed, static, given, the rules are all there. Many become legalists and "fall from grace" because they want to be "rule–book" Christians not "relationship to the Lover" Christians. To walk in the Spirit, to live by the law of Christ, to follow the way of love, requires a dynamic relationship, a daily dependency on the Spirit in intimacy with Christ. When we do live in the Spirit we will fulfil the spirit of the Law – as Paul will make clear: "the righteous requirement of the law" will be "fulfilled in us, who walk not according to the flesh but according to the Spirit" (Romans 8:4).

The story is told of a minister going into a church and seeing an old chap weeping as he stares at two plaques on either side of the pulpit. On each plaque five of the Ten Commandments are beautifully written in gold leaf. The minister asks if the chap is all right, and he smiles through his tears... "I see it! These are not commandments, they are promises." God's Law, re-presented and re-written, can and will be fulfilled in us as we follow the law of Christ, led by the Spirit, filled with love for God and neighbour.

25

Laws at War (7:14–25)

In our last study we considered Paul's statement that we have died to the Mosaic Law. We are now free to wed another as we live by the law of Christ, the law of the Spirit, and the law of love. These form the basis of our moral framework and our ethics. Being a Christian and also being wed to the Torah is rather like living with your new spouse, while dragging your old spouse around in a coffin!

However, it has to be said that liberty from the Torah brings relief to many, yet insecurity to some. How will I know what to do? What not to do? How will I know how well I'm doing? How will I gauge how well others are doing? Will dying to 613 laws of Torah lead to antinomianism liberalism, relativism?

The first part of Romans 7 says we are free from the Law. The second part says we definitely do not slide into lawlessness. On the contrary, Paul shows a desire to obey God's inner law, and disdain for personal sin is intensified in the believer – to the point of agony. "I delight in the law of God, in my inner being, but I see in my members another law waging war against the law of my mind and making me captive to the law of sin that dwells in my members" (7:22–23).

There are few other scriptures that have brought me more encouragement. There is nothing worse than thinking you are the only one with an issue, the only one trying to love God while battling sin and temptation. In *Shadowlands*, the movie about C. S. Lewis, one of Lewis's pupils comments: "My dad always says, 'We read to know we are not alone'", and when I read this I breathe a sigh of relief: Paul – you too? I am not alone.

The war within

There has been much debate about which part of his life Paul is speaking about in this passage. Four main options are proposed:

1. This is Paul in his previous life as a Pharisee under the law of Moses.
2. This is the ego, representing humanity, Adam's heirs, conscious of sin.
3. This is Paul as a Christian currently struggling with his own sin and failure to fulfil the law of the Spirit, the law of Christ and the law of love.
4. This is any Christian who tries to defeat sin in their own strength, or by legalism, rather than by walking in the Spirit.

Reasonable arguments may be marshalled for all, but I follow the church fathers and the Reformers who generally regard this as Paul the apostle in his ongoing struggling to resist sin, which wars with his desire to follow the Spirit. Consider the following four factors.

1. Its place in Romans

This is a chapter on the believer's sanctification, so why would Paul be talking about a pre-Christian struggle here? If this were about the struggle for purity before he met Christ, it would have made more sense if it were found in Chapter 2.

2. Its present tense

Paul is moving from the past to the present tense. If it represented his life as a Pharisee before Christ, it would make more sense to have spoken in one of the various past tenses – pluperfect, perfect, or aorist. The present tense suggests a present struggle.

3. Its personal pronouns

In just nineteen verses (verses 7–25 in the ESV), Paul refers to "me", "my", or "I" nearly fifty times. This is among the most concentrated present-tense, first-person passages in the New Testament. It would be a most strange construct if we were to regard it as generic of humanity in the past tense! Significantly, Paul also confesses his personal struggles with specific named sins (covetousness). This does not feel like human history; it is personal, confessional, and autobiographical.

4. Its practical experience

This passage portrays the ongoing struggle that all Christians experience with sin and their hatred of it. I have never met a pagan who desired to fulfil God's law and who felt distraught by their own sin – have you? Significantly, we must note that Paul uses very similar language in Galatians 5:17 to describe the struggle the Galatian believers are currently experiencing with sin, and how the sinful nature wars with the Spirit "so that you do not do what you want" (NIV). There is no question that this is a current battle the Galatians are in, where their reliance on the Law, rather than being led by the Spirit, has left them powerless to resist the desires of the flesh.

For these reasons I believe it most likely Paul is speaking of his own struggles as a Christian to conquer the sin that the Spirit of God and the law of Christ have exposed in him.

The believer's battle

There is, Paul tells us, "another law waging war against the law of my mind and making me captive to the law of sin that dwells in my members" (7:23).

Warfare is a way of life for the believer. Martin Luther says of becoming a Christian: "He enters the warfare for God."[157] C. E. B. Cranfield speaks of our "severe and relentless warfare".[158] Dietrich Bonhoeffer in *The Cost of Discipleship* wrote: "When all is said and done, the life of faith is nothing if not an unending struggle of the spirit with every available weapon against the flesh."[159]

Paul speaks of a civil war between "Paul in Christ" and "Paul in Adam". The spiritual civil war is between the will of God and the will of sin in the flesh; between the old operating system of the sinful flesh and the new operating system of the Spirit. Paul speaks of "sin" eleven times in just a few verses, and twice of evil. Paul thinks of sin not as the "absence of good" but rather as an active presence; a will, a power, a law, a rule. Paul does not personify this in terms of a demon or malevolent spirit, but rather he conceptualizes it as a distinct law or principle or pattern within his members that operates in opposition to the will of God in his mind and spirit. What Paul presents here is the internal war between the will of the born-again Christian, who delights in God's rule and desires to obey it, and the antagonist inherited in Adam, the body of sin which continually reasserts itself against God's law, promoting sin and provoking us to it.

The Christian body and soul is a battlefield with two laws at war – the law of Christ and his Spirit versus the law of sin; the born-again "ego" in Christ and the old "ego" in Adam. There is a remarkable scene in the movie of Tolkien's *The Lord of the Rings* where Sméagol and his degenerate alter ego Gollum have a conversation with each other. The Sméagol "ego" wants to help Frodo; the Gollum "ego" wants to steal the ring.

> *Gollum: We wants it, we needs it. Must have the precious. They stole it from us. Sneaky little hobbitses. Wicked, tricksy, false!*
> *Sméagol: No. Not master!*
> *Gollum: Yes, precious, false! They will cheat you, hurt you, lie.*
> *Sméagol: Master is our friend!*
> *Gollum: You don't have any friends; nobody likes you!*
> *Sméagol: I'm not listening... I'm not listening...*
> *Gollum: You're a liar and a thief.*
> *Sméagol: No!*
> *Gollum: Murderer.*
> *Sméagol: Go away!*
> *Gollum: (smiles) Go away?*
> *Sméagol: I hate you, I hate you.*

For a long while the Gollum ego has held ground, but now Sméagol reasserts himself. Sadly Gollum is never far away. What Paul is offering us in Romans 7 (and what Tolkien is offering in his work) is not the divided personality of the schizophrenic but the civil war experienced by Paul and by every Christian – between their ever insistent, flesh-desiring sin and the Spirit of God who has awoken their spirit to God.

In Tolkien's first book in the *Lord of the Rings* trilogy, *The Fellowship of the Ring*, under the telling chapter heading "Shadows from the Past", the wizard Gandalf is explaining to Frodo the power of the ring and the control it has over Gollum. Frodo asks,

> *"But if he hated it, why didn't he get rid of it, or go away and leave it?"*
>
> *"You ought to begin to understand, Frodo, after all you have heard," said Gandalf. "He hated it and loved it, as he hated and loved himself. He could not get rid of it. He had no will left in the matter."*[160]

Our flesh loves sin; our spirit alive to Christ hates sin. Whereas Gollum had no will left to resist, *we definitely do*. Defeat is a choice: the renewed will of our spiritual being, alive to Christ, Spirit-filled, can truly triumph over this death rattle craving of the sinful flesh.

The believer's battle ground

Paul says that "sin... dwells within" (7:17, 20); "nothing good dwells... in my flesh" (7:18); "evil lies close at hand" (7:21); and he is "captive to the law of sin... in my members" (7: 23).

Sin in us is the result of the programming of our inherited flesh in Adam, programmed by our willing sinning, in our body. Though we died to Adam in Christ, we still walk around in this body while we await a resurrected body. Just as tuberculosis germs can remain dormant in the body for years, even decades, before awakening and bringing disease to the host body which becomes contagion to others, so the law of sin is like a germ or virus in our inherited Adamic flesh, in our fallen human body, living in a fallen human world.

I recall a minister confessing to me that, at a time of weariness, he had fallen into a pattern of sin that had been part of his life for many years before he had become a Christian. Now suddenly it had reasserted itself. He had thought it was long gone, but it had simply been dormant in his flesh, and when he was tired his guard came down and the sin rose up. The first statement of the Reformed creed, the Westminster Shorter Catechism, is that "the chief end of man is to glorify God."[161] Meanwhile the selfish gene of sinful flesh says: "The chief end of man is to gratify man... and disobey God."

In his commentary on Romans 7 Karl Barth thundered against liberal, optimistic, idealistic humanism:

> *Paul, good man that he was, longed to be without sin, but to it he was chained. I too, in common with many others, long to stand outside it, but this cannot be. We belch forth the vapours of sin; we fall into it, rise up again, buffet and torment ourselves night and day; but, since we are confined in this flesh, since we have to bear about with us everywhere this stinking sack, we cannot rid ourselves completely of it, or even knock it senseless. We make vigorous attempts to do so, but the old Adam retains his power until he is deposited in the grave.*[162]

In Christ we are given a new heart and our spirit comes alive to God; but we are still in our flesh, dirty old Adam's members that need subduing. We struggle with sin in our flesh, until we receive resurrection bodies. Battle is inevitable, defeat is not.

The believer's battle scars

"I do not do what I want, but I do the very thing I hate" (7:15). "For I know that nothing good dwells in me, that is, in my flesh. For I have the desire to do what is right, but not the ability to carry it out" (7:18). "For I delight in the law of God, in my inner being, but I see in my members another law waging war against the law of my mind and making me captive to the law of sin that dwells in my members. Wretched man that I am!" (7:22–24).

Paul takes personal responsibility for personal sin. He does not put the blame down to the fact that he was a short man, or a short-sighted man, or a Jew oppressed by the Romans, or a tradesman tent-maker and not a aristocrat. People will blame just about anything except themselves for their sin: poor education; society; parents; being dropped on their head as a baby; lack of parental affection; being fat; being thin; not being someone else. Paul specifically names his issue as covetousness – but his reference to sin in the mind and the body's members suggests more than just the one area of struggle over sin. Paul's confession here is not of a man who is living a backslidden life but of a man who is being transformed into Christlikeness. It is Paul's proximity to God that exposes the sin in his flesh. It is Paul's delight for the Law of God that arouses his hatred of failing God and falling into sin. At times we feel so weak and impotent against the onslaught of lusts and passions of the flesh. Just as we deal with one sin, two more appear. No wonder the apostle declaims, "Wretched man that I am!"

Professor Cranfield wrote on this passage: "A struggle as serious as the one here described can only take place where the Spirit of God is active."[163] If Paul was not a Christian desiring God, filled with the Spirit, he would neither notice nor care about the sin within.

I recall going to my bishop for a personal pastoral interview at my retreat before being ordained. I was painfully aware of the temptations in my mind that seemed more intense than ever. I shared this with the bishop who prayed for me. The following year at my retreat, before being priested, again I had personal, pastoral time with my bishop, and I confessed the same ongoing struggles and temptations. This time the bishop seemed somewhat shocked: "Yes, yes, we spoke about that last year."

"I know. It's this year's struggle too."

Praise God, if I were to see him today it would not be the same issues that I would be confessing. But it was then, at that holy time of separation for service to the Lord, as I was seeking his anointing on a life of ordained ministry. Even as I was pressing into God, sin was pressing into me. It's when we are not worried about pressing sins that we need to be worried.

The believer's battle cry

"Who will deliver me from this body of death?" (7:24).

In desperation Paul cries out, spent of his own resources. But his cry does not fall on deaf ears – God hears. The question "Who will deliver me?" receives the answer, "Thanks be to God through Jesus Christ our Lord."

The Japanese battle cry *Banzai* means "Long life!" Superhero He-Man's battle cry is "By the power of Greyskull!" The believer's battle cry is *kyrie eleison* – "Lord have mercy!" And he does.

The power of self-will cannot overcome the inherent, insistent will of Adam. I need one stronger than I. All the while Paul has been speaking of the "ego" – me, my, I. And perhaps that's half our trouble:

while we look to ourselves, look inside ourselves, rely on ourselves, we lose. We need to "look to the Lord" – when Paul takes his eyes from himself, his sin and his struggle, and looks to his Saviour, he is delivered. Many Christians take too strong a dose of "Vitamin I"; they are too introspective, too internalized; they search for victory within rather than with-him. We cannot save ourselves, neither can we sanctify ourselves. We need a saviour and a sanctifier. And we have one.

Missionary Stephen Olford in his book *Not I, But Christ* says, "The victorious life is the victorious Lord living in you and me in utter mastery."[164] Paul does not despair: sin will not win, deliverance is close to hand. Whosoever calls on the name of the Lord shall be delivered.

The wonderful organization Alcoholics Anonymous proposes a twelve-step programme to deliverance. The first three are profound:

1. We *admit* we are powerless over alcohol.
2. We *believe* that a Power greater than ourselves can restore us.
3. We *decide* to turn our will and our lives over to the care of God.[165]

Deliverance, transformation, overcoming the craving and programming of the flesh, is progressively possible through admission of need, dependence on God, and active rejection of the vice. Paul describes the Corinthians' former lifestyle as "unrighteous" – "sexually immoral… idolaters… adulterers… men who practise homosexuality… thieves… greedy… drunkards… revilers… swindlers" and then celebrates, "such *were* some of you. But you were washed, you were sanctified, you were justified in the name of the Lord Jesus Christ and by the Spirit of our God" (1 Corinthians 6:9–11). The vice of sin was broken, nature and actions were transformed; Christ by his blood, the Spirit by his power, worked a revolution.

Johann Blumhardt was a pastor in Möttlingen in nineteenth-century Germany. The doctors brought to him a young woman named Gottlieben Dittus, who suffered severe psychosis and whose household was troubled by poltergeists. The medical professionals recognized that here was something beyond their ken. Blumhardt discerned this was a genuine case of demon possession. After two months of counselling and of not getting anywhere, he realized what was needed was deliverance, not discipleship. He and Gottlieben prayed: "Lord Jesus, help us. We have watched long enough what the devil does; now we want to see what the Lord Jesus can do." They began soaking the girl in intercessory prayer and ministry, and finally came the moment of crisis. At a decisive point, as Blumhardt's prayers and the girl's physical and emotional manifestation and torment were at their height, Gottlieben's sister, who had recently come under demonic oppression herself, in a strange voice suddenly screamed in Latin, *Christus Victor*! "Christ is Victor!"

It was all over. Gottlieben was never troubled again. Revival broke out in the village, many people, including the emperor, pilgrimaged to this village. Many were healed, delivered, and saved. *Christus Victor*.[166]

Sin in us is rarely a demonic presence, but it is a demonic programming, a demonic principle in the flesh. The one who cries in faith to God, "Who will deliver me?" and who looks to the deliverer, will also be able to cry: "Thanks be to God through Jesus Christ our Lord."

26

Two Propositions, Two Prepositions (8:1–4)

In the classic cult movie *Bill and Ted's Excellent Adventure*, the two likely lads interview various historic figures as they travel through time, gaining wisdom for their school project, and they record it all on camcorder. Abraham Lincoln says this: "Seven minutes ago... we, your forefathers, were brought forth upon a most excellent adventure conceived by our new friends, Bill... and Ted. These two great gentlemen are dedicated to a proposition that was true in my time, just as it's true today. [He then proposes two propositions.] Be excellent to each other. And... party on, dudes!"

If Bill and Ted had visited Paul, he may well have said the Christian life is "a most excellent adventure conceived by God, dedicated to two propositions" – "We can be without blame," and, "We can be without blemish." Each of these propositions is dependent on a preposition: without blame *in* Christ Jesus; without blemish *by* the Spirit.

Proposition 1: life without blame

"There is therefore now no condemnation" (Romans 8:1).

The word "condemnation" translates the Greek word *katakrina*, which means "judgment against, passing sentence on, pronouncing guilt, damning". In the Greek Old Testament it was used to describe the destruction of Sodom and Gomorrah and of the death sentence pronounced on Daniel; in the New Testament it was used of Jesus being handed over to death; and Paul in Romans 1–5 uses it to describe the just judgment of God against sin that brings death.

Ever since our ancient ancestors stood naked and ashamed before God, having opened Pandora's box of evil and closed the door to paradise in Eden, our DNA has echoed with their condemnation and separation from God. There is a universal fear of condemnation in the soul of humankind – a fear that one day all we have done, said, and thought will be brought beneath the bar of God – judged and ultimately condemned.

Hans Selye, the twentieth-century endocrinologist and leading expert in the study of stress, said that "as much as we thirst for approval, we dread condemnation".[167] He argued that feelings of condemnation lead to stress, and stress to distress. Deep within our soul we feel the displacement from Eden and we fear the displeasure of God.

Some try to compare themselves with those they consider more sinful so as to justify themselves. It won't do, for the standard of comparison is God. Some try religious efforts, attempting to balance the scales of good over bad in their favour, living morally, doing good works. That won't do either; how can a good work atone for a bad? The bad is done.

Some follow philosophers and atheists seek to argue God away, for where there is no God, there can be no condemnation. They are simply burying their heads in the sand as the storm gathers. Some seek psychological help from counsellors in the hope that they will be told they are neither mad nor bad. In 1912, a band played on as the Titanic sank in the North Atlantic Ocean. In twenty-five years of Christian ministry I have constantly met and prayed with folk troubled by memories of wrong things done and said years – even decades – before. Their consciences condemn them – and the accuser sticks the boot in. Satan tempts us to sin then condemns us for our sin. I have sat with aging men as the sins of their youth return to terrorize them – they are not losing their minds, they're beginning to see really clearly. And they call for the priest they have avoided all their lives. Men confessing horrors committed in long ago wars; confessing secret sins buried in their memories. Hounded and haunted, they need a confessor.

There was a time when there was no escape from the condemnation of God's just judgment against us. But now there is no condemnation. As C. S. Lewis says: "God has forgiven the inexcusable in you."[168]

The word "now" is crucial: Paul is picking up on points he has already made. Now, because Christ has died as substitute for our sins (3:21–25)… now, because we have died to the law that held us captive and condemned us (7:6)… there is no longer condemnation.

"Now" signals a whole new epoch, ushered and offered through Jesus. No condemnation means:

- mercy triumphs over justice
- our sins don't get what they deserve
- the accuser's accusation is silenced
- my slate of sins is wiped clean
- we are justified, acquitted, righteous
- there is no obstacle between me and God
- my past does not determine my future
- I am free from guilt and shame and fear.

Well, a proposition is a presupposition without verification. On what basis is there no condemnation? There is only one, and that is all that's required. The righteous wrath of God that must condemn sin was not discarded or disregarded but directed to God's Son (8:3) who came in the likeness of human flesh and who bore our sins and God's condemnation.

Preposition 1: "in" Christ Jesus

"… for those who are *in* Christ Jesus" (8:1, my italics).

The proposition "no condemnation" requires the preposition "in Christ". There is no condemnation for those, for all, for everyone, for anyone, who is *in* Christ Jesus. And the converse is also true: there is condemnation for those, for all, for everyone *outside* Christ Jesus. It is only by being in Christ Jesus that the benefits of his death for us are imputed to us, and the annulment of condemnation at the cross is transferred. This is God's economy of salvation – and this is the great motive for mission to herald this great news. "God did not send his Son into the world to condemn the world, but in order that the world might be saved through him. Whoever believes in him is not condemned, but whoever does not believe is condemned already, because he has not believed in the name of the only Son of God" (John 3:17). One popular writer recently argued that God would not really condemn anyone to hell for ever, quoting the first half of verse 17 as proof: "God did not send his Son into the world to condemn the world". Sadly the author failed to finish the sentence: "whoever does not believe is condemned already". The difference between condemnation and no condemnation is trust in Christ's death for us and being credited with the benefit of his death for us.

Many Christians don't like the "whole counsel of God". They want it piecemeal. They'd rather be inclusive, expansive, affirming, increasing the options of prepositions. Spirituality is the big thing – whether Zen or Christian or unicorn or purple crystals. It won't do. It is Christ or nothing; it's all of Christ or nothing. The Bible's exclusive and particular conception of salvation is that the benefits of Christ's death are mediated fully, removing all condemnation, to those, and only those, who are found in Christ.

The English Literature don, Charles Williams, one of the members of the Oxford literary discussion group, the Inklings, along with C. S. Lewis and J. R. R. Tolkien, wrote, "How accurate one has to be with one's prepositions. Perhaps it was a preposition wrong that set the whole world awry?"[169] The preposition that puts the world right is simply being *in* Christ.

Proposition 2: life without blemish

"... in order that the righteous requirement of the law might be fulfilled in us" (8:4).

While all religions focus on justification and sanctification, what is unique to Christianity is the order in which these come. In most other religions, you sanctify yourself and are then justified; in Christianity, God justifies you, and then helps to sanctify you.

In practice what this means is that we will always have a church full of people who may be saved but not yet sanctified! At justification the principle or seed is planted which awakens sanctification; many are content to ignore it, to settle for less. The *crisis* of justification must be followed by the *process* of sanctification. "No condemnation" must lead to "no contamination".

The word "fulfilled" (*plerothe*) is a spatial term and means "filled right up". Paul envisages not a half-measure-holiness but one that is filled full. Holiness is not something Paul thinks the Christian dips his toe into.

What would that holiness look like? Jesus alone lived a perfect life and fully satisfied the moral requirements of the law. Holiness therefore looks like Jesus. It is the imitation of Christ. John Stott, in his very last sermon at Keswick given at the age of eighty-six, said,

> *I want to share with you where my mind has come to rest as I approach the end of my pilgrimage on earth as it is. God wants his people to become like Christ. Christ-likeness is the will of God for the people of God.*[170]

When I was a teenager I read a book about a Christian imprisoned and tortured for his faith under the Soviet's communist regime. If being a Christian was an imprisonable offence, I reflected, would there be enough evidence in my life to get me arrested? What evidence of being a Christian could be marshalled? One day the Christian prisoner was asked by the officer who had overseen his torture what this Jesus whom he was suffering for was like? The prisoner immediately replied: "He's just like me." The guard converted to Christ. Could I ever say, "Jesus is like me"? Paul urged the Corinthians to "be imitators of me, as I am of Christ" (1 Corinthians 11:1). That is holiness. Christ is our model.

Note the passive tense here in verse 4: the righteous requirement is "fulfilled in us". We cannot do it alone. Just as we cannot save ourselves, so we cannot sanctify ourselves. We are dependent on the Spirit. To attempt to be holy and fulfil the righteous requirement of the law in one's own strength leads to legalism and Pharisaism. There's a lot of it around, and it makes religious people look like they are wearing underpants three sizes too small.

Preposition 2: "according to" the Spirit

"... who walk not according to the flesh but according to the Spirit" (8:4).

Spirit-fullness is the only means to Christ-likeness. The Puritan scholar John Owen discussed the mortification of sin through the inhabitation of the Spirit:

> *For it is he who mortifies and subdues our corruptions, who quickens us unto life, holiness and obedience as he "dwelleth in us" that he may make and prepare a habitation meet for himself...* [171]

Owen says the Spirit plants in our minds the contrary inclination to the flesh, and then the Spirit gives us grace to live to this new spiritual principle he communicates to us. Following in this tradition, Bible teacher Errol Hulse has written: "Every method put to use to mortify sin which is not by the Holy Spirit is doomed to failure."[172]

The preposition that applies to this proposition is *kata pneuma* – "according to the Spirit". The word *kata* literally means "down from" and implies movement from the higher to the lower. Holiness comes as a movement down to us from the Spirit.

The Spirit is the great focus of Romans 8. In chapters 1–7 he is mentioned five times, and chapters 9–16 there is a total of eight times; in chapter 8 alone the Spirit is mentioned twenty-one times.

The Law can be lived, but this is done by being filled with the Spirit; in being filled by the Spirit, we "full-fill" the moral requirements of law. The concept of "walking in the Spirit" suggests accompaniment, process, journey; it is not a one-off event, a baptism, a second blessing. It is a walking: the Greek *peripatousin* is a participle, signifying an ongoing constant process and not a one-off event. As we walk in intimacy and dependency on the Spirit, daily attentive to his highlighting and removing of sinful acts and attitudes, we will gradually be transformed and conformed into the likeness of Christ. Sanctification comes through keeping in step with the Spirit. Paul, in Galatians 5, says there are two ways of living: according to the flesh or according to the Spirit. You cannot walk in two opposite directions at the same time – though some appear to try! We must choose whether we will walk following the appetites and dictates of the flesh or the desires and delights of the Spirit.

I'm often telling one of my sons to walk properly. He is really into street dance and he walks, or rather "swaggers", from side to side as if he is a cool gangster in Harlem. This is not helped by his trousers being worn half-way down and his wearing flat-footed basketball trainers. He has watched too many clips of hip-hop dancers and learned to walk badly! (Six weeks' basic training in the Grenadier Guards and he would soon walk tall and straight!) We need to learn to keep in step with the Spirit and, as we do, we will find we conform to the likeness of Christ.

There are two propositions of the Christian life: life without blame and life without blemish. There are two prepositions for the Christian life: in Christ Jesus and according to the Spirit. This is the God-given way to live a life that is pleasing to God.

27

The Spirit of Holiness (8:4–11)

The American spiritual writer A. W. Tozer said, "The whole purpose of God in redemption is to make us holy and to restore us to the image of God."[173] Sadly, though holiness is God's gift to us and his goal for us, holiness is seldom the all-consuming desire for many Christians. George Barna, the leading Christian social statistician, conducted a survey of values and lifestyles of the evangelical church in the USA in 2000. He concluded that rarely were substantial differences between the moral behaviour of Christians and non-Christians found, and as a result there was uproar among many evangelicals who challenged the findings. The Project Director, Meg Flammang said: "We would love to be able to report that Christians are living very distinct lives and impacting the community... the evidence suggests the opposite."[174] New life in Christ should bring a new lifestyle. Those made righteous positionally (justified) must become righteous practically (sanctified). The crisis of conversion must be followed by the process of sanctification.

In Romans 8 Paul says there are two ways to live, two Chief Executive Officers, two operating systems: the flesh or the Spirit. Jesus said that two masters cannot be served by one person (see Luke 16:13), but many Christians try. In *The Importance of Being Earnest*, the Victorian wit and satirist Oscar Wilde, wrote, "I hope you have not been leading a double life – pretending to be wicked, but being really good all the time."[175] Many Christians lead a double life, pretending to be good but really living sinfully. Living by the Spirit and by the flesh. I trained for ministry with a priest who was a bigamist – supporting a wife and children in two different continents! He led a double life. There are too many Sunday singers, Monday sinners.

So there is the "Spirit-led" person and the "flesh-led" person. Which are you?

Paul in Romans 8 mentions *pneuma* – the spirit or Spirit – twenty-one times, and he mentions *sarx*, meaning flesh, twelve times. In the Greek text there is no distinction between upper and lower case words, which means great care must be paid in translation and interpretation as to whether Paul means the "Holy Spirit" or the "human spirit". *Sarx* in Greek refers to flesh and blood. In Paul's usage *sarx* represents not meat or muscle but rather the carnal, fleshly, base passions and desires of human nature that oppose the Spirit. The NIV version translates *sarx* as "sinful nature"and I think that is an accurate sense of Paul's meaning. It is the sin-filled, selfish, lustful, fleshly appetites of our fallen human nature inherited from Adam and programmed by our sin.

In 8:4–12 Paul lists the consequences of living according to flesh or Spirit: the flesh-led person is dead (verse 6), hostile to God (verse 7), won't submit to God's Law and cannot comply with the Law (verse 7), is incapable of pleasing God (verse 8). Conversely, the Spirit-led person loves and lives God's moral requirements (verse 4); has life and peace (verse 6); experiences life from righteousness (verse 10).

Until we die and are given resurrection bodies, we will be in the sarcophagus of flesh, programmed with an inherited DNA of sin. However, as Professor Cranfield said, for the Christian the fallen human nature "is not left to itself".[176] It has the Spirit to transform it.

1. A Spirit-sought walk

"... in order that the righteous requirement of the law might be fulfilled in us, who walk not according to the flesh but according to the Spirit" (8:4).

You need a leader

The Spirit does not walk according to us – we walk according to the Spirit. He is the guide, he takes the lead. We are led. The flesh is like a 250-pound Rottweiler on a lead who wants to pull its owner after a scent or a cat. The spiritual person, the mature Christian, is led by the Spirit, not dragged by the flesh. Indeed, the spiritual Christian is like a champion display collie at a dog show who does not need any leash, but walks alongside its master attentive to every turn and twist and whistle and look, delighting in simply obeying.

You need direction

The Spirit does not lead you in circles. The Spirit lays out cat's eyes on a road towards holiness and fruitfulness.

This walk in the Spirit is a daily complying as we follow the pathways of God – his directions for holy living, according to the laws of the Spirit, Christ, and love. I remember being with the friend I mentioned in the introduction to this book, the former Sergeant Major in the élite SAS. His training made him attentive to every detail. We were going to a restaurant that I knew and he didn't. He kept asking, "Where next?" I would reply, "Second left, twenty yards." Then, as soon as we had made the move, he would say, "Where now?" I'd reply, "Thirty yards, turn right." And on we would go. He wanted directions at every point.

We should be like that with the Spirit – not to the point of neurosis, expecting him to tell us what colour socks to wear; but walking in the Spirit, in all our ways acknowledging him, and him making straight our paths along the highway of holiness (see Proverbs 3:6).

An intimate partnership

You cannot walk with the Spirit from a distance. To walk with someone means you have to "keep in step".

To walk with someone means you don't lag behind, or run ahead, or go aside. To walk with someone demands a measure of intimacy, conversation, and attentiveness to the guide. The Holy Spirit doesn't carry you to holiness – you walk and work with him. Although justification is a *monergist* work (God saves us singlehandedly, while all we bring is faith alone) nevertheless sanctification is *synergist* (a joint work). Salvation is by faith alone, but sanctification is definitely not. Scripture gives us repeated numerous imperatives and instructions, commands that we comply with by the Spirit's assistance, to enable us to become more like Christ. Gradually, as we walk with the Spirit long enough, responding to his prompting, his values, and his voice, then his vision become ours.

Process and progress

You can't walk standing still. Whereas salvation is a momentary crisis, sanctification is a process. Holiness is not given in an instant, as with Wesley's notion of "perfect love", or some ideas of a second baptism by the Spirit, or the Keswick Convention's spirituality of the "higher life" by the instant recognition of a second "dying to sin". Sanctification comes not as a crisis moment but in a process. Walking in the Spirit is a daily "where now/what now Lord?"

Too many are stuck where they were ten years ago; they haven't followed the Spirit: they went off on their own path, attracted by tempting sirens; or they stayed put and made no effort to move forward. The remarkable Nelson Mandela in his autobiography *Long Walk to Freedom* wrote: "With freedom comes responsibilities and I dare not linger, for my long walk is not yet ended."[177]

It's no walk in the park

Walking with the Spirit is not easy; it's often an uphill walk. The Spirit will often lead you where you do not want to go – where the flesh will resist and protest. A friend once wrote to me all flustered. She had received a request to help someone who had previously done her a personal and very real harm. She could not believe the request, yet only she was in a position to help. She asked my opinion, already knowing the right course of action. I said, "You won't learn to be gracious unless you are insulted and have to learn to show grace." God had brought this situation into her life to reveal the flesh – unforgiveness and resentment, cherished hurts; she had an opportunity to win a victory over the flesh, to follow the Spirit and become more holy. My friend knew what the Lord would have her do, and eventually agreed to show grace, to step over the offence. And when she did, her character was transformed, just that little bit more, by one degree, into the likeness of Christ as she walked in the Spirit.

2. A Spirit-taught worldview

"Those who live according to the flesh set their minds on the things of the flesh, but those who live according to the Spirit set their minds on the things of the Spirit. For to set the mind on the flesh is death, but to set the mind on the Spirit is life and peace. For the mind that is set on the flesh is hostile to God, for it does not submit to God's law; indeed, it cannot" (8:5–7).

Five times Paul speaks here of the "set of the mind", the mindset. The Greek term is *phronein* which is not the pre-occupation of your thoughts but your worldview, the mindset that determines how you conceive the world, how you live in the world. A holy life reflects a holy mindset. John Stott saw clearly that "the major secret of holy living lies in the mind".[178]

It is often said that you are what you eat. The Bible says you are what you think (see Proverbs 23:7, KJV). We need to learn to mind our manners, to think before we speak and act. We need to cultivate the mind of Christ; the Christ-like mindset. A worldview, technically termed *Weltanschauung*, is the way in which we view the world. It is our understanding of how the world operates, the framework or philosophy of life. The Christian worldview is directly opposed by the triplet of the New Atheism (Richard Dawkins, Christopher Hitchens, Philip Pullman), the New Hedonism (promiscuity, pleasure, materialism) and the New Imperialism (radical totalitarian Islamism). The spiritual man, the Spirit-filled woman, needs to have their worldview formatted according to the biblical worldview, a God's eye view.

Often we subtly absorb the worldview or value systems of our surrounding culture. Paul begins his letter to the Colossians, "to the saints and faithful brothers in Christ at Colossae" (1:2). There are two clear spheres of influence here: the sphere that influences them (being in Christ) and the sphere that they are to influence (being in Colossae). From our life in Christ we are to live in Colossae, or Oxford, or London, or wherever. But we are to be the influencers of where we are rather than the other way round. Sadly we are often more influenced by our Colossae than influenced by Christ and influencing Colossae.

The Corinthians easily conformed to the culture of Corinth. They were self-indulgent when it came to the gifts of the Spirit, and they turned the Lord's Supper into a dinner party that excluded the poor. The church was marked by cliques and people easily aligned with one personality over another. They were marked by immorality, in one instance tolerating a member having sex with his mother-in-law (1 Corinthians 5:1).

The liberal church succumbed to the worldview of a scientism that posited truth as only that which could be verified, repeated, and observed. Consequently the liberals rejected the miraculous to the point of denying the incarnation and resurrection. The twentieth-century church in Germany largely bought into the Nazi worldview, baptizing Hitler's lust for power. This is not merely an intellectual value judgment. To set our mind according to the divine mindset is to find peace and life. However, when we set out mind to follow the mindset of the world – the flesh – we find ourselves set against God, hostile to God. And who, in their right mind, would want that?

3. A Spirit-fought war

"If you live according to the flesh you will die, but if by the Spirit you put to death the deeds of the body, you will live" (8:13).

This is fighting talk. Onward, Christian soldier. The enemy is the flesh, the sinful nature, Adam's foul recessive gene. To put to death or mortify the misdeeds of the flesh is the Greek term *thanatoute*. It is a present tense that suggests a constant battle. And it is an imperative, a command – we are under orders. We must put to death the sins in us that Christ was put to death to pay for. Holiness cannot be attained without a sustained fight. It is the invasion of the soul and flesh by the Spirit of God evicting the squatting of resistant patterns, programs, and principles of sin. Your body, soul, and spirit are not neutral territory in this war – they are the battleground. These are the occupied territories where the evil one would seek to conform you into his likeness rather than allow God to transform you into Christ's. You cannot win if you don't fight. Thomas à Kempis wrote,

> *The devil does not sleep, nor is the flesh yet dead; therefore you must never cease your preparation for battle, because on the right and on the left are enemies who never rest.*[179]

Sin won't simply go away if you ignore it – it breeds and spreads. On almost a weekly basis, once the school term begins, we go through my sons' head looking for lice. Tiffany doesn't say, "Ah, look at that amazing creature, *pediculosis capitis,* resistant to almost everything, living by burrowing into the scalp and drinking my son's blood – what an amazing eco-system!" No, she combs out the ticks and their eggs and crushes them between her fingers and the comb. We need to ask God by his Spirit to comb through our body and soul to show any persistent patterns of programmed sin, and repent, receiving the cleansing of the blood of Jesus and welcoming the power of the Spirit to walk a transformed life.

You fight for what you love. If armed burglars entered your house while you were asleep next to your spouse, with your children in the next room, and you suddenly woke up, would you roll over and go back to sleep? Never. You would get up, turn on the lights, make a noise, protect your children and your home, call the police, and perhaps take up a weapon. Yet many Christians, metaphorically, turn over and allow the intruder of sin to ransack their spiritual home.

Paul does not envisage that the squatters of sin will win. Victory is ours to take. We can put sin to death by living "according to the Spirit". Holiness will come, but not by will power but by walking in the Spirit's power. Paul reminds us in this passage that we have available to us "the Spirit who raised Jesus from the dead". This is a Spirit of power – power to raise the dead, power to reverse the forces of evil and sin. That power – submitted to, called upon, in the battle of temptation – is the power with which we can overcome. No sin has ever come our way that a sincere call upon and following of the Spirit cannot overcome. If you continue in sin, you have not relied upon the Spirit. Holiness is not a walk in the park – it comes through a warring in the Spirit, a walking in the Spirit, cultivating a worldview of the Spirit.

John Milton, in *Paradise Lost,* depicts a divine voice calling from a golden cloud: "Servant of God, well done, well hast thou fought the better fight"[180] – may that be spoken over us on judgment day.

28

A Father to the Fatherless (8:14–17)[181]

Consider these startling statistics:

- 85% of children exhibiting behavioural disorders come from fatherless homes
- 90% of all homeless and runaway children come from fatherless homes
- 80% of all rapists motivated by displaced anger come from fatherless homes
- 70% of juveniles in state-operated institutions come from fatherless homes
- 85% of all youths sitting in prisons grew up in fatherless homes.[182]

The article from which these statistics are drawn concludes, "Pick a social ill at random and you will find that the correlation with fatherlessness is clear and direct... suicide, dropping out of school, teenage pregnancy, drug abuse."

In sum, fatherless children are:

- 5 times more likely to commit suicide
- 32 times more likely to run away
- 20 times more likely to have behavioural disorders
- 14 times more likely to commit rape
- 9 times more likely to drop out of school
- 10 times more likely to take drugs
- 9 times more likely to end up in a mental institution
- 20 times more likely to end up in prison

In one British study it was claimed that fatherless children were thirty-three times more likely to be abused. In the UK, the Office for National Statistics[183] informed us that in 2012 there were almost 2 million one-parent families in Britain, 92 per cent of which were lone-mother family units. We live in a society that is fatherless. The moral laxity arising from the sexual libertarianism of the post-1960s has reaped disastrous consequences both for the many children born into this culture and for wider society as a whole. In the thirty years between the early 1970s and 2004 single parent families rose from one in fourteen to one in four.

In the West a fatherless generation is growing up. Now, in some respects, this has often been the case – centuries of military conflict when "the men went off to war" resulted in children growing up fatherless. The war now is more subtle, but no less dangerous and disastrous, especially for the children left behind. At least in the past, they could consider their father as a hero dying for a cause; but most today have no such noble epithets to imagine. Many have never known their dads at all; many knew their fathers as absent, abusive, or adulterous.

Of course, we must recognize that some single-mother families are the result of tragedy or a legal system that may discriminate against the father, not always allowing him to be the father he wanted to be. But even where there are outstanding mothers who, alone, do their utmost to nurture their children against the backdrop of much financial hardship, children who grow up without a father inevitably suffer. Deep-felt rejection, an inner sense of abandonment, fear, lack of appropriate role modelling or paternal disciplining, may leave deep scars, and sow potential emotional, psychological, and social problems which surface later in life.

It is not moralistic to lay considerable blame at the sexual revolution, and the ease with which divorce is available, or the lack of dignity and respect many young men show their girlfriends, getting them pregnant without taking responsibility for the consequences. We need to ask why it is that so many young women think it acceptable to get pregnant out of marriage, or even out of a serious relationship.

We live in a fatherless generation. We need to point them to God's paternal, compassionate, restoring, gracious desire, and offer to make up that which is missing.[184]

Prodigal sons and prodigal Father

There is a longing in our generation for a father. And there is a Father longing for this generation. If we can heal the longing in this fatherless generation for a father, we can heal society. The traditionally named parable of the prodigal son (Luke 15:11–32) reveals to us the nature of God as a longing Father who is looking for his lost son. I am uncomfortable with the usual title of this well-known parable, focusing our thinking on the state of the sin of the rebellious boy, rather than on his restoration and the staggering generosity and affection of the Father. The Father is every bit as prodigal (extravagantly wasteful) with his affections towards his son as the son is prodigal with his inheritance.

We know the story well: the son asks for his share of the inheritance. Even though his father is not dead yet, he wants what is coming to him and to cut loose. The father graciously gifts the son who then leaves and squanders everything on wine, women, and song. When everything is spent, a famine comes and the boy hires himself to work, feeding pigs (not the best thing for a good Jewish boy). He is slowly starving to death, longing to eat the pigswill, when he finally comes to his senses and realizes that his estranged father's servants at least get fed. So he returns intent on begging to be a servant of his father.

And here is where we see what God is like: the father is waiting and watching, scanning the horizon on the edge of his land, looking longingly as he clearly has done every day since his son left. When he catches the silhouette of his boy, knowing intimately how he carried himself and walked, the old man begins to run and run, and when he gets to his son, breathless, wet with perspiration and tears, he pauses, then crushes his pig-stinking, bag-of-bones boy in his arms of love.

The son tries to resist, unworthy, guilty, but Dad will have none of it. He calls his servants "quickly" so as not to waste time; "bring… the best robe" – not any old covering, but the best robe reserved for the guest of honour. "Put it on him, and put a ring on his hand, and shoes on his feet" (Luke 15:22). A robe of honour, a signet ring of sonship, shoes worn by the free. He calls to have *the* fatted calf – the special one, the one they'd been saving – and a party is thrown in his honour.

Why? Because the dead has come alive, the lost has been found, a son is with his dad.

That is the blistering good news. That is what God is like. He is not malicious, capricious, vengeful, or resentful. He is ecstatic, forgiving, generous, honouring – utterly extraordinary. And that is the Father God desires to be – as King David celebrated, "Father of the fatherless… is God in his holy habitation" (Psalm 68:5).

"For all who are led by the Spirit of God are sons of God. For you did not receive the spirit of slavery to fall back into fear, but you have received the Spirit of adoption as sons, by whom we cry, 'Abba! Father!' The Spirit himself bears witness with our spirit that we are children of God, and if children, then heirs" (Romans 8:14–17).

This passage unveils to us perhaps the most beautiful and glorious insights into the work of the Spirit in the life of the believer. Through faith, the believer has been justified (Romans 3–5; Galatians 2:16; 3:6) and simultaneously has received the Spirit (Romans 5:5; Galatians 3:2). They have moved from being slaves, living in fear and servitude before the Law and the devil, to being free sons of God. The Spirit who regenerated them confers adoption in that same moment. It is not a higher order benefit for the élite Christian, but for *all* who are led by the Spirit.

Paul speaks of the "Spirit of adoption". Calvin lists this as the first title of the Spirit, corresponding to what must be seen as the highest of the privileges of redemption, namely sonship.[185] Gordon Fee says, "the ultimate evidence of this sonship is their use of the Son's own address to the Father in prayer – Abba."[186] The Catholic preacher Raniero Cantalamessa says, "The first thing the Holy Spirit does upon coming into us is to make us see God in a different way."[187] The Spirit shows us the true face of God. Not taskmaster, but papa.

This adoption as sons is an upwardly mobile move to a privileged position of dignity, authority, and responsibility. We become heirs of God with Christ. Our new position as sons of God is written and ratified publically in blood on Golgotha's hill, but it is known by us existentially. The Spirit in us whispers and witnesses with our Spirit that we are God's children, that he is our Abba. From deep within rises the child's cry of delight and desire for Abba. Fifth-century Diadochus of Photike says:

The Spirit acts as would a mother teaching her baby to say "daddy" and she repeats that name to her baby until the baby becomes so used to calling "daddy" that it can call even in its sleep.[188]

Adopted as sons

Paul makes much of the status of the regenerate as *adopted sons*. Even as Christian men must come to terms with being described as the bride of Christ, Christian women must learn to appreciate they are adopted sons. We must not let concerns about gender and inclusive language – understandable though they are – cloud the real issue here. This is not about sexism but status. Women remain women but take the honour of firstborn son. Paul uses the term adoption five times (Romans 8:15, 23; 9:4; Galatians 4:5; Ephesians 1:5). The Greek term he employs *huiothesia* is a conjunction of *huios* meaning "son" and *thesis* meaning "secured position": so "adopted as a son".

The believer becomes an adopted son in the family of God. We take a place of dignity, authority, and responsibility. We are cut off from our past and the future is legally binding, secured by blood and Spirit. We become what we were not. As Berkhof notes,

If they are adopted as children by God, it shows they are not children of God by nature as liberals believe. You can't adopt your own children.[189]

We gain what we did not have. C. H. Spurgeon declared that at regeneration we are given the nature of children, but at adoption we are given the rights of children. Distinctive in effect, they occur simultaneously. At great cost we were bought and then given great honour. The Spirit does not procure adoption – the blood of Christ does that; but in terms of the believer's experience of salvation, the Spirit is the Spirit of adoption because he actualizes adoption for the believer.[190]

This cry of "Abba" is involuntary and emotional. *Krazo* means to "cry aloud, shriek, scream" and was vocal, violent, unmistakable (Matthew 20:31; Mark 1:26; 5:5). New Testament scholar Douglas

Moo says that, in using this verb, Paul is stressing that our awareness of God as Father comes not from rational consideration or from external testimony alone, but from a truth deeply felt and intensely experienced.[191] The Spirit of sonship crying Abba is the heartbeat of a truly charismatic theology.

We cry "Abba!" Though this term is only found three times in the New Testament (Mark 14:36; Romans 8:15; Galatians 4:6), scholars generally agree that it is a term that expresses the very core of Jesus' religious life and relationship with his Father God.[192] That God's own Son should call his Father Abba is perhaps understandable; that he should allow us to share that same relationship is unfathomable, except in the light of limitless love.

Catholic writer Brennan Manning notes:

> *Jesus the Beloved Son, does not hoard this experience for Himself. He invites and calls us to share the same intimate and liberating relationship.*[193]

This embracing of an untranslated, undiluted Aramaic–Jewish term in the Greco–Roman church reinforces the claim that its origin and its transmission is from Christ. While it is possible to conceive of "father" in rather abstract or impersonal or respectful terms, as progenitor (biological male parent) or institutional originator (founding father), to speak of God as *Abba* can convey only one meaning. Ascribed to God, it may have seemed almost blasphemous to the devout religious Jew, who would avoid directly uttering God's name; to the sinner outside the worshipping community it must have been utterly miraculous that they could ever be allowed to comprehend, let alone converse with God in such terms. Intimate, familiar, childish, embarrassing, preposterous, glorious – God invites us to call him "Papa"; to call him "Daddy".

Professor Clark Pinnock said,

> *We are invited inside the Trinity as joint heirs with Christ. By the Spirit we cry Abba together with the Son as we are drawn into the filial relationship and begin to participate in God's life.*[194]

However, the experience we have of God as Abba is not exactly parallel to that of Jesus. It comes through Jesus. Jesus is the eternal Son of Abba. He was born of flesh to make us who are born of the flesh eternal sons of Abba. Jesus knows Abba through his eternal generation as divine Son. We may know God as Abba only through adoption.

Jesus utterly revolutionizes this perspective and makes "Father" the normative description of God and personal address to him. To those who accept him as their Saviour Jesus came to reveal and mediate the Father (see Luke 10:22; John 14:8–9). Over 250 times in the New Testament, 175 times in the Gospels alone, Jesus refers to God as the Father. This was clearly how Jesus understood his relationship to God, as Son to Father, but it was the same relationship he invited his disciples to enjoy, instructing them in something that would have been revolutionary: to pray, "Father" (Luke 11:2).

The musician Michael Card has said that to experience God as Father is to begin to know him as Jesus knows him. German theologian Wolfhart Pannenberg has rightly shown that Jesus' referential use of the title "Father" for God shows that the personal character of the God whom Christians worship is inseparably bound up with this concept of God as Father. It is who he is.[195] The God Jesus came to reveal to us, and bring us to, is the God who is fundamentally Father. To fail to worship God as Father is to call into question which God we do worship.

We have been made sons of God; a party has been thrown in our honour, with status, dignity, inheritance, and authority conferred on us. We can live like sons in the Spirit or like slaves – it's up to us. The Galatian Christians chose to live like slaves. The second son in the parable of the prodigal chose to live like a slave, bemoaning "all these years I've slaved for you" while in fact "all the father had was his". Such a revelation of our position before God, on the basis of the decree of the Father, the death of the Son, and the deposit of the Spirit, should revolutionize our lives. God is Abba – our Father. I am his son, not his slave. I serve him freely and without fear – I relax in my sonship: security, identity, inheritance, and freedom from anxiety and fear. Being God's own sons should cause us to wonder and worship with all our heart. It should cause us to walk with our head held high, that such dignity has been conferred upon us, sons who perpetuate God's name and inherit his estate. It should compel our passionate witness to this broken, lost, fatherless generation.

In conclusion

Let me quote one of the fathers of charismatic renewal in Britain in the 1970s, Dr Tom Smail:

> *Within the charismatic renewal today, there is a good deal more talk about spiritual gifts than exercise of them; more discussion about the power of the Spirit than actual experience of it. One of the main reasons for that is most people just do not have the confidence that God has accepted them and loves them just as they are as his children, and therefore will not let them be led astray by what is fleshly or demonic but will give them all that he has promised – his robe, his ring, his shoes. This confidence will not be created by repeated acts of laying on of hands, but only by an awareness of the Spirit's cry of Abba at the creative and motivating centres of our lives. This is what releases from the paralysing fear of God and man that grips so many – and it is not a technique that we can master but a sovereign work of the Spirit which must liberate us.*[196]

29

The Spirit of Adoption (8:14–17)

Colin Urqhuart wrote a book called *When the Spirit Comes*. In it he tells of his experience of the Spirit when, as an Anglican vicar, he read Watchman Nee's book *The Normal Christian Life*.

> *It was like a great flash of light. Something I had been searching for had suddenly been discovered. "I am a son of God". That truth transformed my life and ministry... I had been taught to be highly suspicious of experience and subjective Christianity. God was often portrayed to be great, but remote; to be believed in, to be worshipped, but definitely not to be experienced in a personal way. What mattered above everything else was objective truth: that we "believed" in God's existence and his love. Now something was happening to me: something that can only be described as an experience. I felt different, I was different. I was bubbling over with joy. It seemed as if the whole room, the whole house, everyone and everything around me had changed. I wanted to go dancing and skipping about the house shouting, "I'm a son of God, I'm a son of God, I'm a son of God!" This experience is the birthright of all who embrace the gospel.*

"For all who are led by the Spirit of God are sons of God. For you did not receive the spirit of slavery to fall back into fear, but you have received the Spirit of adoption as sons, by whom we cry, 'Abba! Father!' The Spirit himself bears witness with our spirit that we are children of God, and if children, then heirs" (Romans 8:14–17).

The cry for a father

As discussed in the previous chapter, there is a deep cry in the human soul for a father, for a home.

In the Oscar-winning movie *Cider House Rules* – a powerful and provocative film about life in a 1940s' American orphanage for unwanted babies – we see some children grow into their teens as they wait to be chosen by a family and given a home. In one scene a child, Curly, is standing alone by a window in the corridor, waiting longingly to be chosen. A suitcase is next to him. But soon the truth dawns… no one has asked for him. No one ever wants him.

Ever since Eden an orphan spirit has been programmed into the human soul. There is a deep sense of estrangement, abandonment, exclusion, and a spirit of rejection. Many recognize this angst but don't know what it's a cry for. They try to palliate it by finding intimacy in relationships, sexual promiscuity, or pornography, or by driving for achievement and recognition, or by spoiling themselves with goods, hiding in a bottle, or hitting out angrily at the world in pain. Deep within it is a cry for adoption by God, for a home-coming into the divine family. It's as if we live looking out of the window, suitcase packed, waiting for someone to come for us. God wants to heal you of your rejection, to welcome you to his family, to put your suitcase away, and to give you a home.

Not all welcome such a revelation or such a God.

The father of modern psychoanalysis, Sigmund Freud, argued that to conceptualize God as Father was the result of neurotic humans projecting our needs, privations, and aspirations onto a divine figure – a kind of grown-up version of a little child's invisible friend. Freud argued that calling God Father was a neurotic compensation for our bad experiences with our dads, positing an ideal divine Father-figure.

It is true that some people struggle to relate to God as Father because of their poor relationship with their own father. It is not easy to get intimate with God as "Abba" when you called your father "Sir" and knew him to be absent or aloof. It is not easy to appreciate your adoption when you know you were an unwanted child, a mistake, or when you're a girl and your dad said he always wanted a boy. It is not easy to connect with God as Father when your dad beat up your mum, or left the home. It is not easy to appreciate God as Father when you were sent away to school and only saw your dad at holiday time; or when you feel he was more interested in work than you, or that he loved your siblings more than you, or that he only ever appreciated you when you managed to do well in your studies.

Your own father at his best is a poor analogy of the love of Father God. Your father at his worst bears no resemblance whatsoever to God. Many here will have inadvertently allowed their relationship with their dad to adversely affect their relationship with Father God. We need to invite the Spirit to establish in us and mediate to us the subjective experience that God is our loving Father – to heal us of the pain and rejection we may have absorbed through poor relations with our natural father.

The cry of the Father

Our cry for God is drowned out by God's cry for us.

When Paul says we are "adopted as sons" he uses a Greek word, *huiothesia,* which is a conjunction of *huios* meaning "son" and *thesis* meaning "a secured position". This is the practical and legal transference of a person from one family into another.

In the ancient Roman world of the New Testament era adoption was a common practice among the patrician and senatorial ruling classes. Several Roman emperors were adopted to ensure that an appropriate successor could take over and manage the family's wealth, rather than trust the luck of genetics and birth. So an appropriate male "heir" was found, often a young, distant cousin who was known to be healthy, had distinguished himself in his leadership abilities, and had shown courage in battle. The parents of both families would agree the adoption, money would be exchanged, legal documents and public ratifications secured, and the son would be transferred from one family to the other. Instantly the young man in question lost all rights with his biological family and gained all rights as son and heir in the new adoptive family. This was always an upwardly mobile move. Paul may well have this framework in mind as he writes to the church in Rome: God has chosen to make us royal heirs.

I have already mentioned the painful scene in the movie *Cider House Rules,* where the boy Curly is waiting forlorn for someone to adopt him. There is a second scene in that movie that stands out, towards the end. Homer, the manager of the orphanage, is tucking the children into bed, speaking tenderly over them. "Goodnight, you princes of Maine, you kings of New England." They are not to see themselves as orphans but as kings. And so with us. In a very real sense we who have been adopted sleep well, for God has spoken over us, princes and princesses of God.

The Father is not reluctant to adopt us – he is eagerly seeking sons. It is not simply that we are orphaned and desiring a father we are estranged from; God himself feels that orphan loss and he himself cries out for us. There is a longing in the human heart for God and there is a longing in the heart of God for us. Since Eden God has been crying out in loss and dereliction, "Adam, where are you?" God is not a reluctant adopter. His Spirit of adoption is his *yes* to us, his election of us, his taking us by the hand and bringing us home. God initiated the first "Hide and seek" – Adam and Eve hid and God sought them. And he is still seeking us as we hide away in sin.

Another group that have not welcomed the revelation of God as Father is those with a feminist perspective. Christian and secular feminists have often objected to the conceptualizing of God as Father, seeing this as a power play by men who oppress women. If God is Father, goes the logic, then God is understood as masculine, and if God is masculine, then women feel diminished. If God is male, males can easily think they are God and oppress women. Feminists claim a religion with a father figure as God leads to a patriarchal system of male dominance and suppression of women.

But as we have already seen, the term "adopted as sons" need not upset women. We must not let understandable matters of gender and inclusive language obscure the point Paul is making here – this is about the status being conferred. Women remain women but gain all the honours of the firstborn son, just as men remain men when they are part of the bride of Christ.

The cry "Oh, my father!"

"... you have received the Spirit of adoption... by whom we cry, 'Abba! Father!'" (8:15).

The Spirit who gives us new birth also confers adoption on us.

Adoption is the consequence of our regeneration. The Spirit of adoption delivers us from an inappropriate fear of God and slavery to sin and slavery to obedience as a means of winning God's approval. The perfect love of God, love experienced by the adopted, the wanted, drives out all fear. Both texts that speak of the Abba cry by the Spirit, in Romans and Galatians, juxtapose it with slavery and fear. The Spirit of adoption delivers me from insecurities, anxieties, and slavery to sin – from a performance-driven life that sought to win God's and man's approval.

This Spirit of adoption makes me secure in my identity.

The Spirit of adoption releases a cry within – Abba!

This cry is involuntary and emotional. As we have already commented, the cry is a loud shriek or scream. The cry would be powerfully loud; there would be no missing it. Professor C. H. Dodd observed that it could be ascribed to those moments of religious fervour in revival when restraints and inhibitions are broken up and the inner life is expressed. Professor James Dunn says,

> *Paul would have had little personal sympathy with a purely rational faith or primarily ritualistic religion. The inner witness of the Spirit was something... at the heart of what distinguished his faith as a Christian from what he had known before.*[197]

The Spirit of sonship crying Abba is the heartbeat of a charismatic experience and theology. The Spirit shows us the true face of God – not taskmaster but dear dad. The Spirit in us whispers and witnesses with our spirit that we are God's children, that he is our Abba. From deep within rises the child's cry of delight and desire for Abba. This is about comfort, security.

Read carefully this testimony by the famous Welsh evangelist, Howell Harris, a contemporary of Wesley and Whitefield, a man much used by God to stoke the flames of the eighteenth-century Welsh

Revival. Here he describes how he encountered God and experienced for himself what it meant to be God's son:

> *June 18, 1735, being in secret prayer, I felt suddenly my heart melting within me like wax before the fire with love to God my Saviour ... longing to be dissolved and to be with Christ; then was a cry in my inmost soul, which I was totally unacquainted with before, Abba Father, Abba Father, I could not help calling God my father, I knew that I was his child and that he loved me and heard me. My soul being filled and satiated, crying, "'tis enough, I am satisfied."*[198]

Are you satisfied? Do you know the Father's love? It is your birthright as a child of God. Ask the Lord to renew it in you today.

God as Abba is the unique revelation of God through Jesus.

- The ancient Greeks had no notion that we could call God Father – only a Hercules who was the product of sex between a divine and a mortal could consider God as a father.
- In Hinduism, despite the plethora of gods, none is specifically father, and the supreme source and creator Brahma is impersonal.
- In Islam there are ninety-nine names for Allah, but no mention of God as father. Indeed, a remarkable book by a Muslim convert to Christianity is titled appropriately *I Dared to Call Him Father.*[199] To predicate our intimacy with God as analogous to that of a father to child is uniquely Christian.

The Jewish Christian scholar Joachim Jeremias said that the designation of God as *Abba* was one of the most authentic utterances of Jesus, being almost unique in religious usage. He says, "We are confronted [here] with something new and astounding. Herein lies the great novelty of the gospel."[200] It has no parallel in the Old Testament, nor in the Judaism of Christ's time. Only one late first-century source is found in rabbinical Judaism, and that is placed as a prayer on the lips of children, then echoed by a rabbi. We must not soften the scandal of its intimacy by bringing a more mature, hands-off interpretation as *father*. This was the affectionate, intimate word a child uses of their dad at home – "dear papa". Jesus called God Abba and he invites us into the same relation with God that he had. We are welcomed into the home life of the Trinity.

In conclusion

As I was writing this chapter I heard of an epic tragedy in Majorca. A father and son were on rocky outcrop by the sea when a wave dragged the son into the water. The father instantly jumped into the sea to save his son, but both were washed away and drowned. We were told that the father couldn't swim – he had never learned – but he jumped into the waves anyway, knowing there was a high chance that he would die, in order to be near his son, to try and save him. That's what a father does. And that is what happened when God in Christ jumped into the stormy seas of sin and death and judgment, and did so knowing he would forfeit his own life. But in our case, he held us aloft that we might be saved.

30

The Privileges of a Prince (8:17–30)

To be born a royal brings great privilege: wealth, fame, comfort, the best education, servants at your beck and call, never needing to queue at the doctor's surgery, or at a supermarket till, or at the job centre, or for a restaurant seat, or airport check-in. And sometimes you get to marry people better-looking than yourself. The monarch has diplomatic immunity in other nations and immunity from prosecution in court.

However, being royal does not mean that one is not immune to suffering many of the usual exigencies of humanity: sickness, loneliness, relational breakdowns, sorrow, death. The early-twentieth-century French novelist Jean Giraudoux once wrote, "One of the privileges of the great is to watch catastrophe from a terrace."[201] Perhaps, but royals are not strangers to their own catastrophes.

In Romans 8:12–17 Paul has explained that the person who has embraced Christ, who has trusted in his death for them, for their sin, becomes a member of the divine royal family, having been adopted by God, become children of God, heirs and co-heirs with Christ, with free access to address God as Abba – dear Father. This is the jaw-dropping marvel of Christianity, that we are taken from the darkness like a beetle under a stone and seated on a throne with God.

But just as being a royal with all its privileges does not exempt a prince or princess from many of life's hardships, so being a child of God does not make us immune from trials and sufferings of many kinds.

"... we are children of God, and if children, then heirs – heirs of God and fellow heirs with Christ, provided we suffer with him in order that we may also be glorified with him" (8:16–17).

Many Christians probably did not think they were signing up for this... possibly because evangelists and preachers do not always preach the "small print" and do not explain the need to carry the cross and count the cost of following Jesus.

1. The sons of God suffering

"... fellow heirs with Christ, provided we suffer with him... For I consider that the sufferings of this present time are not worth comparing with the glory that will be revealed to us" (8:17–18).

Many may be surprised to see this emphasis on suffering in the context of being the adopted sons and heirs of God. But divinity is no stranger to suffering. Sonship and suffering go hand in hand. Being a Christian, far from exempting you from suffering, actually qualifies you for it. In fact, one can almost say that if you are not suffering your sonship is called into question.

Now, suffering is not the preserve of the saints and sons of God; it is of course generic to humanity. The German philosopher Friedrich Nietzsche rightly saw that "as deeply as human beings look into life, so deeply too they look into suffering".[202]

There is natural suffering – that which stems from the creaking creation we inhabit: tsumani waves, earthquakes, famines, droughts, the ecological crisis. Based on widely quoted statistics it is safe to estimate that over 500 people will starve to death during the time it takes you to read this chapter (3.6 per second).

There is also man-made suffering – that which is caused by human being against human, evidenced in the irresponsible handling of creation, wars, violence, theft, greed, and wickedness. There are an estimated 30 million slaves or bonded slaves in the world today,[203] more than at any time in recorded history. That number may in fact exceed 100 million[204] if we include sex-trafficked people and child labour. Worldwide, $2.4 trillion dollars are spent annually on an industry that creates or manages violence (the defence industry), while a tiny proportion – $175 billion – could eradicate world poverty with one investment.[205]

And then there is suffering particular to Christians. Being a disciple of Christ invites hardships, from discrimination to persecution. In all except thirty of the world's 200 nation states Christians face oppressive measures, ranging from deprived economic or human rights to actual threat to life. And we must add to this the bitter war waged by the enemy of our souls, who aims well his targeted temptations, torments, and trials because we follow Christ.

It is impossible to close our ears and shut our eyes to suffering. It is constant and it is everywhere. How do we respond? The philosophy of Buddhism is in part an attempt to understand life's suffering. Its answer is that suffering (*dukkha*) is not actual reality (*dharma*) but essentially illusory (*mara*), a dream world. Through enlightenment that comes via meditation and good works establishing *karma*, one is liberated from the illusion of suffering through the reincarnation cycle towards nirvana, where illusion makes way for reality, and suffering makes way for oneness with the One. But there's nothing illusory about a lonely person longing for marriage, nothing illusory about a couple unable to conceive, nothing illusory about being in debt, or slowly dying of cancer, or burying your son or daughter who has been killed in a car crash. Suffering is not a dream that many wake up from.

Marxism was a philosophy conceived against the backdrop of suffering. It believes that suffering is the net result of an economic system preferentially biased towards the élite few at the expense of the majority. Karl Marx, a Jew who was baptized Lutheran, subsequently rejected Christianity for offering a future hope and not a present one. He believed religion – Christianity in particular – was the opium of the masses, drugging people into inactivity, fobbing them off with a false hope of a future better life in heaven, rather than seeking, by force, to get a better life in the here and now. Marx's ideology believed violent revolution was required to overthrow the wealthy oppressors and bring about a just society. The fruit of his philosophy did little more than redistribute the wealth to a new powerful élite, while causing untold suffering and poverty for millions, including the murder of 50 million people in the Soviet Union and 30 million during China's Cultural Revolution. A philosophy that seeks to remove suffering by causing greater suffering is hardly worth spit.

Atheistic evolutionism regards suffering as a necessary mechanism for the advance of life as we know it. A godless evolutionism is predicated on suffering as the soup in which the strong survive and thrive. Philip Kitcher of Columbia University in his book *Living with Darwinism* argues there is nothing *kind* in evolutionism, which is by nature self-serving and violent, and he claims that if there were a God presiding over life, "it is extremely hard to equip the face with a kindly expression".[206]

Unlike Buddhism, Christianity does not claim suffering is illusory, a dream world one need to escape from by your own personal enlightenment. Suffering in all its forms is very real, and is ultimately evil. This evil is that which Christ came to conquer through his death at the cross and the establishing of his kingdom, and one day he will return to restore all things and rid for ever the causes and effects of suffering.

Unlike Marxism, the violent revolution is one God experiences himself at the cross, and the church and God's kingdom are to be the true egalitarian society which communism apes.

Against atheistic evolutionism, the whole of history is driving towards encountering God, not evolving into gods ourselves. God is bringing his kingdom. The mark of God's kingdom is kindness; in his kingdom there is the rule of love, not the rule of the jungle. It is a kingdom where only the kind can enter. Suffering in this groaning creation, suffering caused by human wickedness – both will end when Christ returns and recreates and rules.

Meanwhile God's people, Spirit-filled, with a vision of love and justice, glimpsing his glorious new creation, seek to transform the suffering of others here and now, to echo in advance the eternal perfect kingdom of heaven coming from the future.

Paul states two significant points about the experience of suffering by the Christian. First, it is suffering "with him" (verse 17) – we share in Christ's suffering and Christ shares in ours. He does not abandon us, but walks with us through it. We are not alone – God is with us, God is for us in this. Secondly, our suffering is in the "present time" (verse 18) – our suffering is not perpetual, its time is running out. For the believer it ceases at death, and for the world it ceases when Christ returns.

2. The sons of God sighing

Three times in this passage Paul speaks of groaning or sighing: the sighing creation (verse 22); the sighing sons (verse 23); the sighing Spirit (verse 26).

The words "groaning" or "sighing" translate the Greek term *stenadzo,* which had the sense of to narrow or squeeze. Suffering so constricts, crushes, that we feel our life being squeezed out of us; words fail, and all we can utter is a deep, involuntary, internal groaning. This groan does not go unheard by God.

Paul says creation groans: it too is touched by the Fall, exhausted by its cycle of life and death and decay and life again. American writer Henry Thoreau wrote, "Even trees do not die without a groan."[207] Paul says (verse 19) that the whole of creation is longing "for the revealing of the sons of God" – the great day of creation and recreation when the chaos in nature, which erupted when Adam and Eve unlocked hell, is calmed, and all that was tarred and marred by evil is renewed in the new heavens and new earth – the new heaven on earth.

And Paul says we who have the Spirit groan inwardly as we await the great and glorious day when Christ returns and embraces us. We possess the Spirit but we still grown. This is important. Possession of the Spirit does not end or even dull our sighing and crying. Possession of the Spirit brings a deep joy, but it is joy amidst grief. We who have the Spirit still groan. Perhaps we groan more so. For possessing the Spirit, we posses the mind of Christ, and we see even more keenly the suffering in the world. And yet we also see by that Spirit the new world that is to come. And the chasm between the reality and the hope produces a deep longing and sighing.

I recently watched news of wicked abuses in Uganda comprising child sacrifice and child trafficking. I groaned aloud, and told my wife to turn the TV off. I could not take it. The next day I was sitting in town when an African woman carrying a small child walked by me, and I instantly recalled the TV reports, the abuse of the children, and I involuntarily groaned aloud in pain. The Spirit within was moving me to groan at the pain in the world. God who sees all must be continually groaning.

And so we groan between the gulf of what is and what will be, and that groan becomes a prayer, a deep crying to deep for change.

Karl Marx said, "Religion is the sigh of the oppressed creature."[208] He was right. But he did not believe it was a cry that was heard by God, and so he exhorted man to rise up and revolt. But our cry *is* heard and joined by God. Moses records in Exodus 2:23–24, "the people of Israel [in Egypt] groaned because of their slavery and cried out for help. Their cry for rescue from slavery came up to God. And God heard their groaning, and God remembered his covenant with Abraham".

Please take note: if you are crying, sighing, groaning, it does not fall on deaf ears. John Bunyan, author of *The Pilgrim's Progress,* spent a total of twelve years in jail for preaching the gospel – something prohibited to all but licensed and ordained Anglican vicars! He wrote, "The best prayers have often more groans than words."[209]

"The Spirit himself intercedes for us with groanings too deep for words" (8:26).

Our groan evokes the groan of God. God is neither absent nor indifferent. He is present and attentive and responsive – even if we don't always perceive him as such at the time. He is there, deep within, and by his Spirit he joins his sighs to ours as a joint offering to the Father in intercession. In verse 26 we see a wonderful triplet: the Spirit helps us, the Spirit intercedes for us, the Spirit groans for and with us. God is not passive – he is not in this context an unmoved mover! He is groaning by his Spirit, praying within us, praying for us, praying on behalf of us… groaning God.

Incidentally Paul is not referring to the gift of tongues. He speaks of groanings "without words", whereas tongues is speech with unknown words. Shakespeare wrote, "Sigh no more ladies, sigh no more"[210] – a theme popularized in a recent successful Mumford and Sons song. Well, God doesn't say, "Sigh no more." He says he will sigh with us, until that point when he promises that sorrow and sighing will flee away (Isaiah 35:10).

3. The sons of God shining

"... provided we suffer with him in order that we may also be glorified with him. For I consider that the sufferings of this present time are not worth comparing with the glory that is to be revealed to us" (8:17–18); "the glory of the children of God" (8:21); "And those whom he predestined he also called, and those whom he called he also justified, and those whom he justified he also glorified" (8:30).

Suffering and sighing are not the last word. Glory is. The Anglo-Saxon father of English history, the Venerable Bede, wrote some 1,300 years ago: "Once we have entered our eternal reward, the years spent suffering here below will seem like no time at all."[211] Paul has used the metaphor of all creation groaning with labour pains. Groaning and pain are not always life-taking, of course. They can be the accompaniment to life, a prelude to birth. Jesus said, "When a woman is giving birth, she has sorrow because her hour has come, but when she has delivered the baby, she no longer remembers the anguish, for joy that a human being has been born into the world" (John 16:21). For those who reject Christ, suffering in this life is a phantom pregnancy without life at the end, but for the sons of God suffering is often the birth-pangs that climax in eternal life. The last word, the last impression, is glory.

The Chinese church statesman, Watchman Nee, who was imprisoned from 1952 until his death in 1972, said, "God's purpose in redemption is glory, glory, glory."[212] Groaning is replaced by glory. But what is this glory with which we are glorified? Glory is God shining out. It is his essence, effulgence, excellence, magnificence, pre-eminence – the weight of the matter of God. God clothes us with his divinity, with his glory, something we forfeited at the Fall. God wraps us in himself, he honours and exalts us in himself.

Humankind spends its life looking for glory – to stand out from the crowd and be honoured, applauded, exalted. We want to shine. We look for it in academic success, sporting achievement, looks, the acquisition of wealth, existential experiences of wonder, travelling to places of outshining beauty. There is a longing in the human heart for what has been lost – a longing to be restored to a pre-fallen state.

I often think of glory as a "wow" moment. I've had a few wow moments – the day I was saved; the day I was first filled to flooding with the Spirit; the day I saw Tiffany coming down the aisle to actually marry me; the day I was ordained to the priesthood; the days my sons were born. Yes, I have had a few glory days. But I have had far more grey days, dark days, suffering days. And yet the shadow of these will quickly fade, and all tears be wiped away, and all bruises healed, in the glory that will be revealed as the perpetual state of eternity. In all our suffering, whether natural to the human condition or particular to the Christian, we know life is not as it should be, but our momentary woes will give way to eternal wows.

Suffering and sighing will make way for shining. This glory far, far outweighs the current suffering (8:18). Indeed, in Romans 8:17–30, Paul mentions suffering twice, sighing three times, and glory four.

In conclusion

"... for those who love God all things work together for good, for those who are called according to his purpose" (8:28).

The saints will suffer. The Christian faith and the love of Christ do not insulate or inoculate us from the everyday exigencies of human existence. Indeed, such allegiances to Christ and his kingdom will invite further suffering by those forces opposed to Christ's kingship. Paul was no stranger to suffering, and he knows only too well that those he writes to will be the same. His mention (8:35) of "tribulation, or distress, or persecution, or famine, or nakedness, or danger, or sword" is as much prophecy as it is rhetoric. But in the economy of God, in the eternal kingdom of God, what the enemy intended for harm God will work for eternal good. Sufferings and ignominies endured for his name's sake will be rewarded with honour. And even those sufferings all too familiar to our kin can be redeemed to produce character and perseverance, and to fuel our hope in the future. With God nothing is wasted.

The three most difficult experiences of my life have been the loss of several children through miscarriage, extended periods of almost debilitating stress and depression, and a cycle crash that left me in hospital for many days, with two operations, months in a wheelchair, and years in recovery. In all these I begged God to intervene miraculously, and yet this was not forthcoming.

However, now, as I look back, I believe that good came from the harm. I would not want to revisit those experiences, but I can honestly say I am now grateful for what God taught me and told me through them. I learned more about myself, my weakness, and my fleshly propensities to self-pity, fear, doubt, and unbelief, than I would have without them. How quick I could be to forget and forsake God when he remained silent! I learned to understand the human condition far more – I learned to appreciate what I had rather than what I thought had been taken. I believe God worked in me character and perseverance and faith, and he gave me a greater sense of hope and anticipation and longing for Jesus' return when all wrongs are righted. And I learned that God is faithful; he is present, and he is powerful, and he is for us. And I know that, one day, these scars earned here will be treasured like medals in heaven.

31

God is For Us (8:31)

Many people suffer from the soul-sapping dis-ease of paranoia. In recent years there have been a number of studies conducted to assess levels of paranoia in an attempt to discover whether people were experiencing thoughts about others doing them harm. The researchers were surprised by the levels of paranoid thoughts exhibited by the participants, which were almost as high as those for depression and anxiety. In one UK survey, 21 per cent said that there had been times in the past year when they had felt that people were against them, and 9 per cent believed that their thoughts were bring controlled or interfered with by an outside force or person. In the US, 10 per cent believed other people were following or spying on them while 6.9 per cent thought they were being plotted against of that others were attempting to poison them.[213] I confess, at times of stress, I do have a tendency to paranoia. (Of course, maybe I'm not paranoid... maybe my worries are true!) During one bout of mild paranoia I shared my anxieties with a friend. It drew this brusque but helpful reality check from my pal, Frank: "Simon, forget it, you're irrelevant – no one cares about you!"

Many people fear that God is against them, that God is out to trip them up.

Many Christians live with a deep dread, a gnawing anxiety that, if they put a foot out of line, God will send disaster their way, or won't answer their prayers, or will make them suffer somehow. Negative religious experiences can fuel this, as can fierce, firebrand preaching. I heard a gifted preacher lay it on thick with these words: "Some of you – God hates you. Some of you – God is sick of you. God is frustrated with you. God is wearied by you. God has suffered long enough with you. He doesn't think you're cute. He doesn't think it's funny... He doesn't care if you compare yourself to someone worse than you – he hates them too. God hates, right now, personally, objectively hates some of you."[214]

Sure, God hates sin, but does he actually hate sinners? Tens of thousands of people have downloaded that sermon, presumably most because they connected to this view of God toward them. But is it true? No! I agree with John Stott who wrote, "God does not love us because Christ died for us, Christ died for us because God loved us."[215] In Romans 8:31 Paul states: "If God is for us, who can be against us" The "if" here is rhetorical. Paul is saying, "*because* God is for us we can know that none can stand against us".

I believe this gets to the very marrow of the gospel.

Deus pro nobis – God for us – was the core to Dietrich Bonhoeffer's conception of the person and work of Jesus:

> *Every Christology which does not begin with the assumption that God is only God for me, Christ is only Christ for me, condemns itself.*[216]

It's one thing to believe God is. It is an altogether different thing to believe God is for me. Do you believe that God is *for* you? Only in grasping and being grasped by this fact will you be the person and live the life God desires for you.

1. God is for us in his substitution

"He who did not spare his own Son but gave him up *for us* all" (8:32, italics mine).

Here is the very heart of Paul, of the gospel, of the Christian faith – that God is for us. There are over forty verses in the New Testament that specifically emphasize the death of Jesus "for us", in the place of us, as a substitute for us.

Consider some of them:

- while we were yet sinners, Christ died *for* us Romans 5:8
- Christ suffered *for* us (1 Peter 3:18)
- Jesus was a propitiation *for* our sins (1 John 4:10)

- This is my body/blood given *for* you (Luke 22:20)
- Jesus died *for* us (Romans 14:15)
- God made him who had no sin, become sin *for* us (2 Corinthians 5:21)
- Christ became a curse *for* us (Galatians 3:13)
- Christ Jesus who gave himself as a ransom *for* all (1 Timothy 2:6)
- Christ loved us and gave himself up *for* us (Ephesians 5:2)
- By the grace of God he might taste death *for* us (Hebrews 2:9)
- He is the atoning sacrifice *for* our sins, and not for ours only, but for the sins of the whole world (1 John 2:2).

On the Mount of Olives, while the disciples slept, Jesus accepted the cup of wrath and dripped drops of bloody sweat, going through agonies *for us.* When Jesus was betrayed, blindfolded, slapped, mocked, and spat on, he took it all *for us.* When Jesus was handed over to the Romans, stripped and flogged and mocked and beaten again and again, God cries, "Look, this is all *for you*!"

When they hammered iron through his flesh and tendons, through his Son's screams God cries, "It was worth it, it's all *for you*!" And when the punishment for our sin fell on his sinless shoulders, when God turned away and turned out the lights, it was all for you. All this was always all for you… because God so loved the world.

Because God is for us in his self-substitution, no charge can be brought against us (8:33), no accusation at us will be entertained, no condemnation pronounced upon us, and no eternal separation from God for us. No wonder the great twentieth-century theologian Karl Barth challenges us:

> *Look once again to Jesus Christ in his death on the cross. Look again and try to understand that what he did and suffered, he did and suffered for you, for me, for all of us. He carried away our sin, our captivity, our suffering, and did not carry it in vain…* [217]

2. God is for us in his provision

"He who did not spare his own Son but gave him up for us all, how will he not also with him graciously give us all things?" (8:32).

God who gave his Son for us promises to graciously give us all things. God's giving flows from grace, he is ever the benevolent and generous God. The Greek tense of "give" here is future-orientated; it is not a promise of present prosperity.

God giving us all things does not mean we get everything we pray for here and now. We should probably read the words "all things" in the light of Ephesians 1:22 which states that God "put all things under his feet". Paul here in Romans 8:32 is speaking of our share, our portion in Christ's bounty. Being in Christ, we share in the royal inheritance as sons of God. In Matthew's presentation of judgment day, the King will say to the sheep (his saints), "Come, you who are blessed by my Father, inherit the kingdom prepared *for you* from the foundation of the world" (Matthew 25:34, my italics). On the night of the last supper, betrayal, and arrest, Jesus told disciples he would shortly be leaving them and returning to his Father: "In my Father's house are many rooms… I go to prepare a place *for you*" (John 14:2, my italics).

Every year my sons excitedly look forward to their birthdays. Sometimes they begin thinking about what they want and planning their party six months before the actual day! I'm trying to forget how old I am getting, but for them it's not an "age" thing, it's a celebration thing. They read magazines, look online and think about what they'd like as a gift, what they'd like to do for their party, who they will invite, what meal they'd like to eat. Months of anticipation, preparation, and excitement go into that day. It's because they sense that this one day of the year is their day, and it's all for them.

Just so, every day in eternity is a day to give glory and live to the glory of Christ. And Jesus has spent the last 2,000 years preparing a party for us, a wedding feast for his bride. He has an army of angels sorting things out – every detail – the presents, the wedding clothes, the food. No expense is spared.

3. God is for us in his intercession

"... the Spirit himself intercedes for us" (8:26); "Jesus ... at the right hand of God, who indeed is interceding *for us*" (8:34, my italics).

The whole of the Godhead is involved in praying for us. The Spirit intercedes for us. The Son intercedes for us and the Father is constantly searching our hearts to read the Spirit's mind (verse 27) for prayers prayed according to his will, so that he might answer. God is praying for you.

There is a famous play called *The Six Degrees of Separation*. It is based on the premiss that you can get to anyone in the world, even the President of the USA, within six contacts. So, for example, we could say:

1. You know me;
2. I know a Rhodes scholar who is friends with a
3. US Senator who meets for breakfast with
4. the President's Press secretary who can mention my name to
5. the President's PA who can make an appointment for you and me to
6. see the President.

Now, some Christians relate to God that way, through "degrees of separation", conceiving that divine grace flows from God, through the pope, through the cardinals, to the bishops, to the priests, through the Eucharist, to me. Others think they get the ear of God by petitioning Mary who is nearer to God, or pray with or through the saints who may have influence and are regarded as "one step nearer" to God than they are.

We don't need any degrees of separation. The Spirit is praying for us, Jesus is praying for us, God is praying for us, before we pray ourselves. We have access and may approach God boldly with confidence – we do not need any other mediator, go-between, fixer, or intermediary (see Romans 5:2; Ephesians 3:12; Hebrews 10:19–22).

Your name and your needs are on the prayer list of Jesus, and on his praying lips. Your prayers are getting through directly.

The Scottish saint, Robert Murray McCheyne, once said:

> *If I could hear Christ praying in the room next to me I would not fear a million enemies – yet distance makes no difference. He is praying for me. Christ is still in the next room praying for us. He ever lives to make intercession.*[218]

4. God is for us in his great affections

"Who shall separate us from the love of Christ? Shall tribulation, or distress, or persecution, or famine, or nakedness, or danger, or sword?" (8:35).

Paul is not talking in the speculative abstract. Hardships, persecutions, famines, nakedness (by beating or poverty), and dangers will come, but Paul says these sufferings do not in any way imply that God's love has fled. New Testament Professor Thomas Schreiner writes, "The God who is for us will see to it that we are never severed from his love."[219] Paul repeats this point so that we do not miss it: "For I am sure that neither death nor life, nor angels nor rulers, nor things present nor things to come, nor powers, nor height nor depth, nor anything else in all creation, will be able to separate us from the love of God in Christ Jesus our Lord" (8:38–39). The universe could never conceive of anything that could stand between us and God's great love for us. God will never be persuaded not to love us. Corrie ten Boom, the famous Dutch church mother imprisoned in the death camp Auschwitz for aiding Jews during World War II, and who saw her father and sister die yet herself survived, was once asked by an academic what was the main lesson she had learned in the annihilation camps. She didn't hesitate: "That God's love still stands when all else has fallen."[220] Everything in life fails in one way or another; all is flux; change is the only constant – except for this one thing: God, being perfect, cannot change, and so God's great affections remain. They never wane or weary or get worn out – his mercies are new every morning (Lamentations 3:22–23). Dietrich Bonhoeffer wrote:

> *This being pro me is in turn not meant to be understood as an effect which emanates from him, but it is to be understood as the essence, the being of the person himself.*[221]

Nothing good we do can make God love us any more, and nothing bad we do can ever make God love us any less. He saw us from afar, steeped in sin, and still he loved us. He died knowing every sin we would ever commit, and he loved us. Jesus is the only God the world has ever heard of who loves sinners.

There is one further point we must not miss with this revelation of God's inseparable love, and that is the thematic link to the next section in chapters 9–11 with their focus on the people of Israel, the Jews. Just as nothing can separate us, the redeemed elect in Christ Jesus, from God's fierce, loyal love – so nothing can separate God's first covenant elect people Israel from God's faithful covenant-keeping love.

So, God is for us. He really is. Do you know that?

5. Are we for God?

God's affection and actions for us precede any response we offer. They are not conditional on our being for him. Christ was born to die for you long before you were born. God's gifts are given without conditions and strings attached… that is what grace is, gratis. Having said that, however, having tasted that the Lord is good, we will willingly want to give our all for him.

In the early eighteenth-century the young Count Zinzendorf was in an art gallery in Düsseldorf. There he was captivated by and meditated on a portrait of Jesus hanging on the cross. What struck him were the words painted below: "All this I did for thee, what hast thou done for me?"[222] Utterly gripped by this, he dedicated his life to live for Christ who died for him. He founded the Herrnhut Community in Saxony, Germany,[223] which, for 100 years, held 24-7 prayer meetings. This tiny village amazingly sent 1,000 missionaries to such far-flung places as Jamaica and Greenland. Their sense of God's reality stirred a revival in John Wesley who became the spark that lit the eighteenth-century English revival, and he helped fuel the American Great Awakening. Remarkable ripples of revival flowed out from this one young Austrian aristocrat who was gripped by the love of God for him and devoted himself to live for God. And the same Jesus asks us the same question: "All this I did for thee – what hast thou done for me?"

Sacrifice for Jesus

Jesus promised that "And everyone who has left houses or brothers or sisters or father or mother or children or lands, for my name's sake, will receive a hundredfold and will inherit eternal life." Matthew 19:29. But the promise is predicated on the forsaking, leaving everything for him. He who left heaven for us calls us to forsake all for him and follow after him. He wants everything – our ambitions, our relations, our possessions, as the worship hymn exhorts: "Jesus, all for Jesus, all I have and am and ever hope to be."[224]

C. T. Studd, the notable Eton, Cambridge, and England cricketer, gave up fame and fortune for Jesus and spent his life on mission fields in China and Africa. He founded WEC, the world's largest missionary organization. His life motto was: "If Jesus Christ is God and died for me, then no sacrifice can be too great for me to make for him."

Speak for Jesus

Paul says, "we are ambassadors for Christ, God making his appeal through us" (2 Corinthians 5:20). The term Paul uses here for "ambassador", *presbeuo*, was used of the official Roman legates who functioned as the emperor's administrative representatives in scattered provinces of the empire, and who accompanied the generals in war and set out the terms of peace for the vanquished enemies, offering them the conditions of citizenship. As Christ's ambassadors we are his official representatives of the heavenly kingdom, presenting Jesus' terms of peace and bringing people into heaven's citizenship.

Suffer for Jesus

"It has been granted to you that for the sake of Christ you should not only believe in him but also suffer for his sake" (Philippians 1:29). Every month twice as many Christians are targeted and murdered for their faith in Christ as the total number killed in the Twin Towers bombing in America in 2001. But it never even makes the news! You cannot face this in the flesh. Peter said he was willing to die for Christ, then denied him three times (Luke 22:34). Only after seeing Christ die for him, and having been filled with the Spirit, would Peter willingly suffer martyrdom. Even as I write this, I am suddenly aware that some reading this may be called to lay down their lives for Christ. Grace to you.

Scorned for Jesus

We are "fools for Christ's sake" (1 Corinthians 4:10). The message of a crucified God will always be treated with contempt. Our gospel is always foolishness to the intellectual Greeks and a stumbling block to the religious Jews. Those who live by this message will incur ridicule, mocking, derision, and scorn. We are not to attempt to make the message palatable and acceptable to "cultured despisers", as for instance the German scholar Friedrich Schleiermacher did, who whittled away whatever was not acceptable to those championing the new Enlightenment. Richard Dawkins derides belief in God as delusion. Memorably he said, "By all means be open minded, but not so open minded as to let your brains drop out!" Many think us fools for believing in and giving our lives, tithes, and time to God and church, but as martyr Jim Elliot wrote in his journal before he went to the mission field, "He is no fool who gives what he cannot keep to gain what he cannot lose."[225]

I'd rather be a fool in man's eyes than in God's. God's perspective is that the fool says in his heart there is no God (Psalm 14:1)! To the man who lived to amass wealth Jesus said, "Fool! This night your soul is required of you" (Luke 12:20).

Serve for Jesus

In the context of feeding the hungry, clothing the naked, visiting the prisoner, tending the sick, welcoming the stranger, Jesus said, "whatever you did" for them, "you did *for me*" (Matthew 25:40, NIV).

Jesus takes compassionate service to others very personally. And the converse is true: that when we fail to act with compassion, mercy, or generosity towards the needy, poor, and outcast, Jesus takes it personally, as though it were not done to him. And he judges us for it. This is one of the most shocking statements in the gospels. We recoil against it and try to slip exegetically or hermeneutically from it. Nevertheless, one consideration on judgment day will be evidence of acts of mercy. We need to learn from the likes of Mother Teresa whom the cynical satirist Malcolm Muggeridge visited and through whom was drawn to Christ. He asked Mother Teresa why she did what she did in all the sin and degradation of the dying in Calcutta. Her simple reply: "I wanted to do something beautiful for God."[226]

We are to love him who first loved us. As a good father or mother loves their child unconditionally, yet longs for the reciprocity of their children in love, so God desires our love. The first and greatest commandment, on which all the other 613 Old Testament laws hang, is to love God – with our affections, our will, our intellect, our strength. God desires it and God deserves it. The medieval mystic Margery Kempe had a revelation of this one day when she heard God say:

> *Daughter, I have suffered many pains for thy love – therefore thou hast great cause to love me right well, for I have bought thy love full dear.*[227]

We have a great God to love, and we have a great cause to love God.

32

Longing, Belonging, Prolonging (9)

Paul devotes the next three chapters, Romans 9–11, to the question of the Jews. This is the longest single theme in this particular letter and, I believe, the very centre of Paul's concern. While Protestantism has often taught the Epistle to the Romans as if it only has eight chapters with its main focus being the theology of "justification by faith in chapters 3–5, I am of the opinion that Paul's main focus is the place of the Jews in relation to God and his church, as presented in chapters 9–11. The centre is not justification by faith but Paul's justification of the ways and word of God. Far from Romans 9–11 being, as some liberal scholars once claimed, a parenthesis to the main argument, or even an old synagogue sermon of Paul's sewn into his letter, I believe these three chapters are the interpretive key to the letter, revealing to us the ways of God, his faithfulness, promises, election, salvation, and glory.

The question Paul is asked and answers in 9–11 is: What about the Jews? That is a question that has been asked throughout history, ever since Abraham's family grew into a nation in Egypt three millennia ago. Pharaoh asked the question, so did the Philistines, the empires of Assyria, Babylon, Persia, Greece, Rome, the Ottoman empire, the Holy Roman empire, Napoleon, the Nazis, Britain, the League of Nations. Today the Islamic nations, the United Nations, the press, the politicians, everyone is asking: "What of the Jews?"

The early church in Rome, containing Jewish and Gentile converts, were asking this question. Paul has just stated that nothing can separate us from the love of God in Christ Jesus. But if that is true, what about the Jews? Why haven't they accepted Jesus as Messiah? Has God's affection, his purposes and promises, finished or failed? The Jewish members of the congregation are asking whether their Jewishness still matters now that they have embraced Jesus as Messiah. Both Jewish and Gentile members of the church in Rome are asking the question: what about the Jews, now that the gospel has come to the Gentiles?

Paul's *longing* for his people

"I have great sorrow and unceasing anguish in my heart. For I could wish that I myself were accursed and cut off from Christ for the sake of my brothers" (9:2–3).

There are two equal and opposite religious errors regarding the Jews.

Perpetually saved?

The first error is to believe that all Jews are perpetually saved on the basis of Abraham's bloodline. One example of this error is the profoundly flawed statement produced in 2002 by the twenty-two members of the Christian Scholars Group who represented different Christian denominations: "In view of our conviction that Jews are in an eternal covenant with God, we renounce missionary efforts directed at them..."[228] There are liberals and even conservative evangelicals who subscribe to the notion that Jews are saved by their Jewishness, the covenant with Abraham, and not by faith in Christ Jesus, not by the gospel. They would conceive of the gospel as the New Covenant for the Gentiles, while the covenant ratified at Sinai with Israel runs in tandem. A misunderstanding of biblical theology, influenced perhaps by an awareness of the centuries of Jewish abuse at the hands of Christians, have led to this. It is well meaning but profoundly mistaken.

I have a friend, an Anglican priest, who actually lost his licence to preach the gospel and officiate in Anglican churches because he ran a mission preaching the gospel to the Jews. When a few members of the Jewish community along with some influential Anglican representatives complained, he was punished for his commitment to the gospel work. The same people presumably would have thought the same and acted the same to Peter and Paul in their mission to convert their Jewish brethren.

Perpetually cursed?

The second error, and evil, is the notion that all Jews are perpetually cursed because their ancestors killed Christ. This despicable view has in fact dominated and been deeply inculcated in the church mindset throughout history, and indeed is held still by many. The rejection and crucifixion of Christ by the Jewish authorities is not seen as part of the mystery of God's economy, but as part of the demonic DNA of the Jews.

In Matthew's Gospel we see that Pilate tried to have Jesus released, but the crowd insisted on crucifying Jesus. Pilate declared that he was innocent of Jesus' blood, and the Jewish crowd shouted, "His blood be on us and our children!" (Matthew 27:25). Throughout history, much of the church has believed that this self-invocation of blame, of a curse, means that *all* Jews, in *every* generation, for *all* time, must suffer the curse they invoked on themselves.

In the fourth century the most famous preacher of his day, John Chrysostom ("John the golden-mouthed"), wrote a rabid treatise entitled *Discourses against Judaizing Christians* and in it sought to suppress any and all connection between the church and her Judaic roots. He stated:

> *The Jews are the most worthless of all men. They are perfidious murderers of Christ. The Jews are the odious assassins of Christ and for killing God there is no expiation possible, no indulgence or pardon. God always hated the Jews. It is incumbent upon all Christians to hate the Jews.*[229]

Such views justified Hitler 1, 500 years later. Hitler declared in 1938, "In the gospels the Jews called out to Pilate when he refused to have Jesus crucified, 'His blood be upon us and upon our children!' Perhaps I have to fulfil this curse."[230] Many millions, inside and outside the church, embraced such evil.

Thus there are two opposite errors: first, that all Jews are already saved and do not need the gospel; and secondly, that all Jews are always accursed. The consequence of both errors is that gospel mission, which is meant for the Jew first then the Gentile, is actually withheld from them.

Paul here puts the lie to both of these notions. He is heartbroken because many of his fellow Jews have rejected Jesus as Messiah and for this reason are accursed, cut off from God. And yet he himself is a Jew, and proof that salvation may come to the Jews. Paul always preached the gospel first to the Jews because it's their gospel first. Let us not miss the apostolic heart that compels Paul. Paul himself says he would be willing to forfeit his own salvation to save others.

I wonder what I would be willing to lose to see loved ones of mine saved? A night's sleep, perhaps? Many of us are not willing to be made uncomfortable or embarrassed by inviting someone to an Alpha Course, or a carol service, or even to admit we are Christians. Have you ever asked God to fill your heart, to break your heart, with compassion, with tenderness for someone who does not know Jesus? I promise you this: if you pray that and become that prayer, God will use you to draw them to Christ.

That statesman of revival, Leonard Ravenhill, in a sermon in his old age reminisced about Hugh Price Hughes, one of the greatest Methodist preachers of his generation. Hughes's daughter gave Ravenhill a huge biography of her father, and she said this:

> *When he came back on a Sunday night from the service, if no one had been saved, he would be inconsolable. You couldn't comfort him. He wouldn't eat, he wouldn't drink. He wouldn't even take his long coat off. He threw himself over his bed and he sobbed and he sobbed and he sobbed and said, "Why? Why? Why?"*[231]

The psalmist said: "He who goes out weeping, bearing the seed for sowing, shall come home with shouts of joy, bringing his sheaves with him" (Psalm 126:6).

God's gifts *belonging* to Israel

Twice Paul states (9:4–5) that to the Jews "belong" a whole catalogue of divine gifts. The Jewish people stand in a unique relationship to God. God created them and graced them with revelation and vocation. Victorian British Prime Minister Benjamin Disraeli once replied to an English MP who had sneered at his Jewishness:

> *Yes, I am a Jew, and when the ancestors of the right-honourable gentleman were brutal savages in an unknown island, mine were priests in the temple of Solomon.*[232]

This is the privileged relationship that Israel knew, and of which Paul reminds us.

Theirs is the adoption

God told Pharaoh through Moses, "Israel is my firstborn son" (Exodus 4:22). Firstborn here relates not to the order of birth, but the order of status – a status as the Father's heir. God says he is Israel's Father and they his firstborn heir. Classic nineteenth-century liberal theology waxed lyrical about the "universal fatherhood of God and brotherhood of man", but this is nonsense. Of whom is God Father? First, God is eternal Father of the Son Jesus. Secondly, God is the Father of faithful Israel. Thirdly, God is Father to all who accept his Son Jesus.

Theirs is the glory

Glory is given to Israel by their unique creation, election, and relation to God. Glory is the manifest presence of God. And to Israel God gave his glory, God gave himself. His glory was displayed in mighty miracles. It was given in the Torah that came with glory. And it was pre-eminently displayed in his abiding presence, dwelling among them in Tabernacle and Temple.

Theirs are the covenants

God established his universal covenants with all humankind through Adam and Noah. But God entered into a particular and exceptional union with Israel. God covenanted with *Abraham*, and reiterated it with Isaac and Jacob, to make him a great nation, possessing a land, to be blessed and a blessing to the world. Whenever we hear the triplet "The God of Abraham, Isaac and Jacob" invoked, God is saying he is the covenant-making God with Israel (Exodus 3:6; 6:3; Matthew 22:32; Acts 3:13). God covenanted with *Moses* to make Israel a people for his own possession, a holy nation, a kingdom of priests. God covenanted with *David* that he would never fail to have a descendant king on a throne. God promised a new covenant for the *house of Israel,* that he would write a law on their hearts.

Theirs is the Law

Every people group and society pragmatically constructs law – a set of rules and regulations for the ordering of society. In part this will stem from the law written on the human heart, the conscience, the divine witness, the trace of the *imago dei* in humanity. However, only to Israel did God draw up a particular divine decree to order life.

Theirs is the Temple worship

Most people groups try to meet God and devise religious structures to facilitate this – temples, sacrifices, liturgies, sacred texts, offerings, and intercessions to encounter their god. But only to the Jews does God give precise details for worship.

Theirs are the promises

As a husband I have made promises to love, protect, and provide for my wife. As a father I have made similar promises to my sons. God as Israel's Father, as Israel's bridegroom, has made beautiful promises to her, and he is faithful to them. Pastor Mark Dever has written a book with the apposite title, *The Message of the Old Testament – Promises Made.*[233] Most of those promises were made to Israel and fulfilled in Israel's Messiah, Jesus (2 Corinthians 1:20).

Theirs is the human ancestry of Messiah

"... who is God over all, blessed forever" (9:5). This is an amazing Christological statement presenting Jesus in both his natures – human and divine, his human ancestry as a Jew at the same time as being God over all, eternally praised. Paul finishes his list of Israel's blessings from God with Christ because Christ is the pre-eminent gift of God to Israel. Jesus is also the fulfilment of all the preceding gifts, promises, and covenants that are types and shadows prefiguring and anticipating Jesus.

Christianity is a Jewish religion. Christians worship Yahweh, the Jewish God, the God whose eternal Son became a Jew.

Privilege comes at a price. The unique revelation and vocation to Israel brought both responsibility and resentments. Since they were created they have often found their calling a burden, and certainly the demonic and jealousy of others has turned on Jews. The Jewish nation, by virtue of her election, represents something of the divine and Satan despises her for it. Being Jewish is a heavy load to bear at times. In a telling scene in *Fiddler on the Roof*, the Jewish father, Tevye, weighed down by his burdens of poverty and anti-semitic pogroms, dialogues with God: "I know, I know. We are Your chosen people. But, once in a while, can't You choose someone else?"

God's promises *prolonging* for Israel

"It is not as though the word of God has failed. For not all who are descended from Israel belong to Israel… it is not the children of the flesh who are the children of God, but the children of the promise" (9:6, 8).

Paul anticipates a protest: if Israel stands in a unique relationship to God, if Israel has a unique election and vocation, then why have most of those to whom the promises were given rejected the fulfilment of promise? Has God's word actually come untrue? Have God's promises failed? Paul states emphatically: the promises of God have not failed. The Greek word Paul uses is *ekpipto* which was used at those times of the withering of a flower as it fell to the ground. Not so God's Word. God's promises may have been misunderstood by those who received them, but God's promises prevail. They never fail.

Paul's argument here is rather hard to grasp; to some it is even scandalous. The logic of verses 1–5 demands we see that God stands in a unique covenant relationship to the Jews generically and ethnically. Paul speaks of his "brothers, my kinsmen according to the flesh" (9:3),

"Israelites" (verse 4), descendants of "the patriarchs, and from their race, according to the flesh" (verse 5), and to these belong the Law, prophets, patriarchs, promises, temple, adoption, Messiah. And yet, and yet... Paul also says that not all who are descended from Israel belong to Israel. Paul is not, as some have suggested, implying that the church is the true Israel, that the church replaces Israel – this is very far from his thought here. Verses 1–5 prove Israel's unique role before God is not annulled nor seceded. Professor Cranfield rightly states:

> *Paul is not continuing to disinherit the majority of his fellow Jews – to write a charter for anti-semitism.*[234]

Sadly such verses have often been taken and abused to do so. This is not about the church as the "wider" spiritual Israel beyond ethnic Israel; on the contrary, Paul is actually saying there is a narrower Israel within Israel.

Verses 1–5 show that all ethnic Israel is the elect of God for particular revelation and particular vocation. Notwithstanding, a second election takes place *within* those elected to revelation and vocation, which is an election unto salvation. Paul sees an elect within the elect, an Israel within Israel, a remnant of Israel within the race of Israel. Again, this is not the church, per se, but this remnant, who went on to embrace Christ, become part of the church, along with Gentile believers.

God is neither fickle nor inconsistent. He has always worked this way. Paul marshals two illustrations from Israel's history to show this: first (verses 7–9), from the same seed of Abraham came Ishmael and Isaac, but it was only Isaac not Ishmael that God chose to fulfil his promise. Secondly, in verses 10–13 Paul argues that from the same womb of Rebekah came Jacob and Esau, but it was only through Jacob and not Esau that God chose to fulfil his promise.

Paul is clear that Israel's own ancestry and history demonstrate a God who, according to his wisdom, foreknowledge, and eternal mysterious decree has always chosen one over another. Put simply, God never promised all Israelites salvation. The elect of the elect will be saved. And for those who protest, Paul is robust in his response: the potter can choose to make from the same clay two pots for different uses, one noble, the other ignoble. Yes, all ethnic Israel are elect to the privileges of revelation and vocation; but only remnant Israel are elected (at this stage) to salvation in Christ.

But the story does not end there. There is a mystery that Paul will address in chapter 11, where he will claim that God has partially hardened the majority of Jews to Christ, in order that he might have mercy on the Gentiles. However, Paul sees that, one day, when all the Gentiles God has elected to be saved in Christ have come in, then "all Israel will be saved" (11:26). Why? Because they are the *elect* and *beloved* of God (11:28); and because God's gifts and call to them are *irrevocable* (11:29). Thus, in the end, the remnant, the Israel within the Israel, the elect within the elect, will be so great as to encompass the whole.

Paul's anguish at the start of Romans 9 will make way for his jubilant joy at the end of Romans 11.

33

Paul's Type of Christian (10)

What sort of Christian are you? I sometimes hear people say, "I don't like categories – I'm just a Christian" as if they are a higher Platonic pure-form. When I hear this I tend to think: "Ooh, get you!" Such comments are about as helpful as going to the butcher and saying, "I want meat." The butcher replies: "You've come to the right place. Now, do you want: lamb, beef, pork, veal, poultry, or offal? Is it for stewing, braising, roasting, frying, or baking? Would you like it minced, steaked, boned, rolled, stuffed, breaded, marinated, or diced?"

What sort of Christian are you? I took two online quizzes to define the type of Christian I am; one said I was an "evangelical" and the other defined me as a "Billy Graham-type Christian" – both are fine by me. According to the definitive *World Christian Encyclopedia,* in 2001 there were an estimated 38,000 different denominations or branches of the Christian church. There is Anglican, Baptist, Orthodox, Catholic, each with sub-sets of liberal, evangelical, conservative, charismatic – and one could add the prefix "post" to all of these categories. Born-again, Spirit-filled, fire-baptized, circumcised, fully immersed, dipped, dunked, dabbed; emergent, emerging, emo. Dress up, dress down, high, low, middle, tee-total or G&T, Sunday sort or seven days a week. What choice!

What sort of Christian are you? In Romans10 we see the sort of Christian Paul was and what sort we should be.

1. Paul was a Jesus type of Christian

"Christ is the end of the law" (10:4 where the Greek *telos* is the goal, the climax, the be-all-and-end-all); "if you confess with your mouth that Jesus is Lord and believe in your heart that God raised him from the dead, you will be saved" (10:9); "the same Lord is Lord of all... 'everyone who calls on the name of the Lord will be saved'" (10:12–13); "faith comes from hearing, and hearing through the word of Christ" (10:17).

Christianity is Christ. Fourteen times in a few verses Paul refers to Jesus; fives times the personal pronoun "him" is used. Additionally, Paul focuses down on three key predicates: Jesus, referring to his humanity and destiny as Saviour; Lord, referring to his eternal and divine nature; and Messiah or Christ, referring to his sovereignty as Son of David, King of Israel, King of the Jews.

Error comes when we fail to hold all three of these in balance.

Jesus Christ is the criterion of everything and the conclusion of everything. Jesus Christ is the bedrock of Christianity. Christianity is Christology.

As evangelist J. John says, "Take Christ out of Christian and you are left with Ian, and Ian can't save you." Many who claim to be Christians are simply Ians. There is often so little of Christ in their life as to be almost non-existent. They are Christian homeopaths who have diluted away the essence of the faith. A. W. Tozer wrote:

> *For the true Christian, the one supreme test for the present soundness and ultimate worth of everything religious must be the place our Lord occupies in it. Is he Lord or a symbol?*[235]

When I was a young curate, I heard of one interfaith adviser recommending to the clergy that in our discussions with Muslims we avoid the "J" word. He was not referring to potential incendiary words like jihad or Jerusalem. No, this church-employed interfaith worker was warning us not to use the word Jesus. He wanted the more abstract, less defining, less dividing word, "God". But when Jesus Christ as Lord is not the be-all-and-end-all, then we are not Christian. The founder of the Moravian mission, Count Zinzendorf, declared, "I have but one passion, it is He, it is He alone."[236] That was Paul's sort of Christian. Paul was a Christian with a capital Christ.

2. Paul was an affection type of Christian

"Brothers, my heart's desire and prayer to God for them is that they may be saved" (10:1).

Paul was among the most brilliant minds of his age. But he was no unmoved, detached, donnish intellectual. He was an enthusiast, a passionate man, a man on fire. The leader of the eighteenth-century American Great Awakening, Jonathan Edwards, once wrote:

> *But yet it is evident, that religion consists so much in affection, as that without holy affection there is no true religion; and no light in the understanding is good, which does not produce holy affection in the heart.*[237]

True religion is defined as loving God and loving your neighbour as yourself. Love is a passion, an emotion, an affection that leads to action.

In a 1996 lecture at Westminster Abbey entitled "When Shall We Live?" atheist playwright, Sir David Hare, expressed how disappointed he was with the church. He spoke scathingly of a London clergyman he knew who was "drier than the driest martini". He continued, "A Labour party which does not dare use the word 'socialism' is one thing. But a church that does not dare say 'Christ' is quite another." And he showed insight into the core of our faith by stating: "The Christian faith after all is based on the idea of intervention… I cannot see how, if the facts of Christ's life are true, they do not change everything."[238]

I have been around religious folk – whether evangelical, catholic, or liberals – who have as much passion for Christ as wax dummies in Madame Tussauds in London. They approach their ministry with less passion than an orthopaedic surgeon faced with a bunion. Paul's religion was of the heart – a heart filled with passion for God and his people and their eternal destiny. He was a man on fire, a man of desire. C. S. Lewis once said, "Our Lord finds our desires not too strong but too weak."[239] Oh, how often and how easily we are fobbed off by lesser things than the God who offers himself.

3. Paul was an intercession type of Christian

"Brothers, my heart's desire and prayer to God for them is that they may be saved" (10:1). Paul's affections led to his intercession. He cared and he prayed. We would pray more easily if we cared more deeply. Paul was a praying man. In his epistles we hear him talk about "every prayer of mine for you" (Philippians 1:4); not ceasing "to give thanks for you in my prayers" (Ephesians 1:16). Paul prayed all the time for all of his church because he wanted them to receive all that God had for them and be all that they could be for God. Paul believed his prayers were heard, that they were effective. Paul firmly believed in the sovereignty of God – he didn't believe we could twist God's arm – but he knew that prayer puts God's plans into practice.

I do not find prayer easy. In fact I have always found prayer the most difficult of things. Why is this? Perhaps because it's the most spiritual, most powerful, most resisted by the flesh. The missionary James Hudson Taylor once wrote to a Canadian couple embarking on missions to a demanding part of China: "Brother, if you would enter that Province, you must go forward on your knees."[240] Prayer is contestation and so prayer is contested.

I can fall asleep in any position praying... and consequently have employed numerous techniques or practical prayer-focusing activities to stop my mind from wandering. I have tried prayer-walking, prayer stools, candles, rosaries – even rotating a fifty-pence coin around my hand and praying for an individual each time I touch one of the five edges. I have prayed in tongues, cited scriptures, prayed lying down, standing, rocking like Orthodox Jews, sitting, kneeling, walking. I used to have my wife drop me five miles form my house so I would walk back praying. Prayer lists, staring at icons, liturgical set prayers, Jesus prayer, writing prayers, reading prayers. I still feel a failure and a complete novice.

But I have found two things that focus my prayers and keep me awake and attentive: times of personal trial and praying for those friends and family who do not know Jesus. When my prayers are for the lost, I find that there is faith, and fire, and I know the Spirit guiding me. If you are having trouble praying, make a list of ten people who do not know the Lord and commit to praying for them daily.

4. Paul was a salvation type of Christian

"Brothers, my heart's desire and prayer to God for them is that they may be saved... everyone who calls on the name of the Lord will be saved" (10:1, 13).

Paul is very focused in his prayers: he prays for them to be saved. This presupposes that, as far as he is aware, they are not saved. Those who have called upon the Lord are saved, and those who have not are not. Paul saw the world in binary – those saved and those unsaved. There were for Paul, as for Jesus, only two categories which divide humankind: the lost and the found; the wheat and the tares; those on the narrow path to life and those on the broad road to destruction; those in Christ and those outside.

Following the sinking of the Titanic in the North Atlantic Ocean in 1912, the ship's owners, the White Star Line in Liverpool, placed two noticeboards outside its offices. They were marked "Known to be saved" and "Known to be lost". As the fate of passengers was made known, their names were added to one or other of the boards. The same is true eternally for all the world drowning in sin: either their name is in the book of life (known to be saved) or it is not (those known to be dead). Our intercession and our mission is to seek to empty the list of the lost and place their names on the list of the found.

In July 2007 in an interview with *Christianity Today* pop singer Sinead O'Connor said she considered herself a Christian and that she believed in the core Christian concepts about the Trinity and Jesus Christ. She also said, "I think God saves everybody, whether they want to be saved or not. So when we die, we're all going home... I don't think God judges anybody."

That is a very widespread opinion or hope. And it is not just ill-informed pop stars who say such things. Highly influential church leaders like Rob Bell and Brian McLaren have in recent years published similar theology to widespread acclaim. In the second major release from the US Religious Landscape Survey,[241] the Pew Forum states that 70 per cent of Americans with a religious affiliation say that many religions, and not just their own, can lead to eternal life. The detailed survey indicates that 57 per cent of those attending evangelical churches also agree that many religions can lead to eternal life. Only 36 per cent chose the alternative: "My religion is the one, true faith leading to eternal life." It boils down to the basis of our belief. If we are orthodox and follow tradition, if we are biblical and follow revelation in Scripture, we cannot avoid the nature of the inclusivity and exclusivity of the Christian faith, as we considered earlier. And this becomes the great impetus for prayer and evangelism.

5. Paul was a justification-by-faith type of Christian

"... being ignorant of the righteousness of God, and seeking to establish their own, they did not submit to God's righteousness... righteousness based on faith... For with the heart one believes and is justified, and with the mouth one confesses and is saved" (10:3, 6, 10).

Paul speaks of being saved in the same breath as being righteous. One is saved on the basis of being declared righteous. This righteousness, Paul says, is not based on belief in God per se, nor in religious effort in good works and self-purifying for God. Paul's Jewish brethren believed in Yahweh and served God with their religious devotions, and sought purity through their obedience to the Torah, and yet, despite the fact they had belief and zeal for God and had worked hard at establishing their own righteousness, they remained unsaved and without knowledge of God's righteousness.

This was Paul's great heartache: the Jews awaited their Messiah who would save them, yet when he came they rejected him and tried to save themselves by themselves. As such they are the archetype of all who seek to be right with God but reject the revelation of God and the terms of God. David Pawson helpfully states:

> *I am afraid that among Christian Zionists there can arise a feeling that Jews are OK, that they are safe in God's sight, that they do not need to be evangelized... Listen, the greatest need of every Jew is to be saved. Those who love Israel ought to be in the forefront of evangelism of Jews, of giving the gospel of their Messiah, hard though it is. It is so much easier to cheer them and comfort them and love them, but the real love is to save them. That was Paul's desire, and it should be ours too. They are lost in*

> *self-righteousness and need to be saved from it and brought into the righteousness of God.*[242]

This is the great scandal of Christianity – that salvation comes by grace alone, through faith alone, in Christ alone; and that without grace, faith, and Christ, no one will be declared righteous.

6. Paul was a mission type of Christian

"How then will they call on him in whom they have not believed? And how are they to believe in him of whom they have never heard? And how are they to hear without someone preaching? And how are they to preach unless they are sent?" (10:14–15).

Paul's logic is faultless. If people are lost, unsaved, and if Christ alone is the Saviour, and righteousness and salvation come not by religious zeal or works but only by faith in Christ and confession of him as Lord, then it is imperative that the world understand the invitation and the preconditions for salvation. And that demands that someone must be sent to tell them the good news.

C. H. Spurgeon in a sermon voices the cries of those who have never heard the gospel or received Christ. Like the Macedonian man who called to Paul – so they cry out to us in our comfortable churches enjoying our comfortable faith: "It is not for yourselves you have received it, but for us. Oh! Give it to us. Preach the gospel to us, for it is designed for us."[243] The first time I met my wife Tiffany's parents was the same time I asked her father for his blessing on our marriage. Tiffany's mother was shocked – she looked at Tiffany and said, "You never told me!" How many walking towards hell will look back over their shoulders at the Christians on judgment day, shaking their heads and saying, "You never told me. Why? Why not?"

The fabled Baron Münchhausen could not pull himself out of the swamp he had got stuck in by his own hair. If you are having a heart attack, you cannot give yourself CPR.

We must not put the onus on the non-Christian to try and find Christ for themselves. It is our responsibility, our duty, and our privilege.

Mission, evangelism, and sharing the greatest news, fail for one of three reasons. Either:

1. We do not believe people are lost and so do not tell them they are and how to be found;

2. We do not believe people are saved exclusively by faith in Christ as Lord and so we leave them to find their own way;

3. We do not care either way.

I have a study and an office but I do not find either the best place for writing. For years I have worked from coffee shops. The problem is that word quickly gets around about where the good coffee is, and so you often find the best coffee shops crowded out with noisy people. Recently I found a superb coffee shop with lighting, space, the finest flat-whites, good snacks at reasonable prices, great service. And they let you stay for hours! I have taken a few people there but always urged them not to tell anyone about the place. Some people are like that about their discovery of heaven. It's their secret.

No. Good coffee shops we keep secret. Good news must go public.

34

Good News for Whom? (10)

by Joseph Steinberg[244]

A few years ago I was asked to be a keynote speaker at a special day called together by the UK Evangelical Alliance to consider what response it should have to President Bush's "Road Map" to Peace with regards to Israel and evangelism in the Middle East. My brief as final speaker was to point a "way forward" for the seventy leaders who had gathered. And as things heated up during the day, that was exactly what we needed. I was disappointed throughout the day as not a single speaker addressed the possibility of Jesus being the only real, lasting solution to peace in the Middle East. All we heard was arguments about injustices against both sides. When I finally got up to speak I tried to pull us back together. "Surely, as evangelicals," I said, "there must be one thing we can all agree on – proclaiming the good new of Jesus to both sides, whether Jew or Arab. The only hope for peace in the Middle East is found in the Prince of peace, the Messiah Jesus." Unfortunately, not everyone there agreed with me. There were some who spoke out against that belief, who basically did not agree with what Paul is saying here in Romans 10.

But this kind of peace with God is exactly what Paul desires when he writes here in Romans 10:1, "Brothers, my heart's desire and prayer to God for them [the Israelites] is that they may be saved."

The first thing Paul wants to say in Romans 10 is that we need to place a priority on sharing Jesus with the Jewish people, because like all people, they need to be saved. But there are Christians who love the Jewish people so much that they would contradict Paul here. They would say that today God has two covenants – one for the Jews and one for the rest of the world. They would say it is right to share Jesus with the world and it is fine that Gentiles should follow Jesus. But they would go on to say that preaching the gospel to Jewish people is entirely inappropriate and offensive. They would say the Jewish people are the people of the Book – they have the Old Testament Law. And as Jews seek to keep the law and maintain a Jewish lifestyle they have a covenant relationship with God.

But anyone who takes the time to study the Mosaic covenant will quickly discover three things:

First, Jewish people can't keep the law – no one can. In fact it's impossible to keep it without the Temple we lost in AD 70, where we offered the sacrifices that brought us peace with God.

Secondly, Hebrews 9 states, "The blood of bulls and goats could never take away sin." That is why the sacrifices had to be offered day after day. The sacrifices were pointing us to the Messiah Jesus who would be the once-and-for-all-time sacrifice.

And thirdly, in Jeremiah 31 God made it clear that my people – the Jewish people – had irrepairably broken the Mosaic covenant. But because he is eternally committed to us in his love, like a husband, he would make a New Covenant with the houses of Israel and Judah. He promised to write his law on our hearts instead of on tablets of stone. And Jesus tells us that, in his blood, he has instituted that New Covenant.

There are not two covenants – one for Jews and one for the rest of the world. "Christ is the end of the law for righteousness to everyone who believes" in Jesus (10:4).

The Scripture is so plain and simple here, and so I struggle with why there are so many Christians who are confused on this issue. But when I spoke to that EA gathering and reminded everyone of who the true Peace of Jerusalem is – and the need to remain committed to gospel proclamation among both Jew and Arab – I was openly opposed. After my address, an advisor to some of the top church leaders in the UK spoke out and directly challenged me. Claiming Jewish people have their own way to God, they warned the entire gathering that we must not offend Jewish people by telling them about Jesus. After the meeting closed, they rebuked one of my fellow

Jewish Christians – calling him a traitor to his people because of his faith in Jesus.

I wonder what this church leader would say to Paul here in verses 1–4 when he writes: "Brothers, my heart's desire and prayer to God for [the Israelites] is that they may be saved. For I bear them witness that they have a zeal for God, but not according to knowledge. For, being ignorant of the righteousness of God, and seeking to establish their own, they did not submit to God's righteousness. For Christ is the end of the law for righteousness to everyone who believes" (Romans 10:1–4).

Paul wants to make sure we understand that we must tell the Jewish people about Jesus. We must not keep from them the *only* means of salvation! God does not love Judaism, he loves Jewish people, and they need the righteousness that comes only through faith in the Messiah Jesus.

Telling people about Jesus isn't only at the centre of Paul's longing – it is central to Jesus' heart too.

I have observed in life that the last thing someone says say before they go away is the most important. For me, when I go away, the last thing I say is "I love you." That way, if that plane I am getting on turns into a blazing tube of fire – at least my family will remember my love. So, if this principle is true, what was the last thing Jesus said to his disciples before he went away? What was that which was most important to the heart of God?

Jesus said, "Go ... and make disciples of all nations ... you will receive power when the Holy Spirit has come upon you, and you will be my witnesses in Jerusalem and in all Judea and Samaria, and to the end of the earth" (Matthew 28:19; Acts 1:8).

So the most important thing Jesus wanted for his disciples was for them to go and make many more disciples. He wanted them to reach the world! But don't miss the irony of what Jesus is asking here. Jesus came as the Jewish Messiah – and by his own decision, his mission was almost exclusively to Jewish people. The Jewish religion of the day did not allow Jews to mix with Gentiles, who were considered ceremonially unclean. So now Jesus is turning everything on its head. He is telling a group of Jews to go out and make disciples... of *everybody*, everywhere, all-inclusive. But Gentiles were not in the disciples' thinking. They never mixed with them. And besides, wasn't Jesus the Messiah for the Jews? And so, despite Jesus commanding them to go to the uttermost parts of the earth, they stuck with Jerusalem and Judea and ignored Samaria and beyond. Finally, in order to get the disciples' attention, God gave Peter the same dream three times. He dreamed of unclean animals coming down to him in a sheet and was told to get up and eat. What was God's message to Peter? Gentiles can believe in Jesus too. In fact, they need to hear the message and believe in Jesus in order to be proclaimed kosher – clean – by God; in order to be saved.

Today the roles have been reversed. Then the Jews had a problem evangelizing Gentiles. Now the church has a problem evangelizing Jews. There is a prejudice against sharing Jesus with "my people". And we have it bad in two ways: we either hear one side that romanticizes Judaism into a religion that saves – an idea that says, "The Jews have their own way to God through their own religion," or the opposite idea that has permeated church history, the insidious idea that says, "The Jews rejected and killed Christ, so God has rejected them – the church has replaced Israel."

Sometimes I wonder whether God needs to give the church today the opposite dream he gave Peter: does the church need a God-given dream of Jewish food coming down from the sky and God saying, "Go and eat – bagels are good! Chicken soup is good!" Paul demands we do not forget that his Jewish people need Jesus to be proclaimed kosher and forgiven. They too need to call on his name to be saved. That is what Paul writes here in verse 13, quoting the prophet Joel: "everyone who calls on the name of the Lord shall be saved" (Joel 2:32).

In verses 14–15, which are normally used for mission to all peoples, Paul is making a priority call for evangelism among his Jewish people when he boldly writes:

> *How then will they call on him in whom they have not believed? And how are they to believe in him of whom they have never heard? And how are they to hear without someone preaching? And how are they to preach unless they are sent? As it is written, "How beautiful are the feet of those who preach the good news!"*
>
> ROMANS 10:14–15

The church has a God-given responsibility to ensure it has beautiful feet – to ensure that Jewish people hear the only message that can offer them real, life-changing salvation and peace with God. Psalm 122 asks us to pray for the peace of Jerusalem (verse 6). We hear this request a lot. But I wonder if Paul would ask what kind of peace we seek for the Jewish people today? It seems so many Christians are fixed on the issues of the land of Israel and the city of Jerusalem that they pay for a *piece* of Jerusalem instead of pray for the *peace* of Jerusalem. Paul's heart's desire for his people is that they would be saved. He wants them to know the peace of God. Jesus is the peace of Jerusalem. Taking the words of Jesus into today's context: "What does it profit a man or woman to gain a piece of land but to lose their own soul?" Paul says his heart's desire and prayer to God for his people is that they be saved.

So, imagine if all the funding that was poured into Israel by Christians was for the evangelization of the people living in that region. What a difference that would make! Imagine if we prioritized *peace* over *piece* and ensured that Jews and Arabs heard the gospel. And yet finding Christians who are committed to making sure Jews or Arabs have a chance to hear about Jesus is so rare. And of course there is also that natural problem we all feel when faced with sharing Jesus. How do you tell someone, using Paul's phrasing here in verse 13, that they need to be "saved"? Who wants to do that? And yet this is exactly what Jesus and Paul tell us to do. There are many followers of Jesus who prefer the peace of not sharing Jesus than the polarization that could come through sharing Jesus with their Jewish or Arab friends – or any friends for that matter. Well-meaning churches and Christians who are involved in work with Jews or Arabs would say they love their friends and don't wish to offend them with the gospel.

But is this the kind of love we are called to show? Again, Paul asks us: "How can they believe in the one of whom they have not heard? And how can they hear without someone preaching to them?"A person who will not share Jesus with their friend for fear of offending them is really saying they care more about what their friend thinks of them than they care about what God thinks of their friend. We need to share God's love with *all* people – from Judea (the Jews) to Samaria (the Arabs) to the uttermost parts of the earth.

I am eternally grateful that a Christian friend risked my anger to share Jesus with me, to challenge me as a Jew to consider Jesus' claims to be Messiah. My friend lived out his peace with God consistently before my eyes, making me envious of the relationship with God he had – one I knew I did not have.

And that is exactly what Paul is speaking of in verses 19 and 20 when he quotes Moses and the prophet Isaiah as saying, "I will make you jealous of those who are not a nation; with a foolish nation I will make you angry... I have been found by those who did not seek me; I have shown myself to those who did not ask for me."

Why does God want to make the Jewish people envious? Why does he want to provoke us to anger? Because he wants to save us! Again verse 1: "My heart's desire and prayer to God for [the Israelites] is that they may be saved." And how will this happen? Paul tells us it is the Gentile church's responsibility to make Jewish people envious, jealous of the faith you have – and it works! I am living proof that this is true and I know too many other Jewish people who have come to faith through the loving witness of Christian friend to count them all.

So what, now what?

You will notice the last verse of this chapter where it says, "All day long I have held out my hands to a disobedient and contrary people" (10:21). My people are known for not endorsing Jesus' claims to be the Messiah. But does this disqualify us from participating in receiving God's mercy? Notice the very next verse (remembering this letter originally had no chapter headings): in light of the obstinate nature of my people Paul asks, "So then did God reject his people?" And in the strongest terms he writes, "By no means!"

So why all this talk about the Jews? What does it matter? Who cares? In the scope of all the people who have lived through all time, why should such a small and insignificant people really matter? Why so much space and time given to them here in Romans and the New Testament? Well, it matters because of what it says about God and how he deals with you and me as those who trust in Jesus and his New Covenant.

Because if we worship a God that will stop loving us when we fail at obeying his commandments, or if we fall short of his expectations, or one who grows tired of us constantly going our own way and doing our own thing; if we worship a God who can, because of our constant selfishness, decide to replace us with somebody new – then you and I are in big trouble. As much as we may want to say Israel broke the commandments, and failed in their commission as lights to the world and rejected their Messiah, I wonder if any other nation would have done any better? I don't think so. Sin and failure are a universal human problem.

I believe this harks back to the thrust of this whole section from Romans, and it really starts near the end of chapter 8: "For I am sure that neither death nor life, nor angels nor rulers, nor things present nor things to come, nor powers, nor height nor depth, nor anything else in all creation, will be able to separate us from the love of God in Christ Jesus our Lord" (8:38–39). As I re-read this I see Paul's Gentile Roman reader express the question, "Well, if we cannot be separated from the love of God, what about the Israelites? Aren't they?"

And so Paul says in 11:1 – "By no means!" The fact is that Scripture is clear on God's ongoing and eternal commitment to the Jewish people. And it is clear on his ongoing and eternal commitment to save *all* of those who call on his name. We all break his commandments, failing to live up to the high call of Christ and daily reject God's rule. And so concerning us all God says, "All day long I have held my hands out to a disobedient and obstinate people." So Paul asks, Does God reject you? By no means! "Everyone who calls on the name of the Lord will be saved" (10:13).

A dream of the future

In verse 17 Paul writes: "faith comes from hearing, and hearing through the word of Christ."

In 2002 I attended a rally in Trafalgar Square in London that drew 30,000 Jewish people together to support Israel. I went to do some street evangelism – but soon realized I would be lynched. While there I noticed a wall of scaffolding and flags. On the other side of the wall was a smaller group of a few thousand Palestinians gathered to demonstrate their support for Palestine. As I cast my eye over the huge crowd gathered around the square on that day, I took a moment to dream. I dreamed of what it would be like if that middle wall of scaffolding were torn down and all those who were present, both Jew and Arab, were there united and rallying to proclaim Jesus to the nations; rallying to be his witnesses; rallying in preparation to go out to share Jesus with the world.

Imagine the impact that would make: one great wave of witnesses, with a testimony of reconciliation, reaching out to a world in need of reconciliation with God. It would be like life from the dead. That is why the apostle Paul tells us of a future blessing in Romans 11:15 when he writes: "For if their rejection means the reconciliation of the world, what will their acceptance mean but life from the dead?"

35

For the Jew First (11:11, 14)

The gospel of salvation, appropriated by faith in Jesus the Messiah, is for the Jew first (1:16). They are the womb in which it was conceived. They heard it first, they received it first, they were appointed to herald it first. They were also the first to refuse it. Paul has expressed his anguish that his own people in large part had rejected their Messiah (9:2), while only a remnant received it. Paul has conveyed his incessant intercession that they might embrace their destiny and deliverer (10:1). Paul has exhorted the church to preach the gospel to the Jews (10:14). In Romans 11 he brings a new nuance to shape the church's relations towards the Jewish people: "Make them jealous."

"Salvation has come to the Gentiles, so as to make Israel jealous ... I magnify my ministry in order somehow to make my fellow Jews jealous, and thus save some of them" (11:11, 13–14).

Paul extolled his ministry about God's goodness and kindness towards the Gentiles. He waxed long about the miracles and the mercies God poured out on the Gentiles – how Yahweh had included the Gentiles in God's royal priesthood, God's chosen people; how he had extended his embrace to the Gentiles to come under the divine Shepherd's tender care. In all this he wanted not to provoke the Jews, not to rub their noses in it, not to incite them to anger, but to arouse a deep jealousy for God, a deep longing that they too might experience what these Gentiles were experiencing, and so come to accept Jesus as Messiah, and so be saved. Never a one-upmanship, never a boast to put the other down, but always a provocation, a making the Jews jealous so that they too would want and receive Jesus. The church makes the Jews jealous, not to make them bitter, but to provoke hunger and to awaken their hearts to the gospel of their Messiah.

In Luke15 we read the story of the prodigal son and the prodigal Father. It has many levels of interpretation, but the embrace of the prodigal son by the father incurs the jealous protest of the old brother who resents this rebellious son being received and celebrated while he had "been slaving" (Luke 15:29, NIV) for years for his father. The father does not rebuke the older brother, but says, "Son… all that is mine is yours" (verse 31). Just so, it is the hope that the embrace of the sinful, prodigal Gentile Christians by the Father will cause a questioning from the older brother who will then understand his identity and, instead of slaving for the Father, will experience the embrace of grace.

The church makes the Jews jealous through many ways:

- their inclusion into the people of Yahweh and experience of the promises of Yahweh
- their experience of forgiveness declared through faith in the Jewish Messiah Jesus
- their lives transformed through faith in the Jewish Messiah Jesus
- the divine love experienced through faith in the Jewish Messiah Jesus
- the hope enjoyed through faith in the Jewish Messiah Jesus
- knowing Yahweh as Father, through faith in the Jewish Messiah Jesus
- the promises received through faith in the Jewish Messiah Jesus
- the Law fulfilled through faith in the Jewish Messiah Jesus
- the new covenant entered by faith in the Jewish Messiah Jesus.

The church ought to so live a life with Yahweh through Jesus the Messiah that the Jewish people say, "You have what we have waited for and wanted for so long. How ever did you receive it?" But woe to the church – for far from provoking a jealousy for Jesus among the Jewish peoples, the church, through her arrogance and insistence on her replacement of Israel in God's purposes, has caused the Jews to despise the church. Far from precipitating a godly jealousy for God, the church has cursed Israel and withdrawn from her the very bridge to salvation. After 1,700 years of pogroms, expulsions, forced conversions, ghettos, ovens, and annihilations the church and Christ has become to the Jew the fragrance of death and not the fragrance of life.

Rose Warmer was a cultured Jewess growing up in post World-War-I Hungary who became a Christian and an active evangelist to her Jewish people. In the Nazi purge in Hungary she volunteered to join a train to Auschwitz to witness to Christ to Jews. Remarkably, she survived. On the day of liberation Rose awoke to silence, rather than the accustomed shrieks and whip cracks of the SS guards and their barking dogs. She was free to make her way to the single water tap on the parade ground. As she queued for a drink, a large Ukrainian prisoner turned and saw her struggling for water, and immediately punched her to the ground screaming, "Get away from me, you Christ-killer."[245] How could this Ukrainian woman, who had shared and survived the same hell as Jewish Rose, have such deep-seated hatred towards her as to act and speak in the same spirit towards her as their SS captors? Shared humanity, shared womanhood, shared nightmare in Auschwitz, shared need for water, shared Christianity – so much shared could not so quickly bridge the gulf between this "Christian" Ukrainian and this Jew.

"Christ-killer" has long been the cry of the church against the Jews – from two millennia ago to modern times. A notorious 1930s German children's book *The Poisonous Mushroom* instructed Aryan children: "When you see a cross, then think of the horrible murder by Jews on Golgotha."[246] For many Christians the cross became not simply the symbol of a crucified Jewish Christ, but the symbol of Jews as Christ-killers. And indeed subsequently the same cross for many Jews became a symbol of Christians as Jew-killers.

Auschwitz survivor and Nobel Prize winner, Elie Wiesel, once wrote:

> *you must understand that the cross for you is a symbol of love and compassion; for us Jews it is a symbol of suffering and oppression.*[247]

I will never forget one American Jewish scholar telling me that she grew up believing that, if she looked at a cross on a church, she would die. How on earth did we get here?

1. The great divorce: separation between synagogue and church

We have already seen that Christianity is Jewish. Christians worship the Jewish God Yahweh, and are saved by the Jewish Messiah Jesus, and their religion is the fulfilment of the Jewish Law and the prophets. The Jewish story is the Christian story. Christians are late-comers joined to the Jewish narrative.

Nevertheless Jews like Jesus of Nazareth, Paul, and Peter did not always have the nicest things to say about some of their own people. Jesus told the devout Pharisees who prided themselves on their Abrahamic ancestry that they were of their father the devil (John 8:39–44). Paul speaks of "the Jews, who killed both the Lord Jesus and the prophets, and drove us out, and displease God and oppose all mankind by hindering us from speaking to the Gentiles that they might be saved" (1 Thessalonians 2:14–16). Peter's Pentecost sermon addressed the gathered crowds of pilgrim devout Jews and talked brazenly of "this Jesus whom you crucified" (Acts 2:36). Such descriptions were specific to the Jewish leaders, and perhaps included the manipulated crowds who conspired and cried out against Christ, but later they would be taken and applied generically to all Jews.

Paul, who celebrated the divine gifting to Israel and declared such love for his own people that he cried out to be cut off from God so as to save his people (Romans 9:3), nevertheless could also seemingly dismiss his Jewish credentials. He claimed that his circumcision on the eighth day, being from the tribe of Benjamin, a Hebrew of Hebrews, a Pharisee, faultless in obeying the Torah, were as "dung" (Philippians 3:5, 8). Even allowing for hyperbole and rhetoric, and his main point being a contrast with the surpassing greatness of knowing Jesus, nevertheless this seems a stark statement that many have read as an apparent negation of Jewishness and, for some, even grounds to dismiss or demonize Judaism.

In his first epistle Peter applies to the church the predicates God ascribed to Israel: a holy nation, a royal priesthood, God's elect, people belonging to God. The writer to the Hebrews is clear that the Law, the sacrifices, the priestly duties, were all merely shadows that have made way for a new and better covenant. In two of Jesus' letters in Revelation (to Smyrna and Philadelphia) Jesus speaks of "the synagogue of Satan" and provides what has been taken as grist for the mill by those who embrace replacement theology, saying, "They call themselves Jews but are not." The destruction of the temple in AD 70 and the Diaspora – the scattering of the Jews among the nations – has been seen as symbolic and prophetic: God not only making Judaism redundant but Judaism being under divine judgment.

Evangelical New Testament Professor Douglas Moo summarizes the material to suggest:

> *The New Testament can justly be said to be anti-Judaic in the sense that it claims to leave no room for the claims of Judaism to mediate salvation through the Torah. But the New Testament is not anti-Semitic.*[248]

But the church would not make such subtle theological distinctions. For many this potential anti-Judaism became anti-Semitism. It is of course very easy to present a totally opposite argument from Jesus and the apostles, to show the continuity between the church and Judaism; however, increasingly the church ignored this and focused on what divided, not what united. Significant to the breach was the hunting and harassing of Messianic Jews by Orthodox Jews and Jewish authorities. While many Messianic Jews in the first century wanted to hold their Jewish roots, many Jews refused to recognize them. Such persecution by the Jews of the Christians did little to endear Judaism to the converts. As we will see, this persecution of Christians by Jewish authorities would soon be reversed.

2.The great abuse: ecclesiastical fratricide

During the so-called patristic period (AD 100–451), as the church gained ascendancy, eventually becoming the state religion of the Roman empire, one struggles to find a single positive comment about the Jewish people among the leading scholars and clerics. The luminaries among the church fathers consistently identified the Jews with the demonic and sought to exorcise all trace of Jewishness from Christianity. In the early second century Ignatius, who was later martyred in Rome, wrote in his Epistle to the Philippians that "if anyone celebrates the Passover along with the Jews, or receives emblems of their feasts, he is a partaker with those that killed the Lord and his apostles".[249] Clearly the implication is that Jewish roots and ceremonies were still part of the Christian identity of some, but it was not welcome by the leading church authorities and thinkers.

The second-century apologist and defender of the faith, Justin Martyr, in his *Dialogue with Trypho the Jew,* claimed that the Jews suffer, with their cities burning, their harvests stolen, "justly, because they slew the Just one". He is among the first to present a so-called "replacement theology" where the church replaces the Jews in God's economy, when he speaks of "true Israel" being those who have been led to God through this crucified Christ.[250] In the late second century St Melito of Sardis was perhaps the first to declare that all Jews were perpetually guilty of deicide in the crucifixion of Christ, a charge eagerly adopted by many in the church ever since. He claimed that they had committed the "unforgivable sin" and explicitly claimed that the Jews had been replaced by the church in God's purposes.

Early in the fourth century the paradigm-shifting Emperor Constantine befriended the church, whether for religious or pragmatic reasons, or both. Conscious of the church's schisms and rifts, he sought to unite the church and clarify its doctrines through calling the First Ecumenical Council in 325. Present at the Council of Nicea, which took place in Bithynia (modern-day Turkey), were 318 bishops from throughout the empire. Not one bishop was of Jewish extraction. Gentile hegemony prevailed by then in the church, and no messianic believer was represented. Here doctrines on the nature and divinity of Christ were settled once and for all and formulated in the Nicene Creed. This is well known. What is less known was the council's attempts to further separate the church from her Jewish roots by adopting a different church calendar from the Jewish one which had been much utilized until then.

Following the Council of Nicea Constantine expelled all Jews from Rome, forbade Jewish proselytizing, and changed the date of Easter to no longer fall during the Jewish Passover. He sent an official letter to church dignitaries stating that Christians should not "tarnish their soul by communication with such wicked people [the Jews]".[251]

When the Roman emperor Theodosius I ordered the rebuilding of a synagogue that had been burnt down, the distinguished Bishop Ambrose of Milan (who discipled Augustine) wrote to him boasting: "I hereby declare that is was I who set fire to the synagogue; indeed I gave orders for it to be done so that there should no longer be any place where Christ is denied."[252]

Late in the fourth century our "golden-tongued" John Chrysostom proved in fact foul-mouthed in his infamous *Eight Sermons against the Jews*. What aroused the full force of his rhetoric, or venom, was that some Christians had actually been fellowshipping with Jews. Chrysostom called this "disease". He was on the warpath, stating, "It is against the Jews that I wish to draw up my battle."

We have already quoted the following extract in Chapter 32, but it is important we read it again, slowly, to see the depth of hatred targeted against the Jews by such an influential church leader. Such things set the trajectory of church-Jewish relations for more than a millennium, and its stench remains.

> *The Jews are the most worthless of all men. They are perfidious murderers of Christ. The Jews are the odious assassins of Christ and for killing God there is no expiation possible, no indulgence or pardon. God always hated the Jews. It is incumbent upon all Christians to hate the Jews.*[253]

What chance did the Christians have in understanding and embracing their Jewish roots when their leading churchmen made such decrees!

Reckoned among the greatest theologians of the church, Augustine of Hippo, who lived during the third and fourth centuries, sadly also used some of the same deriding terms to speak of the Jews as Christ-killers. However, uniquely, he preached that they should not be harmed but allowed to wander as a perpetual prophetic symbol of God's justice and judgment against God's killers. But he also believed that far from finding in Christ the fulfilment of their Jewish roots, Jews were to see their Jewishness as a defilement to be exorcized. This concept of exorcizing the evil of Judaism was formalized in the rites of conversion for Jews to Christianity. The church of Constantinople required them to make this vow:

I renounce absolutely everything Jewish, every law, rite and custom, above all I renounce Antichrist, whom all the Jews await in the figure and form of Christ, and I join myself to the true Christ and God.[254]

3. The great assault: from verbal abuse to extreme violence

The anti-Semitism of the patristic period continued into the Middle Ages, unabated in its venomous assault on Jews. But the theological rhetoric of the patristic period now becomes violent and murderous, as we see the medieval unholy trinity of forced conversion, separation, and eradication.

In the West a papal bull decreed that Jews be separated from non-Jews to live in ghettos. This word, derived from an Italian word for "district", was coined for the special place of separation for Jews.

In the East, under Byzantine rule, the Jews had a slightly easier time, but were still forbidden to hold government office, proselytize, or have servants. The Crusades had been fought to recapture the holy sites from Muslim rule ever since the seventh century. Christian armies under the pope's blessing and the sign of the cross (the word "crusade" is from the French word for taking up the cross) hacked their way through Europe, killing Jews and stealing their wealth, to finance the Crusade. Rabbi Eliezer bar Nathan commented of the persecutions of 1096,

Now it came to pass that as they passed through the towns where Jews dwelled, they said to themselves: "Look now, we are going to seek out our profanity and to take vengeance on the Ishmaelites for our messiah, when here are the Jews who murdered and crucified him. Let us first avenge ourselves on them and exterminate them from among the nations so that the name of Israel will no longer be remembered, or let them adopt our faith and acknowledge the offspring of promiscuity."[255]

By July that of year, in just two months, 10,000 Jews in Germany were dead, including many of those in the Rhine Valley, Bohemia, and Prague. Arriving in Israel the Crusaders were not simply fighting the Saracens, they were annihilating remnant Jews who lived peaceably alongside the Muslims. In 1099 during the siege of Jerusalem, Crusaders filled Jerusalem's chief synagogue with women and children, old and young, and burned it to the ground, allegedly kneeling and singing "Christ we adore thee", swords raised as crosses, tears rolling down their faces, believing their brutal acts were devotions received by Christ.[256]

The Blood Libel[257] was a sinister anti-Semitic slur that began in Norwich, England, in 1144, but was enthusiastically adopted in various forms even into the twentieth century. The lie was levelled that Jews had taken a Christian child at Easter, tortured it, and on Good Friday hung it on a rod. It was claimed that the Jews desired real blood, Christian blood, for their Passover Matzot. This lie spread like wildfire, fuelling anti-Semitism, with over 150 trials, throughout history, of Jews accused of taking Christian blood at Passover. Most trials led to the execution of those accused, despite their innocence, and spilled over into Jewish pogroms.

In 1213 the Fourth Lateran Council ordered all Jews to wear distinctive garb to curtail their association with Christians. In Italy Jews sewed a disc on their outer clothing; in Germany they wore a distinctive hat; in England two strips of white linen. Every Nazi law against the Jews has precedence in earlier church decrees. The intellectual statesman of the medieval period and architect of Catholic thought ever since, Thomas Aquinas, employed traditional venom in describing Jews. However, he uniquely stands against the replacement tradition in his commentary on Romans 9–11, emphasizing the ongoing purposes of God for the Jews in predestination and election. Extraordinarily, he stated that their rejection of Christ had not brought about God's rejection of them, and God had not revoked his promises and priorities for Israel.[258] What a tragedy this insight was not further taught and applied.

Christendom banned all Jews from citizenship, and created the "wandering Jew". In 1290 King Edward of England was the first monarch to expel Jews from a European nation – not before first ransoming money for 3,000 of the wealthiest. In 1492 Catholic monarchs Ferdinand and Isabella of Spain, after finally defeating the Moors, the very next day decreed the expulsion of 200,000 Jews from their lands. Verbal abuse led to expulsion, which led to forced conversion, which led to extermination.

And so we come to the demonic Papal Inquisition that lasted from the late fifteenth century well into the nineteenth. It was a Catholic witch-hunt. Many Protestants, as well as Jews, died. Initially the Spanish Inquisition ordered Jews to convert to Christianity or else be banished from the nation. However, they did not trust the conversions as authentic, so thousands of the Jewish converts were subsequently killed, after being brutally tortured first, usually in the church. One can still see today on the walls of Toledo Cathedral, and other churches in Spain, the very chains and manacles which held the Jews who were tortured and killed – for being Jews – by the "Christians" in the church.

4. The Reformation: but no change in attitude to the Jews

Despite the revival of a biblical faith, and a stripping away of much church accretion, there are only very rare exceptions, like Reuchlin, who advocated that the church befriend, trade, and learn from the Jews. (He was himself later sent to the Inquisition.) The leading figures of the early Reformation like Luther and Melancthon condemned him as a Jew-lover. Martin Luther initially believed Jews would come to Christ with the Reformation gospel he heralded. He even wrote an important work in 1523, *That Jesus Was Born a Jew*, emphasizing the Jewish roots of Christianity. He apparently paid for a Jewish lad's education and housed a Jewish family. But as he grew old he grew increasingly bellicose, notably against the peasants (who were applying the freedom of the gospel Luther taught) and against the Jews in particular. When the Jews did not convert en masse as he had anticipated, and, as some have claimed, following a violent illness which Luther suspected was the result of being poisoned by kosher food when he was a rabbi's guest, he turned against the Jews, and wrote a despicable tract entitled *Of the Jews and Their Lies*[259] in which he extolled the Christians to burn the synagogues, ban the Talmud, threaten death to rabbis if they taught Judaism, and put Jews to manual hard labour. He stated, "We are at fault in not slaying them."

In Luther's last sermon four days before his death, he raved like a rabid dog that it was a matter of great urgency to expel all Jews from German territory.[260] Neither Luther nor the next father of the Reformation, John Calvin, had any hope drawn from Scripture of an end-time conversion of Jews to Christ, or a restoration of Jews to the land, though contemporaries Theodore Beza and Peter Martyr were more sympathetic.

However, the Reformation's return to a biblical faith, the presence of the Puritans and their Geneva Bible with its 1599 marginal commentary, would soon lead to renewed understanding of the Jews in God's heart and history as stated in Scripture. We will examine this in our next chapter.

In conclusion

The Jews have long memories. Their history of relations with the church, and with those representing the church, is a brutal one, with them more often than not being on the receiving end. The church, Christ, and his cross came to represent rejection, theft, suffering, torture, and death. Paul said that the church was to make the Jew envious, jealous of our relationship to God. Instead we have invited fear, mistrust, and scorn. Given the church's history of horror to the Jew, what Jew in their right mind would betray the blood of their people to embrace the God of their enemies? If the church represents Jesus, and Jesus represents God, what Jew would want a God like that? The fact is, the church has failed to represent the Jewish Jesus in relating to the Jews.

What are you going to do about it?

36

Making Jews Jealous (11:11, 14)

"Salvation has come to the Gentiles, so as to make Israel jealous... I magnify my ministry in order somehow to make my fellow Jews jealous, and thus save some of them" (11:11, 13–14).

Paul enforces the point by twice, in as many sentences, stating that the church is to make the Jewish people jealous and so stimulate them towards desiring the Messiah. Tragically, as we saw in our previous chapter, throughout the history of the church, far from making the Jews jealous of the church's gospel, the Jewish people have instead been filled with fear and loathing of the church through the persistent persecutions inflicted upon them. This has brought great shame upon the church, and I am in no doubt has robbed the church of the favour of the Lord. Four millennia ago God promised Abraham and the nation who would come from him – the Jews – that he would bless those who blessed them and curse those who cursed them (Genesis 12:3). This promise has never been revoked; it has foolishly been ignored. And we, the church, have often found ourselves at odds with God because we have afflicted or not honoured Abraham's descendants.

However, by the grace of God, following the Reformation and the increased accessibility and closer reading of Scripture that ensued, many at last had their eyes opened to God's purpose and plans for Israel and were moved to repent of the church's previous anti-Semitism. Finally they began to embrace God's first chosen people.

The great embrace

Hugh Broughton stands out as the first Englishman to propose a gospel mission to the Jews in the Middle East, the first such mission to the Jews since apostolic times. For centuries the church had anathematized Jews; now Broughton wanted to evangelize them. He intended that a translation of the New Testament be made in Hebrew for the sake of effective witnessing, but his efforts were sadly scorned and squashed by the Anglican bishops of the time. It is remarkable that, on hearing of this pro-Semite's heart and efforts, the chief rabbi of Constantinople wrote to Broughton in 1599 and invited him to come and teach the Jews there.[261]

The seventeenth-century Puritans had a wholly different spirit towards the Jewish people. Due to their closer, more faithful reading of Old Testament prophecies concerning the restoration of Israel, and their particular interest in Romans 9–11, they came to see the place of Israel in the heart and future history of God. The Geneva Bible was the great text of the Puritans and in its marginal notes, written by Scottish Presbyterian divines, a literal and natural interpretation of Romans 11:25–26 was given, expressing hope in the restoration of the whole race of Jews to Christ and thus being joined to the church.

This important text, naturally understood, roused the Puritans to see the Jews in a whole new light as their own soon-to-be brothers and sisters, whose conversion was key to ushering in Christ's return. Whereas almost every patristic father was theologically anti-Semitic, and believed the race was under a self-inflicted curse for their part in Christ's crucifixion, almost every Puritan father was, theologically if not practically, pro-Semitic. Numerous books and tracts were produced promoting the cause and future of the Jews. Widely circulated was Edward Nicholas's *Apology for the Honourable Nation of the Jews*, published in 1648. It reflected the growing view of many Puritans that the English Civil War was God's divine judgment on England for banishing the Jews, and petitioning England to welcome back the Jews. England had been the first nation in Europe to expel Jews back in 1290, and many saw this as incurring divine wrath on the land. Following the establishment of the Protectorate under Oliver Cromwell, and recognizing the Puritan commitment to the

Jews theologically, the chief rabbi from Amsterdam came to England in 1655 and appealed to Cromwell to welcome the Jews to return and make their home here. Cromwell granted this, and the Jews began to return.

Outstanding among the Puritan scholars was John Owen. He believed in the restoration of Jews to the Lord and the Land, claiming:

> *There is not any promise anywhere of raising up a kingdom unto the Lord Jesus Christ in this world but it is either expressed or clearly intimated, that the beginning of it must be with the Jews.*[262]

The Presbyterians in their substantial statement of faith, the Westminster Longer Catechism, a benchmark for Reformed theology for centuries, declared in Question 191:

> *What is "thy kingdom come" a prayer for? We pray, that the kingdom of sin and Satan may be destroyed, the gospel propagated throughout the world, the Jews called, the fullness of the Gentiles brought in…*

Such Puritan and Presbyterian theologies laid the foundation for what would become the normative view in evangelicalism over the next 200 years.

The early modern period

While anti-Semitism was always close to the surface in some quarters of the church, many of the outstanding figures in British and American Christianity were passionately pro-Semitic. As students of scriptural prophecy they expected a return of the Jews to the land and the Lord. The nineteenth century saw several missions to Jews being established, notably The Church's ministry Among Jewish people (CMJ) in 1809, as well as a passion for worldwide mission. Two perspectives on the relationship between the church's mission and the Jews were evident: first, an emphasis on mission to the Jews was driven by the belief that there would be a worldwide revival – "life from the dead" – once they had come to Christ; secondly, an emphasis on mission to the nations sprang from a belief that once the "fullness of the Gentiles" (11:25) were gathered in, only then would the Jews turn to Christ, and this would usher in Christ's return.

In the 1830s Robert Murray McCheyne and fellow Scot Andrew Bonar encouraged the evangelization of the Jews, and both men led missions to Palestine and Jewish communities in Europe. When a revival broke out in his local parish of Kilsyth in Scotland, McCheyne took this as a sign of God's promise to Abraham and his heirs "I will bless those who bless you" (Genesis 12:3). God's favour was upon this church ministry because this church honoured the Jews, the apple of God's eye. Like many post-Puritan evangelicals they believed that the salvation of the Jews brings the restoration of the church.

Charles Simeon was the distinguished rector of Holy Trinity, Cambridge, whose long and faithful gospel ministry there from 1783 influenced subsequent generations of evangelicals. Of him Iain Murray writes, "The conversion of the Jews was perhaps the warmest interest of his life."[263] On one occasion, as Simeon was preaching on the future of the Jews and waxing lyrical with his visions of a return of the Jews to Christ ushering in world-wide revival, a friend passed a note to him stating: "6 million of Jews and 600 millions of Gentiles – which is more important?" Simeon scribbled back: "If the conversion of the 6 is to be life from the dead to the 600, what then?"[264]

The other outstanding evangelical leader of the nineteenth century was Bishop J. C. Ryle. He preached passionately and taught with great clarity of insight on the restoration of Israel to the Lord and to the Land, publishing a series of sermons in 1879 on prophetic themes entitled *Coming Events and Present Duties*. He challenged:

> *If you expect the Jews to take the 53rd of Isaiah literally be sure you take the 54th and 60th and 62nd literally also.*[265]

These speak of God's future blessing for Israel. And again:

> *I can only say that, to my eyes, the future salvation of Israel as a people, their return to Palestine, and their national conversion to God, appear as clearly and plainly revealed as any prophecy in God's word.*[266]

The novel but influential theological movement known as Dispensationalism arose out of studied interest in biblical prophecy in the mid-nineteenth century. Among its proponents were such figures as John Nelson Darby, Edward Irving, the Plymouth Brethren, Cyrus Scofield, and Charles Caldwell Ryrie. Their theological schema divided history into seven divine epochs or economies, the penultimate being the restoration of the people of Israel to the land of Israel and the Lord returning and reigning from Jerusalem over a Davidic kingdom, having evacuated the church in the so-called rapture. This view – the second half of which I find at odds with a plain reading of Scripture[267] – nevertheless has significantly revived an interest and understanding of the land of Israel and the Jewish people as central to the end-time narrative.

While evangelicalism was stirring in support of the Jews in the nineteenth century, the Jews elsewhere were suffering at the hands of the Orthodox Church in Russia, who incited the murder of several hundred thousand people and made two million homeless. Pogroms were normally carried out on religious high days, at Christmas Day, Good Friday, and Pentecost. On the Easter Day pogrom of 1903 Jews were killed and raped, even babies thrown from third-storey windows, to shouts of "Jesus has risen!"[268]

In the late nineteenth century mainstream English evangelicalism began not only to understand that the Jews would be re-joined with the church, but also hoped for a restoration of the Jews to the land of Palestine. The great social reformer, Lord Shaftsbury, prophesied:

> *The ancient city of the people of God is about to resume a place among the nations and England is the first of all the Gentile kingdoms that ceases to tread her down.*[269]

Shaftsbury always wore a signet ring engraved "O pray for the peace of Jerusalem". This mounting evangelical Zionism stirred political opinion and contributed to the Balfour Declaration in 1917, in which the British government promised to assist in the creation of a nation state for Jews in Palestine. Once the Ottoman empire fell, the League of Nations quickly gave Britain the so-called Palestinian Mandate, the governance of Israel to enable her to fulfil her Balfour promise.

Meanwhile, however, perfidious Britain also made contrary promises to the Arabs. Far from facilitating a Jewish homeland, she obstructed it, restricting Jewish immigration to an absurd paltry few thousand a year, while giving unrestricted permission to immigrate to Arabs and anyone else.

After World War II Churchill refused to honour the promises he had made to the Jews, while the new foreign secretary Aneurin Bevan used his considerable power to frustrate Balfour's enactment. Today Middle-Eastern politics is deeply troubled, in no small part due to Britain's double-dealing and double-speaking. Britain reaped what it sowed, and blood is on its hands, dishonour upon its head. Is it mere coincidence, mere geo-political shifts, that saw Great Britain, the greatest empire the world had known, crumble in a handful of years, leaving it broke and gloomy, even as Israel was established and the desert was breaking forth in blossom? Had not God promised Abraham's heirs: "I will bless those that bless thee and curse those that curse thee"! As the lyrics of the folk song "Where have all the flowers gone?" say: "When will they ever learn?"

The great debate

The twentieth century has seen the most enthusiastic pro-Jewish movements in church history, and yet the most anti-Semitic too. The satanic legacy of Luther's anti-Semitism was to raise its demonic head 400 years later in Adolf Hitler, who capped two millennia of anti-Semitism and rose to power courting church support. In *Mein Kampf* he wrote, "By defending myself against the Jews, I am fighting for the work of the Lord." Hitler declared in 1938:

> *In the gospels the Jews called out to Pilate when he refused to crucify Jesus 'His blood be upon us and upon our children.' Perhaps I have to fulfil this curse.*[270]

Every single edict of the Nazis against the Jews has a precedent in earlier decrees by the church. Indeed, Hitler once told Cardinal Faulhaber that he was merely doing what the church had done for 1,500 years. German Protestant church leaders eagerly embraced this.

In a statement in December 1941 they declared:

> *The National Socialist Leadership has given irrefutable documentary proof that this world war was instigated by the Jews... from the crucifixion to this day the Jews have fought against Christendom and exploited and misrepresented it for their own ends. Baptism changes nothing... Christians who are Jewish by race have no place and no rights in this church... we are determined not to tolerate any Jewish influence on German life.*[271]

Germany's foremost New Testament scholar, Gerhard Kittel, editor of the world-famous *Lexicon of New Testament Words*, oversaw a theological think-tank directed toward exorcizing anything Jewish from Christianity and presenting an Aryan Jesus. In his book *The Jewish Question* he stated "extermination would be impractical" – only in later editions adding that it would also be un-Christian. Kittel was later imprisoned for war crimes, but English theologians petitioned and had him released to complete his lexicon.[272] In the 1930s, amid the rise of anti-Semitic actions, the majority of German Christians either said or did nothing, and many wholeheartedly backed Hitler. Those noble few who did protest were among the first to share the same fate as Jews in Dachau and Sachsenhausen.

Karl Barth is regarded by many as the greatest theologian, Catholic or Protestant, since Aquinas. He has been accused of saying too little, even being anti-Semitic, and in his *Church Dogmatics* he echoed Augustine, seeing the Jews as a negative symbol of humankind's rebellion against God. However, he was also clear they remained the elect of God; their existence was proof of God, and he believed they would convert to Christ *en masse*. As early as 1939 Barth would say "Anti-Semitism is a sin against the Holy Spirit," and would personally get involved in helping thousands of Hungarian Jews escape. He wrote in 1967 to his friend, the biographer Bethge, of his deeply held regret that he didn't speak out more clearly.

Barth was an inspiration to Dietrich Bonhoeffer, who was a leader in the Confessing Church and ran a seminary for young ministers sympathetic to the Confessing Church. Bonhoeffer initially held the inherited Lutheran view that Jewish suffering was their "eternal curse" for killing Christ. However, he quickly came to see anti-Semitism as demonic. In 1935 he famously wrote, "Only he who cries out for the Jews may sing Gregorian chants." His point was that there is no point trying to worship God if you do not aid the Jews. At Kristallnacht in 1938 (which occurred on Luther's public birthday) over 100 synagogues were burnt down and another 76 destroyed; 20,000 Jews were rounded up and taken to concentration camps. Over 7,500 shops were ruined and the Nazis had the gall to charge the Jewish community an extortionate sum – 1 billion marks – for the clear-up operation. The next day, as Bonhoeffer read Psalm 74, he underlined verse 8 where it said, "They burn all of God's houses in the land"[273] and wrote in the margin the date "9.11.38". He was clear that the synagogue was God's house and the Jews were God's people.

The Holocaust was never merely an ideologically driven Nazi agenda; it was a deeply ingrained, theologically legitimated Christendom event. The Holocaust could never have happened without the preceding two millennia of forced conversions, expulsions, and annihilations, ostensibly by the church, in the name of Christ.

Post Holocaust

After this there was a modest gesture of repentance for anti-Semitism amongst a few. In 1946 at the World Council of Churches, hosted in Amsterdam, the gathered church leaders formerly confessed:

> *We call upon all churches we represent to denounce anti-Semitism, no matter what its origin, as absolutely irreconcilable with the profession and practice of the Christian Faith.*[274]

Nevertheless, even after the Holocaust, in 1948 the German Evangelical Conference could unashamedly state:

> *The Terrible Jewish suffering in the Holocaust was a divine visitation and a call to the Jews to cease their rejection and ongoing crucifixion of Christ.*[275]

So, the Nazis were not to blame for the Holocaust, the Jews were! This same logic was employed ten years previously when the Jews had to pay to clean up the mess following Kristallnacht! Not until 1980 did we hear German church statements such as that of the Synod of the Evangelical Church of Rhineland repent:

> *We confess with dismay the co-responsibility and guilt of German Christendom for the Holocaust... We believe in the permanent election of the Jewish people as the people of God and realize that through Jesus Christ, the church is taken up into the covenant of God with his people.*[276]

Amen!

In 1948 the establishment of the nation state of Israel was embraced by many Christians not simply as a humanitarian provision for the remnant post-Holocaust Jews, but also as fulfilment of Old Testament prophecies such as Amos 9:14–15, Ezekiel 37:21, and Isaiah 66:8. However, the church remains a house divided over this issue. Despite the marvel of 1948, the church has been in sharp disagreement over whether Israel's return to the land was a biblical event or just a pragmatic historical one, and some Christians even consider it an immoral one. The theological fault line runs between those who see Israel having a future destiny in the land and those who see Israel's destiny fulfilled in the coming of Christ and founding of the church. This divide transcends church tradition.

Reformed South African theologian Albertus Pieters wrote:

> *God willed that after the institution of the New Covenant there should no longer be any Jewish people in the world – yet here they are! That is a fact, a very sad fact, brought about by their wicked rebellion against God.*[277]

Conversely, and thankfully, in the 1960s Pope John XXIII greeted the welcomed Jewish delegation at Vatican II with the prophetically weighty "I am Joseph your brother". Vatican II documents stated, "On account of their fathers, this people remain most dear to God, for God does not repent of the gifts he makes nor of the call he issues." Significantly the Council also declared the Jews "guiltless" of the death of Jesus: "all Jews, then and now, may not be held accountable."[278] Even as I write this, amidst financial collapse in Greece, Orthodox Bishop Seraphim of Piraeus has spewed out old caricatures in the media about a conspiracy by élite banking Jews to enslave Greece and the Orthodox Church. And so it goes on!

So there is a stark spectrum of opinion. Some see *Israel replaced* lock, stock, and barrel by the church, the Jews having fully served their divine purpose in birthing the world Messiah. Others see an *Israel revived* and believe for an end-time conversion of Jews *en masse* (Romans 11:26), though the land is irrelevant to this. Others see *Israel returned* – a pre-millennial restoration in the land of Israel of Jews who will return to the Lord and where the Lord Jesus will return. Some hold to a Dispensational schema, *Israel ruling,* in which the church will be raptured away and Jesus will reign over a renewed end-time Davidic kingdom in Israel.

Thus a theology of Israel unites and divides. Internationally respected ministers like the Baptist David Pawson, Pentecostal Derek Prince, and Israel-based Dwight Pryor, all agree on an unfinished destiny for Israel in the land in God's plan. Yet on the opposite side are internationally respected Bible teachers and church statesmen like Terry Virgo, Tom Wright, and John Stott, who though they may concede an end-time Jewish revival according to Romans 11:26, categorically reject 1948 as a divinely ordained part of God's plan, and they reject Zionism as well.

The church is divided over Israel. Christians stand both sides of Israel's wall. Some question the right of Jews to be in the land, or their exercise of government in the land, and prefer to promote the Palestinian cause while demonizing the Israelis. Others include Christian Zionists, who believe the secular state is divinely sanctioned, and who are politically supportive of Israel's territorialism and dismissive of all Palestinian claims. Accusations of political naivety, biblical illiteracy, and spiritual blindness are hurled by both sides.

In Joshua 5:13–15, when Joshua is about to invade the land and drive out the Philistines by divine decree, a mysterious figure stands in his way. Joshua asks him, "Are you for us, or for our adversaries?" The man merely replies, "No," and then reveals that he is the angelic commander of the Lord's army. Joshua had asked the wrong question. The question is not, "Is God on our side?" but "Are we on God's side?"

In conclusion

1. Anti-Semitism has been *systemic* in the church for almost 2,000 years.

2. Anti-Semitism is *demonic* – its end has been to dehumanize the Jews and destroy them. Why is this? We will shed light on this in the next chapter.

3. Anti-Semitism is *dogmatic*: it is driven by a replacement theology – the view that God has finished with the Jews – and a desire to apportion blame, claiming that God is judging Jews for killing Jesus.

4. Anti-Semitism is *geographic* – it has always sought to dispossess Jews from having a home. Replacement theology leads to displacement.

5. Anti-Semitism is *unique* – we must ask why? What spirit is behind it? Why are the Jews targeted for such hatred, for so long and by so many?

6. Anti-Semitism is always anti-Zionist. However, anti-Zionism is not always anti-Semitic. (Many orthodox Jews are not Zionist.)

7. Anti-Semitism and anti-Zionism are fuelled by political tensions between the Jewish and Palestinian peoples, and these tensions may themselves be fuelled by anti-Semitism.

8. The church must *repent* of two millennia of anti-Semitism and search its soul for its lurking shadows, walk in the opposite spirit and bless what they once cursed.

9. The church must *renew* an understanding of its Jewish roots – Christianity is a Jewish religion. A Christian is a Jew unnaturally born.

10. The church must *reach out* to the Jews with gratitude and love and present the gospel in a culturally appropriate, historically sensitive manner.

11. The church must so celebrate its faith as fulfilment of Scripture and the prophets, and enjoyers of Messiah's goodness, that Jews look over their shoulders at us longingly, jealously.

37

Holocaust Memorial (11:26)

The Nazi death machine murdered approximately 2,000 Jehovah's Witnesses, 10–15,000 homosexuals, 250,000 physically and mentally handicapped people, 200,000 Gypsies, and several million Ukrainians and Poles. Specially targeted were the Jews – 6 million of which were killed.[279]

From the moment Hitler took power in 1933, every Jew knew that a leader had arisen who personified German cultural anti-Semitism. Immediately the Jews suffered severely, but it was not until 1942, at the infamous Wansee conference, that the so-called "Final Solution" was initiated and systemic discrimination, confiscation, and persecution turned to systematic annihilation.

Two-thirds of all European Jews – one-third of all Jews in the world – were targeted for annihilation. The were killed in the ghettos, in forests away from sight, in the streets in full view, in the fifty-two main death camps and the 1,200 SS-run satellite death camps. As well as being hidden away in occupied territories, there were over 600 camps that were part of the life and landscape in Germany and Austria.[280] The Holocaust was no secret; it was the logical conclusion to almost a decade of enacted Nazi ideology and policy. Few did not know about it, many celebrated it, and the personnel to facilitate and administrate its machinery required not simply a few battalions of military SS, but hundreds of thousands, if not several million, very ordinary German folk.

What caused the Holocaust?

What caused this unprecedented evil? There was certainly a complex matrix of causation.

German purity

In the late nineteenth century there was a significant rise in the concept of Aryan volkishness (the movement of national pride in pure Germanic identity and culture), a commitment to the purity of the German race, *Blut und Boden* (blood and soil), and a growing desire to remove what was termed the "Jewish bacillus", or germ, from German soil. This constituted a complex matrix of causation, which led to a perfect storm that would wreak havoc on the world – and especially on Germany.

German anxiety

At the rise of Jewish Bolshevism, the great threat to the German way of life was perceived as communism, and this was understood as Jewish ideology. This fear of communism was in part behind Britain's reluctance to support the independence of the Jewish state, which they worried might be communist.

There was also the added paranoia among the Germans of a conspiracy by Jewish bankers, like the notable Rothschilds, that they wanted to crush the ordinary German people and that they wanted to rule the world.

The German economy

The experience of crippling poverty in the fifteen years following World War I and the Versailles Treaty – a clause of which saw Germany being faced with a bill of $63 billion for reparations – with constant boom and bust, left Germany on the edge of economic collapse. People were starving to death in the streets of Berlin, and resentment was directed to the wealthy Jews who seemed to be prospering. The Nazis initially targeted and destroyed Jewish shops, and they later stole $230–$320 billion assets from European Jews (as estimated in 2003).

German theology

This built on 1,700 years of replacement theology and theologically justified anti-Semitism, with a German national hero in Luther, whose vile bile against the Jews was regarded by Lutherans with all the authority of papal infallibility. The infamous Kristallnacht mentioned in the previous chapter saw the authorities orchestrate a mass pogrom against the Jews in 1938, smashing German shop windows and burning down over 1,000 synagogues, and taking 30,000 Jews into forced labour camps. And all this occurred on Luther's public birthday.

German industry

We must take account of the Germans' sheer efficiency at practically implementing the ideological implications of Darwin's social evolutionary theory and Nietzsche's *Übermensch* (Superman) theory. This particular configuration of sociological, economic, political, and theological factors created the perfect storm directed against the Jews. However, we must also understand what was happening at the spiritual level, not just the natural. I have been a student of the Holocaust since my teens, and its genesis defies simple categories of sociology. A dark spirit, the darkest spirit, hovers over the Holocaust. I believe a spiritual perspective is required to understand it, and I believe this is hinted at in Romans 11.

Many students of biblical prophecy have long seen that two signs precede the return of Christ and his glorious global rule and ruin of all evil. These two signs are the return of the Jews to the land, and the return of the Jews to the Lord (Ezekiel 36:9; 37:21). Bishop J. C. Ryle, the great Victorian evangelical leader, declared:

> *I can only say, that O my eyes, the future* salvation *of Israel as a people, their* return *to Palestine, and their national* conversion *to God, appear as clearly and plainly revealed as any prophecy in God's Word.*[281]

On the opposite side of the theological fence, the Roman Catholic Church in its formal Doctrines, catechism no 674, agrees:

> *The Glorious Messiah's coming is suspended at every moment of history until his recognition by all Israel... The "full inclusion" of the Jews in the Messiah's salvation, in the wake of "the full number of the Gentiles", will enable the People of God to achieve "the measure of the stature of the fullness of Christ", in which "God may be all in all."*[282]

Now, in the late nineteenth century, after 1,700 years of exile from the land, the Zionist movement arose, with the intention of making a Jewish national home. In England in November 1917 the Balfour Declaration was a promise made by the British government which required it to assist the restoration of the Jews to the land. Just five weeks after Balfour's promise, the British defeated the Turks in Jerusalem and the Ottoman empire collapsed. Because of Britain's Balfour Promise, as we have seen, the League of Nations in 1922 gave the British the Mandate rule of Palestine, expecting them to help create a Jewish national home. To that end throughout the 1920s over 100,000 Jews returned, swelling the Jewish population from 11 per cent to 33 per cent – and fomenting the political troubles of today! The surrounding Arab Muslim nations profoundly resented what they saw as the invasion on their turf of this "other people", especially when the influx resulted, for various reasons, in a displacement of the existing residents in Palestine. Sixty-five years on, the worldwide political stage is living with the implications of these events.

One of my catchphrases over the years, popular with my students when I was a chaplain, is, "I've read the end of the book, and the Lamb wins." Just the thing to say when they felt their world was collapsing because they didn't get the degree grade, or girlfriend or boyfriend, or job they wanted, and it felt like their world was collapsing. I tried to infuse them with a sense of divine perspective!

But the devil has read the end of the book too! Bible scholar Derek Prince says that Satan is more attentive to biblical prophecy than many preachers.[283] Satan knows the Bible, he knows about the return of the Jews to the land promised to the patriarchs, and he knows that the return of the Jews to the Lord will bring the return of the Lord and the ultimate ruin of the demonic realm. Satan will do all he can to stop the prophetic clock. I believe the rise of Zionism and the Jewish groundswell of desire to finally return to the land (*Aliyah* meaning ascent), coupled with the evident possibility of such things through the British Balfour promise to repatriate the Jews, and their gaining the power to do so by the Palestinian Mandate, must have sent shockwaves through the courts of the demonic. The spirit of anti-Semitism is the spirit of Anti-Christ. He hates the Jews, not least because God loved them, but the severity of this hatred at this time was because they are one of the last pieces in the prophetic jigsaw puzzle of the return and rule of Christ.

I believe Hitler's Holocaust was a demonically inspired pre-emptive strike to destroy God's elect, to thus thwart biblical prophecy, and to make God out to be a liar; to postpone the return of Jesus and the ruin of the demonic. One classic definition of a military pre-emptive strike is "an attempt to repel or defeat a perceived offensive invasion or to gain a strategic advantage in an impending war before that threat materializes". Such was the Holocaust.

It wasn't the first time. In Exodus 1 the midwives in Egypt were commanded to kill every male child born. This would effectively destroy a nation in a generation, as having no male children to grow and reproduce brings an end to that race. The Holocaust – a conjunction of two Greek words, *holo* meaning "whole" and *kaustos* meaning "burn", thus "burnt whole" – describes fires raging and consuming Jews. I suggest even this was a demonic echo, a wicked parody of the lake of fire that one day awaits the devil and his followers. The devil understood the time and knew what he had to do.

Romans 11 clearly confirms the place of Jews in God's end-time plan.

In Roman 9 we saw Paul's *anguish* at the fact that most Jews rejected their Messiah; in Romans 10 we saw Paul's passionate *intercession* for the Jews and his *insistence* that the gospel be preached to them; here in Romans 11 we see Paul's declared *hope* and *expectation* for Israel's end-time salvation.

- Paul says God has not rejected Israel but preserved a remnant (11:1–5).
- Paul speaks of the hope for Israel's recovery (11:11).
- Paul envisages Israel's future fullness (11:12).
- Paul envisages Israel's acceptance of the gospel (11:15).
- Paul speaks of hope for Israel's re-grafting (11:23).

This turn of events, this turn of Israel to Jesus, will usher in the resurrection from the dead (11:15) – the general resurrection that is associated with the end of time and the return and reign of the Messiah Jesus.

Paul says there is a mystery that he does not want the church to be ignorant of (11:25). Sadly this mystery has remained and still remains a mystery to most Christians! The biblical term "mystery" does not refer to some hidden secret, but to divine secrets now revealed. And what is this open secret? Paul says that the hardening of the Jews to the gospel enabled the gospel to be directed to the Gentiles. Certainly that was part of the economy of Paul's mission (Acts 13:46; 18:6). However, that hardening was only partial and temporary – as Paul says, "until the fullness [the full number] of the Gentiles has come in" (11:25). The fullness of the Jews will come in (11:12) when the fullness of the Gentiles have been gathered in (11:25), and then what? "And in this way all Israel will be saved" (11:26). Do not rush quickly over these few words – on these hang the mystery and wisdom, the promises and purposes, of God.

Who will be saved?

All Israel will be saved

A few scholars, who balk at the implication of this statement for God's future plans for the Jews, have suggested it is an editorial interpolation or gloss not authentic to Paul's letter. Some significant scholars from Augustine to N. T. Wright have understood "saved Israel" here as referring to the total elect of God, both Jew and Gentile. Such an interpretation stems from a wider *a priori* theology in which Christ and the church have now fulfilled or even replaced the place of Israel in God's economy.

But if "all Israel" actually means "all the elect", the true church, then Paul would be offering a nonsensical tautology, in effect saying: "When all the Gentiles are in the kingdom, then all the church is saved." Where is the mystery here, of which some are supposedly ignorant? Who in the church has ever doubted that the church will be saved?

Fortunately, general consensus among today's scholars across the traditions is firmly that Paul is referring to his belief in an end-time conversion to Christ of all ethnic Israel, the Jews.

"Israel" means Israel; "the church" means the church; "Israel" has never meant the church. Of the seventy-two times Israel is mentioned in the New Testament, only once, in Galatians 6:16, does Israel possibly refer to the wider community of the people of God beyond the generic racial Israel. Surely Paul puts the matter beyond doubt in quoting Isaiah 59 and the hope for a removal of Jacob's sins so that all Israel will be saved. The "all Israel saved" of verse 26a is the ungodly Jacob of verse 26b whose sins are removed. Jacob was renamed Israel by God – Jacob has never been the church! The American Great Awakening father, Jonathan Edwards, stated: "Nothing is more certainly foretold than this national conversion of the Jews is, in the eleventh chapter of Romans."[284]

When will they be saved?

"... a partial hardening has come upon Israel, until the fullness of the Gentiles has come in. And in this way [*or* then] so all Israel will be saved" (11:25–26).

Professor Cranfield rightly says that the fullness of the Gentiles "is probably to be explained as meaning the full number of the elect from among the Gentiles".[285]

Ethnic, Jewish, Israel will be saved consecutively and consequentially to the fullness of the Gentiles coming in – it happens afterwards, and it happens as a result. Only after the Gentiles are in the kingdom, grafted into Israel's olive tree – following and flowing from that – will the temporary hardening of Israel come to an end, and all Israel will be saved.

This scandal of particularity offends the minds of many, posing a problem for those who lean towards human autonomy and who reject the Reformed doctrines of the sovereignty of God in election and salvation. Once we manage to accept that God is God, and that God can save who he wants, how he wants, setting all the terms, then the scandal of particularity is resolved.

Who will save them?

"The Deliverer will come from Zion" (11:26). Some suggest that Israel will be saved according to their historic election or covenants, or their adherence to the Torah or their Abrahamic DNA. Not so. To be saved through the means and mechanism of anything other than faith in the finished work of Christ would be to nullify the whole of Paul's argument in Romans 1–5 and 10. Jews will be saved by the gospel; by faith in Jesus' blood, not by sharing Abraham's blood. They are saved by faith *like* Abraham's, not faith *in* Abraham.

All Jews, like all Gentiles, stand condemned in their sin and need a deliverance from the judgment on sin by a deliverer, a Saviour. Romans 1:17 states that salvation is by faith, Romans 10:9 states that faith must be placed in Jesus. Paul cites Isaiah's hope of just such a deliverer from Zion who will turn away Jacob's godlessness and remove her sins. This refers to Jesus not Judaism. This fulfils the longing of the psalmist who twice prays, "Oh, that salvation for Israel would come out of Zion! When God restores the fortunes of his people, let Jacob rejoice, let Israel be glad" (Psalm 14:7; 53:6). God's chosen people – Jacob, become Israel – will be saved by accepting Jesus as Messiah, as deliverer, through their embrace of the gospel by faith, and their entering the community of the kingdom of God.

Why will they be saved?

Because God is God.

Israel will be saved because God makes covenants and keeps them (verse 27); Israel will be saved because God loves them on account of the faith of their fathers (verse 28); Israel will be saved because the gifts of God and the calling of God are "irrevocable" (verse 29 where *ametameleta* means "not repented of, not changed one's mind over, not taken back"); Israel will be saved because of God's great mercy (verse 31) – note the threefold repetition in verses 30–31 of the word "mercy". Certainly salvation is not merited by Israel's faithfulness, holiness, or worthiness. By no means. Their whole existence, perseverance, and salvation are based exclusively on God's grace and God's commitment to honour his word and his name.

Romans 8 ends promising that nothing can separate us from the love of God. Romans 12 starts, "in view of God's mercy" (NIV). These two themes of inseparable love and fathomless mercy underpin the whole of Romans 9–11 and are the presupposition to all God's dealings with Israel.

How are we to respond?

If you are a Jew, let me encourage you to embrace your Messiah while forgiving the great failure of the church.

For Christians, the response must be:

Confession

The Jews have long and deeply scarred memories. They do not pass lightly over two millennia of persecution at the hands of Christians. Christians must privately and publically repent of the atrocities committed by the church in the name of Christ. We must ask God's forgiveness and we must ask the Jews' forgiveness. I am personally moved by the example of German Christian Dr Basilea Schlink's community who, for a year after World War II ended, stood in silence at breakfast, repenting of the Nazi crimes and blessing Israel.

Intercession

We must pray for the peace of Jerusalem, for mission to Jews and Gentiles, for the scales to fall again from the eyes of more Sauls to become Pauls. In the movie based on Tolkien's book, *The Two Towers*, Gandalf says at a time of great need, "At dawn look to the East." We are at a time when we need to watch and pray over political events in the Middle East, and lift up our heads, for our redemption draws nigh.

Provocation

For the kindest of reasons, we are to make Israel jealous (Romans 11:14). We want them to see the blessing of their Messiah Jesus on our lives, so that they are provoked to consider again the one long rejected.

Bible teacher John Hosier writes, "If we have a concern for the Jews, the best way to reach them is to build a glorious church to provoke them to envy and to hasten the coming of the full number of Gentiles."[286]

Benediction

Israel is the root that supports the branches of the church (Romans 11:18) and so we who have received spiritual blessings owe the Jews at least thank offerings of material blessings. Paul clearly encourages the church towards an attitude of gratitude rather than pride (11:25), being in debt to the Jews, because through them we received Christ.

Mission

A twofold gospel outreach – to the Jew first and to the Gentile. No other text beside the Great Commission has so inspired the history of missions than this promise here in Romans 11:25–26. Mission which hastens the return of the Lord, seeking to bring into God's fold the fullness of the elect Gentiles, which will bring all Israel in, which will bring about the general resurrection from the dead (11:15) accompanying the return of the Lord.

The gospel is for the Jews first and last. They were the first to be offered it and will be the last. The gospel and the return of the Jews form the *inclusio*, bracketing God's economy in church history. This future hope must not preclude us from witnessing to the Jewish peoples here and now. For some well-meaning but theologically ill-informed church ministries, it sadly has. This would make Paul sick to his stomach. If we love the Jews, we must seek to share the Messiah with them. Douglas Moo rightly says, "It is the refusal to preach the gospel to the Jews that is anti-Semitic."[287]

In conclusion

In Genesis 50:20 Joseph said to his brothers who'd sold him into slavery: "you meant evil against me, but God meant it for good". The Holocaust did the severest harm to the Jews of Europe, unwittingly motivated by a demonic host who understood the times and attempted to stop the prophetic clock ticking towards Jesus' return and reign and their ruin.

But what the Nazis intended for harm, incited by the demonic,

God worked for good. Following the Holocaust, for a brief window in history, there was a general global compassion for the Jews. The nations understood and supported their need for a homeland, the obvious exception being some Muslim nations who regarded the establishment of Israel as theft of Muslim-claimed territory and a displacement of Muslim peoples.

The Holocaust – that which the enemy meant for harm – God turned for good, and a new exodus brought the Jews home to their ancient land, promised to their forefathers four millennia previously. Named Palestine by the Romans, a corruption of the term Philistine and an attempt to exorcize all memory of the Jews from the land, it was renamed Israel in 1948, a nation born in a day, setting the stage for the Lord's return. Satan's pre-emptive strike had backfired, and would ultimately set the timer for his own destruction.

38

Living Sacrifices in a Lust-Soaked Society (12:1)

Having taught at some length on the place of the Jews in the economy and future history of God, Paul returns to more everyday issues. Dogmatics leads to ethics. A new life in Christ has a new lifestyle. Christianity is a lived out religion. It is not mystical, esoteric, and otherworldly; it is concretely walked out in society. Paul encourages the church to "present your bodies as a living sacrifice, holy and acceptable to God, which is your spiritual worship" (12:1).

Everything we do is an act of worship. The issue is not how, but who. Worship is not simply singing songs; it may include that but it is far more. Worship is, in fact, a life poured out in holiness and obedience, alms-giving and mission, sharing the gospel with the lost, sharing our bread with the hungry, sharing our lives with one another. I believe God receives glory by the very birth of an infant, by bees making honey, by husband and wife making love, when the painter paints, when the singer sings, when the architect designs, the teacher teaches, the athlete competes. Worship in song is just one part, a significant but small part, of glorifying God in worship. A life lived to God, by obedience and faithfulness to his will and word, is worship; a life lived resisting sin and temptation is worship; a life lived honouring God by honouring others, by honouring our bodies – all this is worship.

One of the underlying illustrations Paul employs throughout Romans to illustrate wrong worship, a life wrongly lived, is that of sinful sexual activity. In Romans 1:26–28 Paul specifically highlights homosexual and lesbian sex acts as archetypal sins; in 6:19 he speaks of the Christians' former sexual immorality as presenting their bodily parts "as slaves to impurity", whereas now they are called to present their members as slaves to righteousness leading to sanctification. In 13:9 he highlights the sin of adultery and in 13:13 he instructs the church members not to participate in "orgies and... immorality and sensuality". Would this latter list need stating and prohibiting if such things were not potential issues for these Christians living in the midst of a culture notorious for her obsessive sexual proclivities?

The Romans 1 citation is particularly significant because it equates sexual immorality with spiritual idolatry – and throughout Scripture we see immorality always accompanies idolatry. How we live, how we act, what we do with our bodies is an act of worship. Someone or something is honoured in all we do. When we live a life of holiness, of moral purity, our bodies set apart for God, we become a living sacrifice to God, walking worship. When our bodies are given over to fleshly, sexual indulgences outside of the parameters Scripture sets for sex – heterosexual monogamous marriage – then they become a living sacrifice to self, to the flesh, to the spirit of the age.

Paul's robust rebuke of certain sexual practices has, in many parts of the church, mistakenly resulted in a prudish, puritanical perspective on sex that considers it as something distasteful at best and seriously sinful at worst. This was certainly not Paul's or any of the biblical writers' intention. They knew well that sex is a divine creation and as such a good and godly thing. But the world, the flesh, and the devil have often sullied and muddied it. And it is crucial that the church reclaim and re-present a godly perspective on it – celebrating and safeguarding it in its right context. I want to apply Paul's instruction to present our bodies as "living sacrifices, holy and pleasing to God" to the whole area of sexual purity and to our worship of God by being living a sexually pure life.

I grew up in a devout Christian context where the word "sex" was never even mentioned. If anything saucy came on the TV, my dad would quickly turn it off. No sex, please, we're British. I remember being told the facts of life by my dad when I was about ten, and I thought the man had gone mad. I learned about the female form from peeping at an encyclopedia in the school library when I should have been swotting up on Latin vocab!

The taboo at home on the topic of sex did not stop nature's course, and my teenage years were spent trying unsuccessfully to match my experience to my appetite. How different the society is that my teenage sons are growing up in. Culture evangelizes them with the erotic. Movies, magazines, TV adverts, billboards, comedians... all these and many more bombard them with words and images to rob them of their innocence. The hosts of hell wait in cyber space, just seconds away from connection to the internet. Twentieth-century satirist and playboy-turned-devout-Catholic, Malcolm Muggeridge, once said that in modern society, "The orgasm has replaced the cross as the focus of longing and the image of fulfilment."[288]

What do we need to know, so that we may present our bodies as living sacrifices to God – holy and pleasing?

In the beginning...

... God created sex. It may come as a surprise, but sex was an idea from God, not from the French. It was God who said it is not good for man to be alone (Genesis 2:18), and he didn't mean just someone to talk gardening with. The first mandate to humankind Scripture records is "go forth and multiply" – sex between married couples is the first command. God created Adam and Eve with genitals made perfectly for each other. God's commentary on the purpose of Adam and Eve was highly sexual: the two "shall become one flesh" (Genesis 2:24).

Dr Don Norman once performed a wedding ceremony and got his words mixed up. Instead of saying, "You are now lawfully joined," he said, "You are now joyfully loined." That was good liturgy, every bit as true and scriptural and appropriate to describe God's purposes in marriage. Joyfully loined. Sexual intimacy was given not simply for procreation but for recreation. If sex was simply about producing children, why would the sex drive be so constant, the act so pleasurable, and yet the moment of potential female fertility in her cycle so infrequent? Clearly God intended there to be many occasions of non-reproductive enjoyment.

In the Song of Songs we have a celebration of sexual union and intimacy. It does not refer once to procreation. Paul said a man should marry if he felt he was acting improperly towards a virgin – meaning, get married and fulfil your desires and have sex in its rightful place. Paul saw sex as the fulfilment of desire and not just for procreating (1 Corinthians 7:36). Paul says,

> *The husband should give to his wife her conjugal rights, and likewise the wife to her husband. For the wife does not have authority over her own body, but the husband does. Likewise the husband does not have authority over his own body, but the wife does. Do not deprive one another.*
>
> 1 CORINTHIANS 7:3–5

Paul is clear that sexual satisfaction is a right of marriage.

Joyce Huggett wrote wisely:

> *The ability to be fascinated by the curves and personality of the opposite sex was also built in by God way back in Genesis 1:27–28. And the ability to feel drawn to a magnet was dreamed up by God, created by him. Sexual magnetism was dreamed up and created by God. Sexual excitation, like the sex drive, was God's idea. Hormones and erections, tender breasts and ejaculations and the stomach somersaulting with desire, were God's brain-children.*[289]

That's not pro-creation, but recreation – the pursuit and finding of pleasure in the other.

What went wrong?

Sadly the church long ago undermined sex, declaring unclean that which God made clean. How did this come about? Let me suggest two reasons:

Unattainable role models

The master whom we follow is Jesus who remained celibate. The supreme disciple is our Lord's mother, Mary – who conceived as a virgin. Indeed, the church invented the heterodoxy of Mary's "perpetual virginity" – despite the Bible telling us Jesus had siblings. It is easy to see how, if our Lord and his mother did not practise sex, we ought to imitate them by being celibate. If the greatest role models for the Christian life were themselves perceived as celibate, then those who did not choose this lifestyle could perceive themselves, or be perceived, as being somehow less spiritual, less consecrated to the Lord.

Dodgy theologians

In the early church, a damaging trend of thought that was particularly influential in Gnosticism (the second-century heretical movement) was Greek dualism. This conceived of the world as inseparably divided into the spiritual and material, elevating the spiritual towards the divine, while regarding the material as fallen and sinful and distant from God. If the divine is only encountered in the spiritual, and if matter is fallen and sinful, it followed that the most basic desires of the flesh for sex were somehow alien to spirituality and divinity. What was regarded as base or unspiritual soon led to the notion that "sex is dirty".

Paul stated that sex in the marriage context is a holy thing (1 Corinthians 7:14); and that "women will be saved through childbearing" (1 Timothy 2:15) – women are saved not simply as virgins but as sexually active, child-bearing wives who are able to express their womanhood in motherhood. But sadly it has not been the Bible's affirmation of sex and sexuality that has influenced the centuries; Augustine of Hippo's influence has dominated Western theology instead. He had his own not insignificant issues with sex and lust, and actually delayed becoming a Christian because he wanted to "sow his wild oats" – which he duly did, before settling into a long-term affair. In his autobiography *Confessions,* he speaks harshly about his own sexual passions, and clearly believed that all sexual activity was the triumph of the will of the flesh over the spirit. He believed "original sin" and the effects of the Fall were transmitted through lust in the sex act, and ultimately his views led to sex being associated with something inherently "evil".

Augustine was not alone with such notions. The church father Ambrose of Milan equated married union with sin and shame, and stated that "married people ought to blush at the state in which they are living". Origen, according to the ancient church historian Eusebius, cut off his manhood rather than burn with lust and temptation, only to find being memberless did nothing to dampen his desire. Medieval texts on Christian practical living exhort the faithful to abstain from sex on saints' days, holy days, feast days, before receiving Communion, and so on. The message was loud and clear – God and sex don't mix: the truly spiritual (those in religious orders) are celibate, while the spiritually devout laity abstain from sex on religious days.

During the Reformation, Martin Luther, a former celibate Augustinian monk, characteristically wanting to smash all false religion, married a nun and consummated their union before all his gathered friends (behind a veiled bed) to demonstrate that he had sex... presumably so that none could suggest the nun was just a housekeeper.

2. Husband and wife

God gave the gift of sex to be enjoyed within heterosexual, faithful marriage.

The command to "go forth and multiply" can only be understood in the context of the exclusivity and permanence of the two having "become one flesh". Adam "knew" Eve and no one else, and she likewise.

The provocative author Rob Bell rightly identifies how many men boast about their many sexual experiences, thinking it impressive, when in reality it is really a sign of weakness:

> *committing to a woman for life is going to demand courage, fidelity, and strength... many men don't have what it takes... Sleeping with lots of women gives them the feeling of being a man without actually having to be one.*[290]

I once read a secular sex psychologist who claimed that evidence showed faithfully committed couples who have been together fifteen years or more have the best sex. Sex was never divinely designed to be about a quick superficial "getting laid", but the crowning of a "life laid down for the other". Good sex expresses intimacy – intimacy demands time, not technique.

Another survey I read (incidentally, I don't spend all my time reading sex surveys) showed that, if you take the frequency of the female orgasm as the criterion, then Christian married couples have the best sex![291]

I recall, when I was a university chaplain, a former student telling me that he worked in an ice-cream parlour in his holidays. His young colleagues were always discussing sex. When he shared that he was a Christian with a different ethic, they mocked him for not having sex, giving him the nickname "Virgin". One day, one of them made the acute observation: "It's funny, we are all having sex but our parents are not; you aren't, but your parents [both vicars] still are."

One of the best things I heard about sex came from an elderly couple. She was in her seventies, he in his early eighties. They prepared me for marriage. They said, "We have sex less often than when we were young, but we are better at it."

In creation God mandates sexual relations between male and female in a permanent, monogamous, heterosexual union. Karl Barth stated rightly, "Coitus without co-existence (covenant) is demonic."[292] Society may embrace various forms of sex as being normal or natural or acceptable or legal, but Christians determine their moral frame of reference from God, in his Word. Scripture and not culture sets the moral agenda for us.

Today people think sex is their "right", but the Bible says only sex in marriage between male and female is right! The Colorado Statement on Sexuality – an evangelical benchmark, produced by Focus on the Family – states: "Sex is not entitlement, nor is it needed for personal wholeness or emotional maturity."[293]

Jesus was not sexually active and he was not androgynous or asexual, yet he was the most whole and complete human that ever graced this earth. Sexual intimacy is not the pre-requisite to fulfilled humanity. His full human sexuality was directed not towards release through coitus, but through deep connections in loving and giving and receiving relationships with both men and women.

The Bible does not shy away from the nitty-gritty of sex. In fact the Bible was where I first learned about the variety of sexual practices: bestiality; incest; prostitution; rape; homosexual acts... they are all in there. The Bible presents these as being detestable to

God and prohibited among the people of God; because of such things the Canaanites were vomited out of the land. Israel, God's own, were to be different, separate, holy; and that meant not participating in any such deviant sexual activity.

Judeo-Christianity is unique in its presentation of sexual ethics. First, unlike pagan idols, Yahweh is never presented as sexual – most pagan gods take gender and have sexual cohorts. Secondly, Judeo-Christianity does not sexualize religion: there are no temple prostitutes, no religious orgies, and sex is not seen as a step to the spiritual. Thirdly, Judeo-Christianity is unusual in prohibiting homosexuality, which was widely accepted and practised in ancient religions.

The New Testament prohibits *porneia* (from which we get our term "porn"). This was a generic term in Greek, and is often translated as "fornication" or "sexual immorality". In its biblical use it applies to any and all sexual practice outside marriage.

Jesus did not simply prohibit the acts, but wanted us to be pure in heart, so he elevated his Sermon on the Mount prohibition above the Mosaic Law to include lust – the lust of the eyes and the thoughts of the mind, and not just the act itself. Sex between husband and wife is part of God's creation and is glorious.

But sex is so powerful that it must be harnessed within the nurturing, loving, covenantally committed parameters of marriage.

Safe sex is not sex with a condom – it is sex within a marriage. Sex outside of marriage is like driving a train at full speed without tracks – it's just a matter of time before there's a crash! When promiscuity prevails, where sex is pursued outside of loving covenant relations, then sooner or later people are treated as objects for consumption: pornography and prostitution in all their forms lead to sexual brokenness, both for those exploited and degraded and for those consuming and addicted.

Unrestrained, uncovenanted sex inevitably tears at the social fabric, resulting in unwanted pregnancies, a proliferation of single-parent families, abortions on demand, sexually transmitted diseases, and the psychological and social problems that ensue – not to mention an erosion of the stable building blocks of society, being a burden on the taxpayer, and divine judgment on sin.

Ironically, the pursuit of pleasure in uncovenanted, unbridled sex pushes further away the very satisfaction people are looking for. God ordained the sexual act as a means for a person to become one flesh with another, whole and complete. But where there are multiple partners, I am not becoming whole, I am being joined then torn apart repeatedly – shredded in pieces. Here we need to heed Sigmund Freud, the father of psychoanalysis:

> *when sexual freedom is without obstacle and unrestrained, love becomes worthless and life empty.*[294]

Uncovenanted sex verges on blasphemy, for the union of male and female in marriage mysteriously reflects something of God's own being, male and female being made in his image (Genesis 1:27). Permanent union with distinction. When we have homosexual or repeated sexual relations outside covenant, we violate our vocation to reflect the very unity and diversity of the Three-in-One God, and in its place we create an analogous idol.

3. Christ mends what is broken

Sexuality and desire for sexual intimacy are core to our humanity. But because we are touched by the Fall and sin, most of us continue to wrestle and struggle with sexual purity. Some years ago I asked my quite elderly mentor, then aged sixty-five, "When does the battle with lust end?" He told me that, when he was younger, an old saint in his eighties came to see him about a personal matter and confessed to real struggles with lust. In his eighties! That illustration was my mentor's way of saying that, for some men, the struggle with the flesh never ceases, whether teenage, middle-age or old-age.

Many of the saints in Scripture did not end well because they allowed their sexual appetite to conquer them: Samson and Delilah; David and Bathsheba; Solomon and his thousand wives and concubines, many of whom were pagan worshippers who turned his heart away from the Lord. How many today have drifted away or simply turned their back on the Lord for the sake of sex!

We sadly hear of too many Christian leaders who were running a good race but fell before the finishing line through sexual immorality, adultery, or pornography. We sadly hear of Christian singles who date and marry partners outside the faith and who then soon leave the faith.

I have been a minister long enough to know that there is a great deal of sexual brokenness in the church – frustrations, temptations, addictions, secret sins, scars from abuse. All can be forgiven, healed, restored – Christ's love covers a multitude of sins, his blood cleanses, his name delivers, his Spirit renews, his grace transforms. Samson who fell with Delilah was given another crack at the Philistines that became his greatest victory; David was restored and laid the plans for the temple. Jesus did not condemn the woman caught in adultery, though he told her to leave her sin behind. Jesus did not reject the repeatedly divorced woman at the well but talked theology and offered her eternal life and eternal satisfaction. Jesus told of the "prodigal son" who went a-whoring but was welcome back in the Father's arms without dishonour. Paul speaks about the transformation that Christ can work in us, precisely in the area of our sex and sexuality: "sexually immoral... idolaters ... adulterers... men who practise homosexuality... such *were* some of you. But you were washed, you were sanctified, you were justified in the name of the Lord Jesus Christ and by the Spirit of our God" (1 Corinthians 6:9, 11 italics mine).

Christ's love and mercy can heal all past hurts and remove all sin's scars. I once heard of a woman who was abused as a child and became highly promiscuous and a prostitute. She was saved and finally fell in love, and was married, and testified that God worked such a miracle, wiping away the past, that it was as if she was a virgin all over again. I have a friend who was part of the gay scene, who met Jesus, was saved, delivered, healed, spent a few years working through the what and why of sexual orientation – and gradually he began to find women attractive. I will always remember him telling me with growing surprise and delight how he had started to fancy a woman for the first time. He is now happily married with children.

We held a conference in my church on relationships where a remarkable message was given. I will never forget two men who came for prayer with fear, guilt, and shame issues related to sex and relationships that had rendered them incapable of forming and sustaining a healthy relationship with the opposite sex. The Spirit powerfully impacted them: they both wept and wept and soaked my sweater with their tears. And both were married within the year!

In conclusion

We live in bodies charged with sexual desire and in a permissive society where we are evangelized by the erotic, stimulated, and tempted with numerous opportunities to fulfil the cravings of the flesh. But Paul says, "present your bodies as a living sacrifice, holy and acceptable to God" (Romans 12:1). We are to resist temptation, to walk in the Spirit, to subdue the fleshly appetites.

This is a very real sacrifice. But when we offer our bodies – our physical members – to God rather than to sin, then it is a holy thing, truly pleasing to God. And it is really possible. In order to do this, we need to no longer be conformed to the culture of this world, but be transformed by the renewing of our mind. And this we shall address in our next chapter.

39

Boiled Frog or Frog Prince? (12:2)

There are over 5,000 different types of frogs. There are flying frogs with webbed feet and hands that float over 15 metres down from trees. There are poisonous frogs with enough toxin to kill twenty men or 10,000 mice. There are medicine frogs that secrete a painkiller with 200 times the potency of morphine. There is a frog that secretes a chemical used as an appetite suppressant for dieters. The largest frog is called the bullfrog and can grow up to 3.5 feet long – the size of a lamb! In January 2012, in Papua New Guinea, they discovered the world's smallest frog – 7.7 mm long, about the size of your small fingernail.

Emperor Julian, the last pagan Roman ruler, once described the church as "a council of frogs in a marsh". In this study, I want to consider: if you were a frog, what sort of frog would you be? Paul in Romans 12:2 says, "Do not be conformed to this world, but be transformed by the renewing of your mind." This suggests two types of Christian frogs: we might call them "slow-boiled frog" Christians or "frog prince" Christians. It is an either/or – one cannot be both. Either you are a slow-boiled frog, conforming to this world, or a royally kissed frog prince, being transformed.

Slow-boiled-frog Christian

"Do not be conformed to this world..." (12:2).

It has been claimed that, if you put a frog in a pan of cold water and heat it up very slowly, the frog, if not distracted, won't jump out but will stay in the water, acclimatizing to its environment, and eventually cook to death. Some suggest this is an urban myth, but in the late nineteenth century Dr Heinzmann and Dr Fratscher separately demonstrated it as fact. In both cases the water was heated very slowly, by 0.2 degrees a minute.[295] The slow boiling of a frog has become an established metaphor for those who are slowly conformed to their culture and context. It was used during the Cold War of the creeping influence of communist ideology, and most recently it has been used by Al Gore and Prince Charles of the West's complacency towards the impending ecological crisis. It is the inadvertent or ignorant adapting to one's culture that eventually proves fatal.

That is the principle that Paul is addressing here. He says, "Do not be conformed to this world" (the Greek is *aeon*, an age or period of history). The word translated conformed is *suschematidzo*, a conjunction of two words, *su* meaning "with" and *schema* meaning "scheme" or "pattern". The J. B. Phillips translation gets the right sense of it: "Don't let the world around you squeeze you into its own mould." Do not partner with the schemes and systems of your age.

Paul does not mince his words. This is a robust command, not an option or choice. And Paul would have no need to give this imperative if it was not required. The Christians in Rome in the first century, just like Christians almost anywhere in the twenty-first century, were in real danger of conforming to the spirit of their age, becoming shaped by their culture. We are often as much a product of our culture as we are of our nature. We are often as influenced by media and marketing and our milieu as we are our DNA. Fashions change, but the "spirit of the age", the spirit of this world generally, wears the same guise, one that is almost always antithetical to the kingdom of God.

Richard Foster has shown how the controlling principalities and powers of the age, whether in Rome then or where you are today, are the spirits that promote the worship of money, sex, and power.[296] John identified this when he wrote:

> *Do not love the world or the things in the world. If anyone loves the world, the love of the Father is not in him. For all that is in the world – the desires of the flesh and the desires of the eyes and pride in possessions – is not from the Father but is from the world.*
>
> 1 JOHN 2:15–16

Do not be conformed to this world; do not accommodate to its values; do not be conned by its sales pitch; do not be ship-wrecked by its alluring sirens. The followers of Jesus are not to conform to the spirit of their culture. They are to be seen to be different. Their new life in Christ brings a new lifestyle – a changed value system, a different way to interact. We are to be like Bunyan's Pilgrim who leaves his home for the journey of faith, and who when others call him back puts his fingers in his ears and shouts, "Life, life, eternal life!" The way of the world – that way leads to death.

The follower of Jesus, far from conforming to this world, should stand up and be counted and stand out and be noticed. Professor David Wells writes, "Worldliness is what makes sin look normal in any age and righteousness seem odd."[297] The Christian should should seem odd, counter-cultural, distinctive – not because we are Luddites or like the Amish, wearing plain clothes or talking with Elizabethan King James language, or having weird, forced, cheesy grins... but because we are holy, and holiness is radical, counter-cultural. Our speech, actions, reactions, demeanour, should mark us out – people should know we are Christians not by our fish badge but by our love, by our lifestyle. We are servants of the Lord, divine emissaries, heaven's citizens. Peter tells us we are foreigners in this world, strangers, pilgrims, just passing through; hopefully making it a better place for having been here, shedding abroad the fragrance of Christ. John Piper, drawing on this image rightly says: "Aliens get their cue from God and not the world."[298]

No one should ever be surprised when you tell them you are a Christian. They should see it coming! We should spread abroad the fragrance of Christ. When a Christian is in the room, people should know something is different. To some we are the smell of death, to others eternal life (2 Corinthians 2:15–16).

Some missapply Paul's words here as meaning do not be involved in the world, that a Pharisaical withdrawal from it into a religious clique is necessary, or some sort of monastic cloister. This is not at all what Paul means. You gotta be in it to win it. The leaven, the yeast, needs to be in the dough to do its work. Jesus' model of holiness was never to retreat but to advance. Christ's holiness was not about avoiding contamination but being contagious. Jesus was the enemy of sin but the friend of sinners.

Being in the world and not of the world is difficult, and without reliance on God, on his Word, on life in the Spirit, we succumb to the world. Victorian Bishop J. C. Ryle once said that we are always trying to make religion "pleasant" by sawing off the corners and edges of the cross – we do not want the discomfort of carrying the cross and following Christ.[299]

The history of Israel in the Old Testament is one of constant drift, succumbing to the prevailing culture around it. Repeatedly Israel was warned not to intermarry with the pagans – because, sadly, Israel would invariably accommodate to the pagan nation's ethics, and accept pagan idols, and be unfaithful to Yahweh. Called to be radical, distinct, a city set on a hill, they forgot themselves – they repeatedly forgot their calling and merged like chameleons into their surrounding culture.

Sadly, many Christians can be like Tolkien's Ents in *The Lord of the Rings*, who instead of shepherding the forest and protecting it from Orcs fell asleep and became like the inanimate trees they were called to tend. As mentioned in Chapter 27, social statistician George Barna surveyed values and lifestyles of the evangelical church in the USA and concluded that there was little difference in life and lifestyle – in values, in use of time, money, and aspirations – between evangelical Christians and non-Christians. Evangelical Christians tended to watch the same programmes, got divorced, or entered adulterous affairs, at the same rate as their non-Christian counterparts.[300]

Paul's command about not being conformed to the world is a verb in the passive mood – *me suschematidzesthe*. Often conforming to the world's spirit and standards is not a matter of intention or wilful sin; it's not that we defiantly rebel against God and his laws; rather, slowly, little by little, incrementally, we succumb to the spirit of the age.

The temperature of boiling water kills the frog if it rises very slowly so as not to alarm the creature. And, like that proverbial frog, we are desensitized slowly, slowly, and gradually conformed. What sins, practices, habits, mindsets, do you now hold which you would not dreamed of twenty years ago, and which would make your grandparents blush in shame (Christian or not)?

A friend told me recently about his pastor in the USA who had held a fruitful ministry for many years among students, but had suddenly blown apart and dropped out with prostitutes and drugs. My friend was incredulous – how could this happen? How could a man of such strong calling, gifting, and fruitfulness end up in this mess? My answer was this: "Incrementally."

You do not abandon God for the world in one step. But every little act of sin makes a bigger one more manageable. It's why Jesus went straight to the root and not the branch when he condemned "lust" and not just adultery, "anger" and not just murder. Our permission of an apparently minor sin is the thin edge of a wedge.

Kissed–frog–prince Christian

"... but be transformed by the renewal of your mind" (12:2).

You will know the fairy story of the frog who was kissed by a princess and turned into a prince. I believe this is a powerful metaphor for what occurs through Christ by his Spirit. Betrayed with a kiss, Jesus kisses a guilty world in love, and that kiss transforms an ugly troll frog into a heavenly prince and princess.

The word "be transformed" is the Greek term *metamorphousthe* which gives us our word "metamorphosis", which literally means a change of form or being. It is the word we use for the biological process in which a pupa is beautified into a butterfly. The great hope here is that change is not simply desirable, but truly attainable. As a caterpillar is meant to become a butterfly, so Christians by their new nature are designed to become like Christ. If a caterpillar does not become a butterfly, it was either sick or eaten!

This metamorphosis is referred to in only two other places in the New Testament: first, when Jesus was on mountain and was "transfigured" before the disciples and blazed dazzling white with the eternal glory he had had with his Father in heaven. And secondly, Paul employs the term again in 2 Corinthians 3:18, where he speaks of us all as "with unveiled face, beholding the glory of the Lord... being transformed into the same image from one degree of glory to another." The Greek Orthodox speak of something termed "theosis"; the Roman Catholic tradition calls it the beatific vision, in which someone, having set themselves apart for God and cast aside sin, take on the attributes of Christ as they consistently meditate on him.

At one of our baptism services I saw clear evidence of this kiss of life, this total transformation from bog frog to prince. Two ex-prisoners – one a lifer, the other a drug dealer – testified to the revolution in their life through Jesus. A lifetime of crime, with all its scars inside and out, washed away in the waters of grace. At the same baptism we heard testimony from a former cynical, church-despising, atheistic Oxford scholar who had been humbled by the love of God. The gospel really does work.

Deep in the human soul is a profound longing for transformation – our souls have a thirst for God. We know we are grubby caterpillars made to fly. But sin interfered and frustrated God's design and so all too many die in the cocoon of this world without ever becoming what God intended them to be. Many long for transformation in society, economy, government, the environment, as well as at a more personal, existential level. Some think that, if only they could change their own situation or circumstance, their career, home, partner, garden, body shape, hair, education, they would realize their innate desire. Such superficial changes never deliver.

C. S. Lewis, in his *The Great Divorce*, depicts a shadowy, oily ghost with a red lizard of lust on his shoulder. The lizard keeps annoyingly flicking its tail at the ghost and whispering wicked things in his ears. The ghost keeps telling the lizard to shut up, but it refuses. Then an angel of fire approaches and asks: "Do you want me to keep him quiet?" and, as the blazing angel comes nearer, the ghostly figure protests that he's burning with the heat. The fiery angel offers to kill the annoying lizard, but the ghost draws back alarmed: "You didn't say anything about killing him..."[301] The lizard may oppress the shadowy figure, but he has grown used to it, and become almost symbiotic with it. So he does not really want to be free of it – and he certainly does not want God's fire to burn him.

Some prefer the devil they know to the God they don't.

In Exodus Pharaoh is cursed with a plague of frogs. He asks Moses to remove them in exchange for releasing the Israelites from slavery. Moses asks, "When?" Pharaoh procrastinates. "Tomorrow." Tomorrow? Really? Pharaoh would rather have one more night with the frogs than freedom, one more night annoyed by sin's curse rather than submit to God as Lord? Many are so accustomed to living with the frogs, living like frogs, that they are reluctant to be transformed into princes or princesses by the kiss of God. Rather than be delivered, we choose one more night with the frogs, like a frog.

How are we transformed?

First, Paul says that we are transformed "by the renewal of your mind, that by testing you may discern what is the will of God, what is good and acceptable and perfect" (12:2).

Righteous living requires right thinking. Our minds are often formatted to sin and need reformatting. Transformed thinking leads to transformed living. Paul uses the Greek word *dokimazo* here, which was used for testing or proving the purity of gold: the transformed mind can prove and approve God's perfect will for a holy life. Earlier in Romans 1 Paul argued that sin begins in a corrupted and depraved mind. Sanctification and transformation must, therefore, be a matter of the mind as well as the will and the flesh. Martin Luther King understood that "as long as the mind is enslaved, the body can never be free"[302] – transformation of our bodies, fleshly appetites, sinful desires, comes through regeneration of the mind, a re-orientation along the lines of the mind of the Lord.

The mind's corrupted hard drive needs defragging and debugging. Our schematics, worldviews, patterns of thought, need to be tested, purified and conformed to the mind of Christ. Why we think what we do, and why we think as we do, must be brought to the bar of the mind of Christ, as revealed in Scripture and by the Spirit. In 1 Corinthians 2 Paul says that we have the mind of Christ, but many of us choose not to think that way. The mind of a Christian is to be a Christian mind. The Christian mindset is a mind set on Christ and a mind set by Christ. Paul says we must set our minds on things above, where we are hid with Christ (Colossians 3:1–3). Our mind must be stayed on Christ – through prayer, scriptural meditation, worship, and intimacy.

Secondly, Paul adds that transformation comes through proximity to divinity.

"And we all, with unveiled face, beholding the glory of the Lord, are being transformed into the same image from one degree of glory to another" (2 Corinthians 3:18).

It is not the *act* of beholding in itself that transforms, it's the *object* of our beholding. We become like what we look at. God the Spirit transforms us into the likeness of Christ as we behold Christ. It is God the Spirit who transforms our mind as we read Scripture, written by the Spirit. The German mystic Meister Eckhart said that God is like fire: fire converts wood into fire, and whatever fire touches turns into fire.[303] Similarly, as we come to Christ, we become like Christ. You become what you behold – watch porn, you will become immoral; watch violence, you will become aggressive; study Christ… guess what?

So, our transformation comes through conscious, sustained meditation on the Son of God, revealed in the Word of God, through which we experience the action of the blazing Spirit of God. And so we are kissed by God, and changed from frogs into princes.

40

God's Fire Service (12:11)

I once attended a meeting for experienced ministers who were appointed to train newly ordained clergy. At the meeting, we were presented with the new material and the requirements necessary for a curate to be duly qualified and certified to become the leader of a parish. It was fascinating. As a trainer, I clearly failed the standards I am supposed to produce and assess in those I train. One document pertaining to the skill-base had a checklist to be answered annually with 124 skills to learn. They included all sorts, including how to take a wedding using 350-year-old liturgy, how to be a "representative Christian", and how to "church women" – an ancient rite for the purification of women after childbirth. Much on this checklist was good, practical, and some even necessary, and I was aware of many skills and experiences that I had not acquired. However, there was one significant omission on the list, as far as I could see: it did not mention God once. No doubt the authors would say that God was the presupposition of them all – but sometimes we need to make explicit what we take as read.

The story is told that distinguished W. E. Sangster was interviewing candidates for the Methodist ministry when a young man came before him who was given a chance to speak about his vocation. Rather nervously he said: "I'm not the sort of person who could set the Thames on fire." Sangster immediately replied: "My dear young brother, I'm not interested to know if you could set the Thames on fire. What I want to know is this: if I picked you up by the scruff of the neck and dropped you into the Thames, would it sizzle?"

In Romans 12:11 Paul encourages and exhorts three values, principles and qualities that I believe are worth more than all 124 practical skills in the clergy training handbook, and without which the 124 practical skills are largely pointless. Indeed, no one should be allowed to begin to learn the full 124 unless they have the following three to bind them.

1. Never be lacking in zeal.
2. Be ablaze by the Spirit.
3. Serve the Lord.

1. Passionate about passion

First, Paul is passionate about the need for passion. In the NIV Bible we have "never be lacking in zeal". The Greek literally means "in haste not slow". Do not be slow in being hasty. Get to it. Paul may be inverting the saying of the Roman emperor from the time of Christ, Caesar Augustus, who often repeated the saying, "Make haste slowly." Paul's point is clear: in the things of God, let's not hang around. This is an appeal for zeal – zeal for Christ, for his crown, for his renown. Zeal is the rejection of the status quo, no "more of the same"; it's a refusal to stand still. The Christian zealot has enthusiasm, passion, direction, motivation. "The kingdom of heaven has been forcefully advancing, and forceful men lay hold of it" (Matthew 11:12, NIV).

The so-called "Wesley Rule" (although there is no evidence that John Wesley ever said it[304]) epitomizes the zeal Paul exhorts us to: "Do all the good you can, by all the means you can, in all the ways you can, in all the places you can, at all the times you can, to all the people you can, as long as ever you can." Some 280 years ago, during the Evangelical Awakening, a group of Oxford Methodist students were so passionate and public for Christ in their prayer and witness that it was said "their zeal got them sent down". Cambridge has seen this zeal – in the east-end window of St Aldates is the image of Henry Martyn, outstanding Cambridge mathematician, who gave up academia to do pioneer mission in India. He also worked on the first ever translation of the Bible into Persian. In his journal he wrote the prayer:

> *Lord, increase my zeal that, though I am but a feeble and obscure instrument, I may struggle out my few days in great and unremitting exertions for the demolition of paganism and the setting up of Christ's kingdom.*[305]

An undeniable fact of church history is that those who have achieved most for God are those who gave themselves most to God in zeal.

Sadly, life's trials and exigencies and disappointments can knock the zeal out of us and damp down the fire. Was there ever a time when you were more passionate about Jesus, his honour, cause, and renown?

At times our zeal can be directed to just about everything except God. We can get caught up giving our all to academic success, or professional success, or financial security, or making life comfortable. I recall one college rower here in Oxford where I work telling me that he had trained seven days a week, four hours a day, for months – just to try and make sure that he would win one of the university's rowing matches. And all that was on top of his studies. It made me wonder how many Christians would give four hours a day, seven days a week, to God. How many give four hours a week?

Tragically it can be church folk who are quick to quench zeal, to dampen it down and dismiss it as youthful enthusiasm: "You'll grow out of it; calm down." I once prayed at a university prayer meeting and afterwards a conservative young woman church worker said it was "like having an African" in the group when I prayed! At the time I took it as a compliment… now I'm not so sure that it was intended as such.

Archdeacon Alf Cooper, church planter in Chile and chaplain to its president, told me that at one of his meetings the Spirit of God fell, people sang, worshipped, cried, were overcome by the Spirit and fell down… and bizarrely a conservative evangelical preacher walked about the church shouting, "Stop this!" George Verwer, the founder of Operation Mobilisation, would challenge his congregations with the claim: "A fanatic is someone who loves Jesus more than you do." The church needs more fanatics – like Christ, consumed by zeal for God's house.

Have you ever looked at other Christians and longed for what they have? Do not be jealous of another's walk with Christ, instead be zealous like them. Not only does zeal achieve more for God – it experiences more of God. The zealous Christian knows a special calling and closeness with God, for the Lord "wrapped himself in zeal as a cloak" (Isaiah 59:17).

2. An internal combustion engine

Secondly, Paul wants every Christian to be an internal combustion engine, to be "ablaze by the Spirit".

Zeal is the fuel that God ignites to become a driving force for the advancement of the kingdom. Years ago, when I applied to be Pastorate Chaplain in Oxford, the minister description required "a man ablaze with the love of God". I wrote, "I want to be." I know that there have been times when I've been warmer than at others. I want to be on fire: God needs me to be on fire; the world needs me to be on fire. God is a consuming fire, and I burn to the extent that I have come near and caught fire.

The word I've translated "ablaze" in verse 11 is the Greek *zeo* and it means to be "on fire, aglow, aflame, boiling, seething". It was used to describe metal that had been heated to white hot, and to describe water that had reached boiling point. "By the Spirit" is an instrumental dative: the Spirit is the instrument, the means by which we boil or burn or blaze. Now, some translations render the Greek as "keep your spiritual fervour" but this is a poor translation. I follow the church fathers, Calvin, and many major modern evangelical commentators, who most naturally translate *to pneuma* as "the Spirit" (meaning the Holy Spirit) – as a noun and not the adjective "spiritual" as in the NIV. It's not our own zeal that sets us on fire, but zeal presents us before God who is a consuming fire, and whose Spirit causes us to catch fire. Professor Douglas Moo in his exhaustive commentary on Romans argues conclusively that what Paul was saying was: "Be set on fire in/by the Spirit."[306]

Moses met this fire of God at the burning bush and on Mount Sinai. Jesus is the one who baptizes us with the Spirit and fire (Luke 3:16). Pentecost is God's visitation, a rent heaven, when he comes down and his presence and proximity alight his people in tongues of fire (Acts 2:3). These tongues of fire fell on them all. This fire is not reserved for the few – it is there for all. William Booth, the founder of the Salvation Army, crafted as the motto and symbol for his movement "Blood and Fire" – the cross and the Spirit. When staying with guests, his secretary would send a letter about his personal requirements, in which he was quoted as saying (in a Nottinghamshire accent): "I like me tea as I like me religion – hot, very hot"![307] It was this fire that propelled the Salvation Army to march fearlessly into the very jaws of hell to rescue the last, the lost, and the least.

Leviticus 9:22–24 is a fascinating text on the fire of God. Here Moses and Aaron bless the people of God. "Aaron lifted up his hands toward the people and blessed them" (verse 22), and what was the recorded effect? Nothing. But then in verse 23 we read that Aaron and Moses offer a sacrifice and enter into the Tent of Meeting. Again they blessed the people – only this time the glory of the Lord appeared, the fire of God came down and consumed the sacrifice, and the people shouted for joy and fell face down. The first blessing – nothing happened; the second blessing – the fire fell. What was the difference between the two? Blood and sacrifice. The first time they gave a blessing before they had met with God; the second time they gave a blessing after they had met with God.

Evan Roberts, the great pioneer of the 1904 Welsh revival, had such a revelation of God's love and such a consecration to God's cause that he could write this:

> *the salvation of the human soul was solemnly impressed upon me. I felt ablaze with a desire to go through the length and breadth of Wales to tell of the Saviour.*[308]

Sadly, many Christians have let the fire die down, and allowed the temperature of their soul to become tepid and luke-warm. Watchman Nee noted, "By the time the average Christian gets his temperature up to normal, everybody thinks he has a fever." It is the heart that is tender to Christ that becomes tinder for Christ. Was there ever a time when you were more ablaze for Christ? Have you lost that fire of God's accompanying presence? If so, get it back.

3. Flames of fire

Thirdly, Paul wants us to take a royal commission: serving the Lord (12:11). Bob Dylan reminded us that we've "Gotta Serve Somebody." Who is it you are serving?

In recent years we have seen the shame fall on politicians and bankers who have used their office to serve themselves. In the Old Testament we see Hophni and Phineas, the sons of the high priest Eli, stealing meat that had been offered to God. They were self-serving and not God-serving. This can happen in the church where ministers and members are in it for what they can get from it. Paul says some preach Christ for personal gain! When the fire of God falls and fills a man or woman, there is not only an enjoyment of God but an employment for God. We have all heard of Einstein's $e = mc^2$ which demonstrates that "mass can be turned into energy which can be put to useful work". It is what the sun does, what nuclear power plants do. And similarly, the Holy Spirit fire converts the mass of the church to energy that's put to useful work.

The psalmist declared that God makes his servants "flames of fire" (104:4, NIV). And God's flame of fire makes his servants. When Moses met the fire of God he was sent to lead Israel out of Egypt. When 120 believers at Pentecost met the fire of God, they were sent to win the world. The Spirit's fire calls us to royal service – on the king's commission. As I mentioned earlier, my granny was a royal nanny – she often spoke proudly of being "in royal service". My grandad was a fighter pilot and proudly displayed his King George's commission on his hallway wall. To serve the King of kings is the greatest honour this world affords.

When John Wesley's heart was strangely warmed he went to work tirelessly for the next fifty years, travelling 250,000 miles on horseback, preaching an estimated 40,000 sermons, writing numerous books, waking each day at 4 a.m., preaching by 5 a.m., doing his correspondence as he rode his horse. He died having trained 750 ministers in the UK, 350 ministers in the USA, leaving 140,000 Methodist members, and having fuelled the Evangelical Awakening which saved Britain from sliding, like her neighbour France, into civil war. When others had a revolution, England had a revival, and it was precipitated by a man of God, fuelled by God, serving God.

If you are longing for more of God's fire, if God has set his fire upon you, know that it is not simply for your pleasure but for his pleasure – to set you to work for his purposes and plan. Fire is not self-serving; it spends itself as it warms another, cooks food, brings light. Fire serves and, as it serves, it is spent; and so with the Christian ablaze. The benefit of being consumed by fire is to be fire for the glory of God and the good of the other.

There is an ancient Orthodox Church story of an aged abbot and a young monk. The monk, Lot, came to Abbot Joseph and said, "Father, according as I am able, I keep my little rule, and my little fast, my prayer, meditation, and contemplative silence; and according as I am able I strive to cleanse my heart of thoughts; now what more should I do?" The elder rose up in reply and stretched out his hands to heaven, and his fingers became like ten lamps of fire. He said, "Why not be totally changed into fire!" When we have done all our doing, what is left? Become consumed by God.

And what will that look like? Samuel Chadwick, the Edwardian Presbyterian theologian, described it this way:

> *Spirit-filled souls are ablaze for God. They love with a love that glows. They serve with a faith that kindles. They serve with a devotion that consumes. They hate sin with fierceness that burns. They rejoice with a joy that radiates. Love is perfected in the fire of God.*[309]

Is that you? Why not?

41

Ablaze with the Spirit (12:11)

The greatest need of the hour is for God's people to be endowed with the fire of God, as at Pentecost; and for this great need we have a great provision. Fire is the mark of an encounter with God. The great tragedy is that, so often, those who represent God know little of God's fire. The lukewarm Christian was the scourge of the Laodicean church, and Laodicea is the mark of much that carries the name "church" today, certainly in the soft-bellied West. Jesus bemoans the fact that the Laodicean church is neither cold nor hot – the word translated "hot" in the Greek is the same word we translate "ablaze" in Romans 12:11, where Paul says, "Never be lacking in zeal, but be ablaze by the Spirit, serving the Lord" (my translation).

This aptly describes the church following Pentecost. They were ablaze by the Spirit, zealous for God's fame, burning to proclaim Christ the King, and serving him faithfully and fruitfully despite severe opposition.

There are two ways to serve the Lord: first, you can do it in your own strength, which is tiring, unfruitful, and will lead to burn-out. Or secondly, you can do it in his strength – which is joyful and fruitful. I am filled with sadness as I look back over the last few decades and see so many of my Christian friends, so many folk I trained with or helped train for the ordained ministry, are now out of ministry: some through mental or moral failure; some simply spent out. Too many have stopped serving the Lord; some have even stopped following him. If we are not ablaze with the Spirit in serving the Lord with zeal, we end up doing it reluctantly or even resentfully. Without the internal fuel of affection we grow weary in doing good for God. Are you perhaps weary in serving the Lord –

after years faithfully, dutifully, serving the church. Has the fire of divine love grown dim?

We cannot serve God with zeal alone. Zeal needs fuel. It needs to be ignited by God's fire. The only solution to being burned out is to be burned up. The Greek in 12:11 literally says *to pneumati* ("in the Spirit") *zeontes* ("boiling"). The greatest need of the hour is for God's people to be endowed with the fire of God, as at Pentecost.

God is a consuming fire

"For the Lord your God is a consuming fire" (Deuteronomy 4:24).

The ancients understood that fire sustained life, and many worshipped it. There are over thirty specific gods of fire named in pagan religions. The Judeo-Christian God, Yahweh, is not a god of fire, but the one and only God who reveals himself as fire. Fire is a primary metaphor for God and a key symbol of his presence.

God's theophany to Moses – his divine self-disclosure – was as a burning bush that did not burn up (Exodus 3:2). God broke out in judgment against Sodom and Gomorrah as a consuming fire (Genesis 19:24) and similarly with Korah's rebellion (Numbers 16:35). God led Israel by night in a pillar of fire (Exodus 13:21). He appeared in glory on Mount Sinai as a fire (Exodus 24:17). God accepted Abraham's sacrifice (Genesis 15:17) and Solomon's dedication of the temple (2 Chronicles 7:1) by sending the fire. Elijah asked God to vindicate himself in the confrontation with the false prophets of Baal, and God did so by sending the fire on the altar (1 Kings 18:38). Isaiah prayed for God's fire, God himself, to come and transform Israel: "Oh that you would rend the heavens and come down, that the mountains might quake at your presence – as when fire kindles brushwood and the fire causes water to boil" (Isaiah 64:1–2). The image is of God coming like molten lava, consuming and transforming everything in its path. John the Baptist prophesied that Jesus would baptize with the Spirit and fire. At the end, all who meet God in unforgiven sin will be judged by fire. If we will not embrace the fire of his love we will experience it as the fire of his judgment.

Why fire? God in his aseity (his underived existence) chooses the means and mode of his revelation, and fire is one of them. Fire speaks of life and death – it is elusive, beautiful, unconstrained, unmissable, purifying, wondrous, dangerous. When Paul challenges us to be "ablaze with the Spirit", he is drawing on this tradition; he is saying the mark of the Christian is God's manifest presence and power and glory and purity. Blaise Pascal, the famous French mathematician and philosopher, wrote on a piece of parchment and sowed it into the breast of his doublet, next to his heart, never to forget, an account of an encounter with God that has been called "the night of fire".[310]

> *23rd November 1654 – 2nd Conversion*
>
> *Fire. God of Abraham, God of Isaac, God of Jacob.*
> *Not of the philosophers and scientists... Certitude – Feeling,*
> *Joy, Peace.*
> *God of Jesus Christ, God of Jesus Christ.*
> *My God and your God... Joy, Joy, Joy, Tears of Joy.*

Such an experience focused his writings, later collated in one of the greatest apologetics for Christianity and published posthumously as *Pensées* (Thoughts).

We have a choice: will we meet God as the fire of love or the fire of judgment?

The church was birthed in the fire of God

I have often thought that if I could have a tattoo, it would say "born to burn".

The church was born in a fire. Following the ascension of Jesus, as the disciples gathered together expectantly and obediently in prayer (Acts 1:14), suddenly a sound like a mighty wind filled the house, and from heaven came tongues of fire and rested upon them – all of them were filled with the Holy Spirit – the tongues of fire set their tongues on fire (Acts 2:3–4). The psalmist said "God makes his messengers winds, his ministers a flaming fire" (Psalm 104:4). Without fire his messengers are mere hot air. Prophetically, a bishop's mitre, his headpiece, is always shaped like a tongue to remind the church that she – represented by the bishop – is birthed in a baptism of the fire of the Spirit's presence. Søren Kierkegaard states powerfully, "Christianity is incendiarism."[311] Christianity is fire-setting; a Christian is a person set on fire.

The mid-twentieth century English Revivalist, Leonard Ravenhill, recalls returning home late one day at 2 a.m., after preaching away. He woke up his wife and said, "Come on, let's us go down to the town, there is a mill on fire and the whole town have gathered to watch." Ravenhill suggested it is the same with God when he is manifest, when his glory is resting upon a preacher or a church community: "You don't have to advertise fire – the most self-advertising thing in the world is fire."[312] Certainly at Pentecost a people on fire drew an intrigued crowd, who then listened to the gospel preached, with 3,000 responding to the invitation of God. The first church on the first day was a mega-church! The fire of God draws a crowd and prepares a crowd for God. If we had more of God, more of the fire of love and holiness in our lives, in our church meetings, in our outreach, in our worship, in our witness, we would not be able to stop folk coming to church, even though some would stay clear for fear of the fire.

We fight fire with fire

The world is largely running headlong into hell-fire. Shakespeare wrote, "Be stirring as the time, be fire with fire."[313] When faced with an oilwell fire, the fire fighters will remove the oxygen from the equation by detonating dynamite over the fire. The blast eats up all the local oxygen, leaving nothing to fuel the fire. When a forest is ablaze, firefighters remove the fuel that feeds the ravaging fire by getting rid of combustible underbrush through carefully setting it on fire. Only a church ablaze with the Spirit of God can combat the fires of the evil one. As the American army axiom says: you bring peace through superior fire-power!

We can easily put out the fire

Everyone knows fires go out if they have nothing to burn. Our devotion is the fuel for God. In a remarkable prayer of consecration by Jim Elliot – a missionary martyred by the Auca Indians – he recorded in his diary, "God, I pray thee, light these idle sticks of my life, and may

I burn for thee. Consume my life, my God, for it is thine." In Leviticus 6:13 we read the command that the "fire on the altar shall be kept burning", a symbol both of the constant divine fire of wrath against sin and the constant divine fire of love to those who draw near to God. Fire needs fuel. That fuel is to be our love and life laid down for our Lord. This fire of God sets our hearts on fire when we come to God. Commenting on the Temple's ever burning altar of fire, Jonathan Edwards said:

> *When a soul is drawn to God in true conversion, fire comes down from God out of heaven, in which the heart is offered in sacrifice, and the soul is baptized with the Holy Ghost and with fire.*[314]

Christians in a religious holy huddle may be cosy and warm, but that is not the same as a fire. We cannot kindle this fire. Only proximity to God will set us alight. But many never draw near; and others, having once drawn near, draw back in fear. Sadly, we can all too easily become accustomed to being rather luke-warm, tepid, mild, like the Laodicean church. Paul had to challenge even the young apostle Timothy to "fan into flame" the gift upon him through the laying on of hands. Timothy had clearly let the fire of God's gifting go out. What puts out the flame? There are several things:

Disappointment with church, with self, even with God – we can grow weary in doing good.

Distractions – taking our eye off the Lord and his cause and call on us, focusing our passions elsewhere, to the worries and cares of this world.

Demonic attack – the enemy, like a flood, seeks to pour cold water on the soul's fire.

Deception – false fires, false fuels, false teachers, false faith.

Paul challenges the church: "Do not quench the Spirit" (1 Thessalonians 5:19) – do not put out the Spirit's fire. I recall seeing on our coal fire a large lump that apparently was not burning despite the rest of the coals being red hot. I went over to examine it and discovered it was not coal but a lump of stone! It seemed as if the Spirit said to me, "Many in the church have placed things on their spiritual lives which take up space but do no good; they won't burn, they give no heat and no light." What might these be in your soul? The Scottish prophet James Stuart Stewart declared,

> *When all is said and done, the supreme need of the Church is the same in the twentieth century as in the first; it is men on fire for Christ. I beg you not to commit the fearful blunder of dampening down that flame.*[315]

Catch the fire

Christians shouldn't smoke – they should burn!

Again, the Presbyterian divine Samuel Chadwick, who meditated deeply and wrote profoundly on the spiritual life, summarized: "Destitute of the Fire of God, nothing else counts; possessing Fire, nothing else matters."[316]

How do we possess the fire? Fire breeds fire. We need to come to the burning bush. Jesus is the baptizer in the Spirit and fire – it's his Spirit we need. Proximity to divinity makes us incendiary.

It is said that John Wesley was once asked the basis for his success. He simply replied, "First I set myself on fire; then people come to see me burn."[317] How did he set himself on fire? Zeal for God, zeal for the things of God, zeal for the honour of God. He heard the Moravians had something, and attended their meeting in Aldersgate in London, where he heard the preface to Luther's commentary on Romans read. His journal recorded that he felt his heart "strangely warmed". A fire was lit, and that fire grew and blazed bright.

Having known the fire for himself, he was burdened that his people would know it for themselves too:

> *My fear is not that our great movement, known as the Methodists, will eventually cease to exist or one day die from the earth. My fear is that our people will become content to live without the fire, the power, the excitement, the supernatural element that makes us great.*

Wesley became a burning bush, ablaze with presence of God, and wherever he went others caught the fire, and that fire grew to the Great Awakening. Oh, how we need another in our nation! If we are not set ablaze by God's fire, we will certainly be consumed in hell fire. Fire fights fire.

The first two great English Protestant martyrs were Bishops Hugh Latimer and Nicholas Ridley. They were burned at the stake for their faithfulness to the gospel, in Broad Street in Oxford, by the rabid Catholic monarch Mary. As they approached the place of execution, Latimer steadied his companion with the immortal words:

> *Be of good comfort, Master Ridley, and play the man! We shall this day light such a candle, by God's grace, in England, as I trust shall never be put out.*[318]

Yes, they were going to the fire, but their faith, their faithfulness, their sharing in Christ's sufferings, would light a greater "candle" that would blaze prophetically to the glory of God throughout England and add fuel to the renewal of the church.

William Booth, founder of Salvation Army, often encouraged his men: "Whatever you do, get the fire." May we also hold faithfully to Christ and his gospel and his cause, at whatever cost, and may we also be a lit candle to Christ's glory.

I have a friend who every morning sings or prays this hymn by Charles Wesley. What better way to start the day, and to live a Christian life?

> *O Thou who camest from above*
> *The pure celestial fire to impart,*
> *Kindle a flame of sacred love*
> *On the mean altar of my heart.*
>
> *There let it for Thy glory burn*
> *With inextinguishable blaze,*
> *And trembling to its source return*
> *In humble prayer and fervent praise.*

Jesus, confirm my heart's desire
To work and speak and think of Thee;
Still let me guard the Holy Fire,
And still stir up Thy gift in me.

42

Charisms and Character (12:3–6)

I know a man from a conservative evangelical tradition who, in the 1960s, had an extraordinary experience when he was in hospital sick with pneumonia. As taught in James 5, he called the elders and asked for the anointing with prayer for healing. As they prayed for him, anointing him with oil, he was filled with the Spirit, spoke in tongues, and was instantly healed. Neither he nor the elders had ever expected, let alone witnessed, anything like it. But they all knew that God had come.

He began to minister in the power of the Spirit in the giddy days of renewal. People came to Christ and into deeper experience of God. He developed friendships with other young leaders in renewal, and began to move in renewal circles. But a growing concern crept over him. I recall a comment that went something like his: "I didn't understand how they could turn off the anointing so quickly – they would see God move in power at a meeting, then go straight out to a restaurant and act like nothing had happened, no evidence they had been with and for God." He wanted to continue in a holy attitude, a holy place, with God. Gradually he withdrew from the charismatic renewal and for forty years has pursued holiness, ministering faithfully in chapel contexts where holiness was a value, though sadly the charismatic gifts went on the back-burner. That man was my father.

Charisms (gifts) without character... character without charisms... must we choose one or the other? Is it really an either/or question? Far from it! Indeed Scripture consistently exhorts us to grow in the Spirit's charisms and, in so doing, to reflect Christ's character. Christlike character is charismatic! In both passages in the New Testament that deal with charisms – 1 Corinthians 12–14 and Romans 12 – both also deal directly with character. We cannot divide them. We need giftedness and godliness!

The church is to be marked by her charisms

Paul does not explicate here a full treatment of the gifts, but he offers principles for understanding and employing them:

1. Charity

Paul speaks of the "grace given to me" (12:3), and again that we have "gifts that differ according to the grace given to us" (12:6). The Greek word for gifts is *charismata,* literally " grace-gifts". Paul wants us to understand that these gifts come from grace.

Charisms are divine gifts, not latent abilities. Charisms are not rewards. Charisms are received by God's grace, not achieved by merit, and are to be utilized as grace-gifts to others, for "all things come from you and of your own do we give you" (1 Chronicles 29:14). In Exodus 35 we meet Bezalel and his apprentice Oholiab who are filled with the Spirit and gifted with skills to make the Tabernacle. God gives the gifts that he employs to his glory. Similarly we are given the Spirit and the Spirit gives us charisms, all of grace, which we give back to build the church and extend God's kingdom. The Spirit's anointing, his gifts, tell us more about the nature of the Giver than of the recipient. They tell us God is good, gracious, generous – but they do not tell us anything much about the ones who receive them.

2. Humility

"For by the grace given to me I say to everyone among you not to think of himself more highly than he ought" (12:3). It is important that we grasp that Paul begins his treatment on the charisms by speaking on character. The gifts mark the church, but godliness must mark the gifted. Precisely because they are divine grace gifts there must be no grounds for arrogance, posturing, or superiority. Because God has graced us with the gifts, we must live honouring the gracing God.

When I was a university chaplain I pastored many students from privileged backgrounds who had attended top private and public schools and were now attending one of the world's finest universities in Oxford. I repeatedly challenged them when they were tempted to preen themselves, plum in the mouth, nose in the air, old school scarf prominently displayed, looking down on others, and I would say, "What do you have that was not given to you? Your whole life and all its social benefits were bought by your parents, gifted into your DNA. Thus far, any achievement shows more what has been given you than what you have achieved."

Similarly, Christians are saved by grace, live by grace, are gifted by grace: what do we have that was not given us? Grace leaves no room for pride – only gratitude. No merit of our own can we claim. The one most gifted by God ought to be the most humbled before God. As David said, "Who am I… and what is my house, that you have brought me thus far?" (2 Samuel 7:18).

3. *Diversity*

"… having gifts that differ" (12:6). Paul here lists seven distinct charisms: prophecy, service, teaching, preaching, giving, leading, acts of mercy. This list in Romans is illustrative not exhaustive. In 1 Corinthians 12 Paul offers two further lists of charisms – in verses 4–11 he lists nine gifts, and in verse 28 he lists eight. In Ephesians 4:11 he lists five. Thus, in these four lists, allowing for a certain overlap, there are twenty distinct gifts named in total.

Scripture emphasizes the plurality and diversity of divine gifts. Often churches focus too narrowly on just a few – be they more or less spectacular, according to preference. But God apportions these gifts. Certainly it is for us to seek them, but it is for God to determine what he gives and where.

At different periods God has highlighted neglected gifts, restoring these to the body. However, we too easily become myopic and miss the breadth and beauty of the diversity of God's gracious gifting. Conservatives avoid the more supernatural gifts and focus on teaching and exhorting. Charismatics embrace the more supernatural gifts, going for prophecy, healing, or tongues. Liberals embrace the more practical gifts like giving, leading, and acts of mercy.

I think leaders often replicate themselves: they create a church after their own image, producing carbon copies of themselves, taking their gifting as normative for the whole church. Teachers identify with and raise up teachers; pastors identify and raise up pastors; evangelists equip people to be evangelists. This is not all bad, of course – that is part of their calling; however, it is a secure leader who can release and encourage a diversity of giftings in the church, especially when they are promoting others whose gifts will be more prominent than their own.

4. Unity

"We, though many, are one body in Christ, and individually members of one another" (12:5). Diversity or plurality of gifts must be held within unity and community. Paul's metaphor of the body is one he often employs when speaking about the gifts: a body is one, yet made of many parts, all of which are noble and necessary. Indeed, if a body was all eyes or all hands or all feet, it would not be a body; it would in fact be dead, or something out of a horror movie or a macabre pathology lab.

We must be careful not to think in individualistic categories – "my gift, my ministry, my anointing" – but we must always think communally: "What have I been given for your benefit? What have you been given for me?" With the exception of the gift of tongues, all the gifts we receive are for the benefit of others. And Paul even says that, if we exercise the gift of tongues publically, we must pray for the gift of interpretation so as to be able to use it for the encouragement of others. Paul here does not suggest a hierarchy of gifts, even though our pride often pushes for one. We must resist this. The gifts are given to complement one another, never to compete. He who would be great must be least, the servant of all (see Mark 9:35).

5. Responsibility

"Having gifts that differ according to the grace given to us, let us use them: if prophecy, in proportion to our faith; if service; in our serving; the one who teaches, in his teaching; the one who exhorts, in his exhortation; the one who contributes, in generosity" (12:6–8).

Whatever we have been given, we are to give it away. Solomon the wise taught: "A man's gift makes room for him" (Proverbs 18:16) – but only if you make room for the gift. According to your faith, you need to exercise your gift. If you withhold your gift, you rob the church. Timothy was Paul's protégé – a godly, gifted, faithful missionary partner. In both of his letters to Timothy, Paul has no need to address the issue of Timothy's character. But in both lessons he addresses the charisms Timothy has received, which Timothy appears to have left dormant (1 Timothy 4:14; 2 Timothy 1:6). Do you know what charisms God has anointed you with? If you don't, ask God and a respected church leader and a close friend. Are you nurturing these gifts, learning about them, looking for and praying for opportunities to exercise your gifting?

You must use the gifts God has given you for the good of the church.

The church is to be marked by Christlike character

We place a premium on charisms, but God places a premium on character.

I recall listening to an elderly Judson Cornwall, the distinguished American Pentecostal Bible teacher, who recalled how, in the American healing revival of the 1950s, he had watched a noted healing evangelist pray for a man without an eye whose sight was miraculously restored. That afternoon the same evangelist preached and was seriously dodgy. Judson approached him, saying how much he valued his ministry, but pointed out his teaching was contrary to the Council of Nicea, and that he should get some theology or start to minister alongside a teacher. The evangelist replied, "When was the last time you prayed and healed a blind man?" Cornwall said, "Never, I'm a teacher." The evangelist tragically replied, "When you can heal the blind, then you can teach me." How tragic that, despite our gifting, fleshly character can cause us to reject another's gift. "The eye cannot say to the hand, I don't need you," says Paul; on the contrary, God has placed different gifts, callings, in the body. We need each other, to build one another up and build the kingdom.

Just think for a moment: when was the last time you attended, or even heard of, a church conference devoted to character, holiness, Christlikeness? When was the last time the main speaker was chosen, not because of his gifting but because of his grace, not because of charisms but because of character?

Charisms without character brings chaos. Man looks on the outward appearance – always has; but God looks on the heart – always has.

Samson was anointed by the Spirit to lead Israel, yet he was marked by sexual immorality, deceit, and weakness of character, and so he fell. Saul was anointed by the Spirit with charisms for leadership and prophecy, and yet his character was flawed: he was marked by pride, rebellion, jealousy, anger. David was an anointed warrior king able to prophesy and praise… and commit adultery and murder. These men were walking contradictions. It's almost a cliché, but when one hears of the stratospheric rise of a charismatic leader, one half expects to hear of moral collapse sooner or later – whether through financial impropriety, sexual immorality, or the abuse of power. The who's who of charismatic leadership in the last few decades is littered with public moral collapse. There is even a Wikipedia page devoted to "Scandals involving Evangelicals" which lists allegations and revelations of moral failure by prominent evangelicals and charismatics. It makes sorry reading.

The apostolic Vineyard movement founder, John Wimber, at a period when his senior pastors in the Vineyard seemed to be falling like nine-pins, asked, "Is every Vineyard pastor having an affair?" His very last sermon, as he was dying of cancer, addressed the worldwide Vineyard pastors, a movement synonymous with charismatic renewal. It was his take on 1 John, "the lust of flesh, and the lust of the eyes, and the pride of life" (1 John 2:16, KJV). He said, "Love Jesus, play nice, keep your fingers out of the till, and your zippers up." He knew his movement, having experienced renewal and exercising the charisms, still needed work on character.

I think some people who experience the grace and charisms of God deceive themselves that they don't have to work on their character because God is self-evidently with them, working through them. French philosopher Blaise Pascal wisely wrote: "Orthodoxy of words is blasphemy unless it is backed up by superiority of character."

Gifts are given to the church without reference to our character. They reflect God's character showing that he is a gracious and generous

God. However, a graced church must become a gracious church. The gifts of God are not rewards for good behaviour; character is not a pre-requisite for giftedness, but they must be followed by good behaviour. Paul emphasizes the prime Christian character as love, saying that love must be authentic (12:9), that we must love one another with brotherly love (12:10). Interestingly and uniquely, Paul employs three different words for love in just two verses: *agapē* (sacrificial love), *philadelphia* (brotherly love), and *philostorgia* (non-erotic love between family members). By marshalling these three related terms Paul presents an unmissable, unforgettable, rhetorical exhortation to be men and women marked by love. In the rest of this chapter we have a list of qualities that forms a commentary on what love looks like. Love honours others, love is zealous, love is joyful, love is patient, love is prayerful, love is generous, love is hospitable, love blesses those who persecute, love empathizes, love is peace-making.

Christian Christlike character is demonstrated and inculcated in community.

Almost all Paul's list of character traits must be relationally evidenced. They are not attributes that can be exhibited living alone in a cave praying – they are all qualities exhibited in community. It is reasonably easy to be holy on your own – I'm a saint in my quiet time. It is when I leave the front door and meet folk – especially some church folk – that my character defects are shown up.

Let us pay special attention to Paul's emphases – three times he refers to love; twice he speaks of "blessing" others; twice of "rejoicing"; twice "not responding to evil with evil"; twice of living out a culture of "honour". This thought of being humble and honouring the other higher than oneself (verse 10) is core to the character of a Christian. It's difficult to love someone you look down upon.

Humility and honour are to mark the charismatic Christian. The mark of the fleshly person is to seek honour from others. The mark of the Spirit-filled, Christlike person is to give honour to others. Often the worldly people honour themselves by humbling others. Spiritual people humble themselves and are honoured by God (Luke 1:52). Let us live to make a name for someone else!

The Greek philosopher, Socrates, said, "an unexamined life is worth nothing". Paul would concur. "Examine yourselves, to see whether you are in the faith" (2 Corinthians 13:5) and I think here in Romans 12 we have a useful checklist. Perhaps with a trusted friend, or in a prayer triplet, you might prayerfully go through each character trait, and ask: How do I measure up? Is there any evidence of this in my life?

In conclusion

It is much easier to have God's charisms than godly character, but it is far better to have both. I began this chapter by briefly mentioning my father's journey. His spiritual mentor was Stanley Jebb, another emerging teacher in the 1960s' West Country charismatic movement. He also, in a more public manner, later left the renewal movement disillusioned. In an article entitled "Why I left the Charismatic Movement"[319] he recorded his main reasons, one of which was the number of charismatic leaders that had fallen morally.

> *Yes I know that Reformed and Evangelical leaders have fallen also. But there is this difference: charismatics claim to be filled with the Holy Spirit. Furthermore, they claim to manifest spiritual gifts such as prophecy, which can reveal what is in a person's heart... Why, in the many cases of moral failure in charismatic circles, did no one manifest a "gift" to reveal this?*

Certainly not since the early Pentecostal movement has holiness been a valued virtue of the charismatic movement. I understand Jebbs's decision. However, I think the answer is not to leave the renewal movement, but to see it transformed, encouraging it to pursue with equal tenacity the character of God as well as the charisms. We do not need this bifurcation, this either/or. We need a church that has both the charisms and the character – giftedness and godliness.

43

God and Politics (13:1–7)

It is not always easy these days to be a practising Christian and a public citizen. Several prominent legal rulings have challenged and curtailed the public practice of Christianity in the UK: prayers in certain public council meetings were deemed to violate the rights of the non-religious present; some guest-house owners were fined for morally discriminating against homosexual couples to whom they had refused rooms; some Catholic adoption agencies have been forced to close after being ordered to allow gay couples to adopt, something contrary to Catholic moral conviction.

Trevor Philips, the chairman of the Equality and Human Rights commission, declared in 2012 that Christians must "choose between their religion and obeying the law". He said religious people must leave their rules "at the door of the temple" and, when they are on the streets, live by state law, not religious law. In our secular West it is widely held that, while religion may govern the private sphere, only government may govern in the public square. Notwithstanding that government represents the people, and law is there to serve the interests of the people, several million Christians – not to mention those of other religious faiths – are being forced to choose between religion and state, judged as law-breakers if their faith comes first.

How should a Christian live in society? In Romans 13 Paul addresses this tension of church and state.

1. God *gives* good government

"Let every person be subject to the governing authorities. For there is no authority except from God, and those that exist have been instituted by God. Therefore whoever resists the authorities resists what God has appointed... For he is the servant of God, an avenger who carries out God's wrath on the wrongdoer... the authorities are ministers of God" (13:1–2, 4, 6).

Writing to the church in Rome, Paul has in view the Roman magistrate system that administered law and rule over the empire. Paul describes them as authorities (*exousiai*), governors (*hyperexousai*), and rulers (*archontes*). These terms occur again in Ephesians 6 where Paul speaks of "principalities and powers", and this has led some to understand Paul here as referring to the spiritual angelic governing spirits rather than Rome's rulers. However, the fact that Paul in Ephesians 6 says we wrestle *against* these powers, whereas here in Romans he calls us to support them, would lead us against equating the two.

The preceding verse before the command to be subject to the governing authorities, Romans 12:21, speaks of "overcoming evil with good", and it may be that Paul is applying this by saying we overcome the evil in or behind some expressions of government with good and righteous living. Bad government, bad society, are not transformed by anarchy or aggressive regime change, but by righteous living on the part of the community of faith.

In these seven verses discussing the church's relationship to secular authorities, the most prominent and repeated word is "God". God is not indifferent or absent from the sphere of politics, government, and authority. Of course, not all governments are good and godly, but the principle of government is good and godly. Government is God's way of ordering society.

Government is not a pragmatic social construct, nor the fruit of evolution, nor the end result of a Nietzschean "Lord of the Flies" power struggle in the jungle. Government is a gift of the Lord of the universe. Government is a sign that God has not given up on us and left us with the tyranny of anarchy. Where rulers ruling with righteous rules promote justice and order, and hold back evil, government is a grace. Emil Brunner called this ongoing involvement of God in the structures of society for our good, restraining evil, as *Erhaltungsgnade* – literally, preserving grace – the grace that preserves the good.

Paul does not divinely sanction any particular form of government – theocracy, monarchy, democracy, dictatorship – but he recognizes that God has ordained the structure of authority to uphold "égalité, liberté, fraternité". Paul does not assume that the state even recognizes God, and certainly not that it is wed structurally to the church whose bishops and priests might format her policies. The second-century church father Tertullian once declared that "Caesar is more ours than yours, for our God has appointed him" and that, because of their prayers for those in authority, "Christians do more than you [Romans] for his welfare". The German Reformer Martin Luther spoke of the *Zwei-Reiche-Lehre*, the two-kingdoms rule, arguing that God rules through the church as well as through kings and their governments.

Paul goes so far as to say that governing authorities are like priests. In verse 4 twice he speaks of authorities as God's *diakonoi* – servants, ministers, deacons! In verse 6 he speaks of God's authorities as *leitourgoi* – cultic ministers, priests. Paul thus ascribes to governing authorities the titles used almost exclusively for a religious office. Whether governments recognize it or not, they are in that office to serve God, and for God serve the people. And as servants of God, the government and governors will be judged by a higher power for how they exercise their power: law-makers will be judged by the divine law-giver.

In 1985 Michael Cassidy, leader of a reconciliation ministry in apartheid South Africa, was invited to meet the then president, P. W. Botha. When he entered the room, Botha immediately began reading aloud Romans 13 and then asked, "What can I do for you?" The president was clearly using Scripture to justify his office and authority, and no doubt to intimidate this radical evangelical who was criticizing the powers to come into line. Botha was right to recognize that he held an office possessing God-instituted authority. But with divine authority comes awesome responsibility, and divine accountability. The office may be divinely sanctioned, but the officer holding the office may not be. Botha's racist rule violated its position. The church was right to protest against it, in the name of God.

2. The church *lives* under good government

If the governing authorities and rulers are holding a divinely ordained office as God's ministers, then how should we respond to them? Paul writes that every person must be "subject to the governing authorities" (13:1) and that "one must be in subjection" and "pay to all what is owed them... taxes... revenue... respect... honour" (13:7).

Why was Paul addressing this issue to the church in Rome? We know that in the late fifties AD, just a couple of years after Paul wrote his letter to the Roman church, there was civil unrest due to the heavy taxes being imposed by the state, and a fearful Nero even suggested that all indirect taxes cease in order to keep the peace. We also know that the emperor had only recently welcomed back the Jews to Rome, having expelled them for trouble associated with "Chrestus". And we know that, in Israel, the activist group named the Zealots were stirring up revolt against Rome that would come to a violent head in AD 66 and would result in Jerusalem being raised to the ground in AD 70. Paul is certainly *principled*, and he believes that governing authorities are divinely instituted structures for ordering society. However, given the social context and political climate, I suggest Paul is certainly also being *pragmatic*. He wants Christians to live peaceably, to get on with their lives, their faith, their mission, and not unnecessarily rock the boat or give grounds for unnecessary persecution. Twice, in verses 1 and 5, Paul says that Christians must *submit* to authorities; the Greek term *hypotasso* being a conjunction of two words *hypo*, "under", and *tasso*, "arrange". It was a military term for being under the orders of one's commanders.

As young Christian I recall a local preacher saying that, because we are under grace rather than law, we were not bound by the speed limit! I should have given that as an excuse when I was caught speeding... but actually it's madness! Christians are under the law of the land as long as that does not demand we act contrary to the law of God. Christians should be the best citizens, and the most law-abiding where the laws are just. We bless and honour and pray for the structures God gives for our good. We are the first to pay all our taxes and revenues. The great church apologist of the second century, Justin Martyr, in his *First Apology* challenged the Romans to investigate rumours of Christian misbehaviour, expecting they were groundless. He noted that Christians pay their taxes and pray for the emperor. He asserted that, once the facts were in, Christians would be found to be "moral, upright, and law-abiding citizens who are the empire's best allies in securing good order".[320]

As Christians who understand the reality of sin, and whose worldview recognizes only the kingdom of heaven as the perfect rule, we do not idealize any human institution. We do not expect more from them than they can deliver.

We pray for those who govern in authority, that they be given wisdom and courage, and make righteous judgments. In a democracy the church can also influence political structures through the political action of writing, lobbying, and voting.

That said, I was sad when a friend of mine in the House of Lords told me that it was often noted among MPs that they get bags of mail from Christians accusing or criticizing them. How tragic that this is the perception of many politicians when it comes to the church! Perhaps if we sent letters encouraging them, and assuring them of our prayers, they might listen to our lobbying more readily.

I confess at one time I had resigned myself to believing politics was pointless. I was less than supportive when some of my students wanted me to encourage a pro-political stance, writing to MPs on ethical issues. I did not vote at a local or national level for almost a decade. This was not just laziness or indifference: I had even justified it theologically, based on Jesus saying: "My kingdom is not of this world" and speaking of "the prince of this world" (John 18:38; 12:31; 14:30; 16:11, NIV) suggesting to me then that demonic powers controlled the earth. (I was especially struck by the temptation of Jesus when the devil said that all the authority and glory of the cities was his to give!) But the Lord told me, in no uncertain terms, that I was wrong. Yes the demonic is at work and always has a vested interest in power, but that does not mean Christians are to retreat. Indeed, we advance. We are to be the influence in society for good, as leaven in the lump, as salt in the meat. I used to think I was called to get people into church "ministry" – now I see that Christians can and must be in local, county, or national government – there as ministers of God, and for our good.

3. The church *sieves* good from bad government

"For rulers are not a terror to good conduct, but to bad. Would you have no fear of the one who is in authority? Then do what is good, and you will receive his approval, for he is God's servant for your good... an avenger who carries out God's wrath on the wrongdoer. Therefore one must be in subjection, not only to avoid God's wrath but also for the sake of conscience" (13:3–5).

Government is instituted by God to preserve justice and promote good. I am sure that most politicians are motivated largely by such noble ends. Whether they recognize their authority as divinely derived or not, they function as God's servants and ministers.

However, this is not a carte-blanche legitimation or divine sanction of all authorities. Government, in all its forms, must be tested by whether it governs righteously. Paul offers here not just a description of government but a criterion for it. The Mennonite theologian, John Yoder:

> *They are ministers of God only to the extent to which they busy themselves or in that they devote themselves to the assigned function.*[321]

Governments are God's servants, and are to be obeyed, when and if they approve what is good, and when they do good – which involves exercising in God's place judgment and wrath in punishing the evil-doer. When governments do not approve good, or reward good, or punish evil, then they are not God's servants but agents of evil. When governments who hold the sword to uphold justice turn the sword on the innocent, they are not God's servants but agents of evil.

C. S. Lewis, in his classic *Mere Christianity*, writes:

> *The State exists simply to promote and to protect the ordinary happiness of human beings. A husband and wife chatting over a fire; a couple of friends having a game of darts in a pub; a man reading a book in his own room or digging in his own garden – that is what the State is there for. And unless they are helping to increase and prolong and protect such moments, all the laws,*

> *parliaments, armies, courts, police, economics etc are simply a waste of time.*[322]

God gives good government, but not all governments are God-given. If government as a principle is God's means of exercising justice, the demonic will seek to seize, subvert, and pervert authority structures. When the state seeks to sit on the throne that belongs to the King, Jesus, it becomes an idol, a blasphemy. In Romans 13 we are encouraged to recognize the state as divinely ordained; in Revelation 13 we see the state demonically controlled and the great perpetrator of satanic whim. Ironically Paul, who here is calling the Romans to obey the authorities in Rome due to their being a structure instituted by God, will shortly – after writing this – himself appeal to Caesar to protect and defend him against the assassination attempts of the Jewish leaders. And he will be sent to Rome where eventually he will be executed by Nero!

Sometimes civil disobedience will be patently obviously required:

- Daniel refused to obey the edict to pray only to King Darius for thirty days, and was thrown in the lions' den (Daniel 6).
- Peter and the apostles were forbidden by the Sanhedrin to preach the gospel, but they refused on the grounds that they should obey God not men (Acts 5:29).
- Many Christians in the early centuries of the Roman empire chose martyrdom rather than hand over their sacred scrolls to be burned or blaspheme by declaring Caesar as lord.
- Some Christians, all too few, hid Jews in Nazi-occupied Europe, rather than comply with the wicked law and hand them over to be exterminated.

These are all very clear incidents when civil disobedience was obviously required by faithfulness to Christ. But many times civil disobedience may be a less black-and-white matter. At such times we must act according to our own Christian conscience (13:5), for instance, the Christian pacifist conscientiously objecting to military conscription.

Yes, we render unto Caesar what is Caesar's, but we render unto God what is God's (Matthew 22:21) – and if Caesar wants what is

God's, he isn't getting it. Pastor Martin Niemöller was imprisoned after preaching against the Nazis in Hitler's Germany. The prison chaplain visited him, and asked, "What brings you here? Why are you in prison?" Niemöller retorted: "And, brother, why are you not in prison?"[323] Give to Caesar what is Caesar's, and to God what is God's, but be aware that at times the state will cause us to suffer for not giving to Caesar what is God's.

In conclusion

The rule of the state is part of God's economy in this age. God *gives*, the church *lives* under good government, and the church *sieves* government. Meanwhile we wait expectantly for the coming rule of Christ's kingdom at his return, as Isaiah prophesied: "Of the increase of his government and of peace there will be no end, on the throne of David and over his kingdom, to establish it and to uphold it with justice and with righteousness from this time forth and for evermore" (Isaiah 9:7).

44

Get Up and Get Dressed (13:8–14)

God has allowed me to have teenage sons as a payback for the way I treated my parents when I was a teenager. My sons are amazing – I'm so proud of them. However, their approach to communication is interesting. They do not recognize that the word "no" makes up a complete sentence. They think a "grunt" is a conversation. They think the bedroom is a greenhouse where they can cultivate bacteria, or a workshop where they can strip old computers and solder metal on their bed! They have managed to create a strangely foul odour that seeps from the "green zone" onto the landing.

One of the important phrases that parents of teenagers learn with teens is: "Please get up and get dressed." An infant needs someone to get them up and dress them. A teenager needs to be repeatedly told to get up and get dressed. An adult is able to get up and get dressed himself. The Christians in Rome are somewhat like teenagers who need Paul to say to them, "Come on, it's time to get up and get dressed."

Get up

"And do this, understanding the present time. The hour has come for you to wake up from your slumber, because our salvation is nearer now than when we first believed. The night is nearly over; the day is almost here" (13:11–12, NIV).

In verses 9–10 Paul commands us to live a life of love, fulfilling the law. Here he echoes Jesus' teaching that loving God and loving your neighbour fulfil the law, because love for God and one's neighbour is the whole purpose of the law.

Sadly, some in the church of Rome are following the law of the flesh and not the law of love. Paul's command to live by love is given the incentive: do this, understanding the present time. It is as if he's saying: "Don't you know what time it is? Get up." Paul provokes an urgency to live righteously, for two reasons: first, because evil is pressing in all around them and some are not resisting; secondly, because Jesus is returning soon for them and some are not ready. The metaphor is one of the night being nearly over and dawn approaching. Evil is at hand and Christ's return is at hand. The church must be ready to face their foe and embrace their Lord.

Paul tells them to get up (*egerthenai*) from their slumber (Greek *hypnos* which gives us the word "hypnotized"). These Christians need to awake and arise. The term for rising is generally used in the New Testament of the resurrection of Jesus, and Paul may be implying that they should live in the power of the resurrection. Some Christians in the Roman church are sound asleep as their enemy presses in; they are not vigilant and they are vulnerable. Spiritually and morally they have let their guard down and are in danger of being overrun.

The historic American Civil War Army Regulations article 42 states: "Any sentinel who shall be found sleeping on his post, or shall leave it before he be regularly relieved, shall suffer death, or such other punishment as shall be inflicted by the sentence of a court martial." Why so severe? The fact is that to sleep on duty puts both your own life and those of others in danger. Jesus told the parable of the wheat and the weeds (Matthew 13:25) and said that "while they slept the enemy came upon them, sowing weeds". Had they been awake and alert, they would have seen the enemy and resisted.

Many Christians have become dozy and the enemy has subtly come in and sown weeds in their soul. Ask yourself the question before God: what areas of your soul have become overgrown with weeds? Are there sins, moral weaknesses in your life, that you would never have permitted a few years ago? Are there manners of speech, actions, attitudes, habits, that you would never have exhibited once, when you were most alive to Christ, and yet now compromise, complacency, and conformity to the world have won you over? Is there anything in your life that would make your godly grandmother blush? "A little sleep, a little slumber, a little folding of the hands to rest, and poverty will come upon you like a robber" (Proverbs 6:10–11). Rouse yourself, root out the sin, repent, and allow no rest to come to you until you are all you can be for God.

In the 1930s Britain was weary, recovering from the Great Depression and still feeling the effects of World War I. Trying to get back on its feet, Britain had better things to do than worry about Hitler's rise to power and arming a nation for war. In September 1938 Neville Chamberlain appeased Hitler and waved a bit of paper, the Munich Agreement, which he lauded as "Peace for our time". Britain, along with France and Italy, had agreed to allow Germany to take control of the Sudetenland (a part of Czechoslovakia) in exchange for Germany making no further territorial demands. Only Churchill understood the true nature of the times. Disgusted, he told the House of Commons, "England has been offered a choice between war and shame. She has chosen shame, and will get war."[324] There is an enemy of our souls – there is opposition to the kingdom we belong to and to the King we serve. Spiritual war is upon us (Revelation 13:7). We must choose war or shame. If we sleep, we lose. If we appease, we lose in shame. Better to wake up and fight and win.

Paul's "second incentive" to being awake is so that the church may take the necessary preparations for Jesus' return and not miss the glory of the reward he comes to bring for those who are eagerly looking for his coming. Jesus will return like a thief in the night, but for those who are awake, there is no surprise – their lamps are burning, their eyes wide open. They have done all that is required to discharge their duties and prepare themselves, and he comes bringing reward.

The twelve disciples were always asleep at important moments. They slept through Jesus' agony at Gethsemane (Luke 22:45–46); they slept through his glory on the mount of transfiguration, and it was only "when they became fully awake" that "they saw his glory" (Luke 9:32).

The Bible speaks of a bride who has "made herself ready" for her bridegroom (Revelation 21:2). Was there ever a bride who stayed in bed and missed her own wedding? Never. Remember, too, the Parable of the Wise and Foolish Virgins (Matthew 25:1–13) in which the "foolish virgins" are not prepared for the bridegroom's arrival. "Watch, therefore, for you know neither the day nor the hour." Anticipation of the return of Christ must shape how we live today. Knowing he comes bringing both salvation and condemnation, reward and judgment, we must be ready to greet him and receive our due from him. "Blessed are those servants whom the master finds awake when he comes. Truly, I say to you, he will dress himself for service and have them recline at table, and he will come and serve them" (Luke 12:37). What would you do if you knew Jesus was coming back next week? What changes would you make in your life? What sins would you repent of? What apologies would you offer? What would you give away? What would you throw away?

So, why wait?

I once heard of a man who began every day opening the curtains and enquiring: "Is it today Lord?" If it had been, he was up and ready. Are you?

Get dressed

"So let us put aside the deeds of darkness and put on the armour of light. Let us behave decently, as in the daytime, not in orgies and drunkenness, not in sexual immorality and debauchery, not in dissension and jealousy. Rather, clothe yourselves with the Lord Jesus Christ, and do not think about how to gratify the desires of the sinful nature" (13:12–14, NIV).

Paul says we are to get dressed. But before we can put on our new clothes, we must throw off our old, filthy clothes of the flesh and sin. I know someone who once gave a talk at a public school in his pyjamas, to make a point; but generally, we take off our bed-clothes before adding our work-day clothes.

Paul says "behave decently"; the word "behave" translates the Greek *peripateo* meaning "to walk around". We behave "decently" – the Greek word is *euschemonos,* meaning "good appearance". Belief must affect our behaviour. Christians must be *seen* to be different. How we live, speak, what we read, how we spend our money, our time, what we do, what we do not do, must mark us out as Christian. In particular the hallmark of the Christian is to be seen to live a life of love for our neighbour.

Paul offers three negative couplets illustrating the sort of behaviour that ought never be seen among Christians: "revelry and drunkenness"; "sexual immorality and impurity" (*aselgeia,* the absence of moral restraint); and "strife and jealousy". These things you might expect to see in a city centre in Britain on a Friday night. It's rather surprising to see them listed here, perhaps, yet they are the very things Paul needs to challenge in the church. One may presume that the church in Rome is in danger of absorbing the values and vices of Rome. All such attitudes and behaviour are to be thrown aside like filthy clothes to make way for the new clothing in Christ.

When I was in the meat trade, each day I wore a starched, white doctor's coat. By the end of the day it was smeared in blood, guts, and fat. It was great at the end of the day to take it off, throw it in for washing, have a wash, put on clean clothes, and go out not stinking of visceral animal remains. Paul says we need to cast off the stinking clothes of sin and put on the new clothes that Christ offers. For we have a whole new wardrobe with two new sets of kit: "clothe yourselves with Christ" (13:14) and "put on the armour of light" (13:12).

The Greek term for clothe is *enduo,* which was used of an actor entering fully into their role part, being "in character". To be clothed with Christ means to take on the virtues, characteristics, and intentions of Christ – his beautiful perfections and spotless nature are to become ours. The Christian is not play-acting but assuming their identity in Christ. To be clothed *with* Christ is the privilege of every Christian. To be clothed *in* Christ is to be wrapped in his righteousness, to be freed from judgment and be free to enter God's presence as his Son. To be clothed with Christ is to live like Christ and in so doing to fully fulfil the law – as he did – living a life of love for one's neighbour and for God.

When tempted to boast, we must put on Christ's humility. When tempted to lust, we must put on Christ's purity. When tempted to anger, we must put on Christ's gentleness. When tempted to selfishness, we must put on Christ's self-sacrifice. When afflicted by condemnation, we put on Christ's blood. When tempted to fear, we put on Christ's resurrection victory.

We must also put on the "armour of light". The Greek word is *hoopla.* The Hoplites were an armoured fighting force of Greek soldiers. The word might better be translated "weapons" as elsewhere in the New Testament – these are the "weapons of our warfare" (2 Corinthians 10:4). Armour tends to be purely defensive, to enable us to stand, whereas weapons are offensive as well, enabling us to advance. Certainly Paul's word here suggests both offence *and* defence.

What are these armoured weapons? They are not carnal but spiritual; they include prayer, the gospel, the Word of God, sacrifice, love, the Spirit-filled life and the gifts. And who or what are the foes? The weapons of light counter deeds of darkness – the misdeeds of the flesh won't give up without a fight. If we don't fight we will lose.

In the movie *Braveheart* there is a scene where the Scottish and English armies face each other on the battlefield. After a lengthy speech by the English, intended to put fear into the Scottish ranks, Wallace (played passionately by Mel Gibson) rides towards the English. His friend Hamish asks: "Where are you going?" Wallace replies, "I'm going to pick a fight!" Hamish approves. "Well, we didn't get dressed up for nothing." Paul doesn't want us to dress up in our new identity in Christ and with our new spiritual armour for nothing. We get up and get dressed to fight the good fight.

Someone told me that their recurring nightmare is to be caught in public naked. This is in fact not an unusual nightmare. When Christ returns, do not be found spiritually naked, clothed only in the garb of sin, but in his righteousness, armed for war.

In conclusion

Augustine, right from his teenage years, engaged in revelry and sexual promiscuity. In his twenties, as an academic philosopher, he was aware that his lifestyle was not what it should be. Although the influence of his praying mum was never far away, he was powerless to resist the flesh. We have already made mention of how Augustine was one day overwhelmed by a sense of sin when in the garden. His *Confessions* show his distress at that time – he kept exclaiming over and over: "How long? How long? Tomorrow and tomorrow? Why not now? Why not this hour an end to my depravity?" Having heard a voice instructing him to pick up a collection of the apostle Paul's letters that lay nearby, he opened them up at Romans 13, and read the words we have just been considering, exhorting us not to walk "in orgies or drunkenness".

He was pole-axed. God was telling him how not to live, and telling him that in Christ it was possible to be free, to be clean. "I neither wished nor needed to read further – light filled my heart." In that moment he surrendered to Christ, was saved, healed, and delivered, and became the Western church's greatest ever theologian.

If you act upon them, the truths presented here by Paul will at the very least change your life for the better.

45

Don't Get Edgy with the Veggie (14:1–11)

When I first met my wife, she was a vegetarian and I was a butcher. She took up eating bacon sandwiches and we got married.

When I was Oxford Pastorate Chaplain, we interviewed for an administrator to be my PA. The best candidate, Tom, declared himself on his application forms as a committed vegetarian. At his interview I asked him how committed he was to his vegetarianism and whether he could cope working with a former butcher. He replied, "Very vegetarian, although I don't march with placards saying meat is murder."

My colleagues wanted Tom to work for me, but I could not see how we could possibly work together – to my mind vegetarianism and evangelicalism were basically incompatible! My wise mother told me to employ the best person for the job. Tom was the most qualified and so, reluctantly, I gave him the job. We worked together very happily and fruitfully for seven years. Most days I offered him a bacon sandwich, and he always refused. He was a wonderful colleague, friend, and Christian, and through this I learned not to get edgy with the veggie.

1. The church in Rome

In Chapter 13 Paul has spoken about the need to live in love with one's neighbour, for love fulfils the law. He also warned against the sins of the flesh and highlighted dissension and factions as fruit of the flesh. That was no abstract meditation and exhortation. The church in Rome was being divided down the fault line of Jewish and Gentile religious custom. The Jewish Christians were still expressing their Jewishness by Torah observance and kosher food rules, keeping Jewish festivals and sabbaths. They were abstaining from meat, as it had probably been offered to Roman idols at the point of slaughter and had not been killed in a kosher way.

Conversely, the Gentile Christians, having received Christ, felt no compunction to become Jewish in practice and change and limit their diet. And they were non-plussed about keeping the strict Jewish sabbath observance, probably following custom and instead worshipping on Sunday, the day of Christ's resurrection. So the church was divided over its food and festivals. How could there ever be true fellowship when they could not eat together or meet on the same day?

Paul's principle is pragmatic: "Accept him whose faith is weak, without passing judgment on disputable matters ... The man who eats everything must not look down on him who does not, and the man who does not eat everything must not condemn the one who does, for God has accepted him" (14:1, 3 NIV).

Quarrelling and judging and condemning one another marked the Roman church. Paul uses the Greek word *exouthenein* meaning "to despise, belittle". And this was occurring over the small matter of food. This is sinful and unbecoming in a Christian.

Interestingly Paul does actually describe those who won't eat meat as "weak" and those who do as "strong". It would seem Paul is siding with the meat-eaters and believing those who abstain for religious reasons have a weak understanding of God's new economy and a weak conscience before God. However, while Paul sides theologically with the "strong in conscience", and while he does not regard any day more special than another, nevertheless maintaining unity is more crucial and more important to him than the freedom to eat meat.

American pastor and writer Kent Hughes says insightfully:

> *the easy solution to this problem would have been to form two churches – the church of the Carnivores and the first church of the Vegetarians. Paul fortunately was committed to the nobler, but far more difficult solution.*[325]

At almost all costs the Roman congregation of Jewish and Gentile believers is to try and keep the unity of the Spirit in the bond of peace (Ephesians 4:3).

2. The church through history

Paul suggests they are quarrelling over "disputable matters" (14:1, NIV). The Greek is *diakriseis dialogismon* – these are verbal disagreements over conflicting reasoning. Major credal doctrines are not the issue at stake here. The Puritan Richard Baxter, drawing on Augustine, famously declared: "In essentials, unity; in non-essentials, liberty; in all things, charity."[326]

The great tragedy is that most of the big church splits over the centuries have tended to be over minor matters – secondary issues fiercely fought without charity. The English Evangelical Revival leaders, John Wesley and George Whitefield, who had been great friends and colleagues, eventually fell out over the question of exactly how sovereign God was in salvation; what place "free will" had to play in it. The Arminian Wesley emphasized free will, while the Calvinist Whitefield emphasized divine sovereignty – and a terrible tear in the relationship ensued, with defensive tracts and sermons following. One wonders if the great work of God was being targeted by the demonic and subverted by emphasizing difference over non-credal issues.

One of the great scars in church history was the schism between the Eastern Orthodox and Western Catholic church in 1054. There had been a growing sense of unease for many years but now there was a final and complete breakdown driven by differences of culture, identity, theology, and power play. Some issues were significant. However, bizarrely, many of the presenting causes of tension were over such minutiae as whether the bread at the eucharist was leavened or unleavened, and even more absurd were arguments over hair styles, the Romans wearing the tonsure (shaved crown) while the Greeks wore beards and long hair.

In the modern church Karl Barth and Emil Brunner were great friends and colleagues promoting the values and vision of the dialectic movement and the return to orthodoxy from liberalism. They believed that liberalism's God is not God at all, but simply a deified humanity. Regrettably, they fell out over the question of whether God can be known through creation. They never spoke to each other again, each writing books and tracts to defend his own nuanced position against the other. It was not until thirty-five years later, when Brunner was on his deathbed, that Barth wrote a note to him that went some way towards reconciliation.

Churches split over credal issues that were less than credal: whether women can speak or not speak; whether women ought to cover their heads or not cover their heads; whether women can wear trousers or only long skirts; whether to have modern electric instruments or an old organ and choir; whether the clergy wear robes or go mufty... and on it goes. The issues in Rome dividing the church were not irrelevant but they were not central. They were the basis of discussion not the basis of division. At times there will be need for a robust defence of truth, and even separation or schism if the orthodox faith is being undermined. Such perhaps was the case at the Protestant Reformation. However, such moments are rare. Most splits are in fact over secondary matters.

In an interview with *Christianity Today* magazine in 1996 John Stott was asked what issues would lead him to leave the Church of England. He offered three: first, if the Church of England formally denied the humanity or divinity of Christ; secondly, if the Church of England denied justification by grace through faith; and thirdly, if the Church of England approved homosexual partnerships as a legitimate alternative to heterosexual marriage.[327] All three would show a fundamental rejection of Christian orthodoxy and orthopraxy – doctrine and ethics – and an utter disregard for Scripture, requiring a radical response. However, where there is or is not a breakdown over these defining doctrinal and ethical matters, John Stott could affirm that "the visible unity of the church must allow room for divergence of belief and practice in matters of secondary importance".[328]

3. What about us?

"... and let not the one who abstains pass judgment on the one who eats, for God has welcomed him. Who are you to pass judgment on the servant of another? It is before his own master that he stands or falls. And he will be upheld, for the Lord is able to make him stand" (14:3–4).

It would seem being a veggie- or a meat-eater is not a big deal to God, and consequently it should not matter to us. Paul reminds his readers that vegetarians are God's "servants", God has "accepted them" and they will stand rather than fall, because "the Lord is able to make him stand". Humankind looks on the outward appearance but God looks on the heart. I believe God prefers the person who does the wrong thing for the right reason, over the Pharisee who does the right thing for the wrong motive. I am a stickler for sound doctrine – it is my calling and my training – but I suspect God may be more interested in a soft heart towards him and other people, than he is in those who think they have their doctrine all buttoned up yet sit in judgment over others. My father once told me of two Reformed men he knew, one in Plymouth and one in London, who were so "sound" in their own eyes – the only ones who were right on some obscure doctrine – that they met geographically half way to have communion with each other. There was no church good enough for them to be in communion with. Absurd.

The two greatest evangelical preachers of the nineteenth century were the American D. L. Moody and the Englishman C. H. Spurgeon. When Moody first came on an evangelistic tour to the UK, he paid Spurgeon a visit. Apparently he was met at the door by Spurgeon smoking a big cigar. Moody was shocked and asked: "How can you, a man of God, smoke that cigar?" Spurgeon took no offence but simply pointed at Moody's rather rotund belly and asked, "How can you, a man of God, be that fat?" The fact is, they disagreed on the minor issues of diet and smoking: Moody stayed fat, Spurgeon kept smoking, and they became the very best of friends.

In the powerful movie *The Apostle* there is a telling scene when Sonny, a Pentecostal preacher, watches a Catholic priest blessing a fishing fleet of boats with holy water, all robed up with attending acolytes and crucifers. Sonny says approvingly, "You do it your way and we do it mine, but in the end we get it done, don't we?"

So, how can we avoid getting edgy with the veggie? Let me suggest three ways.

Live with a clean conscience before God

"One person esteems one day as better than another, while another esteems all days alike. Each one should be fully convinced in his own mind" (14:5).

Some things are crystal clear and crucial. There are doctrinal and ethical matters that are simply not open for negotiation. The Epistle to the Romans is quite clear what we are to believe and how we are to behave. But what Paul is addressing are those *disputable* matters – not doctrinal ones – that are not definitively addressed by Scripture. At this point, where there is no direct divine decree, the individual is free to act according to their conscience.

In the Reformed tradition there has been a debate over what is permitted in "worship". There are two main positions, the "normative principle" and the "regulative principle". The normative principle claims that worship must include all that Scripture commands but may *also* include whatever Scripture does not directly prohibit. The "regulative principle", on the other hand, states that worship must include *only* what the Bible commands. Thus, regulative Reformed Christians would say no to icons or incense or drums or electric guitars or dancing because these are not clearly commanded or modelled in the New Testament. However, the normative Christians, like Anglicans, would say yes to electric guitars, incense, icons, dance, and so on, accepting whatever is not directly or indirectly prohibited.

This principle of normative versus regulative may be applied not just to how we worship, but also to issues of ethics in the church. Paul appears to take the normative principle approach here regarding food: whatever Scripture commands us to do we do; whatever it prohibits, we do not do; however, if an issue is neither clearly prohibited nor clearly permitted, Paul allows the individual to use their sanctified common sense and freedom of conscience.

Live unto the Lord

"The one who observes the day, observes it in honour of the Lord. The one who eats, eats in honour of the Lord, since he gives thanks to God, while the one who abstains, abstains in honour of the Lord and gives thanks to God" (14:6).

Paul is no moral relativist; his is not the ethical "Whatever!" He is not advocating a complete free-for-all where anyone can do anything they want. Instead, Paul is looking at the heart motive. If the Christian eating meat and the Christian abstaining from meat are motivated to glorify God, then both the carnivore and the veggie gain God's approval. Again, let us consider C. H. Spurgeon, who was not only criticized by Moody for cigar-smoking but was condemned in print by others for it as well. He replied in a letter to *The Times* in which he said, "I mean to smoke to the glory of God," and in a later letter justifying the use of such language he wrote:

> *When I have found intense pain relieved, a weary brain soothed, and calm, refreshing sleep obtained by a cigar, I have felt grateful to God, and have blessed His name; this is what I meant, and by no means did I use sacred words triflingly.*[329]

He was not being rebellious, and he did not believe smoking cigars was a sin. (Remember, this was before we knew that smoking kills.) Spurgeon enjoyed his cigar as a relaxant, even as pain relief, and smoked it before God giving thanks to God. And I suspect God enjoyed him enjoying it. Paul writes in 14:8, "If we live, we live for the Lord; and if we die, we die for the Lord. So, whether we live or die, we belong to the Lord" (NIV).

So it's not that we "live and let live"; it's that we live to the Lord.

In just fourteen verses Paul refers to the Lord ten times. That is surely what matters here: in all our living, in all our thinking, we must live it for and bring it before the Lord.

Live with your judgment in view

"Why do you pass judgment on your brother?... For we will all stand before the judgment seat of God... Therefore let us not pass judgment on one another any longer" (14:10, 13).

Paul says that the act of criticizing someone else's religious devotion is to sit in judgment over them. And who set you up as judge of them? The ultimate arbiter of our actions is not us, but God. Paul says analogously that "a servant is judged by his master" – that servant is accountable and responsible only to their master. And similarly, it is before God that we must give account – not the Spanish Inquisition!

My own family were Plymouth Brethren for several generations. My grandad was a teaching elder with them but in the late 1960s was "put out" of fellowship. The Brothers debated whether a companion of an elderly Sister could own a radio! My grandad said that it was not strictly forbidden in Scripture (the normative principle) and so, while the Brethren might decide not to own one, the companion was entitled to. However, the elders disagreed with this, and expelled or "silenced" my grandad and my granny for being worldly! As my mother and uncle stayed in, they were cut off from their parents for a time... until they came to their senses and also left!

Paul says that "each of us will give an account of himself to God" (14:12).

The emphasis here is on the individual taking personal responsibility for their own actions, because individually they will be held accountable for them. They will not be held to account for how others lived. Yes, corporately we have a responsibility to study and apply Scripture's instructions and exhortations. However, on non-credal matters where Scripture lacks clear direction, and if its principles when applied still leave a question on what is appropriate, we should allow the individual to take personal responsibility, and we do not prescribe what or how they must act. This is not mere pragmatism, it is the principle Paul operated on. You will be judged by how *you* lived, not how they lived. You will be judged by how you treated your brother, not by how you judged him.

In conclusion

A friend of mine was invited to meet a legendary preacher, writer, and revivalist. He went with a few other church leaders, and they enjoyed an evening speaking about God and his work and recalling great revivals in the past, as well as longed-for future ones. At the end of the evening, as they left, this old saint stood at the door and raised his hand. They waited with bated breath for the oracle to come from this great man of God, and then he spoke: "Remember, no mixed bathing!" My friend shook his head in amazement, not knowing whether to burst out laughing or what. Was that it? Was that the wisdom of the ages from this saintly sage? "No mixed bathing, only single-sex swimming."

Mixed bathing is neither the unforgivable sin nor the handbrake on revival. But even the greatest saint can have religious blind spots.

So, what are yours?

46

Risen and Reigning (14:9)

George Gittoes was part of a UN medical team in Rwanda visiting the village of Kibeho when he found himself in the midst of genocide. The horror of what he saw has branded his soul, and he has produced some of the most incredible painted reflections on the massacre. Commentating on his award-winning picture, *The Preacher*, he wrote:

> *It was horrific, we saw children killed before our eyes. We were going in and getting the wounded out as the people were macheteing and shooting and killing. Suddenly there was this guy standing in the middle of the people who were dying all around us. He just began to give this sermon in one of those beautiful melodious African voices, mingling English, French, Rwandan – quoting those sections of the New Testament to them, those bits which give hope and tell us about the possibility of an afterlife. I thought it took tremendous courage, because he exposed himself, yet he had the presence of mind to know that other people needed some kind of reassurance. He gave it to them. Then the killing closed in.*[330]

What was it that gave this preacher such fearlessness in the face of death, such selflessness to herald the gospel? It was the faith, hope, and love that arise from the fact of the empty tomb on Easter day. For Paul, the resurrection was the *sine-qua-non* – the absolute necessity – of Christianity. Without it Christians are fools, dead men; with it we are sons of God who will live for ever. The resurrection is the foundation of Christianity and the presupposition behind every major theme in Romans – whether the revelation of God in Christ or the doctrines of salvation, sanctification, and glorification. Distinguished Catholic

Professor Gerald O'Collins writes: "In a profound sense, Christianity without the Resurrection is not simply Christianity without its final chapter. It is not Christianity at all."[331]

Jesus is risen. What does this mean for us now? Here are seven glorious aspects or outcomes of the resurrection.

1. Jesus is Lord

Paul writes: "For to this end Christ died and lived again, that he might be Lord both of the dead and of the living" (14:9).

The resurrection of Jesus Christ vindicated his claim to be Lord and God, and guaranteed that one day he would rule the living and raise and rule the dead.

Jesus staked his claims to be divine, and invited people's assessment of him on his resurrection. Jesus was asked on two separate occasions to perform a miraculous sign as proof that he was the Messiah and that he had authority to forgive sins and clean out the temple. On both occasions he responded, not by pointing to the moral perfection of his life, nor the profundity of his teaching, nor even the remarkable power evidenced in his miracles; instead, he said, "no sign will be given… except the sign of the prophet Jonah. For just as Jonah was three days and three nights in the belly of the great fish, so will the Son of Man be three days and three nights in the heart of the earth" (Matthew 12:39–40). On the second occasion he replied: "Destroy this temple, and in three days I will raise it up" (John 2:19).

The resurrection is the great vindication of Jesus' divine authority. In communist Russia, a common theme indoctrinated into children from infancy went along the lines of "Lenin knows everything, Lenin is always with us". In an atheist society, where the right worship of God is forbidden, other constructs receive divine attributions. However, everyone who visits Lenin's mausoleum in Moscow today can see the only way Lenin is still with us is by his being soaked in formaldehyde. But Jesus' tomb is empty – no bones have ever been produced to deny the claim, and significantly there was no pilgrimage to his place of death or burial for 300 years. There was no point, for Christ is risen, Christ is Lord, Christ knows everything, Christ is with us always, and the changed lives of the apostles and the changed world two millennia on testify to his lordship.

My friend John Peters gave one of the most remarkable evangelistic messages I ever heard to a group of tough cynical young men I introduced him to. He began, "I am an exorcist." Having gained their attention, he then said it was the power of Jesus' name that expelled demons. He showed that Jesus' name was powerful over the demonic because Jesus is God. He then showed on the basis of scriptural evidence that Jesus' divinity was proved by his resurrection. It was a tour de force. Jesus' power as Lord stands or falls with the resurrection.

2. Lives can be transformed

Back in Romans 1:4 Paul stated that Jesus was declared to be the Son of God in power by resurrection through the Spirit. And that same power of the Spirit, of the same resurrected Lord, had given him grace and appointed him an apostle. That power changed lives then, and continues to do so today.

Paul had been the assassin Saul. He had held the coats for the lynch mob and had given his approval to the stoning of Stephen, the first church martyr. In his zeal to suppress what he deemed a blasphemous cult worshipping a false Messiah, Saul gained permits from the high priest to arrest Christians, and had set out to Damascus to arrest and punish Christians. He was a man on a mission of murder. But on the road to Damascus a blinding light suddenly shone, and a crystal-clear voice called out. Christ stood before the Christ-killer, and an assassin was stopped in his tracks.

Stunned and terrified, Saul cried out, "Who are you, Lord?" and the chilling reply came, "I am Jesus, whom you are persecuting" (Acts 9:5). Speaking personally, I would have been tempted to break Saul's neck, but Jesus would always rather change a life than end a life. Indeed, the assassin is offered the top job in the company – Apostle to the Gentiles! This revelation of the risen Christ brought a revolution into Paul's life. He would never be the same again. Jesus appeared to Saul – and Paul now knows that Jesus is risen, Jesus is Messiah, Jesus is Lord – and Paul will live ever after for him. Arriving in Damascus, Saul arrives as a new creature and a gospel preacher.

3. The power of a transformed life

I will never forget ministering at a Madrid church for former drug addicts. It was named Betel (Spanish for Bethel which means "God's house") and was founded by the remarkable Elliot and Mary Tepper. It was filled with hundreds of men – strong, hard, scarred, and tattooed – worshipping God for all their worth. Several hundred men who had formerly been criminals, drug addicts – the scum of the earth – had been saved, healed, restored, delivered.

I recall that shortly before I spoke Elliot leant over and pointed out the fact that all the elders and pastors and worship leaders on the stage were in fact all ex-addicts, ex-cons, some even ex-murderers, who had met Christ behind bars. And their wives and mothers sat in church, tearfully worshipping God who had transformed their sons. They had endured the lifestyle of their sons before they met Christ – now they exulted in Christ who had worked miracles.

In Ephesians 1:19-20 Paul prays that the church will know the immeasurable greatness of the power which God exerted when he raised Jesus from the dead – the power of the resurrection is the power of the Holy Spirit (Romans 1:4) and that power is available to all who believe in Christ. The same power that conquered the grave lives in me. I wonder, can anyone tell? I must draw on that power to be a better man, a better husband, a better disciple, to overcome temptation, to transform my inherited programmed of sin in the flesh, to be transformed into the likeness of Christ.

4. Satan is defeated

On Good Friday the devil, a mere angel who would be king, smelled victory.

Christ was arrested, falsely accused, sentenced, condemned, beaten, and crucified. And the source of life suffered death. Stripped naked and caked in his own blood, he was laid lifeless in a stone-cold grave.

But Friday is not the end of the week and it's not the end of this story. The devil did not expect an epilogue; he did not reckon on an Easter Sunday. Yet as the words of the hymn celebrate: "Up from the grave he arose, with a mighty triumph o'er his foes".[332]

Halfway through the decisive battle of Waterloo, Napoleon thought his French armies had victory in their sights and even sent a message to Paris for the newspapers declaring that he had won. It was premature. Four hours later Wellington's British, having been bolstered by the arrival of the Prussian forces, had taken the day, and Napoleon fled the field. Similarly, on Good Friday the devil sent the message to his demons "Victory!" But it was premature. Easter Sunday was just around the corner. Jesus would shatter the bonds of death, throw off the grave clothes, kick away the tombstone, and step out into his victory!

One of the most famous boxing matches in the history of the sport was between Muhammad Ali and George Forema. The fight took place in Zaire (now the Democratic Republic of Congo) and is still often termed "the rumble in the jungle". The great ox Foreman pounded Ali for seven rounds. Punch after punch thundered into Ali who rarely got off the ropes. Everyone thought it was over. But remarkably, this was Ali's strategy, soaking up every punch until Foreman's strength was spent, his arms heavy and stiff with lactic acid. Then, in the eighth round, Ali danced up off the ropes, and in just a few, well-aimed punches Foreman was down and counted out. Later Ali described his technique as "rope a dope". And that is an apt metaphor for Good Friday. The devil had Christ on the ropes: he let go every blow he had, and many thought he had won. But Jesus was soaking them all up, and in the eighth round – or rather, on the third day – he rose again, off the ropes, and dealt the devil the decisive knock-out blow.

5. Sins are forgiven

"Jesus was delivered up for our trespasses and raised for our justification" (Romans 4:25). God is a just judge who must punish human sin; if he did not he would not be holy, good, and righteous – he would not be God. Death is the punishment for sin. We sinned, so we deserve death. But God intervened, God interfered, for us. The crucifixion is the great *no* to sin, as God punishes our sin in the Son. The resurrection is the great *yes* to life, as God accepts the sacrifice of

Jesus for us and in his life we live. If only we say yes to Christ and his cross, we receive God's yes to us. Jesus rising from the dead was God's declaration, and also God's demonstration, that we are forgiven.

There is an ancient rabbinical myth about the Jewish festival Yom Kippur, the Day of Atonement. On this day the high priest offered sacrifices for the nation's sins and entered God's sanctuary, the Holy of Holies, on behalf of the people. It is said that a scarlet thread (representing Israel's sins, red as scarlet) was nailed to the temple door. The nation would stand and wait with bated breath to see if the high priest reappeared; if he did, it would mean the sacrifice for the nation's sins was acceptable to God. And if it was, then miraculously the scarlet thread representing Israel's sins turned white as snow.

A beautiful symbol, if historically unlikely; however, on Good Friday Jesus our great High Priest went into the sanctuary bearing his own blood for the sins of the world, and on Easter Sunday Jesus reappeared, and sin's scarlet thread that hung over humanity turned white. God had accepted his Son's sacrifice for us, and our sins were atoned for.

When we trust in Jesus, when we look to his sacrifice for our sin, then the benefits of his death for us are applied to us: all charges against us are annulled, and we are set free from the sentence of death.

6. Death is defeated

"For if we have been united with him in a death like his, we shall be united with him in a resurrection like his" (Romans 6:5).

Death is the universal human experience. Every community has its cemetery. Death is the great shadow of fear hanging over mankind – not because of the pain that accompanies death but because of an innate, inchoate knowing that judgment awaits us on the other side of the veil.

The fear of death is wed to a longing for life. Shakespeare wrote of "immortal longings". Wealthy Californians spend millions speculating on so-called cryonic suspension – having their brains preserved in a frozen state, just in case future technology will be able to bring them to life again. At a more modest level, desperate housewives attempt to hold back aging with surgery, or botox injections, or anti-wrinkle cream, or desperate dieting, health regimes and vitamin supplements. Mid-life-crisis men join a gym, tattoo their arms, grow their hair long, or have it transplanted from private parts, buy a fast car, or a fast woman, or a fast bike, or trade in their covenant partner for a younger model, hoping to hold back the rapidly advancing years.

God is holy and God is life. Sin separates us from a holy God and the source of life. And so we must die. But if we trust in Christ, if we hide ourselves in his wounds, then he carries us through death to resurrection life, and to God. For the Christian who holds on to Christ's death for them, death holds no fear.

An English gentleman who was imprisoned in Flossenbürg concentration camp in Germany with Dietrich Bonhoeffer, but who survived, wrote this of Bonhoeffer's last moments:

> *They came for him. We bade him goodbye. He drew me aside. "This is the end," he said. "For me it is the beginning of life."*[333]

The prison doctor who observed Bonhoeffer kneeling to pray in his cell, moments before the guards came for him, recalled many years later that, after fifty years practising as a doctor, he had hardly ever seen a man die so entirely submissive to the will of God.[334] Our people die well. Those who truly have met Christ, who understand the gospel, know the best is yet to come.

Some of the most powerful moments I have experienced are when conducting Christian funerals. As we carry the coffin in, confronted by the weighty reality of death, I process with the coffin and proclaim Jesus' promise: "I am the resurrection and the life. Whoever believes in me, though he die, yet shall he live" (John 11:25). But to utter these words at the funeral of a non-believer is a chilling reminder of judgment. In the mines where slave Christians were worked to death by the Romans, those about to die saluted Christ and carved the words, "*vita, vita, vita*" – life, life, life.

7. God's reign is coming

"For to this end Christ died and lived again, that he might be Lord both of the dead and the living" (14:9).

The resurrection advances the rule of Christ. His rule is absolute: he will rule over all, dead and alive, and all will kneel before his throne.

The killing of Christ was a political act, for he was a political threat. The three major power blocks in Israel were: Temple Judaism (the Sanhedrin, high priests); the Jewish monarchy; and the Roman empire. All three felt undermined by this carpenter from Nazareth claiming to be the Christ, the anointed King of God. Jesus was a direct challenge to Caiaphas's religious power; to Pilate's political power; to Herod's sovereign power. All three would breathe more easily if he breathed no more. And so Jesus undermined the balance of power, and they did not want this "king" bringing his kingdom and upsetting theirs. The killing of Christ meant the removal of the competition.

Which means... the resurrection of Jesus proves Jesus *is* Lord, King, sovereign, ruler, the One who surmounts every other claim to power and authority.

The apostolic gospel always links the resurrection to the reign and return of Christ. The resurrection is thus a political event – establishing God's government – and the increase of God's government will have no end (Isaiah 9:7). Paul says that Christ "delivers the kingdom to God the Father after destroying every rule and every authority and power. For he must reign until he has put all his enemies under his feet" (1 Corinthians 15:24–25).

In conclusion

In C. S. Lewis's *The Lion, the Witch and the Wardrobe* Aslan is killed by the White Witch standing in the place of Edmund who had violated the law of Narnia. Justice is satisfied in his being put to death, but it transpires that a deeper magic is at work, and Aslan comes back to life. Narnia has been a cursed, frozen wasteland, where it's always winter and never Christmas. But when Aslan rises, the stone altar of justice and judgment is shattered, and the reign of the wicked White Witch is over. All her armies are undone, evil unravels, the curses work backwards, the snow melts, those frozen by the Witch come alive, and spring is ushered in.

N. T. Wright writes:

The resurrection completes the inauguration of God's kingdom… It is the decisive event demonstrating that God's kingdom really has been launched on earth as it is in heaven… The message of Easter is that God's new world has been unveiled in Jesus Christ and that you're now invited to belong to it.[335]

47

Super-Size, Super-Skinny, Super-Spiritual (14:17)

Anthelme Brillat-Savarin, in the prologue to his ground-breaking book *The Physiology of Taste: Or, Meditations on Transcendental Gastronomy* in 1826 offered twenty-two "apohorisms" which the book went on to explicate. He makes huge claims such as Aphorism number 11: "The fate of nations hangs upon their choice of food." His most famous is number 4, which states: "Tell me what you eat and I will tell you what you are."

"You are what you eat" is a widely repeated dictum that is far from true. I have a friend who weighs under ten stone (140 pounds); he once did a sponsored weight-gain for charity, stuffing chocolate bars and nuts all day long. After a month he had only gained a few pounds. My metabolism, on the other hand, is so slow that I only have to look at a roast dinner and I have gained a pound before anyone has said grace.

"You are what you eat" was a controlling theme in the church in Rome. As we have already seen, the community was divided over what foods were appropriate for Christians to eat. The Gentile Christians were happy to tuck into anything to the glory of God, while the Jewish Christians felt bound by their "kosher" laws (from the Hebrew *kashrut* meaning "fitting, appropriate") and felt morally unable to eat foods not sanctioned by Torah, or meat offered to idols, or animals not properly slaughtered and bled. The Jewish Christians believed "You are what you eat" and ate accordingly; the Gentile Christians believed "You are what you do not eat" and also ate accordingly. This theological disagreement and practical inability to share meals together was tearing apart the unity of the Christian community.

In Romans 14 Paul lays out his table manners, and we look at it again now to dig further beneath what is at stake here. In summary Paul says:

1. There is to be no judging, quarrelling, or dissension over disputable matters relating to food and drink.

2. All foods are clean and acceptable to eat.

3. Those of a weaker faith following restrictive food laws nevertheless remain acceptable to God.

4. Someone's conscience, not the community democratic consensus, dictates what is appropriate for them to eat, and they will ultimately be judged by whether they obeyed their conscience before God.

5. Though you are free to eat and drink whatever you want, you may not use your freedom to cause another to stumble by making them eat or drink against their conscience.

Paul here applies the same ethical model as earlier in his instruction on Christian political engagement. He is both principled and pragmatic; indeed his working principle is to be pragmatic, with Christian freedom and love, and divine judgment, as referents to control the moral decision. Paul is pragmatic: the church must not split over who does, or does not, eat what; Paul is principled: culinary and dietary issues must make way for unity and charity. Paul's axiom counters "You are what you eat" with: "The kingdom of God is not a matter of eating and drinking but of righteousness and peace and joy in the Holy Spirit" (14:17).

What God's kingdom is *not* about

"The kingdom of God is not a matter of eating and drinking" (14:17).

God's kingdom is not concerned with diet. We don't count calories in the kingdom! God's rule and reign in our life is neither advanced nor withheld by what is on the menu. In the new economy of God the citizens of the kingdom no longer express their doctrine and devotion through their diet. Once the Jews had a prescribed diet. The strict particulars on food given to Israel by Moses were not a divinely devised Dukan diet. A website introducing Hebrew thought and practice, called Judaism 101, states:

> *The Torah does not specify any reason for these laws, and for a Torah-observant, traditional Jew, there is no need for any other reason... We show our obedience to God by following these laws even though we do not know the reason.*[336]

Joseph Stern has argued that for many aspects of the law, "their validity depends essentially on divine decree, of which we know only by God's revelation."[337] Faithfulness to the law in its very unintelligibility becomes, therefore, a test of one's faithfulness and obedience to God.

That was then. Under the new economy of God – the New Covenant – things have changed. Peter himself famously had a threefold vision of a sheet covered in non-kosher food while at Simon Tanner's in Joppa. Three times God commanded, "Take and eat." Peter protested, "Lord, I have never eaten unclean food", to which God said, "Do not call that which I have made clean unclean." God was changing Peter's diet and his restrictive attitude to food so that he could eat anything with anyone.

As a consequence the apostles at the Jerusalem Council (c. AD 50) went on to advise that the Gentile believers were free from the Law, with the only exception that they must not eat meat from animals that had been strangled or offered to idols (Acts 15:20). In part, this reflected God's covenant established with Noah (Genesis 9:4). Surprisingly Paul subsequently revises even these limited dietary restrictions, and says: "Eat whatever is sold in the meat market without raising question on the ground of conscience" (1 Corinthians 10:25). The New Testment apostolic teaching is that Gentile Christians can eat and enjoy everything on the menu, and while Jewish Christians *may* continue eating only kosher for cultural reasons, they are no longer bound by them and must never bind Gentiles to them.

The kingdom of God is not about eating and drinking – sadly, many wish to make it so. Indeed, one common distinguishing mark of spiritual error is when matters of food and drink are elevated to kingdom issues. One mark of many pseudo-Christian sects and cults is an emphasis on esoteric diets. The minute any religious leader takes to the pulpit to prescribe on dietary matters, the chances are they are rather flaky. The Pharisees thought they were righteous because of what they ate and how they ate, and what they did not eat, and how they fasted, but Jesus said that it's not what goes into someone that makes them unclean, but what comes out of them – "thus he declared all foods clean" (Mark 7:19–20).

Sadly, a religious super-size, super-skinny, super-spiritual is found in all branches of the church. The Western church traditionally followed a vegan fast through Lent, and Catholic canon law still prescribes fasting meat on Fridays. Why? The medieval Catholic scholar Thomas Aquinas, who dominated Catholic theological thought for centuries, wrote:

> *Fasting was instituted by the church in order to bridle the concupiscences of the flesh, which regard pleasures of touch in connection with food and sex.*[338]

Some have even sought to justify this nutritionally, saying that meat and dairy products are full of zinc, which causes anger and arouses lust. Potty! In 1647 the Puritan parliament banned traditional Christmas foods, like mince pies and Christmas pudding, as well as Easter hot cross buns, because they thought them too Catholic and opposed the idea of religious symbolism on the grounds that it tended towards blasphemy. Philip Stubbes expressed the Puritan view in his 1583 book *The Anatomie of Abuses* when he disdained Christmas:

> *What eating and drinking, what banqueting and feasting is then used more than all the year besides... to the great dishonour of God and the impoverishing of the realm.*

Now that is a religious rebuke – but hardly a scripturally justified and righteous one. Seventh Day Adventists avoid all foods mentioned as "unclean" in Leviticus, despite the plain New Testament teaching that these are only for Jews living according to the Mosaic covenant and were but a shadow of the things to come, now annulled in Christ (see Ephesians 2:15). We need to come out of the shadows into the light and liberty of Christ.

The equal and opposite error was imposed on an African

colleague of mine, a former Muslim imam who had converted to Christ. The day after he came to Christ and was baptized, the church leaders encouraged him to shave his beard and eat pork. No doubt they saw this as both a test of the authenticity of his newly professed faith, and as a sign of real separation from, and renunciation of, his old cultural and religious Muslim ties. But I was pained when I heard this. In Christ we are free to eat anything, even pork, but freedom to eat pork is very different from religious compulsion to eat pork! This was hardly an act that would make it easy for this fledgling Christian to share his new-found faith with his Muslim family; indeed, it was guaranteed to incite scorn.

Recently a friend told me that, when she came to Christ, she had a warped view of what God required concerning food and drink. These became a neurotic focus for her early spirituality: "I thought I had to give up Coca-Cola and bread and butter because it was sinful to have things I enjoyed." Such was the hold this notion had on her that she began to starve herself and became anorexic. This was not because of poor body identity but because of false spirituality, an idea that somehow equated the approval of God with the absence of tasty foods. Thankfully, God set her free as she read Ephesians 5:29: "No one ever hated his own flesh, but nourishes it and cherishes it, just as Christ does the church." She realized she had been hating her body instead of cherishing and feeding it as God wanted.

In my early twenties I was filled with zeal for God but had little wisdom. I somehow came to believe that God would only bless my preaching if I fasted beforehand. I preached often, sometimes a few times a day, and eventually my diet was reduced to little more than bread and soup in the evening after my work was done. The weight dropped off me and I eventually weighed about six stone (80 pounds) less than I do now! I recall a close friend telling me that he and his wife were very worried, believing my fasting lifestyle had become an obsession. It probably had. It had crept up on me. What began as a righteous desire to seek God became the obsessive idea that God's blessing could not be found without self-denial. The photos of me then look like they're of a different person (half the person I am now). Looking back, I see I had developed a religiously motivated eating disorder, internally conceiving that God was only pleased with me and would only anoint me, if I ate next to nothing. Fortunately marriage ended that religious neurosis. My wife was not putting up with such nonsense. (I'm now twice the man she married.)

Paul is pragmatic: eat what you want, whatever your conscience allows. Gentiles can eat anything with thanksgiving. Jewish believers can eat only kosher foods for cultural and racial reasons. In fact if I were a Jewish Christian, or even a Gentile among Jews, I would probably become kosher – for pragmatic, mission-focused reasons.

None of this is to gainsay the wisdom of following certain dietary restrictions and directions on health grounds. Undoubtedly many of us eat the wrong foods and suffer the consequences in our health: skin complaints, being overweight, Type 2 diabetes, high blood pressure, and so on. In kingdom terms, how we eat, and not what we eat, is the most important consideration. In fact, kingdom righteousness is equated with sharing our bread with the poor.

What God's kingdom *is* about

"The kingdom of God is not a matter of eating and drinking but of *righteousness and peace and joy in the Holy Spirit*" (14:17, my italics).

Why does Paul talk about "righteousness and peace and joy" in the same sentence as "eating and drinking"? Probably because the Jews in the church at Rome, and generations of Christians through the centuries, are sincerely seeking to worship God, to experience his kingdom, and they think their diet is the key. Paul wanted the church in Rome to really understand that God's kingdom, marked by righteousness, peace, and joy, will not come and will not be experienced with reference to what, when, and how we eat. The kingdom of God, marked by righteousness, peace, and joy, are a gift from the Spirit of God.

I believe that this theme speaks prophetically to our society today and not just to the religious. Many people, having no awareness of God and no real desire for God's rule, nevertheless are innately longing for a kingdom, a divine rule – for righteousness, peace, and joy. Rather than seek these in the rule of God and by the Spirit of God, they use food instrumentally to bring these into their life. They attribute value to food that can only be met in God.

Elizabeth Gilbert, author of the best-selling popular book *Eat, Pray, Love,* articulated the feelings of many when interviewed on Oprah Winfrey: "I am my best person when I have less on my plate." Conversely, others feel they are better people if they eat more food, or more fine food, or more healthily. It 's simply not true, that we become are better people as a result of what we eat. For many people, food becomes the locus and focus for a spiritual feel-good. The relationship to food takes on religious characteristics – food is accorded the status of an ultimate referent. Whether super-size or super-skinny, or neither, many are obsessed with food. They do not eat and drink to live, but live to eat and drink. I am convinced that our society's food and drink obsession, whether marked by overt desire for food or a deep anxiety towards it, is a misdirected, wrongly attributed hunger for God and his kingdom rule and his benefits of righteousness, peace, and joy.

Many use food as a reward or punishment. They feast when they want a reward, they purge or abstain when they feel bad and "don't deserve" good things. This has all the marks of religious neurosis. Many people grew up in families where their parents used food as a means of reward and punishment. They got large helpings or seconds or pudding or sweets if they were good or impressed their parents; they got plain food or less food or no food if they incurred their parents' displeasure. Consequently food is associated with all sorts of confusing positive or negative emotions.

I grew up somehow absorning the notion that you should not eat everything on your plate because it was a subtle social register that you were hungry, and thus poorly fed. It was "common". Consequently cleaning the plate of everything and having seconds could be misconstrued, not as having a healthy appetite or enjoying the meal, but of being poor. Such things leave scars on the soul and make eating a confusing affair. It was not that my parents ever stated these things, but maybe they modelled these middle-class values out of a relationship to food programmed when they were infants in World War II, and then on into the hard years of post-war rationing.

In our Western glutted culture food has become infused with religious or spiritual overtones. Food critics become the theologians, restaurants the churches, Michelin-starred restaurants the cathedrals, chefs the anointed priests, Michelin-starred chefs the bishops, kitchens the household shrines, dining tables the altar, food the sacrament, eating the sacramental encounter. Forgiveness is achieved by dieting or purging; blessing is achieved by feasting.

We substitute these for the righteousness, peace, and joy that come through the Spirit. Deep down we long for the government of God, but we are ruled by food instead.

It is well recognized that one of the marks of any eating disorder is the thought of taking control. The sufferer feels "out of control" in many areas of their life – often controlled against their will by people or circumstances – and food becomes the one thing they can control. What they long for is the righteous rule of God's kingdom, God's government – only that will bring the peace and freedom they long for.

Geneen Roth, author of *Women, Food and God,* defines all food disorders, whether binging or dieting, as symptoms of what she terms "anorexia of the soul". In a public lecture she said:

> *Weight loss does not make people happy. Or peaceful. Being thin does not address the emptiness that has no shape, or weight, or name. Even a wildly successful diet is a colossal failure because inside the new body is the same sinking heart.*[339]

Roth sees that many believe their relationship with food can make them happy, or peaceful, or not empty, or feels a if they don't have a sinking heart; but she also shows that this false food god never delivers. Her solution is to be found in a sort of self-help-cum-Buddhist spirituality. I believe what we want is not to be ruled by food but to be ruled by God.

Only God's government, only God's kingdom, can deliver righteousness, peace, and joy, mediated by the Spirit. Righteousness – *dikaiosyne* – is mentioned thirty-five times in Romans, and refers to a right relationship, a rightness with God on the basis of the acquittal of sins, through faith in Jesus who died as a substitute for our sins. That righteousness – that rightness with God – brings us also into a right standing with ourselves and with our community. And that means no more condemnation, no isolation, no dislocation – or, as Geneen Roth puts it, no "empty and sinking heart".

The cry for peace is deep in the human soul. We feel restless, anxious, in turmoil, dis-eased. Joy is something we are made for and what we long for. Many experience a measure of peace or joy through either abstaining from food, or eating only certain foods, or indulging in eating whatever they desire. This is a psychological and even chemical reaction. But it is momentary and superficial.

The famed English writer, Anthony Burgess, once recalled eating a Nalli Gosht curry on his travels (lamb shank).

> *This curry was like a performance of Beethoven's Ninth Symphony that I'd once heard… especially the last movement, with everything screaming and banging "Joy." It stunned, it made one fear great art. My father could say nothing after the meal.*[340]

A wow meal – a chemically induced thrill – lasting until the chilies chilled out and the endorphins settled. Righteousness, joy, peace… I believe these are the authentic experience of the work of the Spirit in our life, when we welcome the government of God in Christ, We experience, in Burgess's terms, "everything screaming and banging 'Joy.'"

In conclusion

Food and drink is wonderful – God-given and to be celebrated. The second thing God said to Adam and Eve, after go and multiply and rule the earth, was about food to eat. The first thing God said to Noah after the flood was "eat meat and veg". Jesus' first miracle was turning water into wine; Jesus' most extensive miracle was feeding 5,000 people with a few loaves and fish; Jesus spent lots of his time having meals with tax collectors and sinners and was even accused of being a "glutton and a drunkard" (Matthew 11:19); Jesus described heaven in terms of a wedding banquet, a feast. Divine love bids us welcome to a table that's spread before us in the presence of our enemies, to feast on bread and wine – the body and blood of Jesus. Jesus imparts his Spirit to those who embrace his government, his kingdom – and there they find righteousness, peace, and joy.

48

My Word, God's Word! (15:4)

I grew up with my father modelling a life lived loving Scripture. Since his conversion in 1961 he has read and re-read the Bible every year – during the busiest periods of his professional life he only managed to read through it once a year, but at other times he often managed to read it three times. And this was no superficial skimming, but a deep reading, often in the Hebrew text (in which he is fluent) and referring to the Greek text (in which he is competent), taking notes and writing sermon outlines as he read. He has read the Bible through in excess of a hundred times!

When I became a committed Christian, my father's example of rising early and reading Scripture was a pattern I sought to imitate, albeit poorly. I assumed all Christians desired to know God and to meet him in his Word. Imagine my surprise when I began to train as a minister at theological college, and the Old Testament tutor asked my class of about forty trainee ministers and theologians if they had ever read whole Bible, and only about a third had! Ever. Once. A. W. Tozer said, "Nothing less than a whole Bible can make a whole Christian."[341] And certainly nothing less than a whole Bible can make a whole church leader.

The Edwardian Cambridge theologian, P. T. Forsyth, rhetorically asked, "Why do people not read the Bible more?" He then posited the answer: "Because they have not been in that country, there is no experience to stir and develop."[342] In similar vein Karl Barth wrote of the "strange new world within the Bible"[343] that he discovered after many years as pastor of a little Swiss village church. The liberal theology that had trained him had left the Bible a closed book.

I am from the West Country. It's where I grew up and lived the first thirty years of my life, as did many generations of my ancestors. Whenever I return, I immediately feel at home. I know the climate, the contours of the land, the accents, the highways and byways. It is home, it's in my blood, I have a deep connection to the land. And that is how it should be when we read the Bible. We should feel at home: that this land is my land, this people is my people, this God my God, this story my story.

"For whatever was written in former days was written for our instruction, that through endurance and through the encouragement of the Scriptures we might have hope" (15:4).

The term "scriptures", *graphe,* was used of all sacred inspired writings. Paul speaks of these Scriptures as being "God-breathed" (2 Timothy 3:16, NIV); Peter says their origin is with men moved by Holy Spirit to speak from God (2 Peter 1:21). Peter calls Paul's writings "Scriptures" (2 Peter 3:16) and the church from the earliest era believed the apostolic writings fell into this category, and bound these "New Testament" writings with the body of Old Testament sacred Scripture.

The writings of human beings are the *ipsissima verba,* the "very words", of God. These old words from an old world are eternal words for today's world – and tomorrow's. Paul says that these words, written in the past for them, then, there, were actually written for all of us us, here, now. So what can we expect from them?

The Bible gives us an education

"For whatever was written in former days was written for our instruction" (15:4).

Oxford professor and evangelist for atheism, Richard Dawkins, says, "I am against religion because it teaches us to be satisfied with not understanding the world."[344] Many, however, believe that a lack of a biblical worldview leaves even Oxford professors groping in ignorance. Physicist Robert Milikan, Nobel Prize winner and holder of twenty-five honorary doctorates, states: "I consider an intimate knowledge of the Bible an indispensable quality of a well educated person."[345]

The Bible is indeed an education in and of itself. There are thirty-three massive volumes of the *Encyclopaedia Britannica* offering a synopsis of the sum of learning – what the great minds in their fields think is worth knowing by everyone. Yet in just one single volume, the Bible, comprising sixty-six short histories, essays, prophecies, and letters, we get what God thinks worth knowing.

In these sixty-six short books, written by forty different people over 1,500 years, we learn about literature – poetry, history, prophecy, biography, wisdom. We learn about history – Egyptian, Assyrian, Babylonian, Jewish, Greek. We learn ancient languages, ancient cultures, cosmology, ethics, politics, law, morals, philosophy, geography, futurology, and anthropology. And, of course, primarily we learn about God, his revelation of himself – his nature, character, ways, words, will, and how we are to walk with him. The great English poet Lord Tennyson thought that "the Bible ought to be read… an education in itself"[346] and quoted it over 400 times in his poetry.

Theology, the explication and reflection on the revelation of God, was once regarded as the queen of sciences, the sum of learning that unites all disciplines. It has certainly been the engine that has driven science and the humanities. Take theology out of Oxford University and you would not have a university – for it was founded by monks as a place to meditate on the works of God. There is an ancient ritual, but surely prophetic, that at Oxford degree ceremonies the Doctors of Divinity lead the procession. The university motto is fitting, quoting the psalmist: *Dominus Illuminatio Mea* – "the Lord is my Light". Without the Scriptures, and the literacy they demand to be read, and the encouragement to education they involve, we would be in the Dark Ages. The Bible encourages the pursuit of God, but in so doing also the pursuit of knowledge about God's world.

The UK's prime minister, David Cameron, in a 2011 speech in Oxford celebrating 400 years of the King James Version, said, "The Bible is a book that has not only shaped our nation, but has shaped the world"[347] He proceeded to show how the Bible profoundly promoted the best in the arts, literature, social action, and politics.

I meet lots of people who feel insecure about their education. Perhaps they failed their eleven-plus exam, or the Common Entrance exam, or went to a comprehensive rather than a grammar or public school. Perhaps they did poorly in their O levels or GCSEs. Maybe they failed their A levels and did not get into the university they wanted. Maybe they went to a polytechnic, not an academic university, or a red-brick university and not an Oxbridge one. Maybe they got a 2:2 and not a first, or maybe they did not get the grades to do graduate studies. At any level people may feel insecure about their education.

The Bible is the great leveller and great educator – a deep knowledge is available to all who will commit to it, and anyone may be an expert in it who wants to be. And whatever one lacks in any other form of formal education, a study of Scripture is an education in itself. We need to cultivate a teachable spirit – a willingness to learn and study: "All Scripture is God-breathed and is useful for teaching, rebuking, correcting and training in righteousness, so that the man of God may be thoroughly equipped for every good work" (2 Timothy 3:16).

The Bible gives us edification

"... through endurance and through the encouragement of the Scriptures" (15:4).

I enjoy watching the annual sporting event called *The World's Strongest Man*. As the men perform, their team shouts them on with encouragement, giving advice on timings and letting them know where their competitors are, and when they finish they are at hand with a towel, water, oxygen, bandages. Similarly, the Bible is our personal trainer, or life coach, through which God sets high goals for us and then helps us to attain them. Paul speaks of it giving us "endurance" – the Greek is *hypomone,* and refers to staying power, the capacity to hold out, to bear up in the face of difficulty, to endure with patience, endurance, fortitude, steadfastness, perseverance.

Paul says the Bible also gives us "encouragement". The Greek is *paraklesis,* literally a calling alongside with comfort and exhortation to enable us to fulfil our task. It is the same root word as Jesus used of his own ongoing role with believers, and that of the Holy Spirit (John 14:16). Why does Paul emphasize this particular role of Scripture? Because he knows how much we will need encouragement and endurance. The Christian life is often more a crown of thorns than a bed of roses. Jesus said, "In this world you will have trouble" (John

16:33). We will have affliction, temptations, trials, discouragements, and be buffeted by winds of adversity. Exigencies line up to cause many to desert Christ rather than count the cost and carry their cross.

I have read several accounts of Christians going through the Nazi Holocaust – one thinks of the accounts by Corrie ten Boom and Rose Warmer. These highlight that the one thing they prayed for was a Bible – and when they received one, they treasured it above bread, enabling them to surmount their sufferings, to rise above the squalid terror, to find light and hope in even the darkest of hell's holes. Open Doors is a remarkable ministry working with the tortured church worldwide. On their website[348] the first two of their five stated roles involve the Bible – Bible delivery and Bible training for persecuted Christians. Why? Because what persecuted Christians want from us is not money, or even intervention, but prayer and the encouragement and encounter with God that sustains them through the Bible! Open Doors quotes one persecuted Christian who received a Bible: "We are nothing without a Bible. But we can face anything with it. Your gift of this book is the greatest gift."

When the devil tested Jesus in the wilderness, Jesus stood his ground by standing on God's word. Three times Jesus countered the temptation with the declaration: "It is written", and each time extinguished that particular avenue of attack. He overcame through faith in and faithfulness to the Word of God. He knew that "man shall not live by bread alone, but by every word that comes from the mouth of God" (Matthew 4: 4).

It pains me that many of my own family, once keen Christians, involved in ministry, sadly abandoned the church. Meanwhile a third of those I entered ministry with have left their parish ministry. Why did they cease running the race? Why did they not finish the course? What cut in on them? I suspect the first thing to go was a daily diet of God's word. When that went, when God was no longer speaking daily to them and guiding and protecting them, fellowship with God was lost, and soon faith and faithfulness followed. The Bible is the difference between being overcome or being an overcomer.

I recently deleted my Facebook account. I think Facebook is an extraordinary vehicle for networking and friendship and communication. However, after only a short time I had a thousand cyber-, pseudo-"friends", and my own tendency to OCD meant that going on Facebook became almost the first thing I did in the morning, and the last thing I did at night, checking to see who had requested to be my friend, who had messaged me, or who had added to conversation threads to which I was contributing. I found I was spending longer on Facebook than in the Bible face-to-face with God. I was not disciplined enough to set limits to my time social-networking, and within just a couple of months I felt my spiritual strength sapping away. I chose to permanently delete the account and get back to my routine of reading my Bible first thing and last thing each day. Better to be face-to-face with my friend God, through the divine facebook, the Bible.

The Bible gives us expectation

"... that ... through the encouragement of the Scriptures we might have hope" (15:4).

Many people feel their lives are rather like Groundhog Day. Every day is the same-old same-old. Christopher Columbus wrote in his ship's log on 1 October 1492, "This is killing me. Where is land? We have sailed for days and days and there has been no sight of land."[349] Eleven days later they saw land. But for many there is no El Dorado – a land of gold never comes; they feel they just sail on and on in circles.

Some resign to not having hope. The French existentialist philosopher Albert Camus famously quipped, "Hope as a rule makes a fool," and so we ought to "think clearly and hope no more". He defined life according to the myth of Sisyphus, who was condemned for his sin by the gods to push a stone uphill every day, only to see it roll back down, and each day he would awake to the same wearisome effort. Camus's only answer to this human condition was to "do it with a smile on your face".

I recall writing in my copy of *The Myth of Sisyphus* in large scrawl in the margins, "Is this all you have to offer? Is that it?" He and many others would think so. Many cannot even muster a fake botox smile. As I wrote this chapter a good friend told me, following the huge anti-climax of his Christmas, that on Boxing Day he sat on the toilet and wept. That sums up life for many. So much for national holidays. Statistically, New Year's Day sees the biggest spike for suicide.

Hope needs a foundation. As Christians we do not hope in hope, we hope in God. And God's action for us has proven that our hope is not in vain. In Romans 15:12 Paul says that in Christ, the root of Jesse, the Gentiles will hope. Paul prays in Romans 15:13, "May the God of hope fill you with all joy and peace in believing, so that by the power of the Holy Spirit you may abound in hope." Christians are hope people, and Scripture tells us why and fuels this hope:

- It reveals Jesus Christ as our Lord, Lover, and Saviour.
- It is the vehicle for God's Spirit to infuse joy and peace.
- It shows God is for us and nothing can prevail against us.
- It shows that God is attentive to and answers our prayer.
- It shows that evil will not have last word, and the Lamb wins.

Ravi Zacharias tells the story of a young, keen, Christian interpreter, Hien Pham, who assisted him on a preaching tour of Vietnam in the early 1970s before its takeover by the communist Vietcong regime.[350] Ravi often wondered what became of him, until seventeen years later he had a phone call. It was Hien. His story was incredible, both terrible and wonderful. When Vietnam collapsed to the communists, Hien was imprisoned in a slave labour camp, accused of helping the Americans. He was daily forcibly brain-washed with Marxist indoctrination against Western democratic ideals and Christian faith. After some years, Hien began to doubt his faith. "Maybe," he thought, "I have been lied to. Maybe God does not exist. Maybe the West has deceived me." At last Hien resolved that, when he awoke the next day, he would not pray any more or think of God again. The communist programming had done its wicked work. The next morning Hien woke, and for the first time chose not to turn his heart and mind to God. He was assigned the foul job of cleaning the prison latrines. As he emptied the oil can that was used as a toilet, there in the excrement, on a filthy piece of toilet paper, he noticed some English print. He seized it, pocketed it, later washed it and, once his fellow prisoners were asleep, began to read it.

It was a fragment of Romans 8:

> *And we know that in all things God works for the good of those who love him, who have been called according to his purpose...*

> *For I am convinced that neither death nor life, neither angels nor demons, neither the present nor the future, nor any powers, neither height nor depth, nor anything else in all creation, will be able to separate us from the love of God that is in Christ Jesus our Lord.*
>
> 8:28, 38–39, NIV

Hien broke down weeping. He knew his Bible well enough. He knew there was no more relevant a verse for a man on the verge of abandoning his faith than this. On the day Hien decided to give up on God, God showed he had not given up on Hien, and in the squalid filth broke through and spoke to him of his faithfulness.

As an official in the camp was apparently using an old Bible as toilet paper, Hien asked the commander if he could have the job of cleaning the latrines. Each day he picked out used sheets of Scripture, cleaned them, and collected them into a book for night-time reading. God's Word sustained him through the horrors. Later, remarkably, Hien was freed, and escaped the country on a self-made boat.

What carried him through? It was God speaking and meeting him through his Word of hope, endurance, and encouragement.

49

An Ordinary Priest (15:15–21)

In 2010 *The Guardian* newspaper ran an article "Ten of the Best Priests in Literature",[351] citing clerical depictions from literary luminaries like Charlotte Brontë, Robert Browning, Andrew O'Hagan, and Graham Greene. The chosen "ten best priests" were often those who stood out for their unpleasant personality or sexual liberties.

Priests and ministers often have bad reputations: the Russian philosopher George Gurdjieff once said cynically, "If you want to lose your faith, make friends with a priest." Both the super-star actor Tom Cruise and the movie-maker Martin Scorsese initially trained at seminary, the latter claiming, "I just wanted to be an ordinary priest."[352]

But what is an ordinary priest?

Over two decades ago I was an anxious young man on a selection conference for the Anglican ordained ministry. I certainly felt the odd one out, a lone charismatic putting my big evangelical foot in my mouth, and even I had second thoughts about ordination in the Church of England. During the interview, which was focused on assessing "vocation", a dear old archdeacon asked me how I understood the role and call of a priest. I immediately quoted Romans 15:16, which I understood as the only New Testament description of a New Covenant priest. The verb Paul uses here is *hierourgeo,* which was used to refer to the priestly ministry of offering sacrifices. As the NIV renders it, God gave him the grace "to be a minister of Christ Jesus to the Gentiles with the priestly duty of proclaiming the gospel of God, so that the Gentiles might become an offering acceptable to God, sanctified by the Holy Spirit". I nervously told the archdeacon that I thought that was the job description for a priest and that I felt called to it.

Two weeks later I heard that I had been accepted for the ministry. However, the report on me was no ringing endorsement. The interview panel expressed various concerns about my lack of formal education, my limited Anglican experience, and highlighted what they considered my narrow biblical fundamentalism. Some on the panel had suggested I delay my training – but the report stated that the interview with the archdeacon left a clear impression of a deep insight into the nature of priesthood, and such insight indicated a true vocation to it. A few months later I was at an Anglican seminary.

Over twenty years later I am more convinced than ever that the model Paul presents in Romans 15:15–21 is the true template for the ministry of the whole church corporately as God's royal priesthood, and individually for the church's ministers and priests.

What, then, is an ordinary priest? Paul tells us in the passage we now consider.

Paul's priestly prize

"... that the offering of the Gentiles may be acceptable, sanctified by the Holy Spirit" (15:16).

Old Testament priests, through the ministration of a substitute sacrifice, pronounced the penitent worshipper clean of sin, free of guilt, accepted by God, and welcome within the community of the covenant people. Paul's new covenant priestly ministry is fulfilled by preaching Christ crucified, the Lamb of God who takes away the sin of the world, and presenting those who respond in faith to God as acquitted of guilt, cleansed by the Spirit, and acceptable to God. Paul's priestly ministry is not the sacrifice of a lamb for sin, but the proclamation of the gospel of the Lamb who was slain for sin. The priestly ministry is a preaching ministry; the sacerdotal office is a gospel office. Sadly, some ministers think the ministry itself is the prize. Some deluded ministers even think they themselves are the prize.

The ministry is the means to win the prize, not for ourselves but for God. The church, as God's royal priesthood, exists to present the prize to God. The prize is people being saved through the gospel and presented as living sacrifices to God.

Archbishop William Temple is often credited as saying, "The church is the only organization that exists for the benefit of its non members." That being true, why do we expend inordinate, even extortionate, amounts of time, energy, effort, and money on ourselves, on those within the walls, rather than without? Many evangelical churches pride themselves in giving 10 per cent of their income to mission, even though that means 90 per cent of what they have they keep to themselves, and presumably 90 per cent of what they value is themselves.

I have heard some bishops describing their job as "managing decline" rather than imparting vision and passion for mission.[353] Managing decline? That term is business-speak, used when a new product is being brought to market and the company wishes to sell off the old! "Managing decline" is politician-speak for overseeing the slow dismantlement of former vibrant industrial cities or mining centres because of cheap foreign imports. Is that what we are about?

Currently, decline is a fact of the Church of England – income down, members down, priest numbers down. Statistics show that the Church of England was haemorrhaging in real terms at the rate of 30,000 members a week between 2007 and 2009. The only diocese showing significant growth in a 2011 survey was the English-speaking Anglican diocese of Europe. The question, then, is whether we manage this decline or use all our energies to reverse the decline!

I do not believe Jesus ever envisaged decline. Every metaphor for the kingdom is one that grows. The church declines whenever she takes her eye off the prize. I do not want to "manage decline", I want the problem of "managing revival". I did not get ordained to keep the show on the road, but to win the prize for Christ. May God give us bishops and priests who have courage and vision and who believe and strive for revival as a prize to present to Jesus.

Paul's priestly pride

"In Christ Jesus, then, I have reason to be proud of my work for God" (15:17).

Paul had every reason to feel proud of himself. Just consider his achievements, his spiritual endowments, his apostolic calling, his zeal, his sufferings for Christ, the churches planted, converts won, miracles displayed, revelations seen. Yet Paul's pride was not in these things but in his service for Christ. And it is precisely because Paul had such visions of God's glory, such an awareness of his own sinful creatureliness, that he received such extraordinary grace on grace, that he now could live only for God's crown, fame, and glory. Every pore in Paul cried: To God be the glory, great things he has done!

I have witnessed ministers and priests boast in just about everything but Christ: their church architecture, church history, liturgy, music, membership numbers, local dignitaries who are members, worship leader or choir, vestments, lack of vestments, influence, income, diversity of projects, the name they have made for themselves, of themselves. Surely one of the most dangerous things for a church is to gain a reputation. God may have to take away our reputation if we are seeking to make one. He shares his glory with no one. If we seek to make a name for ourselves instead of him he may have to humble our name.

The church in Laodicea boasted in their prosperity claiming: "I am rich, I have prospered, and I need nothing." Jesus rebuked them for "not realizing that you are wretched, pitiable, poor, blind, and naked" (Revelation 3:17). The church in Sardis prided themselves in their reputation and Jesus rebuked "you have the reputation of being alive, but you are dead" (Revelation 3:1). It is a dangerous thing when the church takes pride in anything but Christ and what he has worked in them.

John Steinbeck, in his 1952 classic novel *East of Eden*, perceived that "maybe the less you have the more you are required to brag".[354] Certainly the churches of Laodicea and Sardis needed a reality check. The reputation and self-appreciation they had was precarious. Ironically, the Lord saw them in the opposite terms to the way they perceived themselves or wanted to be perceived.

A while ago a prominent American preacher stirred up some heat by criticizing the British church, saying there were no world-famous British preachers. I confess I bristled when I read this. "Who does this American think he is… of course we have famous preachers…" And perhaps even deep down part of me wanted one day to be regarded as one of them? But as I have reflected on this, I think the right response should be, "Praise God!" Preachers are not meant to make a name for themselves but for Jesus. That's what Paul lived for.

May all God's priests imitate George Whitefield, the great revivalist, who imitated Paul, boasting only in Christ:

> *Let the name of Whitefield perish, but Christ be glorified... Let my name die everywhere, let even my friends forget me, if by that means the cause of the blessed Jesus may be promoted... But what is Calvin, or what is Luther? Let us look above names and parties; let Jesus be our all in all so that He is preached... I care not who is uppermost. I know my place... Even to be the servant of all... I am content to wait till the judgment day for the clearing up of my reputation; and after I am dead I desire no other epitaph than this: "Here lies G.W. What sort of man he was the Great Day will discover."*[355]

Paul's priestly preaching

"I have fully proclaimed the gospel of Christ. It has always been my ambition to preach the gospel" (15:19–20, NIV).

Preaching is seldom popular, but because we live in the age of the stand-up comedian and theatre monologue I think it may have found a window of opportunity. Regardless of whether preaching is in fashion or out, we are to preach the gospel, for as Archbishop Donald Coggan stated,

> *Here is the miracle of the divine economy, that between the forgiveness of God and the sin of man, stands the preacher; between the provision of God and the need of man, stands the preacher; between the Truth of God and the quest of man, stands the preacher.*[356]

Not all see it that way, not even in the church. When I began to sense a call to preach, an elder in my church told me that preaching was a redundant form of communication (always a familiar theme in trendy, liberal church circles). The devil has always wanted to silence preachers, to stone the prophets (Matthew 23:37). But preaching remains God's major means for revealing himself and his salvation.

Every season of church decline has been marked by a decline in its preaching, and every revival and renewal is marked by a return to biblical preaching.

We must preach the gospel, in season and out of season (2 Timothy 4:2), for it is the gospel that is the power of God unto salvation for all who believe. In 1777, in a letter to Alexander Mather, John Wesley wrote:

> *Give me one hundred preachers who fear nothing but sin and desire nothing but God and I care not a straw whether they be clergymen or laymen – such alone will shake the gates of hell and set up the kingdom of God on earth.*[357]

That was the apostolic approach and that must be ours today.

Paul's priestly praxis

"... by the power of signs and wonders, by the power of the Spirit of God" (15:19).

The book of Acts detailed many of the extraordinary signs and wonders that the power of the Spirit worked through Paul as he heralded the gospel. Paul illustrated his message with signs and wonders following. Today we illustrate our sermons with drama sketches, movie clips, and PowerPoint presentations. The apostles never preached miracles – they worked them. The gospel is not "signs and wonders" but should be accompanied by them. Many today preach miracles but work none. Why?

Paul equates signs and wonders with the power of the Spirit. We must deduce that if there are no signs and wonders there is a lack of the Spirit's power! To make sense of the obvious contrasts between power and fruitfulness, between the apostolic ministry and ours today, some suggest that God only gave miracles at special times to launch or relaunch the church; that his economy has changed, and now that we have church, we do not need attesting signs. Nonsense. Surely in every generation the church needs re-launching and advancing.

In the West, faced by a church in decline and a radical advance of secularism, militant atheism, radical Islamism, surely now more than ever we need the power of the Spirit in the exercise of signs and wonders to confirm the preaching of the gospel. I think the problem is not that God has withdrawn his power but that those who supposedly represent him have lost their Bibles, lost their nerve... even lost their faith. Historian Professor Richard Fletcher in his outstanding book *The Barbarian Conversion* has demonstrated that the conversion of Europe from paganism is inextricably linked to miracles.[358] Though a declared agnostic himself, he said he did not know what to make of his conclusions, but as a historian he must simply report history according to the records received – records that show miracles advanced the cause of Christ and confirmed the preaching of the gospel. Where are these miracles today that advance the cause of Christ and his church? Claims abound. Evidence is scarce. Lord, renew your wonders in our day.

Some years ago a famous Bible teacher spoke at my church. He gave a remarkable exposition on this very passage we are currently considering, describing Paul's ministry mission and motivation, and exhorted us to imitate Paul. It was a mesmerizing presentation, employing all his gifts as a communicator and theologian. However, to my surprise, despite making numerous points and drawing out many insights from the text, he totally ignored verse 19 about the "power of signs and wonders in the power of the Spirit".

During the question-and-answer session that followed, one of my students, a smart young American lass now married to a vicar, asked him why he had avoided this verse in his exposition. He replied that he did not want to tread on toes in Oxford, knowing there were some tensions between charismatic and conservative traditions. Well, that may sound reasonable, but surely it would be better to offend the listener than to offend God and do offence to his Word. We must preach the whole text and, by God's grace, practise the whole text!

The Edwardian theological college principal Samuel Chadwick wrote, "A ministry that is college trained but not Spirit filled, works no miracles."[359] Paul says he demonstrated the power of signs and wonders, by the power of the Holy Spirit. Rather than bending our theology to say God's economy has changed, might we not more faithfully say, "We see no signs of power for we lack the Spirit's power"? Lord, let us live in a day of thy power.

Paul's priestly parish

"It has always been my ambition to preach the gospel where Christ was not known, so that I would not be building on someone else's foundation" (15:20, NIV).

As an apostle Paul was a pioneer, not wanting anyone to die without the chance to hear and embrace the gospel of Jesus. When folk who had already enjoyed his ministry wanted to keep Jesus to themselves, Jesus said, "Let us go on to the next towns, that I may preach there also, for that is why I came out" (Mark 1:38).

Paul was always on the go for the gospel – looking for new places and fresh opportunities to proclaim Christ and plant a church. After three decades exhausting opportunities in Asia Minor, yet still full of faith and fire, Paul was ready to pioneer a mission into Spain. Some ministers prefer to preach to the choir or mentor the mature. Not Paul. Not the apostolic. Some churches are the spiritual equivalent of livestock rustlers: they prefer to grow by sheep-stealing rather than soul-winning. Evangelism is tough. Discipling new converts is like running a crèche. New converts are like babies – messy, noisy, time-consuming, and they don't pay their way!

I am always challenged when I think of my great friend, Robin Gamble, who took the smallest church in the Bradford diocese in the north of England. The congregation consisted of a handful of elderly folk, and despite being under the threat of closure, through creative evangelism the church became one of the largest in the diocese within a couple of years. The growth was almost totally new believers – though not for want of existing believers trying. Robin told me that, once the church gained a reputation, people who were disaffected with their churches, fed up with their ministers, wanting a venue to express their gifts, started coming to his services hoping for a home there. Robin said to them all, "Good to see you here. I hope you have been encouraged today. Do take our blessing back to your home church. If you move into the area you are very welcome to join this church and help us reach out to this parish. But I warn you that those first in line for ministry roles are those who have lived here and served here the longest." Most, looking for a platform for their ministry, quickly left. But the community began to see that here was a man and a ministry and a church devoted to bringing God to them, and the church grew exponentially.[360]

That is apostolic ministry, not wanting to build on another's foundation, not nurturing the flock of another sheepfold, but passionately reaching out to those in your place where God plants you.

C. T. Studd, who captained Eton, Cambridge, and England at cricket, was converted through the preaching of D. L. Moody in the late Victorian era. He quickly got the point. Giving up everything – a large inheritance, title, reputation, and distinguished future among England's élite – he entered fifteen years of fruitful ministry in China, then left for six years' mission work in India. Then at the age of fifty he heard of the mission field openings in Africa, and went there for twenty-five years, establishing vibrant churches. His famous motto was "Some wish to live within the sound of church or chapel bell; I want to run a rescue shop within a yard of hell."[361]

In conclusion

I began this chapter by recalling how, twenty years ago when I was being examined to be an Anglican minister, I referenced this passage in Romans, where we have Paul's description of his priestly ministry: preaching the gospel, in the power of the Spirit, to see the lost rescued, all for the glory of God. I said that was how I understood my call, the call to priesthood. I mentioned that my answer weighed in my favour, and that the archdeacon who had interviewed me went into bat for me to go forward for ordination.

I will never forget that when I gave this answer to him, and quoted this passage, the archdeacon's eyes welled with tears. He simply said to me, "You are a very fortunate young man." What lay behind his vulnerable remark? I suspect that, after many years of ordained service, the venerable archdeacon was pensive as he approached his retirement as a priest, and now heard again Paul's paradigm for priestly ministry. Seeing the zeal and confidence in the unschooled, young candidate before him, did he suddenly have a sense of regret, at pursuing a clerical career rather than an apostolic ministry? Or was he tearful because his spirit was stirred, and he knew the gospel he had faithfully proclaimed at great cost, was being handed on to another generation? I do not know. But I do know he was moved. I know he pushed through my acceptance for training for being a priest because of my commitment to the model presented here in Romans 15.

I sometimes think of that elderly archdeacon and his tear-filled eyes, and his support of me for ministry, and I hear his heart: "Come on, son, aim high; pass on the baton, win the prize!" And I know that, after twenty years, with half of my own ordained ministry over, tears could easily come to my eyes. I am not doing so well against Paul's paradigm for priesthood. But I have still got time to put that right.

Dear royal priesthood, I believe God wants to encourage and re-envision you to live to give glory to God, to herald the gospel, to rescue the lost, to see the kingdom of God advance in our day. And I believe also that some reading this will feel their hearts stirred, and sense a call to be gospel ministers, presenting Gentiles as sacrifices acceptable to God by the Holy Spirit.

50

Give It Up (15:20–29)

In AD 251 plague ravaged the Roman empire, and a staggering 5,000 people per day died in Rome alone. So many were dying that families sought quarantine by abandoning their loved ones to the streets. The authorities were overwhelmed and powerless to help; the pagan priests fled their temples where people had flocked for comfort and explanation. Yet following the plague, the church's reputation soared and her congregations increased. How so?

Christians were not supernaturally protected from sharing in their fellow humans' suffering. Many fell to the plague. They did not have compelling intellectual answers to the very present problem of evil. But they did have water and food and their presence. And this meant that, if Romans knew a Christian, they were statistically more likely to live! Social and political theologian Dr Stephen Backhouse observes:

> *It was not clever apologetics, strategic political organisation or the witness of martyrdom which converted an Empire, so much as the simple conviction by normal Christians that what they did for the least of their neighbours they did for Christ.*[362]

Christianity is believed, and it is also lived. Many love to engage with the Christian faith like a biochemist dissecting a frog: they stand over it, dividing and analysing it. And certainly the faith is intellectual and can well withstand scrutiny. But Christianity is a lived religion, not just a learned one. It is about an encounter with Christ that transforms both how we think and how we act. Every New Testament letter has a practical and ethical dimension. A Christian is as a Christian does.

Now, it has been estimated that 17 per cent of all Jesus' sayings relate to money. As the London *Evening Standard* stated in an article on city bankers: "The use of money is the number one moral issue in the Bible."[363] And what professing Christians do with their money indicates whether in reality they are practising Christians.

In this chapter we will reflect on how our money and God's mission go hand in hand:

We give to partner in mission

"... and thus I make it my ambition to preach the gospel, not where Christ has already been named, lest I build on someone else's foundation, but as it is written, 'Those who have never been told of him will see, and those who have never heard will understand.'... I hope to see you in passing as I go to Spain, and to be helped on my journey there by you" (15:20–21, 24).

Paul has exhausted the opportunities of preaching the gospel around the strategic cities and ports of Asia Minor. He now intends to pioneer a mission into Europe. He plans to visit Rome on the way and anticipates their assistance in what he terms *propempo*, a Greek word meaning to furnish, equip, prepare. In practical terms, this probably meant assisting in financing his mission to Europe. Paul wanted them to partner with him in the evangelization of Europe – and that meant praying and paying.

Mission and ministry cost money. They do not run on thin air – or thin prayer. Jesus was funded in his ministry by wealthy women such as Susanna and many other women of substance provided for the disciples (Luke 8:3). Interestingly, The Women's Philanthropy Institute at Indiana University, in a 2007 report, demonstrated that women in four out of five financial bracket groups give more than men – sometimes twice as much.[364]

Mission takes money. The exiled Chinese apostle Brother Yun, reflecting on life in the underground church in China, challengingly wrote:

> *I even miss the offerings we used to give in China. On numerous occasions the leader of a meeting would announce, "We have*

a new worker who is leaving tomorrow to serve the Lord." Immediately every single person would completely empty their pockets of everything they had. With that money the worker would buy a train ticket or a bus ticket and leave the next day. Often this money was not just everything we had in our pockets, it was everything we owned in the whole world.[365]

Ask yourselves the question: in what way am I furnishing mission to people who have never heard the gospel?

We give to provide for the poor

"At present, however, I am going to Jerusalem bringing aid to the saints. For Macedonia and Achaia have been pleased to make some contribution for the poor among the saints at Jerusalem" (15:25–26).

Paul informs the Romans that, before visiting them, he was going to be taking a collection for the poor saints in Jerusalem. A previous collection had been taken ten years earlier in AD 45 during a severe famine. We do not know the reasons for this offering, but it may be that the saints were now suffering poverty due to persecution by institutional Judaism, perhaps through loss of family support and livelihoods.

David Ruis, songwriter and church planter, devotes much of his ministry and most of his money to the poor. He made a considerable amount of money through his songs, which are sung worldwide in renewal settings. On his arm is a tattoo "Consider the poor". One day he was queuing for a coffee when a woman glimpsed his tattoo, screamed out, "Why should I?" and proceeded to let rip a whole host of bile against the poor – how it was "their problem", why should we have to pick up the bill, and so on.

What is the answer to her question? Why should I remember the poor? Because God says so! If we do not do it out of compassion, let us do so out of obedience. God takes it personally when we ignore the poor. When we do it not for the least of these, we do it not for him. In the levitical law Moses states that farmers must leave unharvested some of their field's crop at the edge so as to be gleaned by the poor and the pilgrim (Leviticus 19:9–10). God supports this command simply stating: "I am the Lord." Alongside a command to consider the poor God puts his name. He stands alongside them; not to do this for the poor is to disregard God himself.

Throughout the Bible, we see that remembering the poor indicates whether we are walking with God. The rich young ruler was told to sell all he had and to give it to the poor to gain eternal life (Mark 10:17–22). But he would not, which demonstrated that his other commitments to the Law were negated. Likewise the rich man sometimes named Dives forfeited eternal life because, despite his great wealth, he did not turn in charity towards the beggar Lazarus at his gate (Luke 16:19–31).

The only instruction Paul received from the Jerusalem apostles was to "remember the poor" – something he said he was keen to do and did not need telling (Galatians 2:10). Some of us are less keen and do need to be told. Throughout the history of the church, many nuns and monks and others have taken vows of poverty. However, I confess I do not believe that that is a general biblical mandate. We are not called to become poor but to alleviate the poor. Being poor is not a virtue. Helping others out of poverty is.

The remarkable Victorian, General Gordon of Khartoum, was a devout Christian who carried with him into battle only a Bible and a walking stick. For his services to China the emperor had a special large medal struck for him, in solid gold. After he died the family looked for it but were unable to locate it. Then they discovered the General had sent it to Manchester during a severe famine, and asked for it to be melted down so the money could be used to buy bread for the poor. In his diary for the date when he sent it, he wrote: "The last earthly thing I had in this world that I valued I have given to the Lord Jesus."[366]

Paul was going to Rome to help the poor. When was the last time you went or spent on behalf of the poor?

We give practically to pay back spiritually

"For they were pleased to do it, and indeed they owe it to them. For if the Gentiles have come to share in their spiritual blessings, they ought also to be of service to them in material blessings" (15:27).

Paul boasts about the generosity of spirit of the Macedonians. Two things stand out in the way they gave: first, they were "pleased" to give – Paul repeats this to make a point. They gave willingly and joyfully. In Isaiah we learn that it *pleased* God to allow Jesus to suffer for our sins (see Isaiah 53:10, KJV). Paul in his letter to the Colossians says it *pleased* God for Jesus to be incarnate and reconcile us (Colossians 1:19–20). It gave God great pleasure to give sacrificially to save us, and when we truly grasp this it will give us great pleasure to sacrificially give back. Often folk ask: "how much should I give?" That's the wrong question, especially if it is short hand for the reluctant "What is the minimum I can get away with giving?" Perhaps the question we should ask is, "How much can I keep?" People make much of giving 10 per cent, and debate whether it should be gross or net of tax. But a tithe is generally what we give as a tip in restaurants! Tithing is like tipping God. We cannot be satisfied with giving God our bare minimum. We need to cultivate the spiritual grace where it "pleases" us to give back to God.

Secondly, Paul says that the Macedonians were pleased to give freely to the poor Jews in Jerusalem because they "owed them". The Greek term is *ofeiletes* and means one who owes another, a debtor. The Macedonian Christians understood that, were it not for the Jewish Christians, through whom came the gospel, they would be lost. Their spiritual and eternal gain elicits a debt repaid in material and practical ways.

Let us never forget that we have our Saviour and our Scripture because the gospel came to us through the Jews, and let us not fail to give back to them generously and gratefully, practically and materially. Bishop J. C. Ryle wrote,

> *If there is such a thing as gratitude in the heart of man, it is the duty of all Gentile Christians to take special interest in the work of doing good to the Jews.*[367]

I grew up being taught this by my dad, but not until I was in my forties did I begin to see it. Dr Wilson, author of the best-selling *Our Father Abraham*, was a student in his early twenties when he had what he claims was an "existential moment". It was not informed by his earlier study of Scripture and theology – it was a revelation. He states:

> *I woke up one day and realized everything that had changed my life, everything that is most important to me as a believer came through the Jewish people: my Lord, my Bible, my value system, my ethics, my understanding of morality and spirituality and worship.*[368]

One of America's leading twentieth-century historians, Thomas Cahill, wrote a remarkable essay, "The Gifts Of The Jews", claiming:

> *The Jews started it all—and by "it" I mean so many of the things we care about, the underlying values that make all of us, Jew and Gentile, believer and atheist, tick... Without the Jews, we would see the world through different eyes, hear with different ears, even feel with different feelings... we would think with a different mind, interpret all our experience differently, draw different conclusions from the things that befall us. And we would set a different course for our lives.*[369]

Even without the gift of Scriptures and Saviour, humanity owes the Jews as a people a huge debt.

Blessed we bless and receive a blessing

"For if the Gentiles have come to share in their spiritual blessings, they ought also to be of service to them in material blessings... I know that when I come to you I will come in the fullness of the blessing of Christ" (15:27, 29).

Paul speaks of material blessings for the Jews who have given spiritual blessings to the Gentiles. In the beautiful economy of God, the blessed bless and receive blessing. The Roman Christians have been blessed by the Jews with the gospel. The Roman Christians bless the poor Jews with material goods. The Roman Christians receive a blessing when Paul comes in the power of the Spirit.

Many fear to give because they think they will lose. Naturally speaking, if you give something away your have lost it. And yet in the divine economy, a gift is gain to both the receiver and also the giver.

The Buddha grasped this. One of his proverbs states: "If you knew what I knew about the power of giving, you would not let a single meal pass without sharing it in some way." I believe this is an inviolable law of Scripture: God honours those who honour him; you reap what you sow; give and it will be given to you. The distinguished evangelist Billy Graham, talking about this cycle of blessing God and others having being blessed by God, said,

> *God has given us two hands, one to receive and the other to give. We are not cisterns made for hoarding; we are channels made for sharing.*[370]

This is not the notion of karma, "what goes around comes around"; it is about God's nature, and you cannot out-give God. God loves to give to those who love to give. The only time God permits us to test him is in the area of giving. Israel was complaining about its poverty and poor crops and God said to his people, "Bring the full tithe into the storehouse, that there may be food in my house. And thereby put me to the test, says the Lord of hosts, if I will not open the windows of heaven for you and pour down for you a blessing until there is no more need" (Malachi 3:10).

I was challenged by Mary's devotion, when she broke the bottle of nard and poured it out with her love upon Christ (John 12:3). The disciples thought this was a waste of a year's wages and yet Jesus loved this act done for him! I reflected: what would I be willing to give, to break and pour over Christ? Now, my almost obsessive hobby is collecting vintage English fountain pens; I thought perhaps I could simply break a rare pen as a wild act of abandon and devotion. Hardly a year's salary, but a treasure to me.

The next day was our church auction to raise cash for an intern mission trip to South Africa. I sensed the Lord say, "Sell a rare pen for me!" I initially thought of auctioning the chance for someone to win their choice of pen from my collection of 200, but then I feared they might take one of the best! Then the Lord challenged me that it was for him, and so I decided to auction the rarest pen, worth several hundred pounds, of which there are less than five copies known to exist in the world.

That Sunday it was auctioned, along with a description of what it was and why it was not just a tired old 1920s' brown rubber pen! It sold for a decent amount and I was pleased. I felt I had offered a genuine act of worship.

The very next day was my birthday and a parcel arrived for me. Lo and behold, in it was my pen. The person who gave it had attended the auction and had heard God say to them, "Buy it for Simon for his birthday." They bought it and intended to keep it until my birthday – which they had no idea was the next day! It was only when they saw my colleagues at the parish office signing a card to me that they realized it was right then, and so they brought it round that evening. I was overwhelmed, and so were they. In God's economy, we were all blessed.

Shortly afterwards, a friend visiting her elderly father in Germany saw an old pen in his desk drawer. She asked if she could have it to give to her vicar, who was me. He said yes, but added it was old and valuable! When she turned up and gave it to me I nearly had a heart attack: it was a German Pelikan Toledo 111T from about 1934. It was among the most sought-after of all pens, worth almost as much as my other 200 pens put together! Only an obsessive pen collector would recognize it and appreciate it. But I believe the angels were smiling. God had orchestrated that a pen-collecting nutter in Oxford should receive a beautiful German pen lost with clutter in a drawer in Germany, because he knew it would bring me pleasure. I believe God did this because I sought to worship him, albeit in an inadequate and reluctant way at first. This is God's economy: give and it will be given to you.

This illustration is not meant in any way to inculcate the error of the so-called prosperity doctrine that is driven my mammon and not worship. It is simply to delight in God's goodness, God's generosity. We do not give out of a motive to get – we give because we have received and we give because the poor have need. But you really cannot out-give God. Give and you will receive, bless and you will be blessed.

51

Is Christianity Male? (16:1–7)

In our study of Romans 15:15–21 in Chapter 49, we considered Paul's priestly ministry of preaching the gospel and offering Gentile converts to God, sanctified by the Spirit. I have preached on that passage twice, and both times I made an appeal for people to offer themselves as gospel ministers and missionaries. Both times more young women responded to the call than young men.

For most of church history a male church leadership has argued that women, by virtue of Eve's forfeiting her virtue, are ruled out of the vocation to priestly ministry. C. S. Lewis once wrote, "Only one wearing the masculine uniform can… represent the Lord to the church."[371] In similar vein the Reformed Bible teacher John Piper has stated that, "God has given Christianity a masculine feel."[372] It is certainly true that male leadership has kept church leadership male. Many men think and teach and run church on the basis that women should be seen and not heard.

The well-rehearsed argument is that God has revealed himself as Father not Mother; the Second person of the Trinity is revealed as the eternal *Son* not Daughter; the Old Testament priests were all men not women; the twelve apostles were all men and not women; in marriage God made husbands not wives the head; 1 Corinthians 14:33–35 tells women to be silent in church; 1 Timothy 2:11–14 is understood in its "plain reading" sense to forbid women from ever teaching or exercising authority over any man in a church context.

Conservative arguments against women exercising teaching or leadership roles in church are generally scripturally drawn and as such not lightly dismissed. However, these so-called complementarians, who regard women and men as equal but different and thus free to exercise complementary but not similar ministry roles, do not have a monopoly on faithfully handling and applying the Scriptures. It is also scriptural that God made humankind in his image: female and male; that the Holy Spirit in Hebrew takes the feminine case; that in Greek the Holy Spirit is neither male nor female but neuter; that God employs several maternal metaphors to describe himself; that in the Old Testament a few women prophesied and ruled; that husbands and wives become one flesh, not one ruling over the other; and last but by no means least, that every woman in Christ has a man, Christ, as her head, under whose authority she can minister.

It is also scriptural that every Christian life begins through being "born again by the Spirit" – giving birth being an exclusively female process. It is also scriptural that Jesus gave no exclusion or exception clause to the Great Commission, as if men only can make disciples and men only are made disciples. If the iterative nature of the Great Commission to go and make disciples, who make disciples, includes women as disciples, then women can make disciples that Jesus says happens through "teaching" under Christ who holds "all authority". Finally, it is scriptural that women were included in the power from on high poured out at Pentecost, which was expressly given to anoint witnesses to fulfil the Great Commission (Acts 1:8).

Given these general truths about the calling of women to exercise a similar ministry in Christ to that of men, including teaching, it is possible to read and interpret as pastorally and pragmatically conditioned the two tough texts that apparently prohibit women from preaching and teaching and exercising authority in church (1 Corinthians 14:33–35 and 1 Timothy 2:11–14). On this understanding, they are not a perpetual prohibition on women's leadership and teaching. Scripture interprets Scripture, and significantly, as we will see, I believe Paul's actual practice of praising and partnering with women designated as apostles and ministers must be brought to bear on any interpretation of 1 Timothy 2 that bars women from forms of leadership simply because they are women.

Paul grew up in a culture where women were not regarded as equal to men. For centuries, and still today, some Orthodox Jewish men offer praise in their morning prayers along these lines:

Blessed are you, Hashem [O Lord], King of the Universe, for not having made me a Gentile.
Blessed are you, Hashem, King of the Universe, for not having made me a slave.
Blessed are you, Hashem, King of the Universe, for not having made me a woman.[373]

The reason generally given is that all three categories – Gentiles, slaves, women – were unable to read the Torah, and so the man who had access to the Torah was blessed and blessed God. This had certainly been Paul's theological culture and nurture. But Rabbi Saul was radically converted, and in Romans 16 he greets twenty-four folk in the church by name, nine of whom are women. However, more significant are the epithets he gives to these women, whom he describes as mother to him, suffering for Christ, hard labourers, apostles, deacons, patrons and co-workers (the exact term he uses of the apostolic leader Timothy in verse 21). My thesis here is that Paul's pragmatic and actual employment and recognition of women in senior church leadership roles must take priority over the two hermeneutically difficult texts that may appear to restrict women in leadership.

The prostate Phoebe

"I commend to you our sister Phoebe, a *servant* of the church at Cenchreae, that you may welcome her in the Lord in a way worthy of the saints, and help her in whatever she may need from you, for she has been a *patron* of many and of myself as well" (16:1–2, italics mine).

Paul entrusted Phoebe with delivering this letter to the church at Rome. She was not simply a courier, delivering the letter like a postman. It was customary in the ancient world for those entrusted with such letters to actually read them to those who were recipients, and even to explain and expound on the content. Two predicates Paul attaches to her are significant – the Greek terms *diakonos* and *prostatis*. They are translated differently, the translation presumably reflecting a prior theological conviction:

Deacon and benefactor (NIV)
Servant and succourer (KJV)
Servant and patron (ESV)
Deacon and help (NLT)
Servant and helper (NASB)

The term *diakonos* can be translated "deacon", "minister" or "servant". Paul applies this title to himself (Colossians 1:23, 25; 2 Corinthians 3:6) and to Apollos (1 Corinthians 3:5) and calls Timothy a "co-worker in the gospel" (1 Thessalonians 3:2). All three are *diakonoi* as well as apostles. Paul consistently ties the ministry of a *diakonos* with preaching and teaching and nurturing in the Word. In Acts 6 we see the seven official deacons appointed to minister in the church, serving by caring for the poor widows. The criterion for this office was that all had to be "full of the Spirit" (Acts 6:3), and two of the seven whose names and ministries we know were Philip and Stephen, who were miracle-working evangelists. In 1 Timothy 3 deacons are official leaders, ministers in the church. In the early church, the Roman governor Pliny the Younger in AD 112 details (in his *Epistles* 10.96,8) his interrogation of two Bithynian church leaders who were two slave women he calls *ministrae* – which is the Latin for *diakonoi*. This is highly significant because one may deduce that these ministrae or deacons were singled out for torture presumably because they were the official ministers of the church. The church was led by leaders who were not only slaves, they were also women.

The use of the term "deacon" in all the above cases was reserved for Spirit-filled church leadership. Note that the term is a masculine noun, though it was a description of a role that could be held by a woman – in this case, Phoebe. It just won't do, as some have tried, to suggest that when we read *diakonos* applied to men we are to think in terms of an official church leader, teacher, and minister, but when we read it ascribed here of Phoebe we are to think of someone more like a "table waiter". It would be more scripturally consistent that we think of Phoebe as a minister of the church in Cenchreae.

Not only is Phoebe called a deacon, she is described as *prostatis* – a patron, helper, or benefactor.

This word *prostatis* is the feminine form of the masculine noun *prostates*, from which we get our current term for the male prostate gland. *Prostatis* is a derivative of two Greek words, *pro* and *histemi*, meaning to "stand before". According to the Greek Lexicon of Liddle and Scott, the term *prostates* referred to a front-rank man, a leader, chief, or administrator; or, secondly, to a president or presiding officer; or to one who protects – a guardian, champion, or patron.

This word was applied to the worship leader in a Graeco-Roman temple. Justin Martyr used it in the masculine form to designate the head of a church – the bishop presiding over the Eucharist.

Translating it as "patron" may well be right here. Phoebe may have been a woman of means who financially supported Paul's apostolic mission. One thinks of Selina, Countess of Huntingdon, who supported Whitefield's ministry, funding the building of sixty-four chapels, contributing to numerous others, and supporting many ministers. In terms equivalent to today, she gave away an estimated £20 million to mission (£100,000 in 1750).

Some very wrongly reduce this word *prostatis* to that of a mere "helper". Calvin suggested she was like a "nurse". We certainly do not want to devalue nurses, but that was not what Paul had in mind! At the very least, as a deacon, she was a church official and minister; however, as Paul's acknowledged patron, far from being a mere "financial donor", patronage in antiquity was hierarchical and the client was obligated, sometimes legally, to the patron who held superior status.[374] It was a term used of the relationship between a general and his troops; of a founder and its colonists. How exactly this worked between Phoebe and Paul we do not know, but Paul unashamedly admits it. Phoebe was a deacon and a patron – she was really something!

The prelate Priscilla

"Greet Prisca [a variant of the name Priscilla] and Aquila, my fellow workers in Christ Jesus, who risked their necks for my life, to whom not only I give thanks but all the churches of the Gentiles give thanks as well. Greet also the church in their house" (16:3–5).

Priscilla and Aquila are itinerant church planters who partnered with Paul's apostolic mission in Ephesus (Acts 18:18; 2 Timothy 4:19) and in Corinth (1 Corinthians 16:19). Both in Rome and in Corinth they are seen hosting a church in their house. They discipled the convert Apollos in Ephesus, explaining to him a more faithful understanding of way of Christ, and he subsequently became an apostle. Paul describes them as co-workers (*synergous*), working together with him to further the cause of Christ and advance his kingdom.

Paul mentions the name of Priscilla – or Prisca – before that of her husband in five of the seven times they are mentioned in the New Testament. Significantly, this was against the common practice of the time. Understanding the scandal of this, the KJV actually reverses the Greek order by placing Aquila before Priscilla. However in the Greek text she is the first named. Why would Paul do this?

It seems highly possible that Priscilla is named first because she is the more prominent minister in this shared ministry. Why should Paul say "all the churches of the Gentiles give thanks (to God) for them"? If it was simply because they had risked their lives for Paul, that would be a hugely self-inflated arrogant comment for Paul to make. No, even if hyperbolic, it must surely be because of their strategic influence in assisting the planting of key churches or discipling key church leaders in Rome, Corinth, and Ephesus. The Brethren theologian F. F. Bruce wrote: "Their service to the Christian cause evidently far exceeded their personal services to Paul."[375] Priscilla did not simply host a home-group in her living room; she was a peripatetic, dynamic, apostolic church-planter – supported by her husband.

The apostolate Junia

"Greet Andronicus and Junia, my kinsmen and my fellow prisoners. They are well known to the apostles, and they were in Christ before me" (16:7).

This couple are relatives of Paul, who also suffered in jail for serving Christ.

Paul states they were "in Christ before me", and given that Paul became a Christian in the early days after Pentecost, it is quite possible that they knew Jesus. Some have wondered at their being among the apostolic mission of the "seventy-two" (Luke 10:1), and others that they were Jewish pilgrims converted at Pentecost.

The phrase "apostles… in Christ before me" echoes what Paul

said of the apostle Peter and the Twelve in Galatians 1:17 who "were apostles before me". Have some translators let their pre-conceived complementarian theology shape a translation away from its implication that a woman was an apostle? The Greek text raises two interpretive issues: first, is *Junian* (the *n* is there because it is in the accusative case) masculine or feminine? And secondly, what is their association to the word "apostles"?

The NIV translates the text as "Greet Andronicus and *Junias,* outstanding among the apostles" – rendering the Greek *Junian* as Junias, a man, and both as apostles.

The ESV translates it as "Greet Andronicus and *Junia,* well known to the apostles" – rendering the Greek *Junian* as Junia, a woman, but that this couple are well known *by,* but not *as,* apostles.

These are both plausible but are they probable? I think not. And it seems a theological pre-judgment has affected both these translations. For them, if *Junian* is a woman, she cannot be an apostle; or if *Junian* is an apostle, she must be a man. But many think that *Junian* is rightly understood as Junia, a woman (as in the ESV) *and* that this person is notable as an apostle (as in the NIV).[376]

Junia was a common woman's name in antiquity, whereas Junias is unknown as a male name. In fact the identity of Junia as a female apostle was unquestioned until the thirteenth century, when translators began changing the gender of the name to the masculine "Junias". There is only one ancient commentator (Epiphanius) who makes Junia a male, but he also makes Priscilla a male… so clearly a theological bias is at work. It seems most probable that *Junian* in the Greek is a woman, Junia, perhaps married to Andronicus.

This woman Junia and Andronicus were "notable" (*episemoi*) among the apostles. The Greek term here is related to a word for a sign, or badge, or coin imprint. It was used to identify and promote a person or a thing from among its other representatives – so one flag stands out from other flags, one ship's head stands out from other ships, one coin stands out from other coins. Employed in describing Andronicus and Junia in the context of the apostles, it is unlikely to mean "well known to the apostles" but rather "standing out" – outstanding among them. The translation of *en tois apostolois* as "among the apostles" is reasonable. The preposition *en* is generally a "marker of position defined as being in a location" (Greek Lexicon of Bauer, Arndt, Gingrich and Danker) – the apostles are those they are placed among.

I am no Greek scholar, but using the tools available I believe the best sense of the Greek is that Andronicus and his wife Junia were "stand-out" apostles. Twentieth-century evangelical translations, with all the weight of tradition to influence interpretation, struggle to conceive of a woman as an apostle. However, we must heed the witness of a natural Greek speaker who would better grasp the meaning of Paul's text, writing in the fourth century, Bishop Chrysostom. He was quite clear *Junian* referred to a woman and an apostle:

> *And indeed to be apostles at all is a great thing. But to be even amongst these of note, just consider what a great encomium [eulogy] this is! But they were of note owing to their works, to their achievements. Oh! How great is the devotion of this woman, that she should be even counted worthy of the appellation of apostle.*[377]

Not only are they notable apostles, but it is possible that they are the apostles of the church of Rome. In Chapter 15 Paul has made it clear that he doesn't want to build on any other apostles' foundations – hence he has delayed coming to Rome. Professor Francis Watson[378] suggests that Paul, by greeting Andronicus and Junia as apostles, is essentially petitioning them as the governing apostles of the Roman church to recognize and welcome his forthcoming mission in Rome.

As I studied and prayed in preparing this text, with no fixed views on women in ministry and a genuine willingness to change my opinions, several times I sensed the Spirit of God nudge me: "Who has authority in this church? Who is Paul addressing as the leader of the church in Rome?" It is important to admit nowhere is Peter referred to. Surely Paul would greet him, make mention of him, and certainly honour him, if he had any apostolic oversight of the church. But the truth is, at this stage Peter probably had no connection with the Roman church. The only apostles mentioned here are Andronicus and Junia. The only other leaders in the list are Priscilla and Aquila, who host a church in their house.

So it seems that what we may deduce is: leadership in the Roman church was plural, involving two couples, and that two women, Priscilla and Junia, were among the first popes of Rome...

Leadership is male... and female

It has often been a mark of missions movements or renewal movements to see women step into apostolic leadership roles.[379] The founder of China Inland Mission, Hudson Taylor, employed effective women evangelists, noting that, "At Pentecost, God did not arrange a special women's meeting." The same unction to fulfil the same commission was given without gender distinction at Pentecost. Consider John Wesley, who licensed a few women to preach in his churches and had women leading the small groups that helped fuel growth. Consider the late nineteenth-century evangelist Phoebe Palmer, who gained an estimated 25,000 decisions for Christ. Consider William Booth, founder of the Salvation Army, who said, "My best men are women." And the Army's growth was dependent on leadership by nearly 50 per cent women officers. Consider, too, C. T. Studd, who said of his Heart of Africa Mission (now WEC) that two of his most effective churches were "manned by women" – and who boasted a cannibal reputed to have eaten over 100 men and who was converted by a woman.

We go on. Consider Karen Lowe's study *Carriers of Fire,* which demonstrated how it was largely women who caught and carried the fire in the Welsh revival. Consider Dr Cheryl Sanders' thesis "History of women in the Pentecostal movement",[380] which proved how Pentecostalism's founding father William Seymour was "largely mentored, guided and offered a context for ministry by women". Pentecostalism is still releasing women leaders – 500 million members later.

Consider David (formerly Paul) Yonggi Cho, founder of the world's largest church of over one million members. As a strict Presbyterian he resisted women leadership until God finally got through to him. Once he let women run cells, growth took off exponentially. An attendee at a Yonggi Cho church leaders conference in Seoul records:

> *Finally, he [Cho] asked all the American pastors in the group to stand. So we did—about twenty of us. "It breaks my heart," he said, "at what you have done to your women. You hold them back and relegate them to rather insignificant places of ministry instead of setting them free to minister. It is no wonder Christianity is struggling in your country. You go into spiritual battle with one hand tied behind your back."*[381]

And let our minds turn to the explosion in the Chinese house church under communism. In the 1980s it was estimated that 85 per cent of leadership was female. I wrote this particular chapter from the vicarage of St Frideswides Church. Frideswide was a Saxon princess devoted to God, celibate, who fled to Oxford and founded a thriving Augustinian priory. Many miracles were associated with her. The Roman Catholic Church made her a saint in the thirteenth century. Was she an apostle?

In conclusion

The texts that appear to prohibit women from senior church leadership roles are the very same ones that appear to prohibit women from preaching or teaching men in any capacity. Consequently I see only two possible positions: all or nothing. Either the passages in 1 Corinthians 14 and 1 Timothy 2 do permanently prohibit women from leading and teaching roles, and the matter is closed... or those texts are not rightly understood or applied as comprehensive prohibitions, and other texts such as Romans 16 that appear to legitimate women's ministries must take priority. If that is the case, then no offices are excluded to women, who may exercise all ministries in the church if they exhibit the Spirit's charisms and character to do so.

And I am now persuaded that in Romans 16 Paul is greeting the local church leadership, recognizing them and ultimately petitioning them for help to pioneer into Spain. There are no solo celibate male popes at the reins. Leadership is shared by apostolic couples whose wives are not mere helpers and may even be more prominent and gifted in the shared leadership than their husbands. Thus Paul's actual practice of recognizing and releasing, praising and partnering with women leaders, must inform how we interpret and apply other texts.

If that was Paul's practice, it must become ours. Women's gifts must be identified, honoured, nurtured, and released, without imposing a stained-glass ceiling. Not to do so is to dishonour the gift-giving Spirit, to dis-empower women made in God's image, to diminish the nature of church, and to damage God's action for the world.

52

Benedictus Benedicat (15:5, 13, 33; 16:25–27)

I have often enjoyed eating at formal hall in Oxford colleges. The students all stand at the long refectory tables as the dons enter, and then, while all remain silent, some will bow their heads, and a nervous undergraduate will say grace in Latin. Some try to memorize it, others read from a discreet little card.

This quaint old grace goes back a millennium to the earliest colleges founded by and for scholarly monks, whose language was ecclesiastical Latin. The grace contains the words *Benedictus Benedicat*. This can be translated to be an invocation to God "the blessed One" to "bless" the food; but perhaps a better rendering is as an exhortation to the one who is blessed (with the meal) to bless the giver (God). G. K. Chesterton described *Benedictus Benedicat* as "very precisely the motto of the earliest Medievalism."[382] It could also be a fitting motto for the church, and a fitting conclusion to Paul's epistle to the Romans. Let those blessed by God – bless God!

We have come to the end of Paul's epic epistle. How does he finish? It is clear that, like all good preachers, he does not quite know how to finish! Like the modern plane he circles round the airport, apparently coming into land and then veering off again, before eventually making the landing.

In Romans 15 Paul has described his role in terms of being a priest offering sacrifices to God. The Temple priests were ordained to two other specific tasks: they were to bless the people in the name of the Lord, and to bless the Lord on behalf of the people (Psalm 134). And, as Paul ends his epic epistle, that is exactly what he does: he blesses the church and leads the church in blessing the Lord.

Blessing God's people

In Romans 15 Paul blesses the people with three invocations or benedictions:

1. "May the God of endurance and encouragement grant you to live in such harmony with one another, in accord with Christ Jesus, that together you may with one voice glorify the God and Father of our Lord Jesus Christ" (15:5–6).
2. "May the God of hope fill you will all joy and peace in believing, so that by the power of the Holy Spirit you may abound in hope" (15:13).
3. "May the God of peace be with you all" (15:33).

It is in the nature of God to bless. He is a blessing God – in one sense he cannot help it – it's what he does. He looks for ways to bless our lives. He wants us to live in his blessing. Some have a really skewed notion that God is looking for ways to get them, to punish them, to withhold from them. They become religiously neurotic, always expecting the worst from the Lord. But as a father looks to give his son not scorpions or snakes but good gifts, so God seeks to bless us (Luke 11:11–13) – if we will let him.

The source of the blessing is God, not Paul

It is the role of a priest to bless. A blessing is not a prayer, it is an invocation and impartation upon the recipient of God's favour. The priest is not the source of the blessing, merely the mediator. Numbers 6:27 reveals the role of a priest to bless: "So shall they put my name upon the people of Israel, and I will bless them." He simply passes on what God gives; hence Paul's threefold use of the phrase, "May God…" God is the one who blesses, and God is the blessing. God gives himself – "so that by the power of the Holy Spirit you may abound in hope" (15:13). That divine blessing comes exclusively through Christ, by the Spirit.

The nature of the blessing is spiritual, not material

It is crucial that we grasp exactly what Paul does bless with and what he does not bless with. There is no blessing of security or prosperity or longevity of years. No easy comfortable life, no new car, no holiday home, no pay increase, no perfect physique or good health, no prosperous living, no fair weather. It's so important we realize the nature of God's blessing, otherwise we will be dissatisfied with what we get, blaming God for withholding something he never promised to give, or blaming ourselves for not having enough faith or devotion or holiness or whatever.

Often we want God to bless the appetites of our "flesh". But God is not a genie in a lamp who gives us our wishes; he is God who gives us his wishes, And his wish list is often very different from ours. God's measure of a successful life looks very different from the world's measure. He is more concerned with our character than our comfort. God is more interested with who we are than what we have.

I recently read a thriving church's statement of faith, in which they claim, "God wants to bless." That is true. But then it went on: "We call it prosperity with a purpose. After all, if we are broke how can we be generous to others?" But Peter, at the Temple's Gate Beautiful, said to the cripple: "Silver and gold have I none, but what I have I give to you: in Jesus' name rise up and walk" (Acts 3:6). The apostles had nothing but the power of God to give away. We have so much, and yet so little power.

There is an apocryphal story of Pope Innocent IV saying to Thomas Aquinas, while counting a tableful of money: "See, Thomas, the church can no longer say, 'Silver and gold have I none.'" And Thomas replied, "True, and neither can it say, 'In Jesus' name rise up and walk.'"

The remarkable apostle of China, Brother Yun, who experienced a proliferation of miracles, says he is frequently asked why we see so few miracles or healings in the West. His answer is clear: "In the West you have so much. You have insurance for everything. In a way, you don't need God."[383] Ironically, could it be that our relative prosperity, far from being a sign of divine blessing, is actually a curse that has insulated us against truly experiencing the power of God?

So what can we expect by way of divine blessing? W. Russell Maltby was spot on when he wrote that "Jesus promised his disciples three things – they would be entirely fearless, absurdly happy, and in constant trouble."[384] That certainly reflects the features of the blessing Paul bestows.

Endurance

The Greek *hypomone* is a conjunction of two words, *hypo* meaning "under" and *mone* from *meno* "to remain". This term concerns perseverance under pressure. Paul does not pray for an end to difficulties, but for staying power. The Christian life is hard work, a hard walk, with many troubles, temptations, obstacles, and persecutions on the way. We can often be tempted to give up, give in, or pull back. Many Christians sadly quit. In the parable of the sower Jesus spoke of plants that were choked by weeds (temptations) and others scorched by heat (afflictions). Paul does not pray for an easy life but for staying power in a difficult one; he doesn't pray that we avoid persecution, but rather that we persevere.

Encouragement

The Greek word is *paraklesis* again, to call alongside, recalling the "Paraclete" who is the Holy Spirit (John 14:16). Encouragement is not there just to stroke but to provoke, to gird, and strengthen, and bring the best out of us. Just as an athlete at the Olympics has a coach alongside them, guiding and correcting, and the crowds cheering, so Paul prays for the Spirit of God to enable us to step up to the mark.

Being of one mind

We have seen that disunity over various doctrinal and practical issues is near the surface in the Roman church. Paul has sought to resolve the theological and doctrinal tensions. Here he is praying for that attitude that will enable them to find oneness of heart and mind.

Paul is not expecting them all to agree on every detail (hence the pragmatic compromise on differing diets and dates in Romans 14). But the church's members – Jew and Gentile, rich and poor, old and young, male and female – are all saved by the same means and adopted into the same family and living for the same Lord, and Paul desires that by the Spirit of God they will be fashioned into one people, with one voice, glorifying the one God.

Hope

The Greek word *elpis,* from *elpo,* usually implies the expectation of pleasure. The Christian lives in the now, the in-between time, living *from* Christ's Easter event and the forgiveness of sins, and living *for* the return of Christ with his full salvation.

God is our hope; our hope is in God. The here and now is not the be all and end all. We are a people not looking to our next birthday, next holiday, our retirement, or pension, but we are pregnant with anticipation and the expectation of eternal life, complete – replete – with God. The best has yet to come. For those who die without accepting Christ, this world is as good as it gets. For those who die in Christ, this world is as bad as it gets.

I remember taking my youngest son to school when he was about six. We got to his school peg, and slowly he hung up his rucksack, then his coat, then his hat, then his hoodie. I was in rather a hurry and said, "Come on, son, just give me a kiss goodbye." He replied quickly, "No, Dad, I save the best till last." He was taking his time before that special moment of giving his dad a kiss and a hug goodbye. Beautiful. And Jesus has saved the best till last for us – we live in hope, not wishful thinking, but expectation that he who died and rose again and ascended into heaven, just as he promised, will return for us and take us to glory, just as he promised.

Joy

The Greek for "joy" is *chara.* C. S. Lewis described joy as "the serious business of heaven"[385] and saw all earth's pleasures at best as hors d'oeuvres for it. We are wired for the joy of heaven, and nothing in this world can suffice. Without God we seek this joy here and there, and snatch moments of it. But it is God's gift and only found when we have found Jesus and are found by him. Many Christians slander God by their miserable and morose nature or glum demeanour. They are more Eeyore than in awe. Paul prays for the grace of God, through the Spirit of God who brings joy even now amidst the tears and fears of life. We can know in advance that heavenly "joy unspeakable and full of glory" (1 Peter 1:8, KJV).

Peace

Our last Greek word is *eirene*. Shakespeare's Juliet says to a panting, weary nurse, "How art thou out of breath when thou hast breath?"[386] So many feel like this so often – out of breath though there is breath in our lungs, weary, anxious, driven, churned up, restless. Although successful, popular, and wealthy, nevertheless H. G. Wells, on his sixty-fifth birthday could say, "I am lonely and have never found peace."[387] Jesus promised: "Peace I leave with you; my peace I give to you... Let not your hearts be troubled" (John 14:27). This peace comes by the Spirit of peace, the Spirit of God, who stills our soul like a weaned child. Paul is blessing the church with this.

The great Reformer John Calvin in his commentary on Ephesians (3:21) stated:

> *Whatever expectations we form of divine blessings, the infinite goodness of God will exceed all our wishes and all our thoughts.*[388]

Yes indeed, God's blessings will always outdo our expectations.

The blessed bless God

"Now to him who is able to strengthen you according to my gospel and the preaching of Jesus Christ, according to the revelation of the mystery that was kept secret for long ages... to the only wise God be glory for evermore through Jesus Christ! Amen" (16:25, 27).

We bless God because he first blesses us. With the psalmist we sing, "Bless the Lord, O my soul, and forget not all his benefits" (Psalm 103:2). We would bless God more readily and more fully if only we considered more clearly his blessing of us. When in the "slough of despond" (to use John Bunyan's words), I have often had to remind myself and others to consider all that the Lord has given us and to not forget all his benefits. We lose perspective so easily.

What does it mean to bless God? It means to honour, thank,

glorify, exalt, and worship God. It is to promote him – his fame, his renown, his crown; it is to join with myriads of angels around the throne, giving glory to God; it is to join with the twenty-four elders who fall before the Lord sat on his throne, and casting down their crowns, their honours, their achievements at his feet, shouting: "Worthy are you, our Lord and God, to receive glory and honour and power, for you created all things, and by your will they existed and were created" (Revelation 4:11).

When do we bless? Paul says we are to bless "now" and "for ever". Now is always now – now is never later. The command to bless God always confronts us in the present; now is never tomorrow. We do not wait to worship, we do not wait to bless God. We do not wait on our feelings, we do not wait to be moved by the Spirit. We do not wait for the next service, celebration, or conference. We have already received from God. Come, now is the time to worship. The Anglican liturgy affirms: "It is our duty and our joy, at all times and in all places, to give you thanks."

"Now" is the when, the who is "to him" who strengthens and saves us by the gospel of Jesus Christ, the mystery of God, the revelation of the ages. Those blessed by God with new life must live a life blessing God. A Christian is someone fixated with Jesus to the point of obsession.

Often it is worship that we worship. We so love the sound of our own voices. We often judge worship on what we got out of it, not what we gave to God. But worship is not for us, not about us, not to us; worship is to him, for him, about him. It is because of who he is and what he has done. We are not the point; our enjoyment is irrelevant.

I once heard a worship leader begin the praise time with the exhortation: "If we do what we have always done, we will get what we have always got." Well, that may be true, but it is hardly a call to honour Christ with our lips, and that is the point of worship! Clearly the worship leader thought that we were gathered to worship in order to get something from God, not give something to God!

I recall attending a church service once and not "getting into" the sung worship time. Someone asked me after the service what I thought of the worship and I quickly answered, "I did not enjoy it," as I hadn't liked the song choices. It was one of those rare times I have heard God speak very clearly – I almost had to turn around thinking he was behind me. He spoke to my spirit and said, "I enjoyed it." And that was what mattered – not whether I enjoyed the song selection but whether the Father received worship in spirit and truth. Worship is a party the church throws to honour and celebrate the Lord. As we worship we encounter God, and he blesses us again even as we bless him. But worship is not for the purpose of being blessed; it is to give a blessing.

Matt Redman wrote a song in which he pointed us in the right direction: "I'm coming back to the heart of worship, and it's all about you, it's all about you, Jesus." Worship is ascribing to God the worth that is due to him – because he's worth it. It's a demonstration of affection and devotion to Christ, a celebration of who he is and of all he has done for us.

Worship is not for our benefit – it is not to make us feel good, even though it usually does. Worship is not there to thrill or stroke our aesthetic or emotional registers. Worship is not an evangelistic tool and not for the benefit of non-church attenders. Worship is not the means to attract the young or the old. Worship is profoundly counter-cultural. Worship does not pander to our consumerist desires; it is God-focused. The difference between idolatry and worship is whether God is the point, the pre-occupation, the prime consideration. If he is not, then it's idolatry. The psalmist said: "Not to us, not to us, O Lord, but to your name give glory."

To the only wise God…

"… to the only wise God…" (16:27).

We worship God alone because he alone is God. He stands all alone, quite alone, in splendid isolation. There is no one else sharing the podium; there are no other gods coming in second place, silver medals on the divine pedestal. God alone, who alone saved us, stands alone, and is worshipped alone.

Paul's letter to the Romans has given us the grounds for the worship of God:

- only he who created us is worth worshipping
- only he who is revealed in creation, canon, and covenant is worth worshipping

- only he who died for our sins on a bloody, lonely tree is worth worshipping
- only he who redeemed us from sin, death, and hell is worth worshipping
- only he who sanctifies us by his Spirit within us is worth worshipping
- only he who adopts us into his family is worth worshipping
- only he who pours out eternal love in our hearts is worth worshipping
- only he who blesses us to bless him and the world is worthy of worship.

... Be glory

"... be glory" (16:27).

That says it all. Romans is about the road to glory. Glory withheld from God, glory misdirected to idols, glory forfeited by humankind, glory restored by Christ, glory experienced through suffering, glory given to God.

Giving God glory is "the goal of all Christian existence" according to the Catholic professor Joseph Fitzmyer.[389] He's right. Similarly, the seventeenth-century English and Scottish divines affirmed this in the Westminster Shorter Confession, which states as its first doctrine: "Man's Chief End is to glorify God, and enjoy him for ever."[390] Giving God glory is the recognition of the Creator by the creature. Giving God glory is the celebration of the Redeemer by the redeemed. We glorify God by:

- repenting of our sin and rebellion and idolatry
- accepting the gospel as the only means of salvation
- living and trusting in Christ alone by faith alone
- dying to sin and living a holy life by the Spirit
- by loving him as our adoptive Father
- embracing his election of the people of Israel
- offering ourselves as living sacrifices, holy to God
- serving the church and the world with gifts God gives
- praying for and honouring authorities instituted by God
- sharing the gospel with whoever, whenever, however.

The story of Romans tells us that, when we refuse to worship and glorify God, we shrink, become vapid, our glory is tarnished, our goal in life is circumvented, we become less than human. Whether we give glory to God or not adds nothing to him, for he is altogether glorious. But not to do so shrivels us. C. S. Lewis wrote:

> *We can no more diminish God's glory by refusing to worship him than a lunatic can put out the sun by scribbling the words 'lunatic' on the walls of his cell.*[391]

But as we bless God we are blessed. As we glorify God we are glorified. *Benedictus Benedicat* – let the blessed bless.

In conclusion

Let C. H. Spurgeon, that great prince of preachers, have the final words on this chapter, and indeed in our study on Romans. In his sermon on Psalm 134, which presents the Temple priests blessing the Lord and blessing the people, Spurgeon gives this call to the church:

> *Oh to abound in blessing! May "blessed" and "blessing" be the two words which describe our lives. Let others flatter their fellows, or bless their stars, or praise themselves; as for us, we will bless Jehovah, from whom all blessings flow.*[392]

Notes

1. Tradition has it that from the earliest period, the letters of Paul were collated in order of length into two distinct groups: first, general epistles to churches and secondly, pastoral epistles to individuals. Logically it would have made more sense to order them according to the date when they were thought to be written. However, because it was unclear when exactly they were written – and to this day scholars remain uncertain as to exactly what date Paul wrote them – they were ordered according to length.

   One ancient source, *P46*, believed Hebrews to be Pauline and thus has Hebrews appearing in between Romans and 1 Corinthians and, against traditional ordering, places Ephesians before Galatians. This latter point is interesting, because in fact Ephesians is longer than Galatians (155 verses and 149 verses respectively) and so really ought to appear before it in our Bibles if a strict collation according to length is followed. It would seem that the lengths of these two epistles were miscalculated at an early stage, and Galatians was thus placed before Ephesians hence the order with which we are familiar today.

2. Martyn Lloyd-Jones, *I Am Not Ashamed: Advice to Timothy*, Hodder & Stoughton, 1986, p. 39.

3. Karl Barth, *The Epistle to the Romans*, Second Edition, OUP, 1968, p. 26.

4. Chapter 16 implies at least five house-holds, house-churches – one that meets in Priscilla and Aquila's house (verse 5) another meeting in Aristobulus's house (verse 10) in Narcissus' house (verse 11) at Asyncritus' (verse 14) and at Philologus' (verse 15).

5. F. F. Bruce, *The Epistle of Paul to the Romans: An Introduction and Commentary*, Tyndale New Testament Commentaries, InterVarsity Press, 1983, p. 11f, italics mine.

6. Philip Schaff, *History of the Christian Church*, Volume 1, 1910, p. 766, quoted in J. Dunn, "Romans" in G. F. Hawthorne, R. P. Martin and D. G. Reid (eds.), *Dictionary of Paul and His Epistles*, InterVarsity Press, 1993, edited by

7. Quoted in Dunn, "Romans", p. 839.

8. C. K. Barrett, *The Epistle to the Romans*, Black's New Testament Commentary Series, Second Edition, A & C Black, 1962, p. 27.

9. Noted by Charles D. Myer's "Romans", in *Anchor Bible Dictionary*, Volume 5, Doubleday, 1994, p. 816f.

10. Martin Luther, *Commentary on Romans*, Kregel Classic, Zondervan, trans. J. Theodore Mueller, 1954, p. xiii.

11. David Pawson, *Israel in the New Testament*, Terra Nova Publications, 2009, p. 95.

12. Leon Morris, "The Theme of Romans", in W. Ward Gasque and R. P. Martin (eds.), *Apostolic History and the Gospel: Biblical and Historical Essays Presented to F. F. Bruce*, The Paternoster Press, 1970, pp. 251, 252.

13. John Chrysostom, *Homilies on Romans*, Homily and Argument, 1. See http://www.hailandfire.com/doctrine_Chrysostom_onScripture.html

14. http://www.desiringgod.org/blog/posts/31-years-ago-today-piper-called-to-preach

15. http://www.greaterreality.com/paul.htm a list of quotes of those who would drive a wedge between Paul and Jesus http://www.metalog.org/files/paul_p1.html

16. http://www.spurgeon.org/sermons/0130.htm

17. Blaise Pascal, *Pensées*, 1670, trans. W. F. Trotter, J. M. Dent & Sons, 1931, no. 257.

18. James Dunn, *Word Biblical Commentary: Romans*, Volume 38A, 1988.

19. John Piper, "Meditations on God is the Gospel", http://www.desiringgod.org/resource-library/books/god-is-the-gospel--2

20. Barth, *Epistle to the Romans*, p. 35.

21. *Larry King Live*, CNN, 16 February 1996.

22. http://www.cynet.com/jesus/prophecy/ntquoted.htm; http://en.wikipedia.org/wiki/Jesus_and_messianic_prophecy

23. C. H. Spurgeon, *The Metropolitan Tabernacle Pulpit*, Volume 28, Banner of Truth, 1971, p. 200.

24. Michel Haar, *Heidegger and the Essence of Man*, State University of New York, 1993, p. 99.

25. William Shakespeare, *King Henry VI, Part II*, Act I, Scene I.

26. Leon Morris, *The Epistle to the Romans*, IVP, 1998.

27. http://www.ndsu.edu/fileadmin/history/God_as_a_Spider_-_Red_River_Conference_Draft_Sean_Volk.pdf

28. Steve Chalke, *The Lost Message of Jesus*, Zondervan, 2004, p. 182.

29. Alan Jones, *Reimagining Christianity*, Wiley & Sons, 2004, p.132.

30. http://www.barna.org/culture-articles/422-diverse-set-of-national-concerns-topped-by-widespread-economic-worries

31. "Ultimate Concern" is Tillich's classic definition of the impulse of religion: Paul Tillich, *Theology of Culture*, Robert C. Kimball (ed.), OUP, 1964. Tillich asserted, "Religion, in the largest and most basic sense of the word, is ultimate concern" (pp. 7–8).

32. C.S. Lewis, *The Screwtape Letters*, HarperCollins, 2001, letter XXV.

33. A. W. Tozer, article: "The Waning Authority of Christ in the Churches – Is He Lord or Merely a Beloved Symbol?" published in *The Alliance Witness*, 15 May 1963; see http://www.thescripturealone.com/Waning.html

34. *London Observer*, 5 April, 1964.

35. Cable reply to Rabbi Herbert S. Goldstein's (Institutional Synagogue in New York) question to Einstein, "Do you believe in God?"

36. http://www.thearda.com/quickstats/qs_153.asp

37. http://www.secularism.org.uk/only38ofbritonsbelieveingod.html

38. The Engel Scale was developed by James F. Engel as a way of representing the journey from no knowledge of God through to spiriutual maturity as a Christian.

39. Augustine, *On Christian Doctrine*, chapter 28, part 29. http://www.ccel.org/ccel/augustine/doctrine.xxviii.html

40. Sermon titled "Don't Forget" by General Booth in 1910. Full text here: http://www.sacollectables.com/blood_and_fire/bloodandfire1_words.html

41. Thaddaeus Barnum, *Never Silent*, Eleison Publishing, 2008, p. 242.

42. Barnum, *Never Silent*, p. 246.

43. http://humanism.org.uk/campaigns/religion-and-belief-some-surveys-and-statistics/

44. Emil Brunner, *The Divine Imperative*, Lutterworth Press, 1937, p. 565.

45. Against Faustus, 17, 3, AD 400.

46. http://en.wikipedia.org/wiki/Moravian_slaves_(story) http://www.sermonindex.net/modules/newbb/viewtopic.php?topic_id=20243&forum=34&9

47. My first New Testament essay was on Romans 1:16–17. However I have often referred to the fact my first assignment was to do an analysis of the Greek text of John 21.

48. http://www.cmalliance.org/devotions/tozer?id=732

49. Roland H. Bainton, *Here I Stand: A Life of Martin Luther*, Abingdon Press, p. 65.

50. A. W. Tozer, *The Pursuit of God*, Arc Manor, 2008. Chapter 6 is devoted to this theme.

51. Dunn, *Word Biblical Commentary: Romans*, p. 57.

52. C. E. B. Cranfield, *Romans 1–8*, International Critical Commentary, Continuum, 2004, p. 114.

53. Some would distinguish between the categories of general revelation and natural theology, suggesting that general revelation preserves the action of God as subject – the one who initiates the encounter with himself through creation – whereas natural theology tends to be more "philosophical", focusing on the intellect and deductive reasoning power of the individual who "finds God" rather than who is summoned by him.

54. As quoted in Simon Ponsonby, "Natural Theology in the Thought of Karl Barth", MLitt Thesis, Bristol University, 1996, p. 87.

55. John Calvin, *Institutes of the Christian Religion*, Hendrickson, 2007, 1:3:3.

56. Material here is drawn from a fuller discussion in Simon Ponsonby, *God Inside Out*, Kingsway, 2007, Chapter 5.

57. Augustine, Sermon, Mai 126.6.

58. http://ewtn.com/library/PAPALDOC/JP2DENVR.HTM

59. Calvin, *Institutes*, 1:5:1.

60. Cited in Ponsonby, "Natural Theology in the Thought of Karl Barth", p. 88.

61. Pascal, *Pensées*, number 449.

62. Quoted in *New York Times* obituary, 19 April 1955.

63. Online version: http://www.reformed.org/documents/wcf_with_proofs/

64. Karl Barth, *Gifford Lectures*, 1937, quoted in Simon Ponsonby, "Natural Theology in the Thought of Karl Barth", p. 275.

65. There is some evidence Barth changed his mind toward the end of his life, embracing a modified doctrine of general revelation.

66. Quoted by Ravi Zacharias in a sermon "The Distinctives of Christ"; see

http://www.oneplace.com/ministries/let-my-people-think/listen/the-distinctives-of-christ-part-1-of-2-228897.html

67. Martin Luther, *Watchwords for the Warfare of Life*, Volume 1, T. Nelson & Sons, 1869, p. 110.

68. http://www.ccel.org/ccel/singh/feet.txt

69. www.sagepub.com/lippmanstudy/state/oh/Ch04_Ohio.pdf

70. http://www.e-n.org.uk/6028-A-battle-I-face.htm

71. This is perhaps an urban legend – but cited in Linda Gaupin, *Embracing the Vision: Sacramental Catechesis for First Reconciliation and First Communion*, Twenty-third Publications, 2007, p. 180.

72. Karl Menninger, *Whatever Became of Sin?*, Hawthorn Books, 1973.

73. Oscar Wilde, *Plays, Prose, Writings and Poems*, Everyman's Library, 1991, p. 320.

74. G. K. Chesterton, *Orthodoxy*, John Lane Company, 1909, p. 109.

75. Letter to his brother Theo, July 1880, as quoted in *Dear Theo: The Autobiography of Vincent Van Gogh*, Irving Stone and Jean Stone (eds.), New American Library, 1995, p. 181.

76. John Henry Newman, *Fifteen Sermons Preached before the University of Oxford*, Rivingtons, 1880, p. 18.

77. William Shakespeare, *Macbeth*, Act V, Scene I.

78. *Albert Einstein: The Human Side*, Helen Dukas & Banesh Hoffman (eds.), Princeton Press, 1979, p. 66.

79. *The Collected Poems of Dylan Thomas*, New Directions Publishing Corporation, 1957.

80. *Dying Testimonies of Saved and Unsaved*, collected by Rev. S. B. Shaw, 1898, pp. 49–50.

81. Joseph D. McPherson, *"Our People Die Well": Glorious accounts of Methodists at Death's Door*, AuthorHouse, 2008, p. 12.

82. Oscar Cullmann, *The Christology of the New Testament*, SCM, 1963, p. 157.

83. Christopher Marlowe, *Doctor Faustus*, Methuen, 1962, p. 101.

84. T. S. Eliot, "Gerontion" in *Collected Poems 1909–1962*, Faber and Faber, 1970.

85. Ronald Eisenberg, *What the Rabbis Said: 250 Topics from the Talmud*, Greenwood Publications, 2010, p. 85.

86. The title Barth gave to his understanding of the mystery of the atonement – Karl Barth, *Church Dogmatics*, IV/I, T&T Clark, 2009, p. 211.

87. C.S. Lewis, *The Lion, the Witch and the Wardrobe*, Macmillan, 1950, pp. 159–60.

88. http://www.childabusecommission.ie/rpt/pdfs/

89. http://www.washingtonpost.com/wp-dyn/content/article/2009/05/20/AR2009052003809.html

90. David Pawson, *Israel in the New Testament*, Terra Nova Publications, 2009, p. 162.

91. http://www.nshn.co.uk/whatis.html

92. http://www.edcole.org/index.php?fuseaction=coleisms.showColeism&id=909&keywords=You+don%92t+drown+by+falling+in+water%2C+you+drown+by+staying+there.&page=

93. Quoted in *The Observer*, 3 December, 1978.

94. Anton Chekhov, *The Seagull*, trans. M. Frayn, Methuen, 1896, Act 2.

95. Stanley Schell (ed.), *Platform and All Around*, E. W. Werner and Co., 1912, p. 128.

96. http://www.youtube.com/watch?v=E1lnSi7QWY8

97. Cited in Brennan Manning, *The Ragamuffin Gospel*, Waterbrook Multnomah, 2000, p. 26.

98. Quote for the meditation on 19 June, *Every Day With Jesus: Treasures from the Greatest Christian Writers of All Time*, Worthy Publishing, 2011.

99. Quoted by Douglas Moo, *The Epistle to the Romans*, Eerdmans, 1996, p. 218.

100. Martyn Lloyd-Jones, *Romans: An Exposition of Chapters 3.20–4.25, Atonement and Justification*, Banner of Truth, 1998, p. 25.

101. *The English Writings of Rabindranath Tagore, Poems*, FF76, Sahitya Akademi, 2004, p. 584.

102. Ravi Zacharias, *Has Christianity Failed You?*, Zondervan, 2010, p. 42

103. See the excellent teaching in the series: Dwight Pryor, *Paul – Jewish Apostle to the Roman World*, CFI Communications.

104. C. H. Spurgeon, *Autobiography*, Volume 1, Passmore and Alabaster, 1899, p. 76.

105. Selections from the Allen Notebooks, in *New Yorker*, 5 November 1973.

106. C. H. Spurgeon, *Justification by Faith*, Sermon 3392 delivered at Newington 28 April 1867, http://www.spurgeon.org/sermons/3392.htm

107. *Form of Concord*, The Lutheran Publication Society, 1914, p. 80.

108. Carl E. Braaten, *Justification: The Article by Which the Church Stands or Falls*, Augsburg Press, 1990.

109. Dr Jack Arnold, "Martin Luther, From Birth to his Conversion", lesson 3 of 11, *IIIM Magazine Online*, Volume 1, no. 3; see http://thirdmill.org/articles/jac_arnold/CH.Arnold.RMT.3.doc

110. Thomas C. Oden, *The Good Works Reader*, Eerdmans, 2007, p. 1.

111. Ravi Zacharias, *New Birth or Rebirth?*, Waterbrook Multnomah, 2008.

112. Rob Bell, *Love Wins*, Collins, 2011, p. 158.

113. "There is a Green Hill Far Away", 1848.

114. http://www.leaderu.com/theology/augpelagius.html

115. Karl Barth, *Call for God*, Harper and Row, 1967, p. 78.

116. Michka Assayas, *Bono on Bono: Conversations with Michka Assayas*, Riverhead Books, 2005, pp. 203–204.

117. Søren Kierkegaard, *Fear and Trembling*, Wilder Publications, 2008, pp. 50–58.

118. http://www.chabad.org/library/article_cdo/aid/112356/jewish/Abraham-Our-Father.htm

119. http://www.canadianislamiccongress.com/docs/abraham.php

120. Cicero, *Essays on Old Age and Friendship, Also His Paradoxes*, McKay, 1896, p. 110.

121. http://www.thefriendshipblog.com/blog/how-many-friends-does-it-take

122. http://sites.duke.edu/theatrst130s02s2011mg3/files/2011/05/McPherson-et-al-Soc-Isolation-2006.pdf

123. Samuel Johnson, "The Decay of Friendship", *The Idler*, no. 23, 23 September 1758.

124. http://www.shakespeare-online.com/sonnets/116.html

125. Jamie Ferreira, *Love's Grateful Striving: A Commentary on Kierkegaard's Works of Love*, OUP, pp. 18, 257.

126. Raymond Brown, Joseph Fitzmyer, Roland Murphy (eds.), *The New Jerome Biblical Commentary*, Second Edition, Geoffrey Chapman, 1990, p. 849.

127. Paul C. Bussard (ed.), *The Catholic Digest*, Volume 21, College of St Thomas, 1956, p. 63.

128. Michael James McClymond and Gerald R. McDermott, *The Theology of Jonathan Edwards*, OUP, 2011, p. 436.

129. *The Letters of Samuel Rutherford*, Banner of Truth, 1973, letter no. 139.

130. Arthur Lynch, *Moods of Life*, Cassell & Co, 1921, p. 130.

131. Anders Nygren, *Commentary on Romans*, Fortress Press, 1949, p. 209.

132. William Barclay, *The Letter to the Romans*, The New Daily Study Bible, Westminster John Knox Press, 2002, p. 91.

133. *Life of Philip Melancthon the German Reformer*, Presbyterian Church in the USA Board of Publication, 1841, p. 17.

134. http://www.rcpsych.ac.uk/pdf/Dein%20The%20Faith%20of%20 Patients.x.pdf

135. John Stott, *Christ the Controversialist*, IVP, 1970, p. 106.

136. George Herbert, *The Complete Poems*, Penguin, 2004.

137. Luther's letter to Melancthon, 1 August 1521. http://www.iclnet.org/pub/resources/text/wittenberg/luther/letsinsbe.txt

138. www.newscientist.com/article/dn13556-10-impossibilities-conquered-by-science.html

139. Cranfield, *Romans 1–8*, p. 299.

140. A. T. Pierson, *George Müller of Bristol*, The Echo Library, 2009, p. 209.

141. Sherwood Eliot Wirt, *Billy: A Personal Look at Billy Graham*, Crossway Books, 1997, p. 22.

142. I have written at length on this peculiar doctrine and the wider concept of holiness in my *The Pursuit of the Holy*, David C. Cook, 2009.

143. "Dead Yet Alive", a sermon by C. H. Spurgeon, delivered 6 August 1876 at Metropolitan Tabernacle. See http://www.angelfire.com/va/sovereigngrace/deadyetalive1.html

144. "Of the Mortification of Sin in Believers", *Overcoming Sin & Temptation: The Classic Works of John Owen*, Kelly M. Kapic and Justin Taylor (eds.), Crossway Books, 2006, p. 51.

145. This ancient tale is retold with different touches, but the meaning is stable; see "Wisdom of the Desert", chapter III, part V – http://maritain.nd.edu/jmc/etext/wd03.htm

146. http://www.winstonchurchill.org/learn/speeches/speeches-of-winston-churchill/103-never-give-in

147. http://news.bbc.co.uk/1/hi/7081038.stm

148. christiannews.christianet.com/1233705288.htm

149. Vatican 11, CCC 2068.

150. http://www.fpcr.org/blue_banner_articles/ryle_sabbath.htm

151. In a lecture delivered at the John Rylands University Library, Manchester, 13 November 1974, full text here: www.biblicalstudies.org.uk/pdf/bjrl/moses_bruce.pdf

152. *ESV Study Bible,* (notes on Romans 10:4), Crossway Bibles, 2008, p. 2174.

153. "Antinomian" is from two Greek words: *anti,* meaning "against", and *nomos,* meaning "law"; the term was developed during the Reformation to refer pejoratively to those who so emphasized justification by faith through grace as to reject the value of and need to comply with divine moral law.

154. Ignatius of Antioch, *The Epistle to the Magnesians,* no. 8.

155. C.S. Lewis, *Mere Christianity,* HarperCollins, 2011, p. 72.

156. Catherine Mumford Booth, *Papers on Aggressive Christianity,* National Publishing Association for the Promotion of Holiness 1883, p.71

157. Martin Luther, *Commentary on Romans,* trans. Theodore Mueller, Zondervan, 1954, p. 116.

158. C. E. B. Cranfield, *Romans: A Shorter Commentary,* T&T Clark, 2001, p. 155.

159. Dietrich Bonhoeffer, *The Cost of Discipleship,* MacMillan, 1951, p. 147.

160. J. R. R. Tolkien, *The Lord of the Rings,* HarperCollins, 1991, p. 68.

161. http://www.creeds.net/Westminster/shorter_catechism.html

162. Barth, *Epistle to the Romans,* p. 263.

163. Cranfield, *Romans 1–8,* p. 346.

164. Stephen Olford, *Not I, But Christ,* Crossway Books, 1997, p. 78.

165. http://www.alcoholics-anonymous.org.uk/?PageID=56

166. Friedrich Zuendel, *The Awakening,* The Plough Publishing House, 1999.

167. Hans Selye, *Stress without Distress,* Penguin, 1975, p. 117.

168. C.S. Lewis from a sermon titled "On Forgiveness" in *The Weight of Glory*

and Other Addresses, HarperCollins, 2001, p. 125.

169. Charles Williams, *The Place of the Lion,* Eerdmans, 1940, p. 199.

170. http://www.cslewisinstitute.org/Becoming_More_Like_Christ_Stott

171. John Owen, *Mortification of Sin,* Christian Focus Publications, 2008, p. 102.

172. thirdmill.org/articles/err_hulse/err_hulse.Mortification.Sin.doc

173. A. W. Tozer, "That Utilitarian Christ" in *The Root of the Righteous,* 1955, Ch 6.; http://lovestthoume.com/Books/RRchapter6.html

174. http://www.religioustolerance.org/chr_dira.htm/

175. Oscar Wilde, *The Importance of Being Earnest,* Penguin, 2007, 1895.

176. Cranfield, *Romans 1–8,* p. 387.

177. Nelson Mandela, *Long Walk to Freedom,* Abacus, 1995, p. 751.

178. John R. W. Stott, *The Message of Romans,* The Bible Speaks Today Series, IVP, 2001, p. 180.

179. Thomas à Kempis, *The Imitation of Christ,* Hendrickson, 2004, p. 45.

180. John Milton, *Paradise Lost: A Poem in Twelve Books,* Penguin, 1996, book VI, line 29.

181. In this chapter I am drawing heavily on material I published in my *God Inside Out,* Kingsway, 2007, chapter 10.

182. See www.quebecoislibre.org and http://thefatherlessgeneration.wordpress.com/statistics/

183. http://www.ons.gov.uk/ons/rel/family-demography/families-and-households/2012/stb-families-households.html

184. http://thefatherlessgeneration.wordpress.com/statistics/

185. Sinclair Ferguson, *The Holy Spirit,* IVP, 1996, p. 182.

186. Gordon Fee, *God's Empowering Presence,* Baker Academic, 2009, p. 405.

187. Raniero Cantalamessa, *Come Creator Spirit,* Liturgical Press, 2002, p. 348.

188. Cantalamessa, *Come Creator Spirit,* p. 346.

189. Hendrikus Berkhof, *Christian Faith: An Introduction to the Study of the Faith,* Eerdmans, 1979, p. 515.

190. Fee, *God's Empowering Presence,* p. 408.

191. Moo, *Romans,* p. 502.

192. Edward Schillebeeckx, *Jesus: An Experiment in Christology*, Collins 1979, pp. 258–63.

193. Brennan Manning, *Abba's Child*, Navpress, 2002, p. 62.

194. Clark Pinnock, *Flame of Love*, IVP, 1996, p. 153.

195. Wolfhart Pannenberg, *Systematic Theology*, Volume 1, Eerdmans, 1991, p. 259f.

196. Tom Smail, *The Forgotten Father*, Hodder & Stoughton, 1980, p. 149f.

197. Dunn, *Romans*, p. 462.

198. "A Brief Account of the Life of Howell Harris", Trefeca, 1791, pp. 12–13, recorded in Brian Edwards, *Revival*, Evangelical Press, 1997, p. 54.

199. Bilquis Sheikh, *I Dared to Call Him Father*, Kingsway, 2001.

200. Joachim Jeremias, *Parables of Jesus*, SCM, 1970, p. 128.

201. Giraudoux, *No War in Troy/The Tiger at the Gates*, Act 2, Scene 13.

202. Friedrich Nietzsche, *Thus Spake Zarathustra*, Robert Pippin (ed.), CUP, 2006, p. 125.

203. http://www.notforsalecampaign.org/about/slavery/

204. http://weightofsilence.wordpress.com/2007/05/24/child-labor-trafficking/

205. http://www.visionofearth.org/economics/ending-poverty/how-much-would-it-cost-to-end-extreme-poverty-in-the-world/

206. Philip Kitcher, *Living with Darwin: Evolution, Design and the Future of Faith*, OUP, 2009, p. 124.

207. *The Heart of Thoreau's Journals*, (30 December 1851), Odell Shepard (ed.), Dover Publications, 1961, p. 69.

208. Karl Marx, "A Contribution to the Critique of Hegel's Philosophy of Right", 1843; see http://www.marxists.org/archive/marx/works/1843/critique-hpr/intro.htm

209. John Bunyan, "A Discourse Touching Prayer", a tract written in jail 1662, published, 1663. http://truthinheart.com/EarlyOberlinCD/CD/Bunyan/text/Discourse.Touching.Prayer/Entire.Book.html

210. William Shakespeare, *Much Ado About Nothing*, Act II, Scene III.

211. Bede the Venerable, "1 Peter", in Thomas Oden's *The Good Works Reader*, Eerdmans, 2007, p. 225.

212. Watchman Nee, *The Normal Christian Life*, Hendrickson, 2006, p. 70.

213. http://www.iop.kcl.ac.uk/apps/paranoidthoughts/information/default.aspx

214. http://www.christianpost.com/news/mark-driscoll-sermons-tells-mars-hill-congregation-god-hates-some-of-you-video-61361/

215. John Stott, *The Cross of Christ*, IVP, 2006, p. 203.

216. Dietrich Bonhoeffer, *Christology*, Fount, 1978, p. 47. (Also published as *Christ the Centre.*)

217. Karl Barth, published sermon "Saved by Grace" in Karl Barth, *Deliverance to the Captives*, Harper & Brothers, SCM Press, 1961, pp. 35–42.

218. Victor Knowles, *Together in Christ*, College Press Publishing, 2006, p. 137.

219. Thomas Schreiner, *Romans*, Baker Academic, 1998, p. 459.

220. Corrie ten Boom, *Tramp for the Lord*, CLC, 2010, p. 50.

221. Bonhoeffer, *Christology*, pp. 47–48

222. Story retold in Henry Blackaby, *Called and Accountable*, New Hope Publications, 2005, p. 40.

223. http://en.wikipedia.org/wiki/Moravian_Church

224. Jennifer Atkinson and Robin Mark, copyright © 1991 Authentic Publishing/Adm. by Kingswaysongs, a division of David C Cook tym@kingsway.co.uk Used by permission.

225. Jim Elliot's *Journal*, 28 October 1949 entry, p. 174.

226. Malcolm Muggeridge, *Something Beautiful for God*, Lion, 2009.

227. Margery Kempe, "III Treatise of Contemplation", no. 144. See: http://www.ccel.org/g/gardner/cell/cell16.htm

228. http://www.bc.edu/dam/files/research_sites/cjl/sites/partners/csg/Sacred_Obligation.htm, notes point 7

229. John Chrysostom, "Discourses against Judaizing Christians" in D. Rausch, *A Legacy of Hatred: Why Christians Must Not Forget the Holocaust*, Moody Press, 1984, pp. 23–25.

230. Robert George Leeson Waite, *The Psychopathic God: Adolf Hitler*, Signet Books, 1978.

231. Sermon "Weeping between the porch and the altar", http://www.ravenhill.org/weeping1.htm

232. http://www.victorianweb.org/history/pms/dizzy.html

233. Mark Dever, *The Message of the Old Testament: Promises Made*, Crossway Books, 2006.

234. C. E. B. Cranfield, *Romans 9–16*, International Critical Commentary, T&T Clark, 2004, p. 473.

235. A. W. Tozer, Sermon "The Waning Authority of Christ in the Churches: Is he Lord or Merely a Beloved Symbol?" http://www.thescripturealone.com/Waning.html

236. Paul Everett Pierson, *The Dynamics of Christian Mission: History through a Missiological Perspective*, William Carey International University Press, 2009, p. 188.

237. *Works of President Edwards, in IV Volumes*, Volume III, Leavitt & Allen, 1851, p. 18.

238. Sir David Hare, *The Eleventh Eric Symes Abbot Memorial Lecture*, published with Via Dolorosa in *Via Dolorosa and When Shall We Live?*, Faber and Faber, 1999.

239. In a sermon called "The Weight of Glory" in *Transposition and Other Essays*, London, Geoffrey Bless, 1949, p. 21.

240. Recalled in the testimony of Rosalind Goforth "How I know God answers prayers?" See: http://christianbookshelf.org/goforth/how_i_know_god_answers_prayer/iii_go_forward_on_your.htm

241. http://religions.pewforum.org/

242. Pawson, *Israel in the New Testament*, p. 147

243. C. H. Spurgeon, Sermon 189, 25 April 1858, http://www.spurgeon.org/sermons/0189.htm

244. Joseph is a director of CMS, an author and co-founder of the Y Course.

245. The remarkable story of Rose Warmer's conversion to Christ, sufferings and Auschwitz and subsequent deliverance and ministry is found in *The Journey: The Story of Rose Warmer's Triumphant Discovery*, written with Myrna Grant, Tyndale House, 1978, p. 150.

246. http://www.calvin.edu/academic/cas/gpa/story2.htm

247. David White, "The Road to the Holocaust: A Brief Survey of the History of Christian Antisemitism" (pp. 59–78) in *Israel: His People, His Land, His Story*, Fred Wright (ed.), Thankful Books, 2005, p. 74.

248. Moo, *Romans*, p. 710.

249. Ignatius, from his *Epistle to the Philippians,* quoted in David Rausch, *A Legacy of Hatred,* p. 20.

250. Quoted in Rausch, *A Legacy of Hatred,* pp. 21–22.

251. From the letter of the Emperor (Constantine) to all those not present at the council. (Found in Eusebius, *Vita Constantini,* Book III 18–20.)

252. Quoted in Rausch, p. 23.

253. John Chrysostom, "Discourses against Judaizing Christians", cited in Rausch, pp. 23–25.

254. Rausch, pp. 25–26.

255. http://www.wwnorton.com/college/english/nael/middleages/topic_3/nathan.htm

256. White, "The Road to the Holocaust", pp.64-66 and Rausch, p. 27.

257. David White in *His People, His Land, His Story,* Fred White (ed.), p. 66.

258. Stephen Boguslawski, *Thomas Aquinas on The Jews: Insights into his Commentary on Romans 9–11,* Paulist Press, 2008, p. 107.

259. http://www.humanitas-international.org/showcase/chronography/documents/luther-jews.htm

260. Rausch, p. 28.

261. Iain Murray, *The Puritan Hope,* Banner of Truth, p. 42.

262. Michael Brown, *Our Hands Are Stained with Blood,* Destiny Image Publishing, 1992, p. 20.

263. Murray, *The Puritan Hope,* p. 155.

264. Brown, *Our Hands Are Stained with Blood,* p. 22.

265. J. C. Ryle, *Are You Ready for the End of Time?* Christian Focus, 2001, p. 144.

266. Ryle, *Are You Ready for the End of Time?,* p. 140.

267. See my study on eschatology, *And the Lamb Wins,* David C. Cook, 2008.

268. http://en.wikipedia.org/wiki/Anti-Jewish_pogroms_in_the_Russian_Empire

269. Paul Charles Merkley, *The Politics of Christian Zionism: 1891–1948,* Frank Cass Publishers, 1998, p. 41.

270. Cited in White, "The Road to the Holocaust", p.72.

271. White, "The Road to the Holocaust", p.73.

272. Discussed in Brown's *Our Hands Are Stained with Blood*, p. 153.

273. Quoted in Eric Metaxas, *Bonhoeffer: Pastor, Martyr, Prophet, Spy*, Thomas Nelson, 2011, p. 316.

274. www.wcc-coe.org/wcc/what/interreligious/cd34-20.html

275. Cited in White, "The Road to the Holocaust", p. 73.

276. White, "The Road to the Holocaust", p. 74.

277. Albertus Pieters, *The Seed of Abraham*, Eerdmans, 1950, p. 123.

278. Quoted in David Torrance and George Taylor, *Israel God's Servant: God's Key to the Redemption of the World*, Authentic Media, 2007, p. 98f.

279. http://hmd.org.uk/genocides/victims-of-nazi-persecution

280. Daniel Jonah Goldhagen, *Hitler's Willing Executioners*, Little, Brown and Company, 1996, pp. 167, 171.

281. Ryle, *Are You Ready For the End of Time?*, p. 140.

282. http://www.vatican.va/archive/ccc_css/archive/catechism/p1s2c2a7.htm

283. Derek Prince, "The Root of Anti-Semitism", www.derekprince.org/Publisher/File.aspx?id=1000021480

284. John F. Wilson (ed.), *The Works of Jonathan Edwards: A History of the Work of Redemption*, Volume 9, Yale University Press, 1989, p. 469.

285. Cranfield, *Romans 1–8*, p. 575.

286. John Hosier, *The Lamb, the Beast and the Devil*, Monarch Books, 2002, p. 125.

287. Moo, *Romans*, p. 726.

288. Ian Hunter, *The Very Best of Malcolm Muggeridge*, Hodder and Stoughton, 2003, p. 74.

289. http://www.ccel.us/dating.ch2.html and *Dating, Sex and Friendship*, Joyce Huggett, 1985, IVP, p. 31.

290. Rob Bell, *Sex God*, Zondervan, 2007, p. 126.

291. http://blog.getrelationshiphelp.com/2009/07/christian-women-have-more-sexual-fun.html

292. Karl Barth, *Church Dogmatics* III/4, T&T Clark, 1978, p. 133

293. http://www.citizenlink.com/2010/06/16/colorado-statement-on-biblical-sexual-morality/

294. Philip Rieff, *Freud: The Mind of the Moralist*, Chicago Press, 1979, p. 165.

295. http://en.wikipedia.org/wiki/Boiling_frog

296. Richard Foster, *Money, Sex, Power*, Hodder and Stoughton, 1999.

297. David F. Wells, *God in the Wasteland*, Eerdmans, 1994, p. 29.

298. http://www.desiringgod.org/resource-library/sermons/the-war-against-the-soul-and-the-glory-of-god

299. From J. C. Ryle, *Practical Religion*, James Clarke, 1977, p. 184f.

300. http://www.barna.org/barna-update/article/5-barna-update/188-faith-has-a-limited-effect-on-most-peoples-behavior and http://www.barna.org/barna-update/article/15-familykids/42-new-marriage-and-divorce-statistics-released

301. C. S. Lewis, *The Great Divorce*, Macmillan, 1948, p. 98f

302. From a speech "Where Do We Go From Here?", 16 August 1967, to Southern Christian Leadership Conference, Atlanta, Georgia.

303. In his sermon "Outward and Inward Morality", http://www.ccel.org/ccel/eckhart/sermons.x.html

304. It would appear this quote is a composite of statements often said by John Wesley: http://www.wesley-fellowship.org.uk/WesleyQA.htm

305. S. Wilberforce (ed.), *Journals and letters of the Rev. Henry Martyn, B.D.*, Seeley and Burnside, 1839, p. 272.

306. Moo, *Romans*, pp. 769, 778, 779.

307. http://4officers.wordpress.com/2010/03/30/the-passions-of-william-booth/

308. http://www.roylefamily.pwp.blueyonder.co.uk/eroberts.htm

309. Samuel Chadwick, *The Way to Pentecost*, Hodder and Stoughton, 1932, p. 43.

310. Blaise Pascal, *Pensées*, quoted in Marvin Richard O'Connell (ed.), *Blaise Pascal: Reasons of the Heart*, 1997, Eerdmans, p. 95f.

311. From an article published in *The Fatherland*, p. 51, 11 April 1855, entitled "Would It Be Best Now to Stop Ringing the Alarm?" See: http://sorenkierkegaard.org/articles-from-fatherland.html

312. Leonard Ravenhill "John the Baptist and the Fire of God". http://www.ravenhill.org/johnbaptist.htm

313. William Shakespeare, *The Life and Death of King John*, Act V, Scene I.

314. Henry Rogers (ed.), *The Works of Jonathan Edwards*, Volume 2, William Ball, 1889, p. 943.

315. James Stuart Stewart, *Heralds of God*, Baker Book House, 1972, p. 219.

316. Chadwick, *The Way to Pentecost*, p. 99.

317. This oft-repeated quote lacks any historic source!

318. *Foxes Book of Martyrs*, "321: The Execution of Ridley and Latimer", http://www.exclassics.com/foxe/foxe323.htm

319. http://stanleyjebb.wordpress.com/2009/11/13/why-i-left-the-charismatic-movement/

320. J. David Cassell, "Defending the Cannibals", Christian History 17, no. 1:15. http://www.libertymagazine.org/index.php?id=440

321. John Howard Yoder, *The Politics of Jesus*, Eerdmans, 1971, p. 205.

322. C. S. Lewis, *Mere Christianity*, HarperCollins, 2001, p. 199.

323. Donald J Dietrich, *Christian Responses to the Holocaust: Moral and Ethical Issues*, Syracuse University, 2003, p. 3.

324. House of Commons, September 1938, *The Book of Military Quotations*, Peter G. Tsouras (ed.), Greenhill Books, 2005, p. 35.

325. R. Kent Hughes, *Romans: Righteousness from heaven*, Crossway Books, 1991.

326. http://www.mun.ca/rels/restmov/texts/unitas/essrev.html

327. http://www.christianitytoday.com/ct/2003/septemberweb-only/9-1-51.0.html?start=4

328. Timothy Dudley-Smith, *John Stott: A Global Ministry*, IVP, 2001, p. 66.

329. http://www.spurgeon.org/misc/cigars.htm

330. This long quote I took from a magazine in which Gittoes was interviewed. I regret I can no longer recall the details. A similar depiction from Gittoes is found here: http://www.commontheology.com/vol1no1july2002/thepreacher.htm

331. Gerald O'Collins, *The Resurrection of Jesus Christ*, Judson Press, 1973, p. 134.

332. Robert Lowry's hymn "Low in the grave he lay".

333. Metaxas, *Bonhoeffer*, p. 528.

334. Metaxas, *Bonhoeffer*, p.532

335. N. T. Wright, *Surprised by Hope*, SPCK, 2008, p. 234.

336. http://www.jewfaq.org/kashrut.htm

337. Josef Stern, "The idea of a Hoq in Maimonides' Explanation of the Law" in *Maimonides and Philosophy*, Shlomo Pines and Yirmiyahu Yovel (eds.), M. Nijhoff, 1986 ,p. 92.

338. *Summa Theologica*, Q147 A6. See: http://www.newadvent.org/summa/3147.htm

339. http://www.wholefigured.com/component/k2/item/46-geneen-roth-and-emotional-eating

340. http://www.timeoutbengaluru.net/food/eating_out_details.asp?code=112&source=5

341. *Gems From Tozer*, Wingspread Publishers, 1980, p. 66

342. P. T. Forsyth, *The Work of Christ*, Independent Press, 1910.

343. A sermon in the volume by Karl Barth, *The Word of God and the Word of Man*, Harper, 1957, p. 28ff.

344. http://richarddawkins.net/quotes/49

345. Quoted in Bill Bright, *Ten Basic Steps Toward Christian Maturity*, Here's Life Publications, 1983, p. 239.

346. Hallam Tennyson, *Alfred Lord Tennyson: A Memoir by His Son*, Macmillan, 1899, Volume VI, p. 258.

347. http://www.number10.gov.uk/news/king-james-bible/

348. http://www.opendoorsuk.org/

349. http://library.thinkquest.org/J002678F/columbus.htm

350. http://www.rzim.org/just-thinking/national-day-of-prayer-address/

351. http://www.guardian.co.uk/books/2010/mar/27/ten-best-priests-john-mullan

352. http://www.americamagazine.org/content/culture.cfm?cultureid=254

353. Bishop Pierre Whalon was told this was his job when he took up a new post heading up Episcopalian Bishops in Europe. See: http://web.me.com/pwhalon/Bp_Pierre_Site/Blog/Entrées/2012/4/5_Manage_decline.html

354. John Steinbeck, *East of Eden*, Penguin, 1980, p. 4

355. This theme was often repeated in his journals: Arnold Dallimore, *George Whitefield*, Crossway Books, 2010, p. 154.

356. Source unknown.

357. John Wesley's Letters: 6:271, 272.

358. Richard Fletcher, *The Barbarian Conversion*, The University of California Press, 1999.

359. Chadwick, *The Way to Pentecost*, particularly chapter 2 "The Church Without the Spirit"

360. The story of this church growth in a tough inner-city Bradford, is told in part in Robin Gamble, *The Irrelevant Church*, Monarch Books, 1991.

361. Norman Grubb, *C. T. Studd: Athlete and Pioneer*, Worldwide Revival Prayer Movement, 1947.

362. A quote taken from private correspondence with me.

363. www.thisislondon.co.uk/news/holy-bankrollers-6366701.html, 10 November 2011.

364. http://www.philanthropy.iupui.edu/womengive/

365. Brother Yun, *The Heavenly Man*, Monarch Books, 2002, pp. 297–98.

366. http://en.wikisource.org/wiki/Eminent_Victorians/The_End_of_General_Gordon

367. J. C. Ryle, "Scattered Israel to be Regathered", sermon 5 in *Coming Events and Present Duties*, Kessinger, 2010.

368. http://www.christian.co.uk/research-or-stats/christians-have-a-lot-to-learn-from-jews-p11082

369. http://www.randomhouse.com/features/cahill/gifts_excerpt.html

370. Harold Myra and Marshall Shelley, *The Leadership Secrets of Billy Graham*, Zondervan, 2008.

371. Essay entitled "Priestesses in the Church", written in 1948 for Lambeth Conference, originally published under the title "Notes on the Way", in *Time and Tide*, Volume XXIX (14 August 1948). It was subsequently reprinted with the above title in the posthumous *God in the Dock* book, published by William B. Eerdmans.
http://www.episcopalnet.org/TRACTS/priestesses.html

372. http://www.desiringgod.org/blog/posts/more-on-the-masculine-feel-of-christianity

373. Gurevich, E., *Tosefta Berachot*, Eliyahu Gurevich, 2010, p. 404.

374. Andrew Wallace-Hadrill, *Patronage in Ancient Society*, Routledge, 1989.

375. F. F. Bruce, *Paul, Apostle of the Free Spirit,* Paternoster, 1977, p. 251.

376. http://betterbibles.com/2006/11/13/junia-the-apostle-part-15/

377. *A Select Library of the Nicene and Post-Nicene Fathers of the Christian Church,* Philip Schaff (ed.), Volume 11, Hendrickson, 1994, p. 555.

378. In "Did a Woman Found Roman Christianity?" http://www.catholica.com.au/gc0/ie2/128_ie_121109.php

379. See Rosie Nixon's historical study of effective women in evangelism and church planting: *Liberating Women for the Gospel,* Hodder and Stoughton, 1997.

380. http://www.fullnet.net/np/archives/cyberj/sanders.html

381. http://www.preachitteachit.org/articles-blogs/ask-roger/post/archive/2012/february/article/did-paul-hate-women/

382. G. K. Chesterton, *A Short History of England,* The Echo Library, p. 32.

383. Brother Yun, *The Heavenly Man,* p. 299.

384. W. Russell Maltby, *The Significance of Jesus: Burwash Memorial Lectures,* SCM, 1928.

385. C. S. Lewis, *Letters to Malcolm: Chiefly on Prayer,* Harvest, 1964, pp. 92–93.

386. William Shakespeare, *Romeo and Juliet,* Act II, Scene V.

387. Quoted by Billy Graham, *Peace with God,* Thomas Nelson, 2012, p. 73.

388. *Calvin's Bible Commentaries: Galatians and Ephesians,* Forgotten Books, 2007, p. 235.

389. Joseph Fitzmyer, *Romans.*

390. http://www.creeds.net/Westminster/shorter_catechism.html

391. C. S. Lewis, *The Problem of Pain,* HarperCollins, 2002, p. 46.

392. http://www.spurgeon.org/treasury/ps134.htm

Bibliography

Allen, W., "Selections from the Allen Notebooks", in *The New Yorker*, 5 November 1973

Assayas, M., *Bono on Bono: Conversations with Michka Assayas*, New York, NY: Riverhead Books, 2005

Augustine, *On Christian Doctrine*, Christian Classics Ethereal Library

Bainton, R. H., *Here I Stand: A Life of Martin Luther*, Nashville, TN: Abingdon Press, 1991.

Barclay, W., *The Letter to the Romans*, The New Daily Study Bible, Louisville, KY: Westminster John Knox Press, 2002

Barnum, T., *Never Silent*, Colorado Springs, CO: Eleison Publishing, 2008

Barrett, C. K., *A Commentary on the Epistle to the Romans*, London: Harper and Row, 1957

Barrett, C. K., *The Epistle to the Romans*, Blacks' New Testament Commentary Series, London: A & C Black, Second Edition, 1962

Barth, K., *Church Dogmatics*, IV/I, Edinburgh: T&T Clark, 2009

Barth, K., *Church Dogmatics*, III/4, Edinburgh: T., & T., Clark, 1978

Barth, K., "Saved by Grace", in *Deliverance to the Captives*, New York, NY: Harper and Brothers SCM Press, 1961

Barth, K., *The Word of God and the Word of Man*, New York, NY: Harper and Row, 1957

Barth, K., *Call for God*, New York, NY: Harper and Row, 1967

Barth, K., *Gifford Lectures*, 1937

Bede, the Venerable, "1 Peter", in Oden, T., *The Good Works Reader*, Grand Rapids, MI: Eerdmans, 2007

Bell, R., *Love Wins*, London: Collins, 2011

Bell, R., *Sex God*, Grand Rapids, MI: Zondervan, 2007

Berkhof, H., *Christian Faith: An Introduction to the Study of the Faith*, Grand Rapids, MI: Eerdmans, 1979

Blackaby, H., *Called and Accountable*, Birmingham, AL: New Hope Publications, 2005

Boguslawski, S., *Thomas Aquinas on The Jews: Insights into his Commentary on Romans 9–11*, Mahwah, MJ: Paulist Press, 2008

Bonhoeffer, D., *Christology*, London: Fount, 1978 (also published as *Christ the Centre*)

Bonhoeffer, D., *The Cost of Discipleship*, London: Macmillan, 1951

Booth, C. M., *Papers on Aggressive Christianity*, National Publishing Association for the Promotion of Holiness, 1883

Braaten, C. E., *Justification: The Article by Which the Church Stands or Falls*, Minneapolis, MN: Augsburg Press, 1990

Bright, B., *The Christian and Obedience (Ten Basic Steps to Christian Maturity)*, San Bernardino, CA: Here's Life Publishers, 1983

Brother Yun, *The Heavenly Man*, London: Monarch, 2002

Brown, M., *Our Hands are Stained with Blood*, Shippenburg: Destiny Image Publishing, 1992

Brown, R., Fitzmeyer, J., and Murphy, R., (eds.) *The New Jerome Biblical Commentary*, Second Edition, London: Geoffrey Chapman, 1990

Bruce, F. F, *Paul: Apostle of the Free Spirit*, Milton Keynes: Paternoster 1977

Bruce, F. F, *The Epistle of Paul to the Romans: An Introduction And Commentary*, Tyndale New Testament Commentaries, Leicester: IVP, 1983

Brunner, E., *The Divine Imperative*, Cambridge: Lutterworth Press, 1937

Bussard, P. C., *The Catholic Digest*, Volume 21, Saint Paul, MN: College of St Thomas, 1956

Calvin, J., *Calvin's Bible Commentaries: Galations & Ephesians*, Easy Reading series, Forgotten Books, 2007

Calvin, J., *Institutes of the Christian Religion*, Peabody, MA: Hendrickson Publishers Inc., 2007

Cantalamessa, R., *Come Creator Spirit*, Collegeville, MN: Liturgical Press, 2002

Chadwick, S., *The Way to Pentecost*, London: Hodder & Stoughton, 1932, reprinted by Christian Literature Crusade, 2001

Chalke, S., *The Lost Message of Jesus*, Grand Rapids, MI: Zondervan, 2004

Chekhov, A., *The Seagull*, trans. M. Frayn, York: Methuen, 2002

Chesterton, G. K., *A Short History of England*, Fairford, Glos: The Echo Library, 2008

Chesterton, G. K., *Orthodoxy*, London: John Lane Company, 1909

Chrysostom, J., *Discourses Against Judaizing Christians,* trans. P. Hawkins, Washington, VA: The Catholic University of America Press, 1979

Cranfield, C. E. B., *Romans 1–8,* International Critical Commentary, London: Continuum, 2004

Cranfield, C. E. B., *Romans 9–16,* International Critical Commentary, Edinburgh: T&T Clark, 2004

Cranfield, C.E.B., *Romans: A Shorter Commentary,* Edinburgh: T&T Clark, 2001

Cullmann, O., *The Christology of the New Testament,* London: SCM, 1963

Dallimore, A., *George Whitefield,* Wheaton, IL: Crossway Books, 2010

Dever, M., *The Message of the Old Testament: Promises Made,* Wheaton, Il: Crossway Books, 2006

Dietrich, D.J., *Christian Responses to the Holocaust: Moral and Ethical Issues,* New York: Syracuse University, 2003

Dostoyevsky, F., *Crime and Punishment,* London: Penguin Classics, 2003

Dudley-Smith, T., *John Stott: A Global Ministry – A Biography: The Later Years,* Leicester: IVP, 2001

Dukas, H., and Hoffman, B. (eds.), *Albert Einstein: The Human Side,* Princeton, NJ: Princeton Press, 1979

Dunn, J., *Word Biblical Commentary: Romans,* vols. 38A and 38B Dallas, TX: Word Books, 1988

Edwards, B., "A Brief Account of the Life of Howell Harris", Trefeca, 1791, in Brian Edwards, *Revival,* Durham: Evangelical Press, 1997

Edwards, J., *The Works of President Edwards, in IV Volumes,* Volume III, New York: Leavitt & Allen, 1851

Edwards, J., *The Works of Jonathan Edwards,* Volume 2, Rogers, H., (ed.), University of Michigan: William Ball, 1889

Edwards, J., *The Works of Jonathan Edwards: A History of the Work of Redemption,* Volume 9, Wilson, J. F. (ed.), New Haven: Yale University Press, 1989

Eisenberg, R., *What the Rabbis Said: 250 Topics from the Talmud,* Santa Barbara, CA: Greenwood Publications, 2010

Eliot, T. S., "Gerontion" in *Collected Poems 1909–1962,* London: Faber and Faber, 1970

Elliot, E., *The Journals of Jim Elliot,* Ada, MI: Revell (Baker Publishing Group), 1978

Erickson, M., Christian Theology, Ada, MI: Baker Academic Press, 1998

ESV Study Bible, Colorado Springs, CO: Crossway Bibles, 2008

Eusebius, *Vita Constantini,* Book III 18–20

Every Day with Jesus: Treasures From the Greatest Christian Writers of All Time, Brentwood, TN: Worthy Publishing, 2011

Fee, G., *God's Empowering Presence,* Ada, MI: Baker Academic, 2009

Ferguson, S. B., *Holy Spirit,* Downers Grove, IL: IVP, 1996

Ferreira, J., *Love's Grateful Striving: A Commentary on Kierkegaard's Works of Love,* New York, NY: Oxford University Press USA, 2008

Fitzmyer, J., *Romans,* Anchor Bible Commentaries, New Haven, CT: Yale University Press, 2007

Fletcher, R., *The Barbarian Conversion,* Berkeley, CA: The University of California Press, 1999

Form of Concord, Philadelphia: The Lutheran Publication Society, 1914

Forsyth, P. T., *Work of Christ,* London: Independent Press, 1910

Foster, R., *Money, Sex, Power,* London: Hodder and Stoughton, 1999

Gaupin, L., *Embracing the Vision: Sacramental Catechesis for First Reconciliation,* New London, CT: Twenty-third Publications, 2007

Giraudoux, J., *Tiger at the Gates* (*La Guerre de Troie, N'aura Pas Lieu*), trans. C. Fry, York: Methuen, 1955

Goldhagen, D. J., *Hitler's Willing Executioners,* London: Little, Brown and Company, 1996

Graham, B., *Peace with God,* Nashville, TN: Thomas Nelson, 2002

Grubb, N., *C. T. Studd: Athlete and Pioneer,* Worldwide Revival Prayer Movement, 1947

Gurevich, E., *Tosefta Berachot: Translated into English with a Commentary,* Gurevich, E., 2010

Haar, M., *Heidegger and the Essence of Man,* Albany, NY: State University of New York, 1993

Hare, D., *Via Dolorosa and When Shall We Live?*, London: Faber and Faber, 1999

Hawthorne, G. F., Martin R. P. & Reid, D. G. (eds.), *Dictionary of Paul and His Epistles*, Leicester: InterVarsity Press, 1993

Herbert, G., *The Complete Poems*, London: Penguin Books, 2004

Hosier, J., *The Lamb, the Beast and the Devil*, Grand Rapids, MI: Monarch, 2002

Hughes, R. K., *Romans: Righteousness from Heaven*, Wheaton, IL: Crossway, 1991

Hunter, I., *The Very Best of Malcolm Muggeridge*, London: Hodder and Stoughton, 2003

Ignatius of Antioch, *The Epistle to the Magnesians*, http://www.ccel.org/ccel/schaff/anf01.v.iii.html

Ignatius of Antioch, "The Epistle to the Philippians", in *A Legacy of Hatred: Why Christians Must Not Forget the Holocaust*, Rausch, D. (ed.), Chicago, IL: Moody Press, 1984

Jeremias, J., *Parables of Jesus*, London: SCM, 1970

Johnson, S., "The Decay of Friendship", in *The Idler*, No.23, September 23, 1978

Jones, A., *Reimagining Christianity*, Hoboken, NJ: Wiley, J., & Sons, 2004

Kempis, Thomas à, *The Imitation of Christ*, Peabody, MA: Hendrickson Publishers, 2004

Kierkegaard, S., *Fear and Trembling*, Radford, VA: Wilder Publications, 2008

King, M. L., *Where Do We Go from Here?* Speech on 16 August 1967, to Southern Christian Leadership Conference Atlanta, Georgia

Kitcher, P., *Living with Darwin: Evolution, Design and the Future of Faith*, New York, NY: OUP, 2009

Knowles, V., *Together in Christ*, Joplin, MO: College Press Publishing, 2006

Lewis, C. S., *Letters to Malcolm: Chiefly on Prayer*, San Diego: Harvest, 1964

Lewis, C. S., *Mere Christianity*, London: Harper Collins, 2011

Lewis, C. S., *The Great Divorce*, New York, NY: Macmillan, 1948

Lewis, C. S., *The Lion, the Witch and the Wardrobe*, New York, NY: Macmillan, 1950

Lewis, C. S., *The Problem of Pain*, London: HarperCollins, 2002

Lewis, C. S., *The Screwtape Letters*, London: Harper Collins 2001

Lewis, C. S., "The Weight of Glory", *Transposition and Other Essays,* London: Geoffrey Bles, 1949

Lewis, C. S., "On Forgiveness", *The Weight of Glory and Other Addresses,* London: HarperCollins, 2001

Lloyd-Jones, M., *I Am Not Ashamed: Advice to Timothy,* London: Hodder & Stoughton, 1986

Lloyd-Jones, M., *Romans: An Exposition of Chapters 3.20–4.25, Atonement and Justification,* Edinburgh: Banner of Truth Trust, 1998

Luther, M., *Watchwords for the Warfare of Life,* Volume 1., London: Nelson, T., & Sons, 1869

Lynch, A., *Moods of Life,* London: Cassell & Co, 1921

Maltby, W. R., *The Significance of Jesus,* Burwash Memorial Lectures, London: SCM, 1928

Mandela, N., *Long Walk to Freedom,* Ilford, England: Abacus, 1995

Manning, B., *Abba's Child,* Colorado Springs, CO: Navpress, 2002

Manning, B., *The Ragamuffin Gospel,* Sisters, OR: Multnomah, 2000

Marlowe, C., *Doctor Faustus,* Drama Classics, London: Nick Hern Books, 2004

McClymond, M. J., and McDermott, G. R., *The Theology of Jonathan Edwards,* Oxford: Oxford University Press, 2011

McPherson, J. D., *"Our People Die Well": Glorious Accounts of Methodists at Death's Door,* Bloomington, IN: AuthorHouse, 2008

Menninger, K., *Whatever Became of Sin?,* New York, NY: Hawthorn Books, 1973

Merkley, P. C., *The Politics of Christian Zionism: 1891–1948,* London: Frank Cass Publishers, 1998

Metaxas, E., *Bonhoeffer: Pastor, Martyr, Prophet, Spy,* Nashville, TN: Thomas Nelson, 2011

Milton, J., *Paradise Lost: A Poem in Twelve Books,* London: Penguin Popular Classics, 1996

Moo, D., *The Epistle to the Romans,* Grand Rapids, MI: Eerdmans, 1996

Morris, L., "The Theme of Romans" in Gasque, W. Ward, and Martin, R. P. (eds.), *Apostolic History and the Gospel: Biblical and Historical Essays Presented to F. F. Bruce,* Exeter: The Paternoster Press, 1970

Morris, L., *The Epistle to the Romans,* Leicester: IVP, 1998

Muggeridge, M., *Something Beautiful for God*, New York, NY: Harper and Row, 1971

Muggeridge, M., *Tread Softly For You Tread on my Jokes*, London: Collins, 1966, and New York, NY: Harper and Row, 1971

Murray, I., *The Puritan Hope*, Carlisle, PA: Banner of Truth, 1985

Myers, Charles D., "Epistle to the Romans" in *Anchor Bible Dictionary*, Volume 5, London: Doubleday, 1994, p. 816f.

Myra, H., and Shelley, M., *The Leadership Secrets of Billy Graham*, Grand Rapids, MI: Zondervan, 2008

Newman, J. H., *Fifteen Sermons Preached Before The University of Oxford*, London: Rivingtons, 1880

Nietzsche, F., *Beyond Good and Evil*, London: Penguin Classics, 2003

Nietzsche, F., *Thus Spake Zarathustra*, Cambridge: Cambridge University Press, 1997

Nixon, R., *Liberating Women for the Gospel*, London: Hodder and Stoughton, 1997

Nygren, A., *Commentary on Romans*, Minneapolis, MN: Fortress Press, 1949

O'Collins, G., *The Resurrection of Jesus Christ*, King of Prussia, PA: Judson Press, 1973

O'Connell, M.R., *Blaise Pascal: Reasons of the Heart*, Grand Rapids, MI: Eerdmans, 1997

Oden, T. C., *The Good Works Reader*, Grand Rapids, MI: Eerdmans, 2007

Olford, S., *Not I, But Christ*, Wheaton, IL: Crossway Books, 1997

Owen, J., *Mortification of Sin*, Tain, Scotland: Christian Focus Publications, 2008

Owen, J., "Of the Mortification of Sin in Believers" in *Overcoming Sin & Temptation: The Classic Works of John Owen*, Kelly M. Kapic and Justin Taylor (eds.), Crossway Books, 2006

Pannenberg, W., *Systematic Theology*, Volume 1, Grand Rapids, MI: Eerdmans, 2010

Pascal, B., *Pensées*, trans. W. F. Trotter, London: Dent, J. M., & Sons, 1931

Pawson, D., *Israel in the New Testament*, Bradford-on-Avon: Terra Nova Publications, 2009

Pierson, A. T., *George Müller of Bristol*, Teddington, Middlesex: Echo Library, 2009

Pierson, P. E., *The Dynamics of Christian Mission: History Through a Missiological Perspective*, Pasadena, CA: William Carey International University Press, 2009

Pieters, A., *The Seed of Abraham*, Grand Rapids, MI: Eerdmans, 1950.

Pines, E. S., and Yovel, Y., *Maimonides and Philosophy*, Dordrecht: Martinus Nijhoff Publishers, 1986

Pinnock, C., *Flame of Love*, Downers Grove, IL: IVP Academic, 1996

Ponsonby, S., *And the Lamb Wins*, Colorado Springs, CO: David C. Cook, 2008

Ponsonby, S., "Natural Theology in the Thought of Karl Barth", MLitt Thesis, Bristol University, 1996

Ponsonby, S., *The Pursuit of the Holy*, Colorado Springs, CO: David C. Cook, 2009

Presbyterian Church in the USA Board of Publication, *Life of Philipp Melancthon, The German Reformer*, Philadelphia: The Board, 1841

Pryor, D. W., *Paul: Jewish Apostle to the Roman World*, Eastbourne: CFI Communications

Rausch, D., *A Legacy of Hatred: Why Christians Must Not Forget the Holocaust*, Chicago, IL: Moody Press, 1984

Rieff, P., *Freud: The Mind of the Moralist*, Chicago, IL: Chicago Press, 1979

Rutherford, S., *The Letters of Samuel Rutherford*, Carlisle, PA: Banner of Truth, 1973

Ryle, J. C., *Are You Ready for the End of Time?*, Fearn: Scotland, Christian Focus, 2001

Ryle, J. C., *Practical Religion*, Cambridge: James Clarke, 1977

Schaff, P, (ed.) *A Select Library of the Nicene and Post-Nicene Fathers of the Christian Church*, Volume 11, Peabody, MA: Hendrickson Publishers, 1994

Schillebeeckx, E., *Jesus: An Experiment in Christology*, London: Harper Collins, 1979

Schell, S. (ed.), *Platform and All Around*, New York: E. W. Werner and Co., 1912

Schreiner, T., *Romans*, Grand Rapids, MI: Baker Academic, 1998

Selye, H., *Stress Without Distress*, Toronto: Penguin Canada, 1975

Shakespeare, W., *King Henry VI, Part II*, The Oxford Shakespeare, Taylor, M. (ed.), Oxford: Oxford University Press, 2003

Shakespeare, W., *Macbeth*, The Oxford Shakespeare, Brooke, N. (ed.), Oxford: Oxford University Press, 2008

Shakespeare, W., *Much Ado About Nothing*, Ware, Herts: Wordsworth Classics, 1995

Shakespeare, W., *Romeo & Juliet*, Ware, Herts: Wordsworth Classics, 2000

Shakespeare, W., *The Life and Death of King John*, Forgotten Books, 2012

Shaw, S. B., *The Dying Testimonies of the Saved and Unsaved*, Chicago: Shaw, S.B., 1898

Sheikh, B., *I Dared to Call Him Father*, Colorado Springs, CO: Kingsway, 2001

Shepard, O. (ed.), *The Heart of Thoreau's Journals*, 30 December 1851, Mineola, NY: Dover Publications, 1961

Smail, T., *The Forgotten Father*, London: Hodder and Stoughton, 1980

Spurgeon, C. H., *Autobiography*, Volume 1, London: Passmore and Alabaster, 1899

Spurgeon, C. H., *The Metropolitan Tabernacle Pulpit*, Volume 28, Carlisle, PA: Banner of Truth, 1971

Steinbeck, J., *East of Eden*, London: Penguin Books, 1980

Stewart, J. S., *Heralds of God*, Ada, MI: Baker Book House, 1972

Stott, J., *Christ The Controversialist*, Leicester: IVP, 1970

Stott, J., *The Cross of Christ*, Leicester: IVP, 2006

Stott, J., *The Message of Romans*, The Bible Speaks Today Series, Downers Grove, IL: IVP, 2001

Tagore, R., *The English Writings of Rabindranath Tagore: Poems*, New Delhi, India: Sahitya Akademi, 2004

ten Boom, C., *Tramp for the Lord*, Alresford, Hants: CLC, 2010

Tennyson, H., *Alfred Lord Tennyson, A Memoir by his Son*, New York, NY: Macmillan, 1899

Thomas, D., *The Collected Poems of Dylan Thomas*, New York, NY: New Directions Publishing Corporation, 1957

Tillich, P., *Theology of Culture*, Kimball, R. C. (ed.), New York, NY: Oxford University Press, 1964

Tolkien, J. R. R., *The Lord of the Rings*, London: Harper Collins, 1991

Torrance, D. and Taylor, G., *Israel God's Servant: God's Key to the Redemption of the World,* Milton Keynes: Authentic Media, 2007

Tozer, A. W., *Gems from Tozer,* Camps Hill, PA: Wingspread Publishers, 1980

Tozer, A. W., "That Utilitarian Christ", essay in *The Root of Righteousness,* Wheaton, IL: Scripture Press, 1955

Tozer, A. W., "The Waning Authority of Christ in the Churches: Is He Lord or Merely a Beloved Symbol?", *The Alliance Witness,* 15 May 1963

Tozer, A. W., *The Pursuit of God,* Rockville, MD: Arc Manor, 2008

Tsouras, P. G. (ed.), *The Book of Military Quotations,* Barnsley: Greenhill Books, 2005

Van Gogh, V., *Dear Theo: the Autobiography of Vincent Van Gogh,* Stone, I. and Stone,J. (eds.), New York, NY: New American Library, 1995

Waite, R. G. L., *Psychopathic God: Adolf Hitler,* University Park, PA: Pennsylvania State University, Signet Books, 1978

Warmer, R. and Grant, M., *The Journey: The Story of Rose Warmer's Triumphant Discovery,* Carol Stream, IL: Tyndale, 1978

Watchman Nee, *The Normal Christian Life,* Peabody, MA: Hendrickson Publishers, 2006

Wells, D. F., *God in the Wasteland,* Grand Rapids, MI: Eerdmans, 1994

Wesley, J., *Letters of John Wesley,* Forgotten Books, 2012

White, D., "The Road to the Holocaust, A Brief Survey of the History of Christian Antisemitism" in *Israel, in His People, His Land, His Story,* ed. Wright, F., Eastbourne: Thankful Books, 2005

Wilberforce, S., (ed.) *Journals and Letters of the Rev. Henry Martyn, B.D.,* London: Seeley and Burnside, 1839

Wilde, O., *Plays, Prose Writings and Poems,* London: Everyman's Library, 1991

Wilde, O., *The Importance of Being Earnest,* London: Penguin Classics, 2007

Williams, C., *The Place of the Lion,* Grand Rapids, MI: Eerdmans, 1940

Wirt, S.E., *Billy: A Personal Look at Billy Graham,* Wheaton, IL: Crossway Books, 1997

Wright, N. T., *Surprised by Hope,* London: SPCK, 2007

Yoder, J. H., *The Politics of Jesus,* Grand Rapids, MI: Eerdmans, 1971

Zacharias, R., *Has Christianity Failed You?*, Grand Rapids, MI: Zondervan, 2010

Zacharias, R., *New Birth or Rebirth?*, Colorado Springs, CO: Waterbrook Multnomah, 2008

Zuendel, F., *The Awakening*, Rifton, NY: The Plough Publishing House, 1999